God's Arithmetic:

How Life Adds Up
In
The
Kingdom of God

by Ron Bodlander

Printed in the United States of America

ISBN 9781624190162

www.xulonpress.com

Contents

Foreword

It is a great privilege for me to recommend this book by Ron Bodlander to you. I have known Ron for about twenty years, and I count him as one of my best friends. I had the wonderful privilege of being his pastor for nine years. Almost every week during that time, Ron would faithfully join me on weekly visitation for the church. No pastor could ever ask for a more faithful and encouraging member to be a part of his flock. Then, when God called us to return to the mission field, Ron became a much treasured prayer partner.

Ron has a powerful testimony due to growing up in a Jewish home. He began to read the New Testament in college, and God brought him to faith as he read and began to understand the gospel. He went on to attend seminary so that he might have theological training. He is first and foremost a Biblical theologian. He is also a faithful and committed Bible student and teacher. All that he writes comes from a careful study of the Scriptures. I hope that readers will appreciate the emphasis that he puts on the Word of God.

I have had the privilege to read <u>God's Arithmetic</u>, chapter by chapter, and I have been impressed by his balanced approach to difficult subjects. All who take the time to read his book will appreciate his Christian maturity and balanced approach. I was asked by Ron to make corrections and suggest any changes or additions to what he had written; however I did not see the need to correct much, and was privileged to add a few things to what Ron has carefully written.

It is my prayer that <u>God's Arithmetic</u> will be read and even studied by a wide audience. I believe that reading what Ron has written in this book, and then putting it into practice, would help in bringing any believer to a greater level of Christian maturity. Even though I have been in ministry for about forty-five years now, I was challenged by what Ron wrote, and I was encouraged to go on in maturity. God's ways are not our ways; and in contrast to many writers today who try to make His ways like our ways, Ron lets God be God. <u>God's Arithmetic</u> is not about easy answers to difficult questions, nor does it encourage casual Christianity. It is about being faithful to what the Bible says, and about being a committed disciple of Jesus Christ, even when it is difficult and costly to do so.

Clifford R. Vick
Pastor and Missionary,
Pretoria, South Africa
August 1, 2012

Introduction

*n his article on his recent book "Maximum Faith",
George Barna writes:

"In essence, the born-again community has invited God
to reside in our hearts, accepting the special gift of love
and forgiveness that He offered, along with His promise of
eternal salvation. Sadly, once we felt certain that we had
His gift securely in hand, we abandoned Him and have continued to operate by the standards and values of the world,
searching for earthly treasures and pleasures. That is why the
research has consistently shown over the past two decades
that the lives of born-again Christians are essentially indis-
tinguishable from those of people who do not claim Jesus
Christ as their savior. We may be "religious" but we are not
truly transformed by our faith in and relationship with God.
Only a tiny proportion of born again adults get beyond their
profession of faith to experience the more robust and significant life that is available through Christ to His followers."

It was early in the year 1974 on a college campus in
upstate New York, that I met Jesus Christ. I say *met* rather
than merely *accepted,* because to me, Jesus was offering
more than a one time special gift of His love and forgiveness.
I had encountered the living Savior, who was offering me an
opportunity to live life in His presence, and to have my life

transformed by His infinite power and intimate care. Immediately, I started to immerse myself in reading the Bible. At first, I had no one to guide me, and there was much I did not understand. One thing was clear to me though: I would never again be the same person I had been before. I began to walk with Jesus, and to follow Him day by day. Any thought of abandoning Him in the way Barna describes, would have made no sense to my newly awakened young mind. Fast forward to 2012. I have come a long way spiritually since those first days after I met Jesus, and I still have a very long way to go; yet one thing has remained the same. . . In the words of the Apostle Paul:

"But one thing I do: Forgetting what is behind and straining toward what is ahead, 14 I press on toward the goal to win the prize for which God has called me heavenward in Christ Jesus." Philippians 3:13b-14 NIV

Throughout this journey, I have sought to follow Jesus Christ as His disciple, and to understand His heart and mind. I have discovered that God intends a life for me that is radically different from a life of conformity with our culture and society. If I were to try to explain this life of discipleship to someone who does not believe in Jesus, it would seem quite contrary to many of their commonly accepted views and practices of our modern culture. This is because Jesus Christ has fundamentally changed my life. As a result, my core motivation, and the basic ways that God wants me to live as a citizen of His Kingdom, often stand in stark contrast to the standards and values of the world (as Barna implies they should). However, it is these seeming contradictions toward the world - found in core Christian values - that form the basis of godly character; character that is produced in the life of a person who follows Jesus Christ in true discipleship.

It is the heavenly lessons of these basic transformational changes in our motives and attitudes - along with their resultant effects on our character - which has led me to entitle this book: "God's Arithmetic: How Life Adds Up In The Kingdom of God."

God's Arithmetic - is the metaphor I have chosen for His design to build into our lives - the qualities that characterize His children as citizens of the Kingdom of Heaven. It is God's summation of the kind of transformational living that allows us to add up life from His perspective. God's Arithmetic is the way we must begin to understand all the basic spiritual ideals that He desires to form in our thoughts, actions, and value judgments, while we live as faithful committed disciples of Christ in the world around us. God's Arithmetic is about the heavenly fundamental principles He desires to teach us. It is not about adding, subtracting, multiplying, or dividing numbers; but rather the basic 'math' necessary to successful daily living, as *God's Word* defines success. We experience God's Arithmetic as we begin to see the world through His eyes; to measure our existence as He does; and to allow His Word to shape our reality, instead of trying to forge our own. We become successful in God's eyes, as we take His truth to heart, and initiate the next steps toward ordering our lives in a way that honors Him.

This brief journey through the scripture, is not an attempt on my part to give you all of God's Arithmetic. It is not the final word - but only a beginning. There is yet a 'higher math' that lies ahead for us as believers in Christ, on that day when we enter into the fullness of eternal life. But for now, God's challenge for us, is to grow into Kingdom citizens who have come to learn the truth about the kind of people He intends us to be, and how we can take the next few steps on our journey to becoming like Christ.

These studies in God's Arithmetic have been divided into eight chapters. The strong chords of divine grace, run through each chapter to tie them all together; yet each one stands on its own, as it highlights a particular equation in God's Arithmetic.

Chapter One - **Losing Life To Keep It**; is Jesus' answer to the question of what it really means to follow Him. What are the choices we embrace when we respond favorably to Jesus' invitation? What does it really mean to reject Jesus' offer to follow Him, and to choose to keep our lives for our-selves - to live our own way?

Chapter Two - **No One Wants To Be Last**; is a discussion of the dangers of the wrong kind of 'greatness mentality'. We will look at how Jesus answered the questions, "How do you become a great Christian?", and "What does it mean to be great in the Kingdom of God?" We will examine how Jesus wants us to eliminate self-promotion, arguments, and competition, within the church. We will also consider how walking in Jesus' footsteps of service, leads to a life that is truly blessed.

Chapter Three - **Small Is Large One Cup At A Time**; examines the way we regard our service to Christ and His Church. What are the reasons we give to justify our lack of involvement in Christian ministry? Why do we downplay our ability to make a real difference in the Kingdom of God? How does God truly value the least acts of humble service in His name? How can we bring a new energy and joy into even the most modest efforts to aid our fellow believers? We will also look at the pivotal questions, "What is the meaning of success in God's eyes?", and "What is the true meaning and place of spiritual rewards?"

Chapter Four - **The Surprising Color of Joy**; looks at the unexpected spiritual blessings that advance in our lives, as we experience God's grace while undergoing trials. What attitude does God desire for us to take toward our hardships and difficulties? How can we learn to see opportunities for spiritual growth - in the surprising ways that God wraps His gifts to us? We will join together on the journey toward mature discipleship, as we learn how the joy of Jesus can permeate our lives in all circumstances. We will discover how God is working to *reinforce* our joy, through every situation we imagine is robbing us of it.

Chapter Five - **One For Good Measure**; is an important and meaningful study on the Biblical concept of generosity. What does it mean to be a generous person? What should our motives be as we give? Why should a Christian strive to live with an open hand and an open heart toward others? Is generosity of any benefit to us as believers? What does the spirit of generous giving look like in our lives? Is there any difference between Christian generosity, and the kind of generosity demonstrated by those who do not believe in Christ? We will look at these questions concerning generous giving, and arrive at a new understanding of the Bible's harmony on the matter, from start to finish. We will also learn how God's grace, and not His law, has always been the underlying motivation for Christian stewardship.

Chapter Six - **Be Weak To Be Strong**; will demonstrate that there is a clear path that leads us into an experience of spiritual strength and power — a path unimpeded by our many weaknesses and limitations. Through God's Arithmetic, we will explore the amazing idea that God's power is in fact *made perfect* in our weaknesses. How can a Kingdom citizen come to the realization of the power of Christ on display in their life? If there is a path to this power, how do we get started on it? What attitudes must we adopt to allow God's power to work most effectively in our lives? What are the principles that teach us how to find the most satisfying experience of Christ's power and strength striving within us? We will look at some prominent Biblical examples of these principles, and see how they characterize the lives of those who have been used greatly for God's glory.

Chapter Seven - **Hi Def Pictures Of God's Children**; struggles with the problem of why so many of Christ's followers are portrayed by the world as hypocrites. Why do we lack the distinctiveness that should mark us as His true disciples? Among all the qualities of character that we strive towards as believers — which ones most effectively identify us as children of God? What godly traits mark us out most clearly as individuals who act like Jesus? If we had to choose only three high definition pictures of Christian character that would best demonstrate our likeness to the Lord — what would they be? We will explore the idea that there *are* three such unique qualities of character; virtues that most effectively allow people to recognize that we are genuine ambassadors of Jesus Christ.

Chapter Eight - **When Gain Is Loss**; sets forth from the Bible - humanity's blindness to its true condition: That all people are slaves to sin. Only Jesus Christ can reveal to us our deepest needs, and open our eyes to the truth about how we can obtain a right relationship with God. What makes Jesus unique? What does it mean to know Him? Can this world offer anything that compares with the surpassing value of knowing Him? Why is it important for a follower of Christ to know Him better and better? From the conversion experience of the Apostle Paul, we will explore many commonly asked questions that pertain to our salvation: How many ways are there of obtaining a right relationship with God? Can anyone acquire God's favor through their own efforts? Are all religions really just the same in God's eyes? How can religion be spiritually dangerous? Are sincere beliefs enough to ensure a person of a place in heaven? Why is the Bible unique? What actions matter when it comes to having peace with God - and what actually has no value at all? What does Paul mean when he says that there is a righteousness that comes from God - and how does he assert we may obtain it?. . . and finally: If salvation is truly so easy for us to receive — why do so many people reject the offer God makes to them?

The statistical data from survey takers (like George Barna) may tell us that the lives of most born-again Christians are not that different from others (those who do not claim to know Christ) — but there is no need to believe that this situation is beyond reform. It is with this notion in mind, that God's Arithmetic was written. The intention is to make an appeal to believers in Christ who possess a hunger to grow spiritually. The desire is that these believers will arrive at a deeper, more mature understanding, of what it means to follow Jesus Christ in a world that largely does not. God's Arithmetic is not for the casual disciple. It is for those who are serious about spiritual growth, and who are willing to bring a commitment to it, to think deeply about the meaning of their faith.

It is my hope, that the thoughts on these pages will be part of an ongoing legacy of faithful discipleship that I desire to leave with my family, and to all those who have ever known me, or heard me teach the Word of God. It is also my prayer, that this work will honor the many faithful brothers and sisters who have unselfishly given their lives for Christ and the gospel, so that I might have the opportunity to experience the infinite riches of His grace. My ongoing passion, is to be the kind of disciple that Paul exhorted Timothy to be; and to inspire in other believers, that same devotion and desire:

"1 You then, my son, be strong in the grace that is in Christ Jesus. 2 And the things you have heard me say in the presence of many witnesses entrust to reliable people who will also be qualified to teach others." 2 Timothy 2:1-2 NIV

May God direct this work into the hands and hearts of those it will benefit, and may He use it to bring glory and honor to Jesus Christ, who is God over all, forever praised, Amen.

Ron Bodlander
Mesa, Arizona. March 2012

Losing Life To Keep It!

Is the American dream alive and well? My son doesn't
think so. There was a time when people thought that "a
chicken in every pot, and a car in every backyard to boot"
sounded pretty good. Many Americans have long believed
that with a dream, initiative, and a lot of hard work, a person
can achieve success no matter their background or place of
origin. In today's society there is a new American dream,
my son suggests satirically. He thinks the new mantra is, "I
want to be able to stay home and do nothing." He is not
speaking here of a well-earned retirement after long years of
dedicated labor. Rather, the idea is that we dream of having
the world handed to us on a silver platter. We aspire to have
all the leisure time we desire along with the ability to do
whatever we want whenever we want. We crave this position as an entitlement. All we really hunger for is "the good
life." "Is that too much to ask?", we say. "Surely, I deserve
a life like that." I think my son is correct. I'm not quite certain why this is so. Perhaps it has to do with the false hope
state lotteries offer, that we can have it all for only a dollar.
Or maybe it is the harsh reality involved for most of us in
making ends meet financially, that causes us to pine for easy
living. Then again, it could be the sad fact that most Americans do not enjoy their jobs, which in turn causes a longing

for a life of ease and comfort. Whatever the true reason for this new American dream, it is grounded in the notion that our ultimate kind of lifestyle would not involve effort or struggle. Certainly, not everyone holds to such a self-indulgent ideal. Most of us realize to some extent, that hard work and perseverance in life contribute to our character, and to our growth as human beings. We are not willing to go so far as to say that our dream is, "to be able to stay home and do nothing." Yet many people still reason that the welfare of their soul would best be served if somehow they could have all the things in the world that their heart desires. "Is there a problem with such wishful thinking?", we might ask. Are such desires really so bad? After all, doesn't God want what is best for us? Doesn't His love for us encompass a desire that we have the best things this world has to offer? Doesn't Jesus want His followers to be happy? If we are poor and unhappy, won't that reflect badly on the gospel? Wouldn't those observing our lives be constrained to say, "Why would I want to be a Christian if it doesn't involve a higher standard of living for me and my family?" My intention here is not to put some kind of premium on poverty. What I want to do is to question the value of a certain kind of thinking. There is a prevailing propensity today toward a kind of Christianity that supposes we cannot be faithful followers of Christ, if our aim is not the accumulation of material possessions, and the acquisition of the means to live "the good life." The underlying problem with this type of sentiment is that it does not truly reflect the nature of what it really means to follow Jesus Christ. Actually, the burden for the pervasive influence of this kind of thinking lies with the Church. In our zeal to present the incredible offer of the gospel to every person, we often do so in a manner that appeals to the base part of our human nature. We reason that if we told people the true cost of discipleship up front, then the gospel would hold no appeal to them. We falsely assume that if we present the good news about Christ in a way that sounds too much like a challenge, then those who are seeking after God will shy away from our message. This is not to say that we should downplay grace, and the free offer God makes to each of us when He invites us into a personal relationship with Him. For God's great love was clearly evident when He sent the Lord Jesus Christ to be the Savior of the world. Through the cross, He offers spiritual healing for the widespread bane of sin and suffering that prevails throughout this fallen evil world in which we live. God has established the New Covenant, through Jesus' death and resurrection. From this Covenant, issue the free flow of forgiveness, the transformation of our hearts, and eternal life. All this is lavished upon us at no cost. That is, there is no cost *to us* in the sense that there is nothing whatsoever we can do to earn our salvation or pay for it - Jesus has paid it all at the cost of his own blood. Yet we do a disservice even to those people who are hurting the most, when we fail to make clear to them, at an appropriate time, the conditions of accepting the gospel and becoming a follower of Jesus. In that sense, there is a "cost" to us. This cost is presented in terms of the context of relationship. In other words, the offer God freely makes us, to believe in His Son, requires a response. If we give people the impression that God wants to share His love with us without a meaningful response required on our part, we are distorting what it means to enter into a personal relationship with Him. The Bible teaches us that the Church is the Bride of Christ. Jesus has taken all of His people collectively and each of us individually, into a very intimate relationship with Himself that the Bible likens unto marriage. In a marriage, it is not possible for the relationship to thrive if one of the partners is solely interested in receiving love from the other but is unwilling to give love themselves. Any such partnership could not be sustained. This is not because the loving partner is unwilling to make the marriage work. It is because the person who is unwilling to respond to that love makes it impossible for the couple to share life together in any meaningful way. The person who gets married is expected to adopt the position of a husband or wife. They are committing to act in a certain way with respect to their new spouse. They are in essence saying that they will love that person for life, and behave in a manner that appropriately reflects the love they are declaring for their partner. By refusing to receive or respond to their spouse's love, the unwilling partner corrupts the nature of their joint participation in the relationship. It makes unattainable the union that was intended when they committed to the marriage in the first place. So then, if we attempt to introduce someone to Jesus Christ, and then fail to help them understand what their response must be for the relationship to be viable, we are inviting them to a life that remains self-centered; a life incapable of spiritual growth. A self indulgent life is unable to experience the blessings inherent in a relationship with the Creator of the universe. Such a life will fail to develop character, because that person will primarily be seeking only his or her own will and self interests, and not the interests of Jesus Christ.

What we really need then, is a way of presenting the free offer of the gospel that does not neglect the demand that is made upon the person who would receive such a generous gift. For although the salvation Jesus offers cannot be earned in any way by what we do, it nonetheless carries with it a condition of acceptance. It may surprise you to learn that it was Jesus Himself who made this clear to everyone, both to those who were seeking a relationship with God, and to those who had already chosen to follow Him. We'll come to back to that shortly. As I wrestled with how to introduce Jesus' own invitation to follow Him, I decided to first put forth briefly in my own words, the fitting response to His invitation. This may help us form a healthy Christian perspective, and to better understand the meaning of Jesus' words as they were first spoken to those who sought to follow Him while he was still on earth. When we take Jesus as our Savior, we are also agreeing to own Him as our Lord. The two cannot be separated. As we receive Him into our hearts and are born again, we must understand that God has now firmly placed us into a new relationship with Himself. The New Testament describes this relationship in various ways. One of these fundamental descriptions is that we are now uniquely God's children in Jesus Christ (John 1:12-13; Rom.8:14-17; Gal.3:26; 4:6-7). As a child of God, we are first and foremost disciples of Jesus with all that that entails. To establish us in this new life, God has given us His Spirit to live and dwell within us. Throughout the variety of ways that the Holy Spirit ministers to us (whether it is to comfort, counsel, guide, encourage, rebuke, teach, exhort, or strengthen), He is always working to transform us into the likeness of Christ (Rom.8:29-30; 2Cor.3:18; 1Jn.3:2). For our new nature to be conformed to the humanity that Jesus exemplifies, there are choices we must make. These choices are incumbent upon us in our new status as children of God. Unquestionably, it is God who empowers us to carry out these choices, but we must agree to them. Our agreement means that we will act upon them. In other words, as God makes clear to us from His Word what it means to follow Christ, we will do so willingly, and in a manner consistent with who He has already declared us to be - His children and His Church - which is the bride of Christ.

Here is where God's Arithmetic comes into play. The choices we must make are laid out for us in a way that the carnal mind cannot comprehend. These types of spiritual choices cannot be understood apart from a total willingness to commit ourselves without reservation to Jesus Christ. In God's Arithmetic, as Jesus will present it, one cannot actually follow Him without concurrent choices being made. What then are the choices that must be made when we decide to follow Jesus? To be concise; we give up our old life and exchange it for the new life he brings. This is explained to us effectively in several passages by the Apostle Paul. Look at Romans 6:1-14 MSG:

"So what do we do? Keep on sinning so God can keep on forgiving? I should hope not! If we've left the country where sin is sovereign, how can we still live in our old house there? Or didn't you realize we packed up and left there for good? That is what happened in baptism. When we went under the water, we left the old country of sin behind; when we came up out of the water, we entered into the new country of grace — a new life in a new land!

That's what baptism into the life of Jesus means. When we are lowered into the water, it is like the burial of Jesus; when we are raised up out of the water, it is like the resurrection of Jesus. Each of us is raised into a light-filled world by our Father so that we can see where we're going in our new grace-sovereign country.

Could it be any clearer? Our old way of life was nailed to the cross with Christ, a decisive end to that sin-miserable life — no longer at sin's every beck and call! What we believe is this: If we get included in Christ's sin-conquering death, we also get included in his life-saving resurrection. We know that when Jesus was raised from the dead it was a signal of the end of death-as-the-end. Never again will death have the last word. When Jesus died, he took sin down with him, but alive he brings God down to us. From now on, think of it this way: Sin speaks a dead language that means nothing to you; God speaks your mother tongue, and you hang on every word. You are dead to sin and alive to God. That's what Jesus did.

That means you must not give sin a vote in the way you conduct your lives. Don't give it the time of day. Don't even run little errands that are connected with that old way of life. Throw yourselves wholeheartedly and full-time — remember, you've been raised from the dead! — into God's way of doing things. Sin can't tell you how to live. After all, you're not living under that old tyranny any longer. You're living in the freedom of God."

We see from Paul's illustration that when Jesus died on the cross, He represented all of us. We died there with Him. When God raised Him from the dead, we also were raised with Him. As we undergo Christian baptism, it is a perfect picture of our union with Christ. Because of our identification with Jesus in his death, the power of sin has been broken in our lives. Sin no longer has any control over us. When Jesus rose from death, all those who belong to Him were raised together with Him. The power of the new life that Jesus now has in relationship to God, a life that can never die, has been bestowed upon us as well. Therefore we must consider ourselves as dead to the power of sin in our lives, and as having entered into a brand new relationship with God. The Message (quoted above) paraphrases it this way, "Sin speaks a dead language that means nothing to you; God speaks your mother tongue, and you hang on every word." Since we have now been set free from sin, we are empowered to *choose* to follow after our new nature - which is the regenerated life that God has implanted in us through Jesus Christ. As we just saw, we are not even to give sin a vote as to how we conduct our lives. Rather, we are told to, "Throw yourselves wholeheartedly and full-time — remember, you've been raised from the dead! — into God's way of doing things" (vv.12-14 above). It is important to say at this point, that this life changing transformation is not some sort of religious fiction. It is a spiritual reality that God has declared to exist when we place our faith in Jesus. We are to regard this new life as real, and then to depend on it's power, as we make the choices that are embraced by the promise of our new relationship with God. Paul relates these same concepts in his other letters as well. In 2 Corinthians 5:15,17 (NLT) he states:

"He (Jesus) died for everyone so that those who receive his new life will no longer live for themselves. Instead, they will live for Christ, who died and was raised for them."

"This means that anyone who belongs to Christ has become a new person. The old life is gone; a new life has begun!"

In Galatians 2:20 NCV, Paul expresses our identification with Christ, and our reception of new life, this way:

"I was put to death on the cross with Christ, and I do not live anymore — it is Christ who lives in me. I still live in my body, but I live by faith in the Son of God who loved me and gave himself to save me."

Each of the different ways that Paul expresses these realities, is an echo of Jesus' invitation to follow Him. With that in mind, I want to quote this same verse in Galatians from The Message. This paraphrase highlights the element of choice in following Christ, an element that Paul emphasized:

"Indeed, I have been crucified with Christ. My ego is no longer central. It is no longer important that I appear righteous before you or have your good opinion, and I am no longer driven to impress God. Christ lives in me. The life you see me living is not "mine," but it is lived by faith in the Son of God, who loved me and gave himself for me. I am not going to go back on that."

Each aspect of Paul's commitment to Christ involved choices. It is these choices that sum up for us, what it means to truly follow Christ. What we see here is that Paul's ego has been set aside and his motives have been changed. He has chosen a commitment of faith that is permanently settled in his life.

I related earlier how the Bible uses the illustration of marriage to provide us with a picture of the relationship of the Lord Jesus Christ to His Church. When a couple marries, they will typically exchange wedding vows to solemnize and publicly confirm their lifelong commitment to each other. I would like to pull together an explanation of what it means to follow Christ, by putting it in the form of a wedding vow. Although the vow would be taken by the Church collectively as Christ's bride, we realize that what is true for the Church collectively is also true for each of us individually. Here then is what our personal commitment to follow Christ might look like, if we were taking a "wedding vow" to join ourselves to Him for life.

I take you Jesus to be my Savior. I cease immediately and always from all my own efforts to earn God's favor, because you have completely and forever paid the price for my sins when you died on the cross. I rejoice in my place in your family as your child. I welcome my commission as part of your bride, the Church. I understand that this means that my life must always be joined together with your Church in service to you, since we are all one family. Because you rose from the dead and live forever, I understand that I too have received eternal life solely as a free gift of your love and grace. I take joy in this relationship we have entered. I recognize that I am forever reconciled with God and I share in your oneness and peace with Him. I promise to always remember who I am in you – realizing that my daily living will always be a reflection of our bond of love.

I take you Jesus my Savior to be forever my Lord. I agree to set aside my ego and to place you on the throne of my life. I commit to leave my old life of sin behind and to walk in the newness of life that is mine in relationship to you. I submit myself fully to the direction of the Holy Spirit, given as your marriage gift, who lives in me and makes the actual presence of you and your Father to dwell at home in my heart. I commit to following your path in all the affairs of my life, as your Spirit reveals your will to me through your Word. I will make it my lifelong ambition to be like you in all I think, do, and say. I will always choose to live for you and not for myself. You will be the center, focus, and goal of my life. I will keep my eyes fixed on you to the exclusion of everything that might distract me from following you. I will no longer live to win the approval of people, but I will aim only to please God because I am His child. I vow to never take any glory upon myself, but to give all glory to you, for there is room for only one glory in the Universe and that is yours. I acknowledge the unfailing love of the Father in giving you to me, and I promise to share this gift with everyone I can, all the days of my life.

It may be that some who are reading this will think that such a vow as I have written is excessive. You might feel that this is way too much to expect of a person first coming to Jesus and asking Him for mercy. After all, many who first approach Jesus Christ do so in a state of pain or desperation, and are in no frame of mind to be able to make the kind of commitment described above. You would be absolutely correct to say this. Jesus receives with open arms all who come to Him for mercy, and He does so without partiality or the expectation that the petitioner has anything to offer him in return. However, that is not what I had in mind with this vow. What we are looking at here, is what it really means to make the choice to *follow* Jesus, to become His disciple, and to publicly declare this as your intent. As part of our first steps in obedience to Christ's command, we submit ourselves to believer's baptism. Through baptism, we are in a real sense, doing exactly what we have been describing. That is, we are making known through a public ceremony, our ambition to follow Jesus, and the commitment we have made to do exactly that. Typically, in modern churches, the candidate for baptism is asked a series of questions right before they are baptized. These questions are in essence the candidate's confession of faith in Christ that is being made in front of many witnesses. In many Christian traditions, there is some form of catechism provided to new believers to ensure that they really understand the Bible's basic teaching about Christ and salvation. To give baptism its intended meaning, and to secure the integrity of their beliefs, a church wants to be reasonably confident that the individual really understands the commitment they are making. While it is not my intention to suggest that a person professing faith in Christ be needlessly grilled with graduate level questions of theology prior to allowing them to be baptized - there must be some level of understanding of what is really involved in making such a profession of faith. Whether it is an adult being baptized or a child, they must understand at an age appropriate level what it is to give their life to Jesus Christ. A child cannot obviously appreciate all the implications involved in making such a life commitment. They can however understand what it means to make a promise to someone, and to have another person (in this case God) make a promise to them. A child, like an adult, is capable of a personal relationship with God, albeit one suited to their level of personal maturity. If the heart be sincere, no matter what the age level, God will accept the person and establish the relationship Himself. We can be confident of this based on such scriptural passages as John 6:37-38 NIV:

"All those the Father gives me will come to me, and whoever comes to me I will never drive away. For I have come down from heaven not to do my will but to do the will of him who sent me."

Perhaps our churches are a bit too benignly lenient when explaining to a person what it means to give their life to Christ. We use phrases like, "invite Him into your heart." Words like these communicate well to contemporary ears. However, if we are not careful, we can leave a new believer with the impression that being in a relationship with the Lord is nothing more than a warm-fuzzy convenience, rather than what it really is – a death to our sinful human nature and a birth into a transformed life where all things become new.

Everything we have talked about so far, has been to prepare us for a special invitation. We have been setting the table to come and dine with Jesus. Let us now partake of the bread of heaven and drink the living water set before us in the Word of God. Jesus' invitation to those who desire to follow Him, is given to us in all four gospels. Matthew, Mark, and Luke, all read very similarly, except for some minor differences. John's version of Jesus' invitation is expressed somewhat differently, and I will touch on that later. I have chosen to focus on Luke's narrative of these words, due to his specific inclusion of the need to remind ourselves *daily* of what it means to follow Jesus. You can find the parallel passages in Matthew 16:24-27; Mark 8:34-38; and John 12:23-26.

"23 Then he said to them all: "Whoever wants to be my disciple must deny themselves and take up their cross daily and follow me. 24 For whoever wants to save their life will lose it, but whoever loses their life for me will save it. 25 What good is it for someone to gain the whole world, and yet lose or forfeit their very self? 26 Whoever is ashamed of me and my words, the Son of Man will be ashamed of them when he

comes in his glory and in the glory of the Father and of the holy angels."" Luke 9:23-26 NIV

In normal everyday life, when we lose an object it is gone. The thing we have lost is not in our possession, and it is no longer possible to keep it safe. For example, my brother recently purchased a new cell phone. On a shopping trip to a retail store in a nearby town, he lost the phone somewhere along the way. It had fallen out of his pocket and he was unaware of it. The phone was lost and not retrievable. He had to purchase a new phone despite his regret at losing the original. All of us have had the unfortunate experience of losing something. It may be something small and insignificant, or it may be something that was of great value to us. Either way, whatever was lost is now absent from us and we no longer possess it. Not so in God's Arithmetic. In our walk in the Spirit, what oftentimes appears on the surface to be lost, has actually been preserved. According to Jesus, this is eminently so with regard to our soul – our true life. There are things, Jesus tells us, that we must lose (give up or let go of) to follow Him. As we do so, we discover that what we thought was loss is actually gain. We can illustrate this from Luke's gospel in the following way.

Lose	Gain
v.23 Self determination	God's plan and purpose for us
v.23 A life of ease and leisure	God's direction for a life of self sacrifice
v.24 Safety and Security	Eternal Life

v.24 Living for my own interests	The discovery of life's true meaning through dedication to Christ's message and teachings
v.25 The approval of the world	Your true self (soul)
v.26 A refusal to bear reproach for Jesus sake	Jesus personal acknowledgment of you when He returns

Before we can further spell out these aspects of Jesus' invitation, there are a few specific words that must be clarified. The first of these, is the word *"cross."* The cross represents our willingness to radically commit to God's will for us. This includes whatever suffering, sacrifice, and reproach, that accompanies such obedience - even to the point of death. The next word is *"life."* Life (or *soul* -Gk. Psuche) is your full "personhood" inside and out - your unique inner life and total personality, emphasizing all you are as a human being apart from God. The last word is *"world."* The world represents any and all approbation toward you, based on what is esteemed and valued by the vast societies of people living on earth apart from God. This includes all material possessions, and any other distinction the unbelieving culture holds in high regard. It would encompass any and all things you might be offered that could take the place of God in your life. With these clarifications in mind, we can now examine Jesus' invitation to follow Him. We will look at what this invitation means to both those who are considering following Jesus, and those who have already determined to follow him.

The fact is that Jesus Christ is still reaching out to people all over the world. His invitation to follow Him - is as vital today as it was nearly two thousand years ago. He has commissioned His Church to partner with Him in bringing the message of the gospel to every person in all nations. Anyone wishing to accompany Jesus in the work of sharing God's love with everyone, must follow where He leads. For the would-be disciple, this means a willingness to place yourself geographically where God wants you - but it means more than that. A disciple is a learner. Jesus' desire is to teach us how to live our lives God's way. This teaching will include instruction on how to relate to others and serve their needs. It involves learning how to make priority decisions while experiencing the diverse complexities of life. Discipleship is learning how to live as a human being before God, as Jesus did. It is a life of service, and of looking at the world in a way that may often conflict with the views of our culture. As a result of following Jesus, we may be faced with choices that involve sacrifice or hardship. However, we are never alone or without comfort. To follow Jesus is to find a life that brings the only true peace and fulfillment to the soul of man. In another setting, Jesus put it this way:

"Are you tired? Worn out? Burned out on religion? Come to me. Get away with me and you'll recover your life. I'll show you how to take a real rest. Walk with me and work with me — watch how I do it. Learn the unforced rhythms of grace. I won't lay anything heavy or ill-fitting on you. Keep company with me and you'll learn to live freely and lightly." Matthew 11:28-30 MSG

To live like this in company with Jesus, is to live in the "unforced rhythms of grace." This is another way of saying what it truly means to live as a child of God. To be a fol-lower of Jesus is to experience a life enveloped in God's grace. Jesus' words of invitation only seem harsh or painful to the mind of someone unwilling to follow Him. But for the seeker whose heart has been touched by God, or the disciple who has already chosen to follow after Him, the teachings of

Christ bring blessing, peace, and true life. To wear the yoke of Jesus, to live as he lived, is to move daily in harmony with the will of God. A clear conscience, a peaceful mind, and a light heart, are descriptions that fall short in their effort to describe the blessedness of a life lived in close relationship to God.

In connection to this invitation to follow Him, Jesus adds words that define the nature of the offer. His followers will have to deny themselves, and take up his cross daily. Jesus spoke these words because there are many who would follow him only for what they can get out of it for themselves. A good example of this is found in the gospel of John. Jesus had just fed 5,000 people with a few small loaves of bread and two fish. He crossed to the other side of the lake, and the crowd followed looking for him. When they found Him, Jesus spoke these words:

"You've come looking for me not because you saw God in my actions but because I fed you, filled your stomachs — and for free." John 6:26 MSG

John gives us another example of this in his gospel. Jesus was in the town of Bethany, dining with his friends; Mary, Martha, and Lazarus (whom Jesus had raised from the dead). Mary had taken a very expensive container of perfume and used it to anoint Jesus' feet. Judas Iscariot (who would later betray Jesus), asked why such an expensive gift was used this way, rather than being sold to raise a good deal of money for the poor. At that point, John tells us something about Judas that belies his supposed concern for the poor. We can almost hear John whisper these words to us as an aside, as he says of Judas:

*"But Judas did not really care about the poor; he said this
because he was a thief. He was the one who kept the money
box, and he often stole from it."* John 12:6 NCV

There are a great many people today who are like both
the crowd who sought Jesus only for food, and Judas who
followed him only for personal gain. They are not sincere
in their desire to follow Christ for who He is. What they
are really trying to do is follow Jesus for what they can
get out of it. Kind of a "what's in it for me" attitude. Such
individuals do not really want to learn how to live a life in
close relationship to God. Their real desire is selfish. They
are asking, "how much is God going to give me if I favor
Him with *my* presence?" These are not the kind of followers
that Jesus is seeking. Therefore it was necessary for Him to
make clear to those who were considering His claims and to
those who already were with Him, what it really meant to be
his disciple. When Jesus speaks of the necessity of denying
yourself, it immediately addresses those who might follow
Him for selfish reasons. To deny yourself is to make the
most serious minded commitment to place God's will above
your own. It is to move your entire existence in a direction
that makes love for God your absolute ruling passion. When
Jesus was asked to sum up what it means to fulfill the law of
God, His answer was this:

*"Hear, O Israel: The Lord our God, the Lord is one. Love the
Lord your God with all your heart and with all your soul and
with all your mind and with all your strength.' The second
is this: 'Love your neighbor as yourself.' There is no commandment greater than these."* Mark 12:29b-31 NIV

To deny oneself then, is to place God first in your life
without reservation. It is to love Him in a way that makes
your own personal desires subordinate to His direction in

absolutely everything. It is to take anything or anyone else that you might make as a "god" in your life, and reject it - submitting instead, unconditionally to Christ. It is to place God's Kingdom and His way of life as your highest priority. Jesus put it this way in the Sermon on the Mount:

"You can't worship two gods at once. Loving one god, you'll end up hating the other. Adoration of one feeds contempt for the other. You can't worship God and Money both."

"Seek first God's kingdom and what God wants. Then all your other needs will be met as well." Matthew 6:24, 33 MSG

All of us who desire to follow Jesus, do not have exactly the same issues that could hinder such a full and unreserved commitment to Him. For some, it might be an unwilling-ness to give up material possessions (cp. Luke 18:18-27). For others, it might be personal goals or ambitions (cp. Matthew 20:20-28). For still others, it may be family, friends, or a lifestyle they are unwilling to leave behind (cp. 2 Timothy 4:10a). Whatever it is that is personal and specific to you that stands in the way of your unconditional commitment to Christ - is what you must be willing to deny yourself to follow Him. He is worthy of no less, and will accept no less.

To emphasize this kind of commitment even further, Jesus adds that we must take up our cross. This phrase is very often misunderstood. Our tendency as Christians is to suppose that whenever we are suffering for any reason, we are bearing our cross. Now it is true that we will suffer in this world. A popular recent advertisement for an insurance company declares that the world is filled with "mayhem". We endure pains and sorrows of many different kinds. There are physical pains and illness, financial losses and hardship, emotional heartaches and distress, and the mental anguish caused by our own sins, as well the sins of others. Despite our entire assortment of troubles, Jesus encourages us to take heart:

"I have told you all this so that you may have peace in me. Here on earth you will have many trials and sorrows. But take heart, because I have overcome the world." John 16:33 NIV

Nonetheless, the suffering that is prevalent in our lives is not what Jesus has in view when He says we must take up our cross and follow Him. The cross, as I noted earlier, represents our willingness to radically commit to God's will for us. This includes whatever suffering, sacrifice, and reproach that accompanies such obedience, even to the point of death. What Jesus is saying to us, is that to live in relationship with Him, is never going to be a halfhearted proposition. There is an expression in gambling that is used to declare one's intention to risk everything. A person will say they are "all in." Once announced, there is no going back. They are willing to risk everything on their decision. This is the meaning of the cross. Our life is decided. We risk everything, putting it all on the line to follow Jesus. There is no turning back regardless of the consequences of our obedience to God. Jesus knows we are weak, and that we will falter at times in our commitment. Nevertheless, his invitation to follow Him is intended to make clear the highest sense of service to God and man. Jesus seeks followers who will make their decision with eyes wide open. He wants this for those who are first considering His claims, as well as those who have already trusted Him. We should have no illusions about what is involved, if we want to experience the abundant life that He promises to those who belong to Him:

"My purpose is to give them a rich and satisfying life."
John 10:10 NLT

This life - purposeful, meaningful, and satisfying - can only be experienced as we get under the cross and take up Jesus' gentle yolk; cheerful loving obedience to God, lived out in a life of humble dedicated service to others. There is no need whatsoever for us to fear this kind of life. Some people have the strange idea that if they follow Christ, he will lead them into a life of misery. Nothing could be further from the truth. A spiritually minded person understands that complete dedication to Jesus, is the most satisfying life imaginable. Even if our circumstances turn out to be unfavorable at times, it is an unalterable truth in the Word of God that obedience to God brings blessing. When we follow the Holy Spirit's leading in our lives, the result is life and peace:

"Those who live following their sinful selves think only about things that their sinful selves want. But those who live following the Spirit are thinking about the things the Spirit wants them to do. If people's thinking is controlled by the sinful self, there is death. But if their thinking is controlled by the Spirit, there is life and peace." Romans 8:5-6 NCV

A story was told recently by one of the leading pastors at my church. He was describing an encounter with God he had while on a mission trip to North Africa. Upon observing the single minded dedication of certain Christians who spent their lives serving in sparsely populated areas of that region, his conscience was troubled. He observed the joy and satisfaction these individuals had in giving their lives to bring the gospel to those who would otherwise never hear it. As he was leaving, God spoke to his heart regarding the matter of obedience. To the surprise of his companions, he was compelled to stop their vehicle, and walk out into a private place in the middle of nowhere to settle the matter with his Lord. He was convicted by the selfless dedication and spirit of service these people had demonstrated who were serving the Lord, and seemingly had so little. He realized that it was they who were fully experiencing the life that Jesus promised, due to their willingness to take up his cross and follow him. This pastor then resolved that no matter what the cost, he too would be willing to risk everything in obedience to Jesus. It isn't that we have to go to Africa or anywhere else to take up our cross. Wherever God has planted us, it is there that we must resolve to follow Jesus into a life that is not consumed with our own interests, but with His. Such a life will be joined with a community of other believers, sharing together in the work of bringing the gospel of Christ to a dying, hurting world. A world crying out for meaning, truth, and hope.

Before we move on to the next part of Jesus' invitation, let's look at a word that Luke adds, which the other gospels omit. Jesus says the cross of which He speaks must be taken up by us *daily*. I believe this word is a special reminder that must be weighed by those who are first considering following Jesus, as well as those who have already made that choice. To take up the cross daily, is Jesus' way of emphasizing that this life of willing, obedient, sonship to God, must command our attention every day - all the way to the end of our lives. There is no time of life where we can casually lay the cross aside, and then take it up again at a time of our own choosing. That is not to say that there won't be seasons of life that demand our attention, or consume our hearts. I am thinking just now of a family in my church that has an infant child who is very ill - hanging between life and death. Through the prayers of many people, this baby has already come through several life threatening operations and procedures, just to stay alive. There remains the constant danger of infection, of heart or lungs failing, and the likelihood of permanent brain damage, even should the child recover. Surely, some will say, the cross must be laid aside just now! How can following Jesus be foremost on the mind of those parents at a time like this? It is exactly at a time like this, that we have our greatest opportunity to show the world what it really means to follow Christ, wherever He might lead. To demonstrate unshakable trust in God's wisdom, love, and power in the midst of such a terrible time of suffering, is to allow Him to bring something quite extraordinary into our circumstance. For God can work into the lives of all involved, a demonstration of His love, that will etch into every heart, a confidence in Him that can never be removed or shaken. Only the Lord can take such painful experiences in life, and transform them into a means of help and blessing for everyone involved. Only He can help us see that the tragedy of the moment, is not the end of life. Even in the darkest hour, God is at work to bring the highest possible good to those who love Him, and are called according to His purpose (Rom.8:28). He gives us new eyes. Eyes that see beyond the sorrow of the moment. Eyes that perceive the divine love and purpose that are bringing spiritual blessing, and infusing it into the very occasion that caused the pain. This kind of insight can not always be put into words. It must be experienced by people of faith. We who have lived with Jesus through sorrow, understand that by following Him most closely when circumstances are at their worst, we experience the highest possible outcomes for ourselves and for everyone else in the orbit of our lives. Only God can bring triumph out of tragedy. Only He can bring life out of death. Only He can transform pain and make it a chariot, carrying us upward to a higher life. Daily, the cross is ours, and we lay it aside to our own detriment.

To take up our cross daily, is also a reminder that as we live each new day with our eyes fixed on Jesus, it allows Him to give us eyes like His. We are surrounded each day by people with needs. Oftentimes, we are not aware of those needs. If we follow Jesus daily, we can learn to see with His eyes, to hear with His ears, to feel with His heart. We can develop a sensitivity to others that can not be acquired any other way but through a close walk with Him. For many years, I worked in large Welfare offices. I would often observe customers becoming increasingly angry with our staff as they spoke with them either on the phone or in person. In a great many of these situations, an already unpleasant confrontation could have been prevented from escalating, if our staff had simply taken the time to listen patiently. Instead, they would often respond in haste to people, with no regard for what their real need might actually be. Sometimes a person's real need is not so obvious. What they are saying on the surface, may not be what is really bothering them. We have all had times where we have vented in anger to someone (or they to us), and what is being spoken aloud is not the true reason for the anger. Suppose it's a rainy day, and you say to a member of your family, "It's a great day isn't it?" They reply grumpily, "What do you mean it's a great day? It's a terrible day. It's raining outside. Take your happy attitude and leave me alone!" Your immediate reaction to this might be, "Wow, what's wrong with you?!" Alternately, if you know the person to normally not be quite so grumpy, you might realize their reaction has nothing to do with you, or with the rain, per se. It may be that they were counting on going to a picnic that day, and it had been rained out. They are now somewhat angry or frustrated at not being able to enjoy the picnic. These feelings of disappointment are now being taken out on you, albeit unintentionally. So, after observing and listening carefully, instead of reacting angrily to their reply to your greeting, you choose to respond to them by saying, "What's really bothering you? Can I help?" What you have done now, is what I call *listening between the lines*. It is a way of reading someone's body language, inflections of voice, facial expressions, and character, in a way that really homes in on what their actual need may be. To be alert and sensitive in this way, requires us to live daily with a mindset that is more concerned for others than for ourselves. Only through a consistent and habitual walk with Jesus, taking up our cross daily to follow Him, can we cultivate the ability to see others as God sees them. Then, as we become more aware of the undisclosed needs around us, we can better minister to those individuals whom God has especially placed in our path.

Jesus has begun the invitation to be his disciple by telling us of the necessity to deny ourselves, take up our cross, and follow him. In an effort to help us understand why it is so essential that this is the only way to be His disciple, He now explains the alternative choice. What is the consequence to us if we choose not to follow Him as a disciple? Here again, the language of scripture is the language of God's Arithmetic. We can only understand it by learning to see the big picture of life, God's way:

"For whoever wants to save their life will lose it, but whoever loses their life for me will save it." (v.24)

If you weren't already thinking hard about whether you really wanted to be Jesus' follower, you would certainly do so after hearing this verse and the one following it. For us to understand the wordplay here, we must be absolutely clear on the meaning of the contrasting choices Jesus presents. *Life*, as I explained above, is all that you are as an individual person, inside and out. It encompasses your inner life and total personality - your life in the world as a distinct human being. It is what makes you - *you* - a complete living soul. The contrast Jesus makes here is not simple wordplay. It is about eternal destiny; life and death, salvation and eternal loss. There is for all of us, Jesus is saying, the choice of a path that results in utter and irrevocable loss to ourselves, and a divergent way that ends in everlasting gain. What then does Jesus mean when He says that we must lose our 'life' to save (or keep) it, and if we try to keep (or save) our 'life', we will lose it? It is the message of the gospel, *"There is salvation in no one else! God has given no other name under heaven by which we must be saved."* (Acts 4:12 NLT). For a person to live in this world with no regard for Jesus Christ is to *already* exist in a state of spiritual darkness and death (John 3:18, 36; John 5:24). The voice of God calling out the message of salvation through Jesus Christ, is reaching across the whole earth. It is to anyone who is willing to truly understand what God is offering, that Jesus speaks these words. To lose our life, means to give it to Jesus. To try to keep our life, is to reject the relationship with God that He offers us. When we enter a relationship with Jesus and agree to follow Him, we are promising to make choices in our lives that are guided by the Word of God, the Spirit of God, and the will of God. We are committing to a path of life that involves all we have looked at regarding self denial and taking up our cross. This is what it means to follow Christ. If we refuse this offer, there is nothing else but the loss of our soul - our true self. Death is not the end. Life in this world is a prelude to a destiny that awaits each of us. All that you are as a total person, will either be retained by God and resurrected to new life in Christ, or it will be lost and have to bear forever the terrible consequences of sin. The Bible calls such loss, *hell*. It is God's desire that no person have to experience the inevitable aftermath of a life lived only for oneself, instead of a life lived in union with Jesus. All the choices we make in this world apart from living in relationship to Jesus Christ, no matter how much we may seem to have gained, can only end in irretrievable loss. All the choices we make in this world in obedience to Jesus, will inevitably end in eternal gain, no matter how much we may seem to have lost in the eyes of the world. Therefore, Jesus extends His invitation to each of us, and while he makes plain that we are free to reject his offer, he also makes it known that to do so leaves us with nothing. We will lose our true life with all that signifies. Nothing of our lives here will be retained. Nothing that has any lasting value can be kept with us. All that we are, and all we have been as a person is lost, and can never be reclaimed. Even worse, is that we will never know the meaning of true life - the quality and kind of life that can only be found in relationship to Jesus Christ.

"And this is the way to have eternal life — to know you, the only true God, and Jesus Christ, the one you sent to earth." John 17:3 NIV

Before we leave this part of Jesus' invitation, there is an addition in Mark's gospel that is worthy of mention. Where Jesus says "whoever loses their life for me will save it" (Luke 9:24), Mark adds, "for me *and for the gospel..*" Mark 8:35 NIV. Here is a reminder for us once again, that Jesus and His message are inseparable. We noted earlier that accepting Jesus' invitation into covenant relationship, means that as God's children we are part of a redeemed community of fellow believers - the Church. The Church expresses itself through local bodies of believers joined together to worship, grow, and serve the communities in which we live. Mark tells us that to live for Jesus is also to live for the spread of the gospel. We are to make it our ambition to advance the Kingdom of God by working together with others in our churches, to take the good news to the whole world (Matthew 28:18-20; Acts 1:8). Any talk of our obedience to God cannot be genuine, unless we are willing to do our part in fulfilling the commission Jesus gave to His Church. Although our participation may take many forms (e.g., prayer, giving, witnessing, the support of missionaries, etc.), the truth remains that we cannot say we are truly following Jesus, if we do not give our lives in service to the gospel. By tying together the giving of our lives for Jesus sake, and the sake of the gospel, Mark makes clear that we have not crowned Jesus as Lord unless we have made His goal our goal, His priority our priority, His passion our passion.

There is one thing more to say about losing our lives for Jesus. Should it happen in the course of following Him that we should have to die for His sake and the sake of the gospel, our true life is safe. On one occasion, Jesus spoke these words to alleviate the fears of his followers:

"I tell you, my friends, do not be afraid of those who kill the body and after that can do no more. But I will show you whom you should fear: Fear him who, after your body has been killed, has authority to throw you into hell. Yes, I tell you, fear him. Are not five sparrows sold for two pennies? Yet not one of them is forgotten by God. Indeed, the very hairs of your head are all numbered. Don't be afraid; you are worth more than many sparrows." Luke 12:4-7 NIV

All that we are as living souls - is safe with God. Our work finished on earth, we will be complete again in the glory of the resurrection. Even now, our old sinful self is dead:

"Your old life is dead. Your new life, which is your real life — even though invisible to spectators — is with Christ in God. He is your life. When Christ (your real life, remember) shows up again on this earth, you'll show up, too — the real you, the glorious you. Meanwhile, be content with obscurity, like Christ." (Colossians 3:3-4 MSG)

Here in the United States, in contrast to many places in the world today, it is unlikely that we will face martyrdom for our faith in Christ. I fear that many who call themselves

Christians are living without a willingness to take any risks at all for the sake of Christ. Too often, our decisions are based on a search for safety, ease, and comfort. The American dream as we see it, is for "the good life." For the follower of Christ, this cannot be our goal. Our commitment to deny ourselves, take up our cross, and follow Jesus, must always be our paramount dream and aspiration. Anything less, is a sacrifice of all that makes life truly worthwhile as a child of God.

We have been speaking of Jesus' invitation to follow Him in terms of relationship. We have examined the meaning of the contrasting choices that such a relationship presents. We have also touched on the dire consequences that result from the decision to keep life for ourselves rather than surrender it to Christ, in exchange for the life He offers. We noted that without Jesus in our lives, no matter how much we may seem to have gained in this world, the end of life on earth can only result in irrecoverable loss. This is precisely what Jesus means as He continues to expand on the alternative to following Him. In these words, He asks a question that we all must answer, one way or another:

"And what do you benefit if you gain the whole world but are yourself lost or destroyed?" Luke 9:25 NLT

The answer to this question is self evident. Clearly, I have benefited *nothing* if I myself have been lost or destroyed. Jesus asked the question in this way for just that reason. He wanted everyone to know that apart from life in Him, there is nothing but eternal loss. No matter what you have accomplished, possessed, or gained in this life, it would never be enough to buy back your soul. Both Mark 8:37 and Matthew 16:26 add these words which follow directly after Luke 9:25:

"Or what can anyone give in exchange for their soul?"

Again, the answer is unmistakable. Once this life on earth is spent, and Christ has been rejected, there is nothing whatsoever that we can do to redeem our soul. There isn't anything that you could offer God in payment to save you from death. Our sin has separated us from God, and death is the end result of that sin (Romans 6:23). Death is ultimately separation from God, and from anything that has any real meaning as *"life."* The life of God Himself, which the Bible calls eternal life, is in reality the only life that exists forever. This quality of life, with all the limitless fulfillment that it brings, is a gift of God's grace offered freely to us in Jesus Christ. There are no other alternatives. There exists only life in Christ - and death. Nothing else. This offer of eternal life in Christ, cannot be purchased or earned in this world or the world to come. It must be received as a gift. To receive God's gift, means the same as 'losing' your life for Jesus. The choice to receive salvation and all that accompanies it, and the choice to give yourself to Jesus, are two sides of the same coin. You trust in Him alone for your salvation. You give yourself to Him completely and without reservation. In doing so, you gain your soul.

The Bible gives us an indication that those who die without Jesus will retain at least some memories of this life. Jesus tells an amazing story about two men who died, and the aftermath for each of them. It goes like this. . .

Jesus said, "There was a certain rich man who was splendidly clothed in purple and fine linen and who lived each day in luxury. At his gate lay a poor man named Lazarus who was covered with sores. As Lazarus lay there longing for scraps from the rich man's table, the dogs would come and lick his open sores.

"Finally, the poor man died and was carried by the angels to be with Abraham. The rich man also died and was buried,

45

and his soul went to the place of the dead. There, in torment, he saw Abraham in the far distance with Lazarus at his side.

"The rich man shouted, 'Father Abraham, have some pity! Send Lazarus over here to dip the tip of his finger in water and cool my tongue. I am in anguish in these flames.'

"But Abraham said to him, 'Son, remember that during your lifetime you had everything you wanted, and Lazarus had nothing. So now he is here being comforted, and you are in anguish. And besides, there is a great chasm separating us. No one can cross over to you from here, and no one can cross over to us from there.'

"Then the rich man said, 'Please, Father Abraham, at least send him to my father's home. For I have five brothers, and I want him to warn them so they don't end up in this place of torment.'

"But Abraham said, 'Moses and the prophets have warned them. Your brothers can read what they wrote.'

"The rich man replied, 'No, Father Abraham! But if someone is sent to them from the dead, then they will repent of their sins and turn to God.'

"But Abraham said, 'If they won't listen to Moses and the prophets, they won't listen even if someone rises from the dead.'" Luke 16:19-31 NLT

There are several different spiritual lessons that can be drawn from this story. For the purpose of this discussion, let us focus on the matter of memories. This is really a sad story, and is intended to be so. One of the things I believe Jesus wanted to convey to us, is the connection between choice and regret. We see from the dialogue between the rich man and Abraham, that the suffering man had memories of his life on earth. He remembered the good things he had during his lifetime - and the poverty and want that Lazarus had experienced. He also remembered his brothers and his love for them. His pleading with Abraham shows the regrets he had for the choices he had made in life like neglecting his relationship with God, and having no concern for the poor. This rich man, is now in want and realizes that the life he chose for himself cannot be changed. Not only can he not undo the sins that led to his own destiny, he can no longer do anything to help those he cares for, who are still alive in the world - to make better choices for themselves. This story makes clear that the choices we make in this life on earth, have lasting consequences; and that once made, we cannot get them back. Our lives here and now are often defined in terms of loss and pain. Life holds many sorrows that most of us would gladly do without. When a person suffers some terrible loss, we might hear them say, "I'd give anything in the world if only I could have_____." There are many ways to fill in the blank. We may have regrets, and wish we could have back a choice we made. We may desire to relive a moment of time that caused ourselves or others great sorrow. We may be expressing a want or desire, a yearning for a return to good health, the restoration of a broken relationship, or the recovery of a bitter financial loss. Maybe it's the longing to say something to a departed loved one; something we meant to say, but due to their death, never had the opportunity. Sometimes our losses are the result of our choices, and sometimes they are the result of the sin filled world in which we live. In either case, there are times when we would give anything if only we could have what we long for so much. Let me suggest that there is one loss that surpasses all others. One loss that is so great, that Jesus declares all other losses pale by comparison. That loss is the forfeiture

47

of your soul. No matter what else you might experience in life, when all is said and done - all that is left is you. With all that you really are in totality as a person - your soul is the only thing of value that you ultimately cannot afford to lose. To lose your soul is to lose everything. It is to exist forever with memory of suffering and sorrow, choices and failures, loss and regrets. It is to live in eternal torment, without hope, knowing that your true life, the life God meant for you to have in relationship to Him, is lost forever; and there is not a single thing that you or anyone else can do to get it back again. We must choose life, choose now, choose to follow Christ. His invitation is open today. We must respond to Jesus while the opportunity to follow Him is still available to us.

We have spoken a great deal up to this point, about the alternative consequences of our life choices. Jesus concludes His loving invitation to follow Him, with a statement that confirms the ultimate issue of where our decision (to follow Him or not) leads:

"Whoever is ashamed of me and my words, the Son of Man will be ashamed of them when he comes in his glory and in the glory of the Father and of the holy angels." Luke 9:26 NIV

Have we tried to save (keep) our life, or have we lost (given) it for Jesus? Here we are confronted by this choice one last time, with an exclamation point! The emphasis here is on the time of final judgment. We see this also in another passage of scripture, where Jesus portrays Himself as the Son of Man to whom all judgment has been given:

"Very truly I tell you, whoever hears my word and believes him who sent me has eternal life and will not be judged but has crossed over from death to life. Very truly I tell you, a

time is coming and has now come when the dead will hear the voice of the Son of God and those who hear will live. For as the Father has life in himself, so he has granted the Son also to have life in himself. And he has given him authority to judge because he is the Son of Man."

"Do not be amazed at this, for a time is coming when all who are in their graves will hear his voice and come out — those who have done what is good will rise to live, and those who have done what is evil will rise to be condemned." John 5:24-29 NIV

It will be absolute folly for anyone to disregard the Lord Jesus Christ - the one who is the final judge. We are powerfully reminded in Luke 9:26 that although Jesus' glory was not recognized while he was here on earth (cp. John 1:10,14), He is the one who shares the glory of the Father. He is the heir of all things and it is He through whom the whole Universe was created (John 17:24; Heb.1:2-3; Col.1:15-17). When Jesus returns to judge the world, where will you be found? Will you be an heir of God and co-heir with Christ; as one who united with Him and has suffered for Him (Rom.8:17)? Or, will you be as those who never took God's will seriously, but were only pretenders? Jesus always knows the difference between true and false disciples:

"Not everyone who calls out to me, 'Lord! Lord!' will enter the Kingdom of Heaven. Only those who actually do the will of my Father in heaven will enter. On judgment day many will say to me, 'Lord! Lord! We prophesied in your name and cast out demons in your name and performed many miracles in your name.' But I will reply, 'I never knew you. Get away from me, you who break God's laws.'" Matthew 7:21-23 NLT

How bitter it will be for those who must hear from Jesus those terrible words, "I never knew you." Yet that is the outcome for those who are ashamed of Him now. What does it really mean to be ashamed of Jesus and His words (message, teaching)? What does it mean for Jesus to be ashamed of us when He returns? 'Ashamed' is an interesting word. The Apostle Paul uses it when he declares:

"I am not ashamed of the Good News, because it is the power God uses to save everyone who believes — to save the Jews first, and then to save non-Jews." Romans 1:16 NCV

The word 'ashamed' is defined by dictionary.com as, "feeling ashamed; distressed or embarrassed by feelings of guilt, foolishness, or disgrace." It is further defined as, "unwilling or restrained because of fear of shame, ridicule, or disapproval." Both of these nuances give force to what Jesus was saying. Paul, as quoted above, is a perfect example. He neither felt ashamed by the proclamation of the gospel, nor did he allow himself to hold back from evangelism due to fear of reproach from others. Jesus is not speaking here however, of those momentary lapses when courage deserts us, or of those times when we fail to speak for Him as we should, in situations where we have opportunity to do so. If that were the case, I'm afraid Jesus would have cause to be ashamed of all of us! What we have here again, is the outcome of the choices we have made that decide our eternal destiny. Those who reject Jesus and His teachings, will never stand up proudly on His behalf. They will always have a sense of disgrace or embarrassment because of who Jesus is, and what He has done on the cross. To such people, the cross of Christ and the message of His love and shed blood, will always be nothing more than foolishness (1 Corinthians 1:18,23). They will never live in selfless service to Him, or to others in His name. They will always disassociate themselves from Him, his message, His people, His teachings, and all that truly represents Him. To confess and acknowledge Jesus as their Lord before men, would be unknown to them. This parallels what Jesus told His disciples on another occasion when He said:

"Whoever acknowledges me before others, I will also acknowledge before my Father in heaven. But whoever disowns me before others, I will disown before my Father in heaven." Matthew 10:32-33 NIV

This is also what Paul means when he tells his beloved son Timothy:

"Here is a trustworthy saying:
If we died with him,
we will also live with him;
if we endure,
we will also reign with him.
If we disown him,
he will also disown us;
if we are faithless,
he remains faithful,
for he cannot disown himself." 2 Timothy 2:11-13 NIV

To disown someone, is to refuse to acknowledge that person as belonging or pertaining to you. We might say today that one person is a known associate of another person. Associates are collaborators, companions, partners, co-workers, and friends with that individual. That is what our life in Christ must be. We must be known associates of Jesus. To be identified in this manner, is what it means to not be ashamed of Him. To refuse to join Him in the newness of life that He offers, is to end up with Him refusing to acknowledge you - as one who belongs to Him.

There are many worthy Biblical examples of what it means to be unashamed of Christ. We find faithful people like Joseph, Moses, Joshua, Elijah, Samuel, David, Daniel, Mary (Jesus' mother), Mary Magdalene, Paul, the twelve Apostles, and a host of others. The Bible shares the stories of many such people of faith who boldly identified themselves with God, and refused to be ashamed to bear reproach for His name. I want to point out one Biblical example that we can all readily relate to - someone who stood tall for God despite the fear, ridicule, and persecution he had to endure. For most of this man's life, he was ostracized by others for his stand in the Lord. Yet he, like us, did not always deal with mistreatment without tears or complaint.

The prophet Jeremiah is a man whose life is replete with examples of bearing shame and disgrace for God, and for the message he proclaimed as God's spokesman. On several occasions, he had very honest and intimate conversations with God regarding the struggle he faced to stay faithful to his calling. The Lord needed to continually reassure Jeremiah that he must not be ashamed to represent Him, or the message he needed to bring to his people. God gave him strength for his task, and comfort in the midst of persecution. As we observe Jeremiah's behavior, we see a man who was patently unashamed of God and His Word. Even while he struggled with emotional turmoil, he continued to deny himself, and take up his cross in obedience to God.

From the events in Jeremiah's life throughout the course of his prophetic ministry, we can observe a variety of afflictions that could have enticed Jeremiah to be ashamed of the Lord whom he so faithfully served. An account of these afflictions is extensive: Jeremiah was falsely accused of treason, and then was thrown into a dungeon for many days. He attempted to befriend a king who professed to respect him, yet who would neither listen to his godly counsel nor stand up for him when others sought his life. Jeremiah was often hungry and lonely, with only an occasional friend or supporter to help and comfort him. He was abandoned in a large filthy hole in the ground and left to die, with his only crime being a passionate love for the nation, and a desire to see his people turn back to God and avoid disaster. He was continually brokenhearted over the sins of his countrymen, and often would plead to God with tears for their survival. Despite his steadfast faithfulness to God and country, he was never thanked, appreciated, or praised for his efforts. There was no money in it for him, nor fame, honor (during his lifetime), position, or privilege. He was forbidden by God to ever marry or have a family. After over 40 years of honorable, unwavering, and patriotic ministry, he was rewarded with only his life as a prize. The man who said to the nation, "For I know the plans I have for you", declares the LORD, "plans to prosper you and not to harm you, plans to give you hope and a future", was himself seemingly 'without hope or a future'. He was ultimately taken from his home against his will to Egypt - coerced by cruel and brutal men. There he eventually died, far from the land he loved, and brokenhearted over the tragedy that had befallen his nation. Despite all the sorrow of his life, Jeremiah never lost faith in God or failed to do His will. Some of his final words on record are these:

"The thought of my suffering and homelessness
is bitter beyond words.
I will never forget this awful time,
as I grieve over my loss.
Yet I still dare to hope
when I remember this:
The faithful love of the LORD never ends!
His mercies never cease.
Great is his faithfulness;
his mercies begin afresh each morning.

I say to myself, "The LORD is my inheritance;
therefore, I will hope in him!"
The Lord is good to those who depend on him,
to those who search for him.
So it is good to wait quietly
for salvation from the Lord." Lamentations 3:19-26 NLT

The man who wrote these words was indeed God's prophet, but he was really no different from you and me. As we look at his life, we are reminded that God can also help *us* to take a stand for Christ despite our struggles and weaknesses. Jeremiah's temptations came from the world, the flesh, and the devil, just as ours do. It is because he has been called "the weeping prophet", that he was so likened to our Savior in his heart and spirit (cp. Matthew 16:14). When we review his ministry, we have a most poignant picture of what Jesus meant when he said:

"If anyone is ashamed of me and my message in these adul-
terous and sinful days, the Son of Man will be ashamed of
that person when he returns in the glory of his Father with
the holy angels." Mark 8:38 NLT

I am often reminded of a false notion held by many Christians towards these notable servants of God (like Jeremiah). As we read the wonderful faith exploits of Bible characters, we often think that we could never live up to their level of commitment and faithfulness. What we fail to realize, is that they are all human beings just like we are. God used them in marvelous ways despite the same imperfections, frailties, and shortcomings in their lives as we have (cp. James 5:17; 1 Corinthians 1:26-29; 2 Corinthians 12:9-10). The truth is, it is everyday folks (like us) that God delights to use for His glory. Most of us tend to think of ourselves as very ordinary people. While we admire individuals like Jeremiah, we still wonder whether God can use 'ordinary people' today. Let me introduce you to an 'ordinary' young boy from the church I attend, who God is using to make a real difference in the lives of others. . .

In the spring of 2004, nine year old Austin Gutwein watched a video that showed children who had lost their parents to AIDS. After watching the video, he realized these kids weren't any different from him except they were suffering. Austin felt God calling him to do something to help them. He decided to shoot free throws; and on World AIDS Day, 2004, he shot 2,057 free throws to represent the 2,057 kids who would be orphaned during his day at school. Friends and family sponsored Austin and he was able to raise almost $3,000. That year, the money was used to provide hope to 8 orphan children.

Over the past eight years, Austin's effort has turned into the largest free throw marathon in the world with an estimated 40,000 people in more than 25 countries participating in Hoops of Hope. By doing something as simple as shooting free throws, Hoops of Hope participants have raised more than $2.5 million. The efforts have led to the construction of the only high school in a rural region in Southern Zambia, four dormitories, two medical clinics (which he was told would save an entire generation), a computer laboratory, multiple water projects, as well as the funding of a dormitory at an orphanage in Kenya and a school in India.

Austin has been featured on NBC Today Show, NBC Nightly News, CBS Evening News, CBS NCAA Pregame Show, Time Magazine, Christianity Today and many others. He has had the opportunity to share his story of hope to more than 500,000 people on four continents including stops at the Sec-

ondary School's United Nations Symposium in Montreal and the United States Air Force Academy in Colorado Springs.

Austin's message is one of hope. **A message that anyone, no matter what their age or skills has a purpose and can make a difference that lasts forever.** *His message weaves stories from his many trips to Africa that will leave the listener inspired and encouraged to make a difference.*

In 2009, Austin was selected as one of the Top 10 Most Caring Americans by the Caring Institute in Washington, DC. That same year, Thomas Nelson released his first book, Take Your Best Shot. *Austin's second book,* Live to Give, *is scheduled to be released in August 2012.*

Austin is currently a senior in High School and co-chairs Arizona Governor Jan Brewer's Youth Commission. In the Fall of 2012, Austin will be attending Anderson University in Anderson, Indiana. [1]

If an 'ordinary' 9 year old boy can heed the call of Jesus Christ on his life, so can we. God can use 'ordinary' people in 'extraordinary' ways, if in simple faith, we will follow Jesus wherever He leads. Where does this leave us? What about you and me? Do others recognize us as known 'associates' of Jesus? As people come to know us, does our manner of life cause them to think about Christ? Are we living our lives in such a way that when others speak of us, they are obliged to mention our Savior as well? When we are seen in prosperity, can it be said that the interests of Christ remain the goal and aim of our lives? When we are suffering sorrow and adversity, can it be said that we never cease to hold up the banner of Christ? Is there anything different enough about us, that gives others pause to say, "This person is not ashamed to identify themselves with Jesus."? If we can answer these questions well, without hesitation, we are on the narrow path to committed discipleship. If God's love constrains us to confess an uncertainty in our hearts about our willingness to be unashamed of Jesus, we must think deeply and soberly about His words to us in Luke 9:23-26. Join together with me, as we ask the Lord what is keeping us from placing Him first in our lives without reservation. Then, allow His Spirit to remove anything that stands in the way - of making His Kingdom and His righteousness our highest priority.

As we conclude our overview of what it means to follow Jesus, we turn now to the gospel of John. When we began this look together at Jesus' call to discipleship, I noted that John's gospel recorded His invitation somewhat differently from Matthew, Mark, and Luke. John's narrative reads like this:

"23 Jesus replied, "The hour has come for the Son of Man to be glorified. 24 Very truly I tell you, unless a kernel of wheat falls to the ground and dies, it remains only a single seed. But if it dies, it produces many seeds. 25 Anyone who loves their life will lose it, while anyone who hates their life in this world will keep it for eternal life. 26 Whoever serves me must follow me; and where I am, my servant also will be. My Father will honor the one who serves me."" John 12:23-26 NIV

I have not found a commentary that sees Jesus' words in John as a direct parallel to what is presented to us in Matthew, Mark, and Luke. While it is true that the context in which the words were spoken is different in John, I believe that we can see a direct parallel in meaning between the two forms of invitation. By looking at how John presented the Savior's challenge, we can see once again the importance of taking up our cross daily to follow Jesus.

I am providing here an easy to follow visual reference. We can place the corresponding passages from Luke and John side by side. Then, we can briefly review the meaning in John, and see how it ties together with all we have been considering in Luke.

John 12:23-26	Luke 9:23-26
23 Jesus replied, "The hour has come for the Son of Man to be glorified. 24 Very truly I tell you, unless a kernel of wheat falls to the ground and dies, it remains only a single seed. But if it dies, it produces many seeds.	
25 Anyone who loves their life will lose it, while anyone who hates their life in this world will keep it for eternal life.	*24 For whoever wants to save their life will lose it, but whoever loses their life for me will save it. 25 What good is it for someone to gain the whole world, and yet lose or forfeit their very self?*
26 Whoever serves me must follow me; and where I am, my servant also will be. My Father will honor the one who serves me.	*23 Then he said to them all: "Whoever wants to be my disciple must deny themselves and take up their cross daily and follow me.*

| 26 Whoever serves me must follow me; and where I am, my servant also will be. My Father will honor the one who serves me. | 26 Whoever is ashamed of me and my words, the Son of Man will be ashamed of them when he comes in his glory and in the glory of the Father and of the holy angels. |

The context in John presents this saying as a response by Jesus to the Apostles Andrew and Philip. Jesus and his disciples were at the Passover festival in Jerusalem, just prior to his passion and death. Among those who were worshiping at the festival, were some non-Jewish people. These people (whose number is unknown), came to Philip asking to meet Jesus. Philip in turn told Andrew, and they both approached Jesus with this petition. The request of these Gentiles brings to Jesus' mind what He is about to do and sacrifice, for the salvation of the world. Then, as a preface to a longer and more extensive invitation for the Jews at the festival to believe in Him; Jesus speaks these words from John 12:23-26, in response to the request to meet him by the foreigners at worship there. Even though in their original setting, Matthew, Mark, and Luke, have Jesus addressing only His fellow Jews - all the gospels extend Jesus' invitation to everyone, as we read it today. All people, Jews and non-Jews alike, are invited to follow Jesus, believe in Him, and enter into a relationship with Him that brings eternal life (cp. John 12:47-50). As we begin the comparison between the invitations, we note that John 12:23-24 has no direct parallel in Luke. For John, the glorification of the Son of Man, and the death and reproduction of the kernel of wheat, are a direct reference to Jesus' passion and His death on the cross. Verse 24 emphasizes that through Jesus' death, many people will be brought into new life. This is an echo of our earlier discussion of what it means to lose our life in exchange for the new life Jesus brings. There, we also looked at Romans 6, and the symbolic way that Christian baptism represents the death to our old life, and the entry into the new life Jesus imparts to us. While Jesus' death is not specifically mentioned in Luke, we do see a reference to the cross. And although the cross in Luke refers to something we must take up ourselves, we can readily infer that Jesus had his own death in view, when he gave this invitation to follow him. So while John begins with Jesus death, there is little doubt that for Luke, Jesus had His cross in mind as he invites us to follow Him by making the choices that will lead us inexorably toward final judgment and eternal life. Referring to the chart, we see the parallel of John 12:25 to Luke 9:24. Instead of saying, "saving life/ losing life", John has, "loves life/hates life." Both of these terms are expressions of *choices* we make, in the context of relationship, that determine our eternal destiny. As you look at the chart, note that Luke 9:25 is placed in opposition to John 12:25; even though John has no verse that directly corresponds to it. This is because Luke's meaning in v.25, which is focused on the contrast between salvation and loss, also embraces John's contrast between the loss of life, and eternal life, in v.25 of his gospel. Next, we can see how John 12:26 directly parallels Luke 9:23. Jesus speaks in Luke of denying oneself, and taking up their cross daily. In John, Jesus says whoever serves Him must follow Him, and they will be where he is. This expression in John, conveys the idea of always being ready to serve at any moment in obedience to God's will; and is akin to Luke's "taking up the cross *daily.*" You may have also noticed that set side by side, is v.26 of each gospel. I believe John's meaning is the same as Luke's. Luke, we have seen, tied this part of Jesus' invitation to the day of final judgment. When John speaks of the Father 'honoring the one who serves Jesus', he is also speaking of our final reckoning, and the promise of eternal life. On that day, the Father will bring honor to those who have lived for Jesus; the honor of being part of the resurrection and an heir of eternal life. We may also understand John as expressing that a life lived for God in faithful service to Him, will result in receiving honor from Him *even now*, in this life. Such honor may take the form of respect and recognition from the Church. It may also be received through the blessing of God upon the faithful ministries of service that His followers have undertaken. Or finally, this honor may be experienced when the disciple, like his Lord, abandons himself for others as a seed planted in sacrificial service. The honor is conferred when the seed bears a harvest of fruit; the fruit of new lives being born into God's Kingdom, thereby bringing great glory to the Father (John 15:8).

'Losing Life to Keep It' is a challenge to us; a reminder that to be in a relationship with Jesus Christ - is more than just a convenience. It is a death to our sinful human nature; and a birth into a transformed life, where all things become new. For the serious disciple, this means there are choices we must make; choices that will affect every part of our lives. Choosing to follow Jesus daily, will change the way we relate to others, and how we serve their needs. It is only by taking up the cross, that we will begin to see others as God sees them. It is only as we 'listen between the lines', and stand ready to obey Christ at any moment, that we will know how to serve those whom God places in our path. As we learn to love as Jesus does, it will change how we look at the world around us. We will discover how the Bible transforms our attitudes in a way that conflicts with the views of our culture. By denying ourselves as Jesus bids us, we will face choices that involve sacrifice or hardship; but we will also find a blessing in 'taking up our cross daily' that we never thought possible. Jesus asks of us the most serious minded commitment — to place God's will above our own. Our lives will have to move in a direction that makes love for God our

absolute ruling passion. We will choose God's Kingdom and His way of life as our highest priority — and anything that gets in the way of that will have to take a lesser place.

This is what it means to follow Christ; we give our lives to Him. We make a promise to have our life choices guided by the Word of God, the Spirit of God, and the will of God. Our lives become dedicated to the service of the gospel. We work in unity alongside brothers and sisters in our churches. Our guiding purpose: To advance the Kingdom of God; to take the good news to all the nations. We will risk anything and everything for the sake of Christ. Our priorities will not be based on the pursuit of security, ease, or comfort. The American dream for 'the good life' will no longer be our goal.

In his provocative book *Radical,* Dr. David Platt shares what he believes is the key to taking back our faith from the American dream:

"The key is realizing - and believing - that this world is not your home. If you and I ever hope to free our lives from worldly desires, worldly thinking, worldly pleasures, worldly dreams, worldly ideals, worldly values, worldly ambitions, and worldly acclaim, then we must focus our lives on another world. Though you and I live in the United States of America now, we must fix our attention on "a better country — a heavenly one." Though you and I find ourselves surrounded by the lure of temporary pleasure, we must fasten our affections on the one who promises eternal treasure that will never spoil or fade. If your life or my life is going to count on earth, we must start by concentrating on heaven. For then, and only then, will you and I be free to take radical risk, knowing what awaits us is radical reward." [2]

It is time to ask ourselves whether we really want our lives to make a difference in this world. As we weigh the cost of giving ourselves completely to the Lordship of Jesus, we must decide what makes life truly worth living. Dr. Platt puts the matter this way:

"This brings us to the crucial question for every professing or potential follower of Jesus: Do we really believe he is worth abandoning everything for? Do you and I really believe that Jesus is so good, so satisfying, and so rewarding that we will leave all we have and all we own and all we are in order to find our fullness in him? Do you and I believe him enough to obey him and to follow him wherever he leads, even when the crowds in our culture — and maybe in our churches — turn the other way?" [3]

Join together with me, as we seek the grace to discover the transforming power of God's Arithmetic. If we want life to add up in God's Kingdom - making us true citizens of heaven - we must learn from the Master, those attitudes and actions that will lead to faithful discipleship in our lives.

No One Wants To Be Last

*W*e live in a world that loves honors and awards. There are awards for everything. We have Oscars, Emmys, and Grammys, along with all manner of similar accolades from almost any organization you can think of. In the world of sports there are trophies, rings, gifts, and other presentations, given to teams and individuals, to celebrate their victories and achievements. For Scouts there are merit badges. In the military there are ribbons, medals, and insignias of rank. In academics, there are certificates, degrees, and scholarships. There is even an international committee that awards the Nobel Prize to people who make an outstanding contribution in the fields of Physics, Chemistry, Medicine, Literature, Peace, and the Economic Sciences. It seems like almost every field of endeavor has some way of making a distinction between the average and the excellent, the ordinary and the superior, the losers and the winners. Everywhere we turn, there are the first and the last, the least and the greatest. From the time we are children, our minds and hearts are saturated with a kind of "greatness" mentality. We learn quickly that it's not good to be last. We don't want to be chosen last, to come in last, or to take last place in anything. Among the sweeping variety of distinctions this world bestows, I have yet to see any person or organization present an award for "last place". American culture in particular is very much like this. We live under the banner of Vince Lombardi — "Winning isn't everything, it's the only thing." Americans hate being last. We have to be first. After all, we believe we are the greatest and most powerful nation in the world. We have a responsibility for world leadership. Our way of life is best, and it leads inexorably, we believe, to peace and prosperity for all. The very thought of the United States being anything less than first among the nations, is abhorrent to us as Americans. Whether it's the Olympics, the United Nations, technology, the world economy, or military power, we must be the best. We must be the greatest. We must be first. That's what America is all about. It's in the Constitution isn't it? Okay, it's not — you knew that. Now don't misunderstand. I'm not making fun of America, or of any worthwhile ambition toward achievement. All I'm saying is that our minds are permeated by this "greatness" mentality. We all want to get ahead. We are overshadowed by a world where greatness is displayed by predomination. The leaders and the strong are the great. They surpass others with their authority and influence. They exert controlling power over people and events. They stand out more noticeable and imposing than those around them. This then, is how greatness appears in today's world. It isn't going to change, and we can't escape it. The great have preeminence among us - and while we recognize that we won't all be great, we certainly don't want to be the least. We may strive to be first, but no one, and I mean no one, wants to be last. If you're last, you fail. You're considered weak, a loser, an underachiever, a nobody, or something even worse! Let's stop and hit the pause button right here. I want you to picture for a moment - a person who grows up in our kind of world, and then becomes a Christian. Their heart is now filled with a desire to glorify God; to bear fruit for Him that will last. They pray, "Lord, I want to be a great Christian. I want to be like Jesus.

I want to be known in the Church, among your people, as a first-rate follower of Christ. I want to be the finest, foremost, choicest, unequaled, primo, number one disciple that you've got." Hmm, not bad. A worthy prayer, motivated no doubt by a sincere desire to please the Lord. The problem is, how do you do it? How do you become a great Christian? How do you become foremost among the disciples? If you have ever felt like that, I have good news for you. The Lord Jesus answered those questions. In fact, He addressed them on several occasions, and under different circumstances. All of His insight on this matter of "greatness", is captured for us in the gospels. However, if you examine the gospels, there are a few things that are really going to surprise you. First, is that His disciples just didn't get it. They had the hardest time understanding what He was saying to them. Second, the reason they had such a hard time with His teaching about greatness, is that they lived in a world just like ours; the kind we also have grown up in. And third, what He taught them was so counter-intuitive from everything in their human nature, that they were still arguing over it - all the way up to the time right before Jesus died on the cross. As we read the gospels, many of us enjoy the parts where the Apostles seem the most foolish, human, or immature in their behavior. For some of us, this may be because it is where we see that they are most like us. This gives us hope, because we reason that if the Apostles acted that poorly, and God used them - then He can surely use us, or help us grow into spiritual maturity as they did. For others, we may look at their spiritual immaturity, and think we would have never acted that way. We suppose that if we were there with Jesus, we would have surely done better than they did. Either way we view the Apostles, whether as an encouragement or as a disappointment; Jesus' teaching on the matter of greatness, carries with it some of the most profound spiritual lessons we must learn, for us to be His true followers. The problem for those first disciples, was the same as ours. When we think about what it means to be a citizen in the Kingdom of Heaven, we carry our Kingdom of Earth ideas right along with us. We never suspect that Jesus is teaching us something so radical, so different from what we are used to, that only the power of God at work in our lives can help us to understand and apply it. I'm going to make a confession here. I have been a Christian for a very long time and have served as a Bible teacher to many believers. I thought I had this whole "greatness" thing down pat. Not that I considered myself great by any means, but I thought that at least I understood what it meant to be great in the Kingdom of God. After careful study of what Jesus had to say about this matter, I discovered that I had not grasped some of the key things that the Lord intended for me. I was really in some ways just as confused as the disciples. I have been so much a citizen of the world in which I live, that I didn't even realize the extent that our culture had influenced my understanding of Jesus' words. In my desire to be a better Christian, **I was using my own arithmetic instead of God's Arithmetic**. I invite you now to journey with me, as we meet our Savior along the road to the cross. We will listen, as he strives to help His disciples (and us) learn what it means to be great in the Kingdom of God.

Our exploration begins in Luke 13:22-30. Before we can fully enter into a conversation on the true meaning of greatness, we must make sure our minds are in the right frame of reference. To do this, we will first look at how Jesus answered a difficult question — *"Lord, are only a few people going to be saved?"*

As I have read the Gospels, I have always been in awe of how Jesus went about His ministry. As He proclaimed the message of salvation and forgiveness, He was performing miracles that attested to the truth of His message. We see Him heal every kind of disease and sickness among the people. Evil spirits are cast out. The blind see, the deaf hear, and even the dead are raised to life again. Everywhere He went, huge crowds followed Him. Jesus has a power and charisma that no one else has ever had. I remember when I read the gospels for the very first time as a young man. I had grown up in a Jewish home, but I had never learned about Jesus. When I finally learned about what Jesus said and did, one of my reactions was a kind of anger. It distressed me that the people of Israel rejected their Messiah. Here was a man who was so obviously good, filled with the power and Spirit of God, gracious, and kind. Not only was Jesus rejected, but many people wanted to kill him, including the leaders of the nation! Even most of those who didn't want Him dead, still refused His message. This kind of reaction to Jesus disappointed and angered me. It was not until some time later, that I began to understand why this was so. For one thing, both the Old and New Testament teach that not everyone in Israel was a true believer in the Lord. Many of the prophets, as well as the Apostle Paul, speak of a "remnant" - a small number of people throughout Israelite history. The "remnant" were individuals who had either remained faithful to God, or were chosen by Him to be preserved and rescued, despite the consequences of the nation's overall rebellion against Him. Another thing that contributed to the nation's rejection of Jesus, was their misconception of what the Messiah would be like, and what He was going to do when He arrived. The popular idea at the time, was that the Messiah would be a powerful invincible leader. He would come and quickly defeat the hated Romans, and gather the nation to Himself. Then, it was thought, He would set up an earthly kingdom like the Israel of old, which would rule over the nations. The promises of God to King David and the Patriarchs would be fulfilled, and Israel would rule supreme over the peoples of the earth. In God's plan of redemption, Jesus was not what most people expected. As a result, when He arrived, He was widely rejected just as the prophets had foretold. If we imagine ourselves as part of the crowd who followed Jesus in Luke 9, it isn't hard to understand the confusion many of them must have felt. They probably wondered (as I first did), "If Jesus is the Messiah, why are there so few people accepting Him and His invitation into God's Kingdom?" Or to put it another way, "Are there only a few people who are going to be saved?" When we catch up with Jesus here, He is in the last year of His ministry, and it's only a few months before His death. He is on His way to Jerusalem. This conversation took place while He was preaching about the Kingdom of God in the towns and villages of Judea. Here then, is their encounter, along with Jesus' reply, found in Luke 13:22-30 NIV:

22 Then Jesus went through the towns and villages, teaching as he made his way to Jerusalem. 23 Someone asked him, "Lord, are only a few people going to be saved?"

He said to them, 24 "Make every effort to enter through the narrow door, because many, I tell you, will try to enter and will not be able to. 25 Once the owner of the house gets up and closes the door, you will stand outside knocking and pleading, 'Sir, open the door for us.'

"But he will answer, 'I don't know you or where you come from.'

26 "Then you will say, 'We ate and drank with you, and you taught in our streets.'

27 "But he will reply, 'I don't know you or where you come from. Away from me, all you evildoers!'

28 "There will be weeping there, and gnashing of teeth, when you see Abraham, Isaac and Jacob and all the prophets

69

*in the kingdom of God, but you yourselves thrown out. 29
People will come from east and west and north and south,
and will take their places at the feast in the kingdom of God.
30 Indeed there are those who are last who will be first, and
first who will be last."*

Notice first, that Jesus does not directly answer the question this person asked. Rather, He gives them all an invitation. This does not surprise me in the least. On many
occasions, when I have shared the gospel of Christ with individuals, they raise all kinds of objections to it. Some of these
objections are reasonable questions that the person has been
thinking about; questions that have held them back from a
clear understanding of Jesus' death and resurrection. I will
always try to answer such genuine questions - and then move
on in my efforts to introduce that person to Jesus. However,
there are times when I perceive that a person is raising objections simply to deflect the conversation away from themselves. They do this in order to avoid having to make a
personal decision as to whether they will receive Jesus as
their Lord or not. In those instances, I will try to help the
person see that their objections are not the real issue. Their
true point of contention, is that they do not want to make
the gospel personal. So here in v.24, Jesus, in a similar way,
brushes aside as non-essential, the question of how many
people are going to be saved. He is really saying to them,
what about you? Never mind the question about how many
will be saved, but consider this: "Make every effort to enter
through the narrow door, because many, I tell you, will try to
enter and will not be able to."

The word in the original language for "make every
effort", is the word from which we get the English word
"agonize." It means to put forth a great effort, to struggle, to
strive. Entering the Kingdom is like going through a narrow
door. You must put forth great effort to go through this door,

because many people are going to try to enter, and won't be able to. Why is that? The use of the word "effort" here, is not to say that a person must do good things in their life to earn credit with God, to become worthy of entering His Kingdom. The agonizing struggle Jesus speaks of here, is the battle within ourselves to surrender our will, our pride, and our sin, to Him. This is what He wanted everyone to understand, and it is very difficult for our human nature to accept. We do not want to surrender control of our lives, even to God. That is a very narrow door indeed! Later, Jesus is going to say we must give up everything. We must deny ourselves, our family, our possessions, and even our own lives, if we want to follow Him. We're going to have to change, and become as humble as a little child - if we ever want to get into the Kingdom of God. The agony spoken of here, is actually about repentance. A change of mind. A willingness to let go of everything we have, and everything we are. It is the willingness to turn from our sin - and to trust in God alone. In short, it is the agony of dying to self - our total submission to the Lordship of Christ.

Jesus spoke figuratively in v.25. *He* is the owner of the house who will one day close the door, and listen to those outside who are knocking and pleading to get in. He will answer them all and say, "I don't know you or where you come from." Their reply to Him in v.26 is, "We ate and drank with you, and you taught in our streets." What Jesus is telling them here, is that there will be many people eternally separated from God, who will be shocked that they did not make it into the Kingdom. They will say things like, "We know who you are Jesus. We were there when you traveled around. We saw you do miracles. We heard you teach. We watched what you did. We were right there with you when you fed hungry people! Why are we in outer darkness? How could we miss salvation?" If we bring this into today's world, we find those who think they are Christian because they live in a Christian nation, or because they grew up in the church. Some people assume they are saved because their parents were Christians, or simply because they know all about Jesus - who he was, and what he did. This gets even more lamentable when you compare Matthew 7:21-23 NIV:

"Not everyone who says to me, 'Lord, Lord,' will enter the kingdom of heaven, but only the one who does the will of my Father who is in heaven. Many will say to me on that day, 'Lord, Lord, did we not prophesy in your name and in your name drive out demons and in your name perform many miracles?' Then I will tell them plainly, 'I never knew you. Away from me, you evildoers!'

Today, we might say these folks were part of large "Christian" denominations, and attended large churches. They preached in the name of Jesus, and they worked in the name of Jesus. They even called Him Lord, Lord! But He says to them plainly, even as he did to those in Luke 13:27, "I never knew you. Away from me, you evildoers!." I don't know about you, but this is very distressing to me. There will be many in hell who will be absolutely shocked that they didn't make it to heaven. Why? How can that be? Why does Jesus call them evildoers? Why are they cast out? It is because *Jesus never knew them*. They never had an actual personal encounter with Him. They never entered through the narrow door of repentance. They never truly turned from themselves, and trusted Christ alone for forgiveness. They never understood the meaning of Jesus' death on the cross, and why it was for them. They never accepted His blood as the only atonement for their sins. They were never covered by the righteousness of God, through faith in Christ alone. They never acknowledged God's grace for what it is - a gift, freely given, but only to those who will receive it in humility; only to those who will place everything - the entire weight of their salvation - into the hands of a risen living Savior. Jesus didn't know them. They had no real union with Him; no personal relationship with Him. They were never born again (John 3:3). They depended on something within themselves that was not the work of God; counting on something other than Jesus alone to save them. They never really knew Him.

In Luke 13:28-29 NIV, Jesus said this to the Israelites who would miss the narrow door:

"There will be weeping there, and gnashing of teeth, when you see Abraham, Isaac and Jacob and all the prophets in the kingdom of God, but you yourselves thrown out. People will come from east and west and north and south, and will take their places at the feast in the kingdom of God."

I can almost hear them say, "That can't be right Lord. I'm one of the chosen people. I'm a Jew, a child of Abraham. How can I not be there? How can I be thrown out? How can some of my fellow Jews be there, but not me? And wait.. those from other lands? Gentiles? In the Kingdom? At the feast?" Yes — and there will be weeping and gnashing of teeth. The conscious torment of remorse, and endless grinding shame and frustration.

Jesus' final words to them are, "Indeed there are those who are last who will be first, and first who will be last." Don't miss this. It is vital to our journey along the path to understanding greatness. For the Israelite, they were first. Remember — to the Jew first, and then to the Gentile (Rom.1:16). Some of the Jews listening to Jesus would be astonished - even scandalized by this. *They* would be left out - but there would be *Gentiles* who were in. There will be Gentiles who were last, now first; and some Jews who were first, now last. What does this mean? It means that we are all equal. Jew and Gentile, together in the Kingdom, all equal, all the same.

"In Christ, there is no difference between Jew and Greek, slave and free person, male and female. You are all the same in Christ Jesus." Galatians 3:28 NCV

Let's see if we can pull together this invitation from Jesus. Are there few or many who will be saved? You don't need to know. The question is, are *you* there? Are *you* saved? Are *you* in the Kingdom? All of us are living on borrowed time. Life is short.

"Your life is like a mist. You can see it for a short time, but then it goes away." James 4:14 NCV

It's hard for us to imagine this. Our time here is not long, and our life is not about the accumulation of things or prizes or lots of 'stuff'. Life is really all about eternity, and our preparation for it. We must be certain of our relationship with Jesus. Do we really *know* Him? Have we truly surrendered our heart, our life, our pride - to the only one who can free us from sin? Is our hope of heaven always in doubt? Is our knowledge of Jesus real and personal - or is it merely superficial? We must be sure of this. Let us make certain our stake in Christ. We can trust in Him, and Him alone, to put things right between us and God. Once this is made sure — we have taken our first step towards understanding what it means to be great in the Kingdom of God.

As we take our next step of discovery, we meet a small child. Not exactly the person we might expect to meet when talking about greatness. It seems more likely we should be meeting a King, or a Governor; a rich man, or a prominent landowner. Perhaps even a distinguished Rabbi, or a Jewish High Priest - someone really important, right? But no - a small child. We begin in the gospel of Luke, a short way back from where we just were. Prior to His final Judean ministry, Jesus had spent about a year traveling throughout Galilee. It was just at the end of His time there, that Jesus began to teach His disciples that He was going to Jerusalem. There, He would suffer many things, be rejected by the Jewish leadership, killed, and raised on the third day. Jesus was also teaching the crowds, along with His disciples, what it really meant to follow Him. He used terms like, "deny yourself" and "take up your cross." He spoke of saving life to lose it, and losing life to save it (these sayings are discussed at length in the chapter, "Losing Life to Keep it"). Right after this, in the midst of Jesus' warnings about His death and all that lay ahead for Him, we are surprised to find His disciples arguing with each other. Luke relates the incident like this:

An argument started among the disciples as to which of them would be the greatest. Jesus, knowing their thoughts, took a little child and had him stand beside him. Then he said to them, "Whoever welcomes this little child in my name welcomes me; and whoever welcomes me welcomes the one who sent me. For it is the one who is least among you all who is the greatest." Luke 9:46-48 NIV

In order for us to get the full benefit from this story, we will need to borrow from the parallel passages that relate to the same occasion. They are found in Matthew 18:1-5 and Mark 9:33-37. From Mark, we learn that the disciples stood in silent humiliation when Jesus questioned them regarding what they were arguing about (Mk.9:33-34). After this awkward silence, they actually found the courage to ask Jesus directly what was on their mind. In Matthew 18:1 they ask Him, "Who, then, is the greatest in the Kingdom of Heaven?" I like the way The Message paraphrases this, "Who gets the highest rank in God's Kingdom?" - because this is really what they were asking. Which one of us is going to be the boss? Which one of us gets to tell the rest what to do? Which one of us is better than the others - the big shot? Which one of us is superior in rank, privilege, and position? Luke tells us that Jesus knew their thoughts. That is - he knew what was really in their hearts. Now at this point, you would almost expect Jesus to say, "What is wrong with all of you? Don't you see that I'm on my way to the cross, and here you are arguing over who is the greatest?" But He doesn't say that. What does he do? He takes a little child and has him stand at His side. Matthew says that He had the child stand among them. Mark goes even further and states that Jesus picked up the child, and held him in His arms - so this was clearly a very small child. Then He says to them all:

"Truly I tell you, unless you change and become like little children, you will never enter the kingdom of heaven. Therefore, whoever takes the lowly position of this child is the greatest in the kingdom of heaven." Matthew 18:3-4 NIV

How does a person change and become like a little child so they can enter the Kingdom? Well, what characterizes a little child? Humility, dependence, and trust. Such a child has no rank, no achievement, no claim to greatness. They have accomplished nothing of any real value, and they are completely dependent upon others to provide for their maintenance and survival. So Jesus tells the disciples that they must realize that they are really nothing. Anything they have done or accomplished in ministry, has been through Him - and they have nothing whatsoever to commend their entry into the Kingdom. They have nothing to boast about. They are only going to get in, by acknowledging their utter dependence upon Him, and by repudiating any merit of their own - which they thought could earn them place or position before God. This is exactly what we saw above, where Jesus spoke of entering through the narrow door. Then He says to them, "Therefore, whoever takes the lowly position of this child is the greatest in the kingdom of heaven." Don't miss the *there-*

fore. Therefore, since even entering the Kingdom doesn't depend on your merit or accomplishments, but by placing yourselves humbly at the mercy of God; when you have that attitude of heart and mind, *then,* you are the greatest in the Kingdom of Heaven. Wait a minute. Is this right? You're saying we're all the greatest? Exactly!! Since we all get in the same way - totally and completely on the merit and righteousness of Jesus alone - we are all great. How can it be otherwise? The Bible teaches that it is through Jesus' perfect life and sacrificial death on the cross, that we are made right (justified) before God. God confirmed this by raising Jesus from the dead. His life becomes our life, His righteousness our righteousness, His greatness our greatness. We are heirs of God, and co-heirs with Christ (Rom.8:17). What could possibly be greater than that? So the first lesson we have here is; **that we must always live with the awareness that we stand before God like a little child - with no rank, no achievement, no claim to greatness. It is only by God's mercy that we are made great.**

I want to note in passing, that so closely does Jesus identify Himself with each of us, that when we welcome any of God's spiritual children and serve them, we are directly welcoming Jesus and the Father who sent Him (Lk.9:48; Mt.18:5; Mk.9:37). This will be examined at length in the chapter, "Small is Large One Cup at a Time."

So far, we see that Jesus has indirectly told His quarreling disciples that they need to get rid of their selfish ambition, and quit seeking the glory that belongs to God alone. It seems that if we could really take hold of this, there would be a lot less fighting in the Church - and a great deal more unity. We must stop seeking only what is good for *us individually* - promoting ourselves and our own clever ideas. We must cease seeking the praise of men, and drawing attention to ourselves. If we could focus all our energies only on the advancement of the Kingdom and the glory of God alone - all the while looking out not only for our own inter-ests but also for the interests of others - we would shake the world for Jesus. It is a sad reality that we can look at some Christian churches which are growing larger and more prominent, and still observe a 'greatness mentality'. Their leaders are prideful, with a focus on self-advancement and the desire to make a great name for themselves. Promoting a popular money-making ministry becomes the goal — with great offerings, expensive facilities, and throngs of worship-pers as the proof of "success." The challenge of taking up the cross and producing mature obedient disciples becomes a secondary goal at best. Is it possible that by confronting such a church with a life that goes beyond spiritual entertainment, self gratification, and the praise that comes from God alone - it may actually *lose* some of its members? Yes, it is. But if a church wants to grow in ways that are *pleasing to God,* then selfish pride in all forms must be thoroughly purged from among the body of believers. Furthermore, once pride infects the fellowship of a church, it can destroy unity as quickly as anything in the Devil's arsenal; while humility, with a focus on the needs of others, will provide the soil in which the grace of God will thrive.

We come now to the heart, sum, and substance of what Jesus wants us to understand. After helping the disciples see that they could not claim greatness for themselves, they still needed to learn what greatness looks like for a citizen of the Kingdom of Heaven. So, this is what He teaches them:

"For it is the one who is least among you all who is the greatest." Luke 9:48 NIV

"Anyone who wants to be first must be the very last, and the servant of all." Mark 9:35 NIV

I've reflected on these sayings for quite a while, trying to come up with a clever way to explain them. I finally realized that there is no need to be inventive or fanciful about this. We simply need to be clear about what Jesus is saying. The disciples had been arguing about which of them would be the greatest. Who was going to be the most important? Who would have the highest rank or position? Who would have the highest privileges and most consideration in the Kingdom? Who was going to have first place among them? So Jesus says to them, "Okay, so you want to know about Kingdom greatness? Here is what greatness really looks like. It's just the opposite of what you think it is. You want to be the most important - be the least important. You want the highest rank and position - find the lowest rank and position. You want the highest privileges and the most consideration - give up all your privileges and consider everyone else before yourselves. You want first place - take last place and serve everybody else before you even think of yourselves. Put their needs ahead of your own." This is what a Kingdom person does. This is how they act. All Kingdom citizens are the greatest, and this is how they should live.

Jesus turns our thinking upside down. He calls for a kind of spirit and attitude that is in total conflict with our sinful human nature apart from the Spirit of God. The words I prefer to use to describe this disposition of mind, are lowliness and humility. To be a lowly or humble person is not to have a low sense of self worth, or to lack self esteem. It does not mean that we serve God by allowing everyone to walk all over us. Put simply, it is to possess a modest opinion or estimate of our own importance. It is to be honest in our self evaluation, and to recognize our rightful place before God. He is the Creator - we are the created. He alone is Holy - we are sinful. He is superior - we are inferior. He is the Lord - we are His servants - not His solicitors. To be lowly and humble in a spiritual sense then, is to place our hearts in a position of worship, dependence, submission, and helplessness before the Lord. We are fully aware of our sins, weaknesses, and failures, while at the same time trusting entirely in His all-sufficiency. When this is coupled with the firm personal knowledge of how much God loves us, how much He has given us in Christ, and how secure our hope is of sharing His resurrection glory - it adds a new depth to our character. We are no longer afraid of giving preference to others, because we are secure within ourselves. We don't have to push for first place or position, because we know deep inside us that we already have a place and position in Christ which is vastly superior to anything this world might offer. We can actually take joy in the status of "servant", because we have learned that the only lasting joy comes from allowing Christ's love to flow from us to others. One day, we who have trusted in Jesus will all be like Him. To be like Him, is to partake of eternal life, which is life indeed. All citizens in the Kingdom of God should have an attitude like Jesus:

"Who, being in very nature God,
did not consider equality with God something to be used to
his own advantage;
rather, he made himself nothing
by taking the very nature of a servant,
being made in human likeness.
And being found in appearance as a man,
he humbled himself
by becoming obedient to death —
even death on a cross!" Philippians 2:6-8 NIV

This willingness to be the last and the servant of all is why:

"Therefore God exalted him to the highest place
and gave him the name that is above every name,

that at the name of Jesus every knee should bow,
in heaven and on earth and under the earth,
and every tongue acknowledge that Jesus Christ is Lord,
to the glory of God the Father." Philippians 2:9-11 NIV

Since this is what the very greatest in the Kingdom of Heaven (Jesus) is like; the Apostle Paul exhorts us to have that "self-same" mindset in all our relationships:

"Therefore if you have any encouragement from being united with Christ, if any comfort from his love, if any common sharing in the Spirit, if any tenderness and compassion, then make my joy complete by being like-minded, having the same love, being one in spirit and of one mind. Do nothing out of selfish ambition or vain conceit. Rather, in humility value others above yourselves, not looking to your own interests but each of you to the interests of the others." Philippians 2:1-4 NIV

There is just no way to say this better. The Church needs to be united with one mind and spirit in what we are all about. The commission of Christ to take His message - and make disciples of all nations - can only be achieved when we turn away from wanting to be superior to others, and cease to covet their praise. Unity can never take place when we argue pridefully about positions and hierarchies. It can only come when we learn this first lesson of "greatness": *Lowliness and humility. The least is great, the first is last, and Kingdom ambition must be directed toward service to others.*

One final word on this. There is a great temptation in our churches, especially among those in positions of paid professional ministry, to think of church organization in terms of hierarchies. This temptation is most subtle — and its reasoning sounds very convincing. We point out that there must be structure in the church; for everything must be done "decently and in order" (1 Corinthians 14:40). Everyone must be "in their place", because the church must have a power structure - a pecking order. There must be authority in place so that order can be maintained. After all, the Apostles such as Paul, were given the power by God to delegate authority to others. This was done for the safety, health, preservation, growth, and maintenance of the churches. God is a God of order. So - we have Pastors, Deacons, Elders, Overseers, Ministers of Music and Worship, Ministers of Education, Church Administrators, Youth Pastors, Campus Pastors, and other "Servant Leaders." We delegate authority in our churches to those with almost every kind of title you can think of. The problem isn't with having people in positions of leadership. <u>The problem is the temptation for those in such positions to think of themselves as better than those under their care; to think of the church as a power structure - with them in the higher positions.</u> In the church organizational chart, "I'm higher up the food chain." The church ends up being kind of like the military. I have a higher rank, privilege, and position. There are more stripes on my shoulder. So. . . I must be better than you, more spiritual than you, and more deserving of a place of honor. Welcome to the land of the disciples! Such people may not be overtly arguing about it, but because of their dedicated service to Christ, they feel they are more deserving than the others in the fellowship of believers. Now of course there must be authority in the church. But the authority is not present to confer upon Christians; rank, privilege, and greatness. It is there to ensure order and accountability. It exists to facilitate spiritual growth among the whole body, and to help each member do their part. It is intended to help us stay focused, and to work together toward our task of making and teaching disciples. In the kingdom of God and in the local church, we are all brothers and sisters and really equal. The ground is level at the foot of the cross. I say here - and will say again

- that **God has no favorites**. None of us has the right to say we are better or more worthy of Kingdom honor than anyone else. There is room for only one glory in the church, and it isn't ours. Glory belongs to God alone. When Paul listed the qualifications for leadership in the church, he added this:

"He must not be a recent convert, or he may become conceited and fall under the same judgment as the devil."
1 Timothy 3:6 NIV

This temptation however, is not limited to new converts. Pride in our heart - is a battle we fight throughout our whole lives in this world. The temptation for ministers to want to be great - to want to be first, like the disciples - is one we must guard against - no matter how many years of experience we have in leadership. Even the accolades from those we serve, can be a source of pride; unless we remember that all of God's people are the "greatest." The first will be last, and the last first. Remember the little child. . . for that child is all of us.

We are at a place now in our study of 'greatness in the Kingdom of God', where we must firmly fix in our minds what was first noted in Luke 9:30. *"There are those who are last who will be first, and first who will be last."* In the race to Kingdom greatness, we will all cross the finish line together. We are all equal, all the same, all great, in Jesus. I know this still may not make complete sense - because it certainly didn't to the disciples. (or for a long time - to me either.) Reflect on it as we continue. We are going to look at a parable of Jesus', to make plain the very meaning of the saying, *"But many who are first will be last, and many who are last will be first."*

The parable is about vineyard workers, and is found in Matthew 20:1-15. The aphorism just quoted, actually serves as "brackets" to the parable, because Jesus cites it to introduce the story in Matthew 19:30, and then again immediately following it in 20:16. While it is likely that this proverb and parable is largely unfamiliar to us — we are probably very familiar with the conversation and encounter that led up to them. I am referring to the story of the Rich Young Ruler, that begins in Matthew 19:16 (see also Mark 10:17-31; Luke 18:18-30). Before we attempt to tie together the parable of the vineyard workers and the encounter with the rich young ruler; I think we need to glance back a few short verses to Matthew 19:13-15 and it's parallels in Mark and Luke. We begin just there:

"One day some parents brought their children to Jesus so he could lay his hands on them and pray for them. But the disciples scolded the parents for bothering him. But Jesus said, "Let the children come to me. Don't stop them! For the Kingdom of Heaven belongs to those who are like these children." And he placed his hands on their heads and blessed them before he left." Mt.19:13-15 NLT

This is where everything starts. On the surface, the picture is simple enough. There are parents who want Jesus to bless their children, but the disciples tried to prevent this. They felt that Jesus was much too busy and involved in important ministry, to be bothered by insignificant children. Jesus, on His part, was indignant about what the disciples had done (Mark 10:14). He calls the parents and children to Himself, and blesses them. Now we know that Jesus loves little children; but don't miss what he said to his disciples. He tells them that the Kingdom of Heaven belongs to those who are like these children. He declares that anyone who doesn't receive the Kingdom of God like a child, will never enter it (Mark 10:15). Does this sound familiar? It should. This is exactly what we learned earlier in Matthew 18:3 where Jesus placed a little child before His disciples and said, *"Truly I tell you, unless you change and become like little children, you will never enter the kingdom of heaven.*" He is telling them again that they're only going to get into the Kingdom by acknowledging their utter dependence upon Him, and by repudiating any merit of their own - that they thought could earn them place or position before God. If we read the narrative carefully, we learn that just then, as Jesus was about to continue on his journey, a man ran up and knelt before Him. Why the timing of this is significant, is that Jesus is going to have to repeat - in three different ways - the lesson He had just tried to get the disciples to understand. The positioning of the story of the little children, alongside the rich young ruler, and the parable of the vineyard workers, is not by accident. In fact, we are going to see later that the events which follow the parable, tie in perfectly as well. This issue of who is the greatest - is so important, that Jesus teaches it over and over again. The reason is — it is vital that we and the disciples understand not only how to enter the Kingdom of God, but also that we never forget what this means (with regard to how we relate to one another as fellow Kingdom citizens).

As we pick up the narrative, Jesus had just finished blessing the little children, and a man ran up and knelt before Him. It is Luke that tells us the man was very rich (Luke 18:23); while Matthew and Mark state he had great possessions. In Matthew 19:20, we learn that he was a young man; while Luke 18:18 introduces him as a ruler. Each of these aspects of the man's life are suggestive - as they serve to highlight the impact of his rejection of Jesus' invitation. Along with his great wealth, he was certainly a gifted and promising young man in Israel's spiritual community. A young person attaining to the status of a ruler - a local synagogue official - was probably not an everyday occurrence. That such a man would come running up to Jesus and then assume a posture of worship before Him, marks him as a sincere individual who begins to arouse our sympathy by his receptiveness. He asks Jesus what good thing he must do to inherit eternal life. A very reasonable question. No doubt he had heard Jesus speaking about life in the Kingdom. So he thought about the matter, and asked himself what good deed he had to do, to merit a place in the new age. Thus he seizes this opportunity, seeing that Jesus has a free moment. He runs up to ask Jesus what has been pressing upon his heart. As we read about this man, we often assume that his spiritual problem was the wealth - which held him back from following Jesus. In reality, the man had two problems - and Jesus addressed them both in due course. He first reminded the young man of the importance of keeping God's commandments. (Almost every Bible commentary will point out that the commandments Jesus cites are those which relate to how we treat our fellow man.) This was not an oversight by Jesus. It isn't that Jesus forgot the other commandments. He wanted to help the young man understand something that was indispensable to his salvation. When the man responded to Jesus that he had kept the commandments since he was a boy - Mark tells us that Jesus looked at him and loved him (Mark 10:21). We shouldn't miss this, because it gives us a glimpse of the majesty and tenderness of Jesus. I picture the two of them standing face to face. Jesus looked him right in the eye with a look of love that also contained a challenge and a hint of grief. Then Jesus said to him, *"You lack one thing: Go, sell all you have and give to the poor, and you will have treasure in heaven. Then come, follow Me."* (Mark 10:21 HCSB). We all know the story. The young man went away sorrowfully, for he was very rich. The truth is, Jesus actually said two things to the man. The obvious one - is the command to sell all he had, and give it to the poor. The other one is not so obvious. By giving this command, Jesus is causing him to understand that he really hadn't kept the commandments, for the poor had not been a consideration for him. His failure to respond to the needs of his suffering fellow Israelites, had a direct bearing on his relationship with God. The man had claimed a passive obedience to God's commandments, but Jesus made him see that an active obedience was called for as well. If we look at the very heart of this; Jesus was inviting the man to salvation, the same way he invites us all. First, he wanted to help the young man acknowledge himself as a sinner, who had not really kept the law of God. Second, he invited the man to submit to His Lordship, no matter what the cost. Simple childlike repentance and faith — but his wealth got in the way.

After the man left, a brief dialogue with the disciples followed, where Jesus told them twice, *"Children, how hard it is to enter the kingdom of God!"* (Mark 10:24 NIV). We have to wonder if Jesus tenderly used the word "children", to call to their minds the children they had just seen Him bless, and the teaching He had spoken to them. He is about to reinforce the lesson that entrance into God's Kingdom requires a total dependence on God. Jesus' next words are the famous metaphor of how it is easier for a camel to go through the eye of a needle - than for those who trust in riches to enter the Kingdom of God. When the astonished and somewhat confused disciples heard this, they wondered who in the world could be saved? This is because they assumed, as did many in their culture, that if a person was rich - God's blessing must be upon them. (They practiced and falsely believed in a kind of First Century Health and Wealth Gospel!) They reasoned that if God was blessing someone (the rich), and *that person* cannot be saved, then who can be? It didn't make sense to them. They still didn't understand what Jesus meant when He said that the only way to enter the Kingdom of Heaven - is like a child. In response to them, and with the same kind of eye contact He had with the rich young ruler, "Jesus looked at them and said, *For people this is impossible, but for God all things are possible.*" Mark 10:27 NCV. I like the way this verse is paraphrased in The Message, "Jesus was blunt: *No chance at all if you think you can pull it off by yourself. Every chance in the world if you let God do it.*" What a great and gracious God we serve! No one can save themselves. It is impossible for anyone to take even the first step in God's direction, without God first reaching out to them. No one is beyond the grace of God. Not even those who idolatrously trust in their riches. Anyone may come, even people like you and me:

"Surely you know that the people who do wrong will not inherit God's kingdom. Do not be fooled. Those who sin sexually, worship idols, take part in adultery, those who are male prostitutes, or men who have sexual relations with other men, those who steal, are greedy, get drunk, lie about others, or rob — these people will not inherit God's kingdom. In the past, some of you were like that, but you were washed clean. You were made holy, and you were made right with God in the name of the Lord Jesus Christ and in the Spirit of our God." 1 Corinthians 6:9-11 NCV (underlining is mine)

With God, all things are possible. Even such unrighteous people as we are, can be saved despite our sinful past.

Here is not the place to discuss the spiritual danger of riches - even though it is considerable. I relate the story of the rich young ruler, because we need to see the connection with what follows. How did the disciples continue to react to it? How does it allow Jesus to progress in educating them about the Kingdom? So right about this time, Peter pipes up - and this dialogue ensues:

"Peter answered him, "We have left everything to follow you! What then will there be for us?"

Jesus said to them, "Truly I tell you, at the renewal of all things, when the Son of Man sits on his glorious throne, you who have followed me will also sit on twelve thrones, judging the twelve tribes of Israel. And everyone who has left houses or brothers or sisters or father or mother or wife or children or fields for my sake will receive a hundred times as much and will inherit eternal life. But many who are first will be last, and many who are last will be first." " Matthew 19:27-30 NIV

Peter is saying, "Jesus, we weren't like that guy. We left everything to follow you just like you wanted. You called each of us and we came. We know we needed you. We've been traveling around with you. We're living hand to mouth just like you are. So, what's in it for us?" They all want to know - and I suppose rightfully so - just how this was all going to pay off for them. What do we get out of this? Jesus makes known to them a couple of things. First, when the world is made new, and the Son of Man sits on His throne (i.e. to judge the world), you will be there with me. You will be abundantly compensated for all you have suffered here for following me. You will share in the glory and dignity that is reserved for all the saints in heaven.

Compare this with what Peter later shares with all of us in 1 Peter 1:3-5 NIV:

"Praise be to the God and Father of our Lord Jesus Christ! In his great mercy he has given us new birth into a living hope through the resurrection of Jesus Christ from the dead, and into an inheritance that can never perish, spoil or fade. This inheritance is kept in heaven for you, who through faith are shielded by God's power until the coming of the salvation that is ready to be revealed in the last time."

Then there is this wonderful assurance to us: All who have sacrificed to follow Jesus, will even now receive back a great Christian family, and a hundred times as much in the grace, comfort, and tokens of God's love. No one will ever lose by forsaking all to follow Christ. Anything that might be lost by giving our lives to Him in this world - the Christian life will compensate us a hundred times over. Even under persecution (Mark 10:30), the rewards of life in Christ, experienced through the fruit of the Spirit, will be more than enough to satisfy the deepest spiritual thirst of our souls.

Now comes the climax that we must not miss. It is the great reward the disciples were seeking. Mark puts it like this at the end of 10:30, **"and in the age to come eternal life"** (cp. Matthew 19:29; Luke 18:30). Everyone who follows me is going to receive eternal life. That is your inheritance and reward - and a great reward it is! None of us has the superlatives to describe this gift. It's just here that we come back to the beginning of this segment of our discussion. I said there - that we needed to look at a parable of Jesus to make plain the meaning of the saying, *"But many who are first will be last, and many who are last will be first."* For right after the words of the promise of eternal life leave Jesus' lips - this is exactly what he says. If you look down to Matthew 20:16 which immediately follows the parable, you will see the same proverb with just a slight variation. So it becomes clear that by bracketing the parable with this proverb, Jesus is using the parable to explain the proverb to us.

Before we tackle this parable to arrive at the clear meaning of the proverb, *"many who are first will be last, and many who are last will be first"* — it may be helpful to review some of the many ways this saying has been interpreted. Here are a few of the meanings that have been suggested, to which you can no doubt add your own:

- Those who become Christians later in life may wind up achieving more than those with seniority.

- Those who suffer for Christ in modern times may accomplish more than those who were persecuted in the past.

- God can raise those we least expect to stations of distinguished usefulness; confer on them peculiar talents and higher rewards.

- Some believers who have had only a short life to serve the Lord, may be more useful than those who had a much longer time.

- The early disciples are not more precious to God than those disciples who came much later.

- Seniors in the church have no right to dictate policy simply because they were there first.

- For the Jews, this is to confirm that God has no "most favored nation" clause.

- Since the final judgment is all about motive; those with right motives will be highly rewarded, while those who feel "entitled" may not find it so.

- Prominence in this world means humility in the next (e.g. those who are rich and powerful now, will be poor and unimportant then).

- The "first" are those who think they are pious, and the "last" are like the tax collectors and sinners who recognized their need of God. (So in the end, the tax collectors and sinners will get into the Kingdom, while those who thought themselves righteous will not. A variation on this is that the tax collectors and sinners may wind up being better believers, and so be more deserving of reward than those who were simply self-righteous.)

- Those among the disciples (and us by implication) who thought they deserved to be first (the greatest) in the Kingdom, may find that some of the other disciples are in fact more prominent than they are.

- This represents those who at first refuse to accept the gospel (like Saul of Tarsus) - but later accept it - and become notable disciples (such as the Apostle Paul).

- The judgments of eternity will reverse the judgments of time. (Everything here on earth is valued upside down. On the last day, God will ultimately reverse the values of the world by honoring and rewarding those the world thought were nothing, and bringing to nothing those people whom the world considered great. God will reveal to everyone in the next life, those who were worthy of honor now, but did not receive it in this life. A slight variation of this, would make the world's "great", wind up as least in the Kingdom of Heaven - if they get there at all; while those Christians who are least now - whom God views as great - will wind up with the places of highest rank, privilege, and position in Heaven.)

Now while I have no doubt that there are valid applications set forth in some of these interpretations of this proverb; I believe that none of them are what it actually means. To discover this, we come now to the parable of the vineyard workers:

"For the kingdom of heaven is like a landowner who went out early in the morning to hire workers for his vineyard. He agreed to pay them a denarius for the day and sent them into his vineyard.

About nine in the morning he went out and saw others standing in the marketplace doing nothing. He told them, 'You also go and work in my vineyard, and I will pay you whatever is right.' So they went.

He went out again about noon and about three in the afternoon and did the same thing. About five in the afternoon he went out and found still others standing around. He asked them, 'Why have you been standing here all day long doing nothing?'

'Because no one has hired us,' they answered.

He said to them, 'You also go and work in my vineyard.'

When evening came, the owner of the vineyard said to his foreman, 'Call the workers and pay them their wages, beginning with the last ones hired and going on to the first.'

The workers who were hired about five in the afternoon came and each received a denarius. So when those came who were hired first, they expected to receive more. But each one of them also received a denarius. When they received it, they began to grumble against the landowner. 'These who were hired last worked only one hour,' they said, 'and you have made them equal to us who have borne the burden of the work and the heat of the day.'

But he answered one of them, 'I am not being unfair to you, friend. Didn't you agree to work for a denarius? Take your pay and go. I want to give the one who was hired last the same as I gave you. Don't I have the right to do what I want with my own money? Or are you envious because I am generous?'

So the last will be first, and the first will be last." Matthew 20:1-16 NIV

As I write these words, it is early Autumn. Even in the dry Arizona desert where I live, everyone knows that this is the time of year for harvest. All around our state there are "Oktoberfests", which celebrate the harvest season. Fresh corn abounds, as do massive amounts of pumpkins. This is the time of year we find in the parable. It is during the critical days of grape harvest, that our story finds its setting. The grapes must be secured quickly at just the right time so they are not lost. So we find a prominent landowner who comes seeking day laborers for his vineyard. In the city in which I live, there are established areas where men gather each day, early in the morning. They do so in the hopes that a local employer will pick them up for a full day of work. This is crucial to their family's livelihood and survival. If they do not get chosen to work, they have no money for food, rent, or other necessities. Even though the social structure in Jesus' day was somewhat different than ours; those workers waiting in the marketplace were among the very poorest of the people. When they did find work, their pay was usually low, and they received little for their efforts. So here, their day begins with a landowner who hires them and agrees to pay them a denarius for a full day's work. As far as I can determine — this was a very fair and generous amount of compensation to these workers. A denarius was the daily pay for a Roman soldier. The landowner was not cheating them or taking advantage of their situation. Today we might say, "they received an honest day's pay, for an honest day's work." So off they went at 6 a.m. to work a long 12 hour day in the hot sun. Some 3 hours later, at 9 a.m., the landowner found still others standing around the marketplace not doing anything. Realizing the need for additional laborers, he hires these men, and agrees to pay them whatever was fair and right for their work. The same thing happened about noon, and then again at about three in the afternoon. Late in the day, at 5 p.m., the landowner went back into the marketplace and found still others standing around. He asks them why they have been standing around all day not doing anything. They respond that no one has hired them. Remarkably, the landowner also tells *them* to go out into his vineyard to work. The end of the workday arrives, and the landowner directs his foreman to call the workers in and pay them their wages. The foreman is to pay the workers in reverse order of their hiring. Those hired at 5 p.m. would be paid first, then those hired at 3 p.m., etc. I imagine that those who were paid first, hired at 5 p.m., thought they would receive the smallest minimum amount for their labor. After all, they were there barely an hour. Instead, to their great surprise, they each received a full denarius — a whole day's pay! We can almost hear them talking as they left. "Wow. A denarius, what a deal! My wife is never going to believe this! Wait until I tell the guys!" So off they went, no doubt grateful for the landowner's generosity. The pay line behind them watched this. It seems likely the guys at the end were getting pretty excited. Those hired at the crack of dawn probably looked at each other and said among themselves, "Look, those guys the owner hired when the work was almost done, got a full denarius. We've been working all day long, think what we're going to get!" By their arithmetic, one hour of work = one denarius, so perhaps 12 hours of work = 12 denarii? They get to their turn in line, and they each receive one denarius. One lousy denarius. So they begin to grumble against the landowner. I don't think "grumbling" needs explanation. Anyone who has ever had cause to complain to their boss about how much work they did - in comparison to what they were paid for it - knows how these guys felt. (Personally, I spent many days working in state government, grumbling about how little I was being paid for all I had to endure.) So, being pretty annoyed at this point, they take their complaints to the landowner. To paraphrase what they said: "This isn't fair! You paid those guys who only worked an hour, the same amount as you paid us - and we slaved all day for you in the hot wind and sun." The landowner now turns to one of the grumblers and says, "Look pal, how am I being unfair to you? You agreed to work for me all day for a denarius, right? So take your pay and go. I decided to give those one hour guys the same pay I gave you. It's my money, and I can do whatever I want with it. Or are you jealous because I was good to those people?"

Let's be honest. When we read this parable, don't we feel sympathy with the guys who worked all day in the hot sun? Doesn't it bother us just a little, that those one hour workers got something that maybe they really didn't deserve? It doesn't seem fair. Why did that landowner not appreciate what those laborers did - who worked all day for him? Why did he give so much to those who didn't deserve it? This land-owner bothers us by what he did. *And you know what?* God bothers us too. He bothers us because we are jealous of what He gives to "those people." You know, those who get good things from God that we don't think they deserve. Those who are wealthy. Those who have many possessions. Those who don't have the same problems that we have - even though we've been faithful to Christ and they haven't. Those without faith whom the world applauds - while we as Christians are despised and unrecognized. Or how about those believers who attend church and sit back and watch - while the rest of us do all the work and most of the giving? They're going to heaven just like we are, and they haven't done anything for

Christ! This is all so unfair, Lord. How can you reward those who don't deserve it - who haven't earned it? You might be starting to get it. God is the landowner, Jesus is the foreman, and we are the laborers. This, Jesus said, is what the Kingdom of Heaven is like. Your pay - your reward if you will - is eternal life (Matthew 19:29). Everyone in Christ receives it, no matter who. The last will be first and the first last. We are all the same before God, who is generous to all. There are no "more deserving" Christians. None. Not even one. The first receive eternal life, and the last receive eternal life — and we all possess this great inheritance. Not because we deserve it, but because Jesus Christ has procured it for us - apart from any work of our own. This parable is a rebuke to the disciples and to us. The disciples had continued to argue amongst themselves, as to who was the most deserving. Jesus has to remind them over and over again - that the Kingdom isn't about what they deserve - but about the mercy and grace of God. Remember the little child? The Apostle's envy and jealousy of each other had to cease - and so does ours. Even as disciples in today's churches, we war within our hearts at the depravity that makes us want to feel superior to others. I am better than you are. I deserve more than you do. Why should you have something that I don't? We fight and argue over meaningless trivialities. If pressed, we would barely acknowledge the fact that we're all headed for the same destiny in Christ - the glorious culmination of eternal life (cp. James 4:1-12). To put this in the terms of the parable; eternal life is not dependent on how hard you have worked for God, or how long, or how difficult the conditions of your "employment" (service) with Him are. In the end, you will receive eternal life. Payday is coming, and Jesus will see that you receive your eternal reward.

Practically speaking, what does this mean? It means that service to God and Christ is not drudgery. God has assigned certain tasks to each of us, and provided us with the spiritual gifts to perform them. We are not in a competition to see who can do more than the next guy (so that we can beat him out), to get a better place than his in the Kingdom. Our service is all joy. It is part of God's gift to us in salvation. Remember what God said through Paul:

"8 God saved you by his grace when you believed. And you can't take credit for this; it is a gift from God. 9 Salvation is not a reward for the good things we have done, so none of us can boast about it. 10 For we are God's masterpiece. He has created us anew in Christ Jesus, so we can do the good things he planned for us long ago." Ephesians 2:8-10 NLT

We often hear verse 10 used as if God meant to beat us over the head, and demand that we do good works for Him. To feel guilty for not doing enough for God - is to miss the idea and encouragement of this. The truth is, as part of His provision in our salvation, Paul says that God has given us the gift and privilege of participating with Christ in this new life. This takes place when we do the tasks that He planned in advance for us - to invest our lives in. This isn't about guilt and competitiveness. It's about gift and grace. We serve the Lord with joy - not out of a sense of bondage (like a job in which we feel trapped). We serve as His children; set free in gospel liberty to serve Christ out of love. We are not like day laborers - who serve only for what we can get out of it. We are the bride of Christ, the heirs of eternal life, who will one day be like him:

"Dear friends, we are already God's children, but he has not yet shown us what we will be like when Christ appears. But we do know that we will be like him, for we will see him as he really is. And all who have this eager expectation will keep themselves pure, just as he is pure." 1 John 3:2-3 NLT

There is no need whatsoever, for any of us to be discontent with our lot in life. No need to be envious and jealous of our brothers and sisters in Christ. No need to compete for first place. We all win! We all get eternal life. So enjoy what you've been given to do, and the time you have been given (allotted) to do it in - and serve the Lord with gladness, no matter how "hot and windy" the day gets.

Before we leave this parable and continue on our way along the journey to understand "greatness"; I want to say one more thing about this matter of "what we deserve." We are trying to rid ourselves of this sense of jealousy; the kind that resents the fact that others will receive the same eternal life we will. We imagine that they have not served Christ with the same faithfulness that we have. Why don't we get a bigger throne, or a higher rank, or special colored insignias to show everyone how great we are? There are no second class citizens in the Kingdom of God - whether in Heaven or on earth. There is no place whatsoever for pride or prejudice. I think it's fair to ask however - whether there will be any reward to us personally from God, for the faithfulness we have demonstrated in our individual lives. Doesn't God recognize our unique contributions? Indeed He does. For we all have to stand before the judgment seat of Christ, as Paul stated:

"For we must all appear before the judgment seat of Christ, so that each of us may receive what is due us for the things done while in the body, whether good or bad." 2 Corinthians 5:10 NIV

We will address the entire matter of heavenly and earthly rewards in the chapter: "Small Is Large One Cup At A Time." For now, let me direct your attention to Paul's words in 1 Corinthians 4:5 NLT:

*"So don't make judgments about anyone ahead of time —
before the Lord returns. For he will bring our darkest secrets
to light and will reveal our private motives. Then God will
give to each one whatever praise is due."*

In context, this verse comes while Paul is addressing the
question of how we should evaluate those who perform ministry in the service of Christ. He is going to make the point
that he is not worried about what people think of him. He
had been entrusted by God with a ministry. He was going
to do whatever God assigned him to do in his evangelism,
teaching, and preaching. He was going to be faithful to God,
and there wasn't anyone, including himself, who was truly
qualified to make a proper evaluation of his ministry. So he
commends the matter to the Lord alone; the only one who
can accurately determine the real motives and intentions of
a person's heart. When we stand before the Lord, He will
give to each person whatever praise is due them from God.
I can think of no greater reward than the "well done, thou
good and faithful servant" - from my Master. All that is fully
involved in God's praise, we cannot now know. In my view
— this is somehow related to our own individual capacity
and capability for the service we will be gifted in eternity. In
any case, we can absolutely trust the Lord in all such matters.
We can also affirm that in the Heavenly Kingdom, there will
be no envy, jealousy, pride, or resentment. We all receive a
full share in the glorious inheritance of the children of God.

By now, we can see that Jesus had a great deal to say about
the meaning of greatness in the Kingdom of God. There is
one more leg on our journey here, and it is as entertaining as
it is informative. We pick up the narrative in Matthew, right
after Jesus finished the parable we just discussed. I don't
think that Matthew arranged this material haphazardly. Here
we will see Jesus teach in the most explicit way — what it
means to be great in the Kingdom. Jesus has resumed his

journey to Jerusalem. Mark 10:32 (NLT) gives us a feel for the mood:

"They were now on the way up to Jerusalem, and Jesus was walking ahead of them. The disciples were filled with awe, and the people following behind were overwhelmed with fear."

From here on, the narrative in Matthew (20:17ff.) and Mark (10:32ff.) are almost exactly parallel, except for one small difference. With the disciples unsure of what lay ahead for them, Jesus takes them aside and tells them:

"We are going up to Jerusalem, and the Son of Man will be delivered over to the chief priests and the teachers of the law. They will condemn him to death and will hand him over to the Gentiles to be mocked and flogged and crucified. On the third day he will be raised to life!" Matthew 20:18-19 NIV

Mark even adds the detail that he will be spit upon as well. This is now at least the third time that Jesus has said this to them. I can scarcely imagine how the disciples must have felt upon hearing this. You're probably also thinking that they are somewhat fearful, and not a little confused. Maybe even a touch humbled and discomfited. Strangely enough, what happens next is this:

"Then the mother of Zebedee's sons came to Jesus with her sons and, kneeling down, asked a favor of Him.

"What is it you want?" He asked.

She said, "Grant that one of these two sons of mine may sit at your right and the other at your left in your kingdom."" Matthew 20:20-21 NIV

Now in Mark's version of the story, we are told that James and John (who are Zebedee's sons) come to Jesus with this request. As you notice, Matthew tells us that they brought their mother with them.

I find this especially amusing - due to my professional background. I worked for many years in large welfare offices. Oftentimes, individuals would get frustrated with our agency, because they thought that we had made a mistake on their case, or we were treating them unfairly and dismissing their concerns. Some of these folks felt that they either didn't know how to communicate sufficiently with us, or that they were not capable of being forceful enough to get their point across. I would be sitting in my office and one of the staff would approach me and say, "'So and so' is here to see you, and they brought their mother with them." At that point, I knew I was in for it, because "mommy" was on the case! Mothers can be quite determined — where the welfare of their children is concerned.

James and John wanted a favor from Jesus, and so they brought their mother with them. Beyond the fact that their mother spoke to Jesus for them; is who she actually was. When you review the accounts of the crucifixion in Matthew, Mark, and John — you see four women near the cross that are specially mentioned. There is Mary the mother of our Lord; Mary Magdalene; Mary the mother of James (the younger) and Joseph; and a fourth woman. This fourth woman is identified in three different ways. Matthew calls her the mother of the sons of Zebedee (Matthew 27:56). This is the woman who is with James and John, approaching Jesus here in Matthew 20; so it is clear that she was a devoted follower of the Lord, and stayed with Him until the end. Mark calls her Salome (Mark 15:40), and John refers to her as "his mother's sister" (John 19:25). When you look at the accounts side by side, it becomes clear that this is very likely the same woman. In other words, her name is Salome and she is Jesus' aunt! As we know, James and John are already part of Jesus' "inner circle", along with Peter. They had also recently witnessed the transfiguration. Now we discover that are they are likely Jesus' cousins, and their mother is His aunt. So they are already feeling pretty special and privileged as they approach Jesus; likely with a sense of family entitlement. We're going to see that this went over really well with the other Apostles! Imagine their reaction when they heard about the request of James and John, with their mom kneeling down before Jesus, asking for the places of foremost honor next to Him in His Kingdom. Definitely not good. Their conversation with Jesus continues like this:*" "You don't know what you are asking," Jesus said to them. "Can you drink the cup I am going to drink?"*

"We can," they answered.

Jesus said to them, "You will indeed drink from my cup, but to sit at my right or left is not for me to grant. These places belong to those for whom they have been prepared by my Father." " Matthew 20:22-23 NIV

Jesus says to them, "Fellas, you really don't know what you're asking for." This is something I often imagine Jesus saying to me when I ask for certain things. It's kind of like the way we ask God for various aspects of Christian character, such as patience. We ask for patience, but God sends trials and struggles. Then we ask the Lord why He has sent His poor servant such terrible stress. He answers us by saying, "Well, I'm answering your prayers. You asked for patience didn't you? The only way to give you patience is by increasing your trials." Take love as another example. We ask God to make us more loving; like Jesus. Then He sends some very unlovable person(s) into our lives, to teach us how to really love as Jesus did. The point is, when we pray for something for ourselves, we need to be sure we really want what we are asking for; because the answer may not be quite what we are expecting. My older son knows that I have long asked God to provide me with a suitable Christian helpmate. He will remind me occasionally that I really need to be sure about what I am asking! That's his polite way of telling me that if God grants my request, I may be surprised at the kind of circumstances it will lead to. Over the years, I have learned to be grateful for God's answers, and for His delays. Our Father knows best what we really need. He also knows how to determine when the time is right for us to have what we have requested. I am also thankful that when I don't know how to pray, or what to pray for, the Holy Spirit is there to help me in my weakness (Rom.8:26-27).

As we return to James and John, Jesus asks the brothers if they can drink His cup or share His baptism. These expressions are idioms. Their meaning is clear. Jesus said in Gethsemane, "Father, if you are willing, take this cup from me; yet not my will, but yours be done." (Luke 22:42). The cup is the terrible pain and suffering that Jesus will endure leading up to, and culminating in, the crucifixion. This is what He has been telling them about. He will have to drink it in full, taking upon Himself all the sins of the world. On the cross, He will experience the judgment of God for our sins. A truly horrific experience that none of us can fully know. His baptism is a similar metaphor. It represents His passion, the cross, and being fully immersed in all the suffering and sacrifice involved in taking our place - to suffer the wrath of God, and make an atonement for our sins. Jesus would suffer, and drink the cup of God's judgment. He would be baptized into the fulness of what it meant to die for the sins of all mankind. For the disciples, the cup and baptism didn't mean exactly what they meant for Jesus. They would not die for the sins of the world. But essentially, He told them that it does mean that they too would have to suffer and sacrifice for His sake - and for the sake of the gospel. This would also occur in ways that they were not yet expecting. I love their response to this: *"We can."* This little expression always comes to my mind whenever I hear a Christian (including myself) ask God if (that) He would use them greatly; perform some great ministry through them; or give them a place of prominent influence in the Christian community. These are all honorable requests; but we had better know what we are really asking. God may indeed honor such prayers. I trust He does. However, we can be sure that if we want to glorify God and make His greatness known, that we (like John the Baptist) will have to decrease - so that Jesus can increase. In other words, if we want God to do a great work in our lives, we will have to die to ourselves, humble ourselves, take no honor to ourselves, and make ourselves nothing; so that God will receive all the glory. The self denial involved in this may be quite painful. We must be prepared to suffer for Jesus' sake. For all those who want to live a godly life in Christ Jesus will be persecuted (2 Timothy 3:12), and we must go through many hardships to enter the Kingdom of God (Acts 14:22). I don't know about you - but even though my heart is in it, I think twice before I say to God, "I can." There's nothing wrong with saying that, but we must be sure we mean it - in the same sense of dependence and humility that Paul did when he said, *"For I can do everything through Christ, who gives me strength."* (Philippians 4:13 NLT).

As it turned out, James and John did indeed drink from Jesus cup of suffering. James died early for his faith (Acts 12:1-5). John, early church tradition tells us, died an old man; having suffered persecution. He also took part in the beatings and abuse the Apostles endured in the book of Acts (see e.g. Acts 4:1-22; 5:17-41). However, as for the places of honor at Jesus' right and left hand; He told them that such a grant is determined and prepared for by God alone. (As an aside, I would note that such places at Jesus' right and left hand - are not necessarily those of rank, privilege, or control over others in Heaven - as the brothers may have supposed. God may bestow them as an assignment of duty, or as a token of special appreciation. While such places would certainly be honorable ones, there is nothing in the text that directly implies or guarantees that Heaven will have seats of special rank that all believers will be subservient to.)

We continue with Matthew 20:24 NIV:

"When the ten heard about this, they were indignant with the two brothers."

Yes, I'll bet they were — mother and all! This kind of pride and self promotion, never accomplished anything positive among the disciples, then or now. I am reminded of the countless situations that occupy our churches today. Someone gets it in their head that they are not receiving the recognition they deserve. It may be a position they desire in the church; a feeling of being slighted; or opposition by others - which means they just do not get to have things their own way. I would hope that we did not have to experience such disturbances in our churches. Sadly, it's more widespread than you might think. On one occasion a number of years ago, I was moderating a church business meeting. There was so much of this kind of self-serving behavior going on - fighting over trivialities - that I truly felt more like an umpire than a moderator! Surely the Holy Spirit is not honored by such behavior. Those involved are not allowing Him to direct their minds and thinking. You may have heard of churches that split over such matters as: What color to paint the walls; what kind of carpet to install; what time evening worship should be; or how much to pay church staff. Conflict abounds over whether worship services should be "traditional" or "contemporary." I was once involved with a serious church dispute over whether the patch of land in front of the worship center should be grass or gravel - and what kind of plants it should have; cactus or no cactus (— that is the question!). It sounds funny to say it, but you know as well as I do, that there is no end to the kinds of petty arguments that have ruined a church's witness (and effectiveness) in the spread of the gospel. No doubt you could add stories of your own. I have heard many more issues like these. All of this begins with pride. Like the disciples, we have to be first. Things have got to go our way, or we just won't play anymore. How our adversary the Devil, must raise his fist and gloat, when we act in such childish ways! The time for all such foolish behavior is past. We must grow up in Christ, and learn to love each other. Writing to the church at Rome, Paul exhorts them:

"Love does no harm to a neighbor. Therefore love is the fulfillment of the law. And do this, understanding the present time: The hour has already come for you to wake up from your slumber, because our salvation is nearer now than when we first believed. The night is nearly over; the day is almost here. So let us put aside the deeds of darkness and put on the armor of light. Let us behave decently, as in the daytime, not in carousing and drunkenness, not in sexual immorality and debauchery, not in dissension and jealousy. Rather, clothe yourselves with the Lord Jesus Christ, and do not think about how to gratify the desires of the flesh." Romans 13:10-14 NIV

As Jesus saw the friction that was developing among His disciples, He gathered them together to settle everyone down. Not only was it important to Him that they learn to love one another (see John 13:34-35), but He wanted them to come to a deep understanding of what true greatness would look like, in the Kingdom He was establishing. In a way, we are indebted to their folly; they draw forth from Jesus, these dynamic and powerful words, which provide our most unequivocal look yet, at what it means to be great in the Kingdom of God:

"You know that the rulers of the Gentiles lord it over them, and their high officials exercise authority over them. Not so with you. Instead, whoever wants to become great among you must be your servant, and whoever wants to be first must be your slave — just as the Son of Man did not come to be served, but to serve, and to give his life as a ransom for many." Matthew 20:25-28 NIV

There are three distinct things that Jesus tells them here. *What does greatness look like in the world in which they live? What should greatness look like, in the citizens of the Kingdom of God? What is the ultimate template for greatness that you can look to, when you need strength and guidance?* As the Pastor of my current church is fond of saying, "Let's see if we can unpack this, and find out what it means."

Jesus begins by reminding His disciples of what they have seen and experienced, as they look at the non-Jewish world around them. He speaks of those who rule in high and important positions among the nations. Some of you may be wondering why Jesus didn't speak of those who ruled Israel. Well for one thing, it was the Sanhedrin who ruled the nation - not any one individual. The Sanhedrin (the Jewish High Council) was comprised of 70 elders, chief priests, and various scribes and teachers of the law. They held all the political power in Israel - except in matters of capital punishment (cp. John 18:31). For that, they had to defer to their Roman overlords; which is why Jesus was taken before Roman officials when they desired to put Him to death. So Israel did not have rulers like the Gentiles per se; although we could make the case that the character of some of their leaders was no different than the type Jesus was describing. More to the point, for the true Israelite, only God was their Supreme ruler. Their hope and expectation was that when the Messiah came, he would assume the throne of David, and rule over Israel in the name of God. In light of this, it was the character and behavior of the Gentile rulers, that would be most evident to the disciples. What then are the high and mighty rulers of the Gentiles like? First, Jesus says they lord it over people. The actual Greek word, is the word for "lord", with a preposition in front of it that means "over or above." So these rulers dominate people; they subdue them; they act as despots. They assume an air of importance and authority that others are compelled to recognize and submit to. Then there are those in important positions. Literally, these are "the great ones." They are the big dogs; the ones who like flaunting and exercising all their authority. They want everyone to do their bidding, and acknowledge their big names and titles. They desire to command the utmost respect. In fact, Luke relates that Jesus said these Kings and great men like to be called "Benefactors"; which was a title of honor given to those who benefited the public good (Luke 24:25). I like the way The Message paraphrases this: "(they) love to give themselves fancy titles." Sounds eerily modern doesn't it? My brother has picked up on the whole "title" idea and we joke about it. He is a proponent of all things British, because our father was from England. He enjoys observing how the Queen of England gives titles to various people, particularly celebrities. So he will often say to me, "I want a title too! I want the Queen to give me a title." Well, I won't tell you the titles we've pondered for him – but suffice to say we've had many good laughs over them. These then, are the great among the nations. They dominate others, exercise authority, and throw their weight around. They assume an air of importance, and try to compel others to do their bidding. They want recognition, and they seek honor and respect from everyone. The disciples were not unfamiliar with this. They saw it with

Roman officials, and they were reminded of it by looking around their cities and towns. Daily, they would see Roman Soldiers, tax collectors, and government buildings. Roman law and culture left its imprint throughout the world. There was even the occasional mandatory census. Roman rule was evident everywhere, and there was no shortage of examples of rulers such as Jesus described. The disciples knew of Caesar, Herod Antipas, Pilate, and many other Governors and Kings. Their world was no different from our world. Today, the earth is filled with people whose selfish ambition knows no limits. They will do anything to anyone in order to achieve seats of power, and fight their way to the top. For such individuals, there is no second place. They are driven by pride, unbridled ambition, and the corrupt desire for money and power. They will push themselves to the front by any means possible. In today's technological age, there are a great many new ways for them to do so. Our world is filled with people who have sold their souls to the god of pride and self. Despite their words to the contrary, they have no real motivation to promote and secure the welfare of their fellow man. Do you think I'm exaggerating? Anyone who follows world politics knows better. Even America seems to be stagnating; because our politicians insist on looking out for only their own agendas, instead of the welfare of the American people.

I decided to take a brief detour to discover whether there were still very many dictators and despots in the world today. I did a quick Google search, and was astounded at what I found. Although this number is slowly changing (due to the various social uprisings in our world), there are at least 31 bona fide dictators in the world today. This is based on using the definitions of "dictator" (an individual ruler who rules unrestrained by law) and "despot" (a violent, oppressive dictator.). The list does not include rulers and regimes that were still teetering on the edge of total control, or authoritarian rulers who had only been in office a few years. It also does not include longtime rulers who may have just been the product of an authoritarian system. There is no mention of Totalitarian regimes - where absolute power is centralized within a party or group. Nor does this list encompass those who are elected officials but act like despots - violating the basic human rights of their citizens. It is not my purpose here to list these individuals, but the number of people they represent is staggering. The point is, what Jesus said to His disciples, is just as true today. This is how one becomes "great" in the world. You push yourself to the head of the line. You fight for prominence and control, and you use any means possible to achieve it. You lord it over others, and you exercise all the authority you possibly can. This then, is what greatness looks like in the world around us.

Jesus always seemed to turn things upside down. Christians are called on to be radically different from what we commonly expect from people. This is made strikingly clear by the next thing Jesus said, "Not so with you" (v.26). That is — among you it must be different. You are not to be like that. The Kingdom of Heaven does not look like that. Its citizens do not act that way. Greatness - Kingdom greatness - has an entirely different model. To put this in modern terms — greatness has a completely different paradigm than what you commonly see in the world around you. And so then, He told them what Kingdom greatness does look like:

"Instead, whoever wants to become great among you must be your servant, and whoever wants to be first must be your slave."

I think it's important to note first, what Jesus is *not* saying. The disciples had been fighting continually over which of them was the greatest. Who was going to be first among them? Who would be prominent above the others?

Jesus is not telling them what they must do to achieve this prominence among themselves. He is not telling them essentially what the correct way is to "dominate" over the others, as people do in our world. Allow me to exaggerate a bit to make this clear. Sometimes we understand Jesus words as if he were saying:

"Okay men — you want to be the most famous, celebrated, and important person? Let me tell you the secret of success. You want the power to command, control, and determine the destiny of others? Here's how you do it. You want Heaven to be all about you; Peter, James, and John in charge, with everybody admiring how great you are? Let me tell you how you can make that happen. Thrones and crowns; homage on the golden streets; people cheering when you walk by? Let me show you how you can be the first to achieve it!"

Jesus is not giving the disciples self-help advice on "How to Achieve Fame in the Kingdom." If you miss the subtlety here, you are missing something absolutely vital to Jesus' true meaning. He is not telling these men something that will continue to promote arguments and competition among them. He is trying to help them understand something that will *eliminate* all such behavior. He wants them to stop the arguments, cease from thinking about prominence, and stop thinking only of themselves. Jesus wants them to begin learning how to see the permanent Kingdom reality of all human relationships - in a completely different light. Life among us, as brothers and sisters in the Kingdom, must be lived in a totally different way. It will be unique and wonderful, and something that you never thought possible. Everyone in the Kingdom will be great. As citizens of this new kingdom, the Kingdom of God, everyone should have a transformed attitude of mind and heart. Each person needs to view every other person as so important - that the interests and needs of others will be of more concern to them than their own. Kingdom citizens will be people who should truly love God with all their heart, and their neighbor as themselves. We are to truly be like Jesus. The law of God will find its perfect fulfillment among us, and God Himself will live among us. He will be our God, and we will be His people (cp. Revelation 21:1-4; Jer.31:33; Ezek.37:27). Jesus is telling His disciples, "This is how greatness is characterized in this present world. Among you, my people, the people of God, if you want to become great in the way God wants you to be; to be 'first' in the way God wants you to be first; then this is how you must learn to live and act. This is how 'great' people in His Kingdom live." After telling them that, he gets practical, and goes on to tell them how to do it. It is not complicated, as you might imagine. It is really quite simple. Two words. Two simple words. If we get this in our spirit, or better yet, if we allow the Holy Spirit to get this into us - we will learn what it means to be one of the great (which is all of us) in the Kingdom of God. Are you ready for this? Here are the two words: *servant and slave*. Learn how to be a servant and a slave. It's so ironic to say this, but if Jesus were to go on national television today and say, "Whoever wants to become great among you, must be your servant; and whoever wants to be first, must be your slave" — there would be any number of groups and organizations up in arms. They would decry how offensive, inappropriate, and politically incorrect it is for Jesus to say this. That is due, of course, to the negative connotation these words have come to carry in our society. For many people, these words conjure up images of servitude and slavery — the kind that the dictators and despots of the world subject millions of people to. They think of human rights violations, the oppression of the poor and needy, military brutality, human trafficking, violent drug cartels, greedy giant banks, oil companies, multibillion dollar corporations, totalitarian regimes, and every other form of corruption that seeks to oppress humanity -

and force their will upon those unable to resist their power and control. This is most certainly the very opposite of what Jesus was saying. It does however demonstrate what happens when we try to understand spiritual words with a carnal mind. As Paul taught:

"And we have received God's Spirit (not the world's spirit), so we can know the wonderful things God has freely given us.

When we tell you these things, we do not use words that come from human wisdom. Instead, we speak words given to us by the Spirit, using the Spirit's words to explain spiritual truths. But people who aren't spiritual can't receive these truths from God's Spirit. It all sounds foolish to them and they can't understand it, for only those who are spiritual can understand what the Spirit means. Those who are spiritual can evaluate all things, but they themselves cannot be evaluated by others. For,

"Who can know the LORD's thoughts?
Who knows enough to teach him?"

But we understand these things, for we have the mind of Christ." 1 Corinthians 2:12-16 NLT

Jesus here is using these kinds of spiritual words. When with the mind of Christ we fully understand them - our souls will be liberated from our slavery to selfishness and pride, and set free to a life of righteousness, peace, and joy in the Holy Spirit. What then is Jesus referring to, when He tells us to become servants and slaves? The word for 'servant' that He uses, is the Greek word *diakanos*. It is usually translated as servant or minister. We often think of its meaning as, "a person who waits on tables." This understanding is derived from the verbal form of the word used in Acts 6:1-7, of the seven men chosen by the church in Jerusalem to help serve certain widows who were being neglected in the daily distribution of food. It's also the word used later in the New Testament for the spiritual office of deacon. My younger son is employed in a restaurant which is part of a large chain. He works as a waiter, or as the correct term is today - a server. It's his job to take care of all of his customers by taking their orders for food and beverages, and by making sure they have everything they need while seated at one of his tables. While he is at work, his mentality is that he is going to be the best at what he does - the best server he can be. His customers will lack for nothing they need, and they will receive their requests in a prompt, timely, and courteous manner. Their drinks will stay full, their food will be right, and any problems they have will be immediately corrected. In a very real sense, this is who we are. We are table servers. It is our reasonable service, 24/7, to worship God by being attentive to the needs in the lives of those around us. This isn't about simply doing good deeds for others. It's more than that. Feeding the hungry, helping the homeless, caring for those sick and in prison, aiding widows and orphans - yes, that's part of it. But in reality, our thinking must go beyond even that. Jesus is talking about attitude, character, mind-set, disposition, inner nature. A way of listening, hearing, and responding in love spontaneously, to the needs of those we encounter in the course of our everyday routine. We should live with a readiness to serve others. It needs to be our first thought, the highest impulse of our new nature, a fixed and settled part of our deepest make up. It's the spirit that wants to reach out to others before any thought of ourselves. It isn't that we neglect our own needs - but that we learn to love our neighbor as ourselves. We mature in our thinking by growing toward a constant awareness that our own lives are not the center of the universe; and that we are really here to contribute to the lives of others. We discover we are part of something far greater than ourselves - and it is up to God to determine how our lives will be used and invested, to promote the welfare and salvation of others.

This is not some strange idea or concept that Jesus is calling us to. The general concept of service to our fellow man - is generally understood even by those who are not believers in Christ. We see this in a variety of ways. In the world of business, the term "excellence in customer service", has come to be synonymous with profitability, and recognized as the most desirable business model. This is because most people instinctively know that when a company or organization is attentive to our needs, we are more likely to want to do business with them. We tend to gravitate toward those who put our concerns first. Even in our personal relationships, we are most appreciative and kindly disposed toward those who's actions evidence an interest and involvement in our immediate concerns. In February 2011, I watched with interest as the President of the United States presented the "Presidential Medal of Freedom" to 15 notable individuals who had made what he called, "an especially meritorious contribution to the security or national interests of the United States, world peace, or cultural or other significant public or private endeavors." It was deeply moving for me to see these people from all walks of life, as they were recognized for a lifetime of service and sacrifice that benefited those in their chosen endeavors. This year, for the fifth time, media giant CNN will host an award ceremony called, "Heroes - An All Star Tribute." This cash award is given to 10 "heroes", nominated by the public, who are honored as everyday people changing the world. One of the 10 becomes "Hero of the Year", and wins an additional cash prize to help them in their work. For the 2011 awards, over 10,000 nominations were received. These are individuals who give sacrificially and unselfishly, working tirelessly to improve the quality of life for others. Performers, celebrities, and other prominent individuals, all pay tribute to the spirit of service exemplified by these chosen heroes. We see from all of this - the universal acknowledgment of the value placed on individuals whose lives are given in service to others. What is unique about being a servant Jesus' way, is that it is done out of love for God and for His glory. There is a total dependence on His all-sufficiency to empower our actions and determine the results. Additionally, it is the result of transformed life - a new birth - that is evidenced by those who have faith in Jesus. We serve not with the ultimate motive of self interest - but with passions and intentions which are rooted, initiated, molded, and shaped, by the Spirit of God.

We return now to the second word Jesus uses: "slave." The Greek word for slave is *doulos*. It means exactly that - a slave. I have already noted the negative connotations this word has in our world, as well as the spiritual understanding which Jesus imparts to it. But in what way are we to become slaves? In the world of Jesus' time, a servant was different from a slave. A servant had a job to do — but a slave was under the total direction and control of another. Slaves were owned. They belonged to someone. As Christians, we belong to God. The Bible makes this plain in many ways, but nowhere more so than in Paul's words in 1 Corinthians 6:19-20 NIV. Discussing the need for us to avoid sexual immorality, he declares:

"Do you not know that your bodies are temples of the Holy Spirit, who is in you, whom you have received from God? You are not your own; you were bought at a price. Therefore honor God with your bodies."

Jesus has brought us back to God at the price of His own blood.

"He died for everyone so that those who receive his new life will no longer live for themselves. Instead, they will live for Christ, who died and was raised for them." 2 Corinthians 5:15 NLT.

This imagery of believers being slaves to God - and slaves to righteousness because we now belong to Him - is discussed at length by Paul in Romans, chapters 5-8. Consider Romans 6:11-18 NLT:

"So you also should consider yourselves to be dead to the power of sin and alive to God through Christ Jesus.

Do not let sin control the way you live; do not give in to sinful desires. Do not let any part of your body become an instrument of evil to serve sin. Instead, give yourselves completely to God, for you were dead, but now you have new life. So use your whole body as an instrument to do what is right for the glory of God. Sin is no longer your master, for you no longer live under the requirements of the law. Instead, you live under the freedom of God's grace.

Well then, since God's grace has set us free from the law, does that mean we can go on sinning? Of course not! Don't you realize that you become the slave of whatever you choose to obey? You can be a slave to sin, which leads to death, or you can choose to obey God, which leads to righteous living. Thank God! Once you were slaves of sin, but now you wholeheartedly obey this teaching we have given you. Now you are free from your slavery to sin, and you have become slaves to righteous living."

Jesus and Paul used the word "slave" to help us in our understanding of the new life we possess. Our lives belong totally to God. We have been set free - but we are not free to live selfishly. We are free to live under the power and guidance of the Holy Spirit. Body, soul, and spirit; we are created anew to live in dedication to God. We are "slaves", but it is voluntary. We are free to explore the capacity of our new nature, to learn how we may best find God's will in serving others. We discover the life we are capable of, by thinking of others before ourselves — they are first, we are last. It's a "slave" mentality. Not in a degrading way - but *only* in the highest possible spiritual sense. We allow others to direct us, as unto God, into providing for their need of ministry. We move with compassion toward whatever need they have, that is within our power to meet. Jesus wants us to know that greatness lies in just this. Everyone we meet is a person we may serve. Everyone is potentially our "master" - in the sense that they may direct us how we might do them good. We are slaves to God and righteousness, yet we are completely free. **This is God's Arithmetic, and it is the true measure of greatness.** <u>We become a servant and a slave to everyone, and in doing so, we find God's blessing and praise.</u> In this way, we learn the meaning of John 10:10 (NLT) where Jesus says:

"The thief's purpose is to steal and kill and destroy. My purpose is to give them a rich and satisfying life."

This full and abundant life that Jesus intends for us, is inextricably bound to a heart filled with love, and a mind bent on service.

I have already noted how Matthew was not haphazard in the manner he arranged the record of events in Jesus' life. Immediately following the teaching Jesus gave His disciples after the incident with James and John, we find this warm-hearted story about Jesus' encounter with two blind men:

119

"As Jesus and his disciples were leaving Jericho, a large crowd followed him. Two blind men were sitting by the roadside, and when they heard that Jesus was going by, they shouted, "Lord, Son of David, have mercy on us!"

The crowd rebuked them and told them to be quiet, but they shouted all the louder, "Lord, Son of David, have mercy on us!"

Jesus stopped and called them. "What do you want me to do for you?" he asked.

"Lord," they answered, "we want our sight."

Jesus had compassion on them and touched their eyes. Immediately they received their sight and followed him."
Matthew 20:29-34 NIV

In this passage that I call to your attention, we discover something incredible. We need to focus on what Jesus said to these blind men. Mark and Luke also record this incident (Mark 10:46-52; Luke 18:35-43), although they only mention one of the two blind men. Mark gives us the name of the man - Bartimaeus. For those who are not of Jewish background, he tells us that means, "son of Timaeus." I love this story, and there are many things we can learn from it. For our present purpose, I want us to see something that directly ties in with our focus on Jesus' meaning of being a servant. I just made the point that everyone we meet is a person we may serve. I suggested that everyone is potentially our "master" - in the sense that they may direct us how we might do them good. The wonderful thing about this story, is how Jesus demonstrates to the disciples and to us, exactly how this is done. As He heard these two blind men shouting to Him above the noisy crowd, Jesus stopped and called them to Himself. The gospels all make clear that both men, Bartimaeus in particular, came face to face with Jesus. Now, don't miss this. With tender compassion, Jesus says to them, *"What do you want me to do for you?"* This may be the most incredible thing we see the Lord say. It is greater in some ways than the healing itself. Jesus is taking orders from a blind beggar! Two of them in fact. The Son of God, who has the name above all names, and to whom every knee will one day bow, and every tongue confess as Lord (Philippians 2:9-11), becomes a servant to two blind men who are the outcasts of society. Jesus models for us what it truly means to be a servant of all. This question that Jesus asked - *"What do you want me to do for you?"* - needs to be our question. It is this question that we must ask of others, if we are to learn what it means to be great in the Kingdom of God.

Jesus had taught His disciples about the meaning of greatness, and He modeled it powerfully His whole ministry — but did the disciples get it? Do we get it? Sadly, we sometimes tend to be as slow to understand as the disciples. When the Lord was nearing the end of His ministry, with the shadow of the cross upon Him, He gathered His disciples together for one last Passover meal. As they met in the upper room, He focused on the new covenant that He would seal with His blood. Then, while He spoke of His death, and symbolized it with the bread and wine, it started all over again. The disciples began to argue with each other - again. And do you know what they were arguing about? Greatness in the Kingdom of God. Luke tells us what happened..

"A dispute also arose among them as to which of them was considered to be greatest. Jesus said to them, "The kings of the Gentiles lord it over them; and those who exercise authority over them call themselves Benefactors. But you are not to be like that. Instead, the greatest among you should be like the youngest, and the one who rules like the one who

serves. For who is greater, the one who is at the table or the one who serves? Is it not the one who is at the table? But I am among you as one who serves." Luke 22:24-27 NIV

It's hard to believe, but the disciples just didn't get it! At a critical time when Jesus needed them, and they could have been offering Him sympathy and support, they were arguing once again about which of them was the greatest. These are the men to whom Christ was about to trust the future of His Kingdom! He is depending on them to be the ones to take the gospel to the world. Yet here they are, in the shadow of the cross, fighting with each other. This makes us realize all over again, the kind of love the Lord had for them and for us. If God measured us only by our failures and foolishness, we'd all be cast aside. Thankfully, we have a God who meets us where we are, accepts us fully in Christ, and patiently works in us - to make us more like Him. So here, gently and lovingly, Jesus once again repeated His teaching to the disciples about greatness. As before, He reminded them one more time about how the people of the world demonstrate greatness, and what their great ones act like. Then He adds, *"But you are not to be like that."* You need to learn to think differently. The greatest should be like the youngest, and the ruler like the servant. In that society, the youngest persons were the least honored. The younger ones in a family may in fact have been called upon to do "table service" for the rest of the household. So Jesus told them again, if you want honor, seek service. Remember His words in Matthew: servant and slave. Honor others before yourself. Take on the mentality of a servant. Then in verse 27, He says something extraordinary. *"Who is greater?"*, He asks them. *"The one who is being served at the table, or the one who is serving everyone? Isn't it the one who is being served? But I am among you as one who serves."* During the last supper, Jesus had again become the model of a servant. He wrapped a towel around himself, and one by one went to His proud disciples, and did for them what none of them were willing to do. He, like a servant, washed their feet. John tells us what Jesus said to them right after this:

When he had finished washing their feet, he put on his clothes and returned to his place. "Do you understand what I have done for you?" He asked them. "You call me 'Teacher' and 'Lord,' and rightly so, for that is what I am. Now that I, your Lord and Teacher, have washed your feet, you also should wash one another's feet. I have set you an example that you should do as I have done for you. Very truly I tell you, no servant is greater than his master, nor is a messenger greater than the one who sent him. Now that you know these things, you will be blessed if you do them." John 13:12-17 NIV

In an amazing way, and totally in contrast to what the disciples expected or what our world would expect today, our Lord and King has taken His place among us as one who serves. The assembled universe must marvel at this. The One who created everything, and for whom all things were created (see Colossians 1:15-17; John 1:1-3; Hebrews 1:2-3), dwells among us as one who serves. Matthew 20:28 (NLT) emphasizes this powerful truth for us:

"For even the Son of Man came not to be served but to serve others and to give his life as a ransom for many."

The one worthy of all glory and honor became a servant and served others with a self sacrificing love. Do we think we are greater than Jesus? Are we above serving others? Jesus said, *"A disciple is not above his teacher, but everyone who is fully trained will be like his teacher."* (Luke 6:40 HCSB). So He tells the disciples, *"I am among you as one who serves."*

Every once in a while, I am privileged to meet someone who exemplifies Jesus' attitude of humble self-sacrificing service. Roy F. Sutton was just such a man. Roy was Executive Director-Treasurer of the Arizona Southern Baptist Convention from 1970-80. He first joined the Arizona convention staff in 1946, at a time when the convention included churches spanning nine states, from Mexico to Canada. Dr. Sutton later had a hand in the birth of two other state conventions: The Colorado Baptist General Convention in 1955, and the Nevada Baptist Convention in 1978. In addition to holding numerous positions within the Arizona Southern Baptist Convention, he was present when the Catalina Baptist Association was formed in Tucson, and was its first associational missionary. Among Dr. Sutton's long list of leadership positions is time served as Vice President of Grand Canyon College (now University). He also served as pastor of Emmanuel Baptist Church, Tucson; First Baptist Church, Coolidge; and College Park Baptist Church, Phoenix. Yet in my mind, it was not simply this impressive resume of service that made Dr. Sutton so much like Jesus. It was the way he related personally to everyone around him. He never thought of himself as better than anyone, but was always ready to associate with 'ordinary' people. Roy enjoyed the company of everyone, no matter who they were. He had a way of making you feel as if you were the person who was really important, not him. I met Roy in the late 1970's while I was a student at Grand Canyon College. He was teaching those preparing for the gospel ministry, and he took advantage of every opportunity to build relationships, so he could encourage each individual in their service to the Lord. As I walked around campus from one class to another, I would often see Roy sitting with students and enjoying their company. I remember walking with him on occasion across the school grounds, all the while relishing the fact that such an esteemed man had taken the time just to be with me. His gift of friendship, and the way he believed in God's work in the lives of others, have left a lasting impression on me to this very day. Dr. Sutton was the very embodiment of Romans 12:16 NIV: *"Live in harmony with one another. Do not be proud, but be willing to associate with people of low position. Do not be conceited."* He went home to be with the Lord in May, 2004 at age 95, having touched countless lives with his humble spirit and tireless service.

We conclude our study of 'greatness in the Kingdom of God' with Jesus' words of encouragement to a life of blessedness: *"Now that you know these things, you will be blessed if you do them."* John 13:17 NIV. The path to blessing lies in the servant life. It begins with the renewal of our minds and hearts. Like the disciples, it's our motives and intentions which matter most to God, and drive our journey. The joy of the servant life is attainable, but it is not one that can be achieved in our own strength. We must depend entirely on Christ's power at work within us. Without a life of daily abiding in Him; we can do nothing (see John 15:5). As we allow God to transform our hearts and minds, working from the inside out, we will learn to be like Jesus. The Apostle John said it well:

"Don't love the world's ways. Don't love the world's goods. Love of the world squeezes out love for the Father. Practically everything that goes on in the world — wanting your own way, wanting everything for yourself, wanting to appear important — has nothing to do with the Father. It just isolates you from him. The world and all its wanting, wanting, wanting is on the way out — but whoever does what God wants is set for eternity." 1 John 2:15-17 MSG

To be happy and blessed — we must learn to walk in Jesus' steps. This is God's Arithmetic! It may not add up correctly according to the world's standard of greatness, but it is perfectly accurate and precisely sums up life in the Kingdom of God.

Give the Holy Spirit full reign. Allow Him to show you what it means to live like Christ. Permit Him to shape the highest and deepest impulses of your new nature. For as you do, you find that greatness is not something you must fight for — but is a victory that Christ has already won.

Small Is Large One Cup
At A Time

*E*veryone enjoys receiving a gift. I've never met anyone who didn't. I think the pleasure we derive when we receive a gratuitous gift, is built into us as human beings. We may be skeptical about the giver's motives, but a gift given from a generous heart always seems to delight us. This is especially true when it is done spontaneously or unexpectedly. It's easy to suppose that the larger or more expensive the gift is, the more we will value it. Almost every holiday season, I see a commercial on television where someone receives a new car parked in front of their house wrapped in an enormous Christmas bow. How many of us could watch that and say we don't wish it was us receiving the car?! My oldest son has a standing joke with me along those same lines. When he graduated high school many years ago, he playfully said to me, "Where's my new car?" I would have loved to have been able to get him a new car for his graduation, but I could not afford to do so. Every once in awhile, he'll still surprise me during a conversation and say, "By the way, you still owe me that new car — you're failing in your fatherly duties!" We always have a good laugh about it, but I'm never quite sure if he's being serious or not! Even though we all might like to receive such extravagant gifts, there are times we are reminded that even small acts of generosity can be meaningful to us. When my younger son was in grade school, he came home one day with a fragile looking wooden object, and presented it to me as a gift. When I inquired as to the nature and purpose of this item, he explained that he had crafted it in wood shop and had made it for me as a gift. The object was meant to sit on my desk, and to be an organizer - designed to hold CD's, paperwork, or whatever else I might need to place into it. This little desk holder my son had created for me was not very impressive. In fact, I could have gone to any office supply store and obtained an inexpensive counterpart to it, which would have served me much better. Nevertheless, I greatly valued his gift, and it remained on my desk for at least 10 years - even though it often required some minor repairs. The value I placed on my son's gift, had nothing to do with its size, cost, or excellence. I esteemed his gift because it was given to me from his heart as an act of thoughtfulness out of his love for me. Every time I used it or looked at it, I thought of him and the way he cared for me. There is another reason why a gift such as this might be regarded so highly. My son gave me what he could. It wasn't as if he had a great deal of money, or a wide variety of choices as to what he could offer me. He found an opportunity to do something for me, and he did what was within his power and ability to do. That's all I could really have asked of him anyway. The fact that he did this spontaneously and without any prodding on my part, made his "act of giving" all the more meaningful to me. Another way to look at this, is that my son received a blessing in himself through his generous giving, and I received a blessing by receiving the gift he offered. He also received the reward of seeing the joy his gift brought to me, and I received the reward of sharing in the happiness he found when he completed what he set out to do. In both the giving and receiving of his small act of kindness, we each found blessing and reward. The sense of what

I am saying, is immediately clear to anyone who has been a parent. But even for those who are not parents; experience teaches us how meaningful even the smallest acts of kindness can be. This whole idea of properly esteeming the value of something we give or that is given to us, has a direct bearing on our walk with the Lord. The focus of the matter has to do with how we regard our service to Christ and His Church. Many of us as Christians, tend to downplay the contributions we are capable of making toward the advancement of the Kingdom of God. As a result, it is often easy to justify our apathy and lack of involvement. It seems like everywhere we look, there are people doing great things for God. We read our Bible - and it is filled with believers who dared tremendous peril in His service. We go to church - and see highly gifted individuals teaching, preaching, praying, leading worship, singing, playing instruments, and directing ministries. We listen to the radio and television - and see famous Christians making their mark for our generation in song and story, as they proclaim the message of Christ. We read the Internet and magazines - and are in awe at the heroic exploits of faithful Christians all over the world. We look at all of this and say to ourselves:

"These people are so talented. They are so gifted. I would love to be able to make a difference as they do, but I am not so talented or so gifted. I am so overwhelmed by the business of daily living, and by the commitment it would take to make a difference, that there really isn't much I can do. So, I think I can best serve the cause of Christ by attending church regularly, giving money when I can, and praying for those people who are doing God's work so well."

I believe that many of us have felt this way at one time or another. We resign ourselves to the fact that we may never be able to do great things for God. Once we accept this, it becomes easier to sit back and stop considering how we might make a difference in God's Kingdom. We reason that if the Lord had intended us to do something great, He would have given us great spiritual gifts to do it. I'm here to tell you — That kind of thinking couldn't be more mistaken. **In God's Arithmetic, great things are happening all the time through the smallest actions of His children.** The problem is, we don't recognize the value that God places on even the least acts of humble service in His name. If we would learn to esteem such acts as He does, it would enrich our Christian experience, and bring new energy and joy to what seem to be our most trivial efforts - on behalf of our fellow Christians.

So we turn now to the words of Jesus. Two passages of scripture will provide us with some unique insights into God's Arithmetic. We rarely hear these verses taught, because they can be difficult to interpret and understand. Through them, we will examine how God valuates the service we perform in His name. It is my prayer that we will come away with profitable insights into some of Jesus' most powerful - yet easily overlooked sayings.

Let's begin with Mark 9:38-42 NIV:

38 "Teacher," said John, "we saw someone driving out demons in your name and we told him to stop, because he was not one of us." 39 "Do not stop him," Jesus said. "For no one who does a miracle in my name can in the next moment say anything bad about me, 40 for whoever is not against us is for us. 41 Truly I tell you, anyone who gives you a cup of water in my name because you belong to the Messiah will certainly not lose their reward. 42 "If anyone causes one of these little ones — those who believe in me — to stumble, it would be better for them if a large millstone were hung around their neck and they were thrown into the sea.

To place John's statement to Jesus into context, as well as trying to make sense of Jesus' reply, it is necessary for us to look briefly at the events that led up to this moment. About a week prior to this, Jesus had taken His disciples on a short retreat, to try to help them understand who He really was, and how He was to fulfill God's purpose for His life. He taught them that He, as the Son of Man, must suffer many things, and would be rejected by the nation's religious and political leaders. He told them of His upcoming death, and of how after three days - He would rise again. Summoning the crowd along with His disciples, Jesus gave them all a great invitation to follow Him - explaining what that would truly mean. With His own total commitment to God fresh on his mind, He made clear how becoming His disciple would involve total submission to the will and purpose of God for their individual lives. (This subject was discussed fully in the previous chapter, Losing Life to Keep It.) In the opening section of Mark 9 (which took place six days later), we find what is commonly referred to as Jesus' transfiguration. For the disciples who were privileged to see this event, God intended to affirm Jesus' identity - and the nature of His mission and ministry. The Kingdom of God was at hand, and it was important to Jesus that His close followers begin to understand the kind of living that His Kingdom was really all about. Unfortunately, even as they were returning from the brilliant light of the Mount of Transfiguration, these chosen disciples were still very much in the dark about what Jesus had told them regarding his death and resurrection. It was Peter, James, and John, who had just witnessed this powerful visual and audible phenomenon, and been permitted a glimpse of the glory of Jesus. We can only imagine the impression this made on them, and how important they must have felt themselves to be — to have been the ones chosen to witness this event.

When they came with Jesus to the foot of the mountain, they found their fellow disciples arguing with some teachers of religious law, and a large crowd surrounding all of them.

The crowd watched Jesus in awe as He came toward them, and then they ran to greet Him. Jesus inquired of them what the commotion was all about. A man in the crowd answered Him. The man explained that he had brought his son to Jesus for healing. He believed his son to be possessed by an evil spirit that had been throwing the child to the ground, and into convulsions. Since Jesus had been unavailable, the man told His disciples of the problem, hoping they could drive the evil spirit out of his son. The man told Jesus (no doubt with great sadness), that His disciples could not effect the cure his son so desperately needed. Jesus then called for the boy to be brought to Him. When the evil spirit saw Jesus, it immediately threw the child into a violent convulsion. The boy's father pleaded with Jesus for help and compassion, saying, "Do something if you can." Jesus replied to him with words now familiar to many believers. Quoting the boy's father, Jesus said, "If you can? Everything is possible for one who believes." Immediately, the father exclaimed, "I do believe; help me overcome my unbelief!" (Mark 9:23-24 NIV). As the crowd gathered to the scene, Jesus rebuked the evil spirit, and commanded it to leave the child and never enter him again. The spirit screamed, convulsed the child again, and then left him for dead. But Jesus took him by the hand and lifted him to his feet, and he stood up. Afterward, when Jesus went indoors, the disciples asked Him why they could not drive the evil spirit out. Jesus replied that this kind of spirit can only be cast out by prayer (or as one gospel writer says, "with prayer and fasting"). Shortly thereafter, when Jesus and the disciples left that place and passed through Galilee, He once again spent time privately with them. He continued to try and help them understand what lay ahead for him — betrayal, death, and coming back to life after three days. Yet once again, they didn't understand what He meant, and they were afraid to ask Him about it.

The events just described, prepare us to understand some very dynamic and dramatic lessons that Jesus was about to teach His disciples. Jesus and the twelve, now arrive at Capernaum. They settled in at the house where they would be staying. Jesus recognizes that the time is now right to teach them some critically important principles about life in the Kingdom of God. He asks the disciples, "What were you arguing about on the road?" Now I believe that Jesus knew full well what they had been arguing about. Kind of like when a parent observes a child doing something they should not be doing, and then asks the child, "What were you doing?" The parent knows exactly what the child was doing, but wants to confront them with their actions. The intent is that the child will be compelled to self examination, and confession of what they had done. The parent hopes the child will either self correct their motives and behavior, or at least enter a teachable state of mind and heart. At that point, the parent can impart truth that will be a catalyst for needed change on the part of the child. This is exactly what Jesus was doing when He asked this question. The disciples were ashamed and didn't answer Him, because while Jesus had been talking about His death, they had been arguing on the road about which one of them was the greatest. The Message paraphrases this well by saying, "The silence was deafening"(9:34). Seizing upon the propriety of the moment, Jesus now provides them with an object lesson. We pick up the narrative in Mark 9:35-37 NLT:

35 He sat down, called the twelve disciples over to him, and said, "Whoever wants to be first must take last place and be the servant of everyone else."

36 Then he put a little child among them. Taking the child in his arms, he said to them, 37 "Anyone who welcomes a little child like this on my behalf welcomes me, and anyone who welcomes me welcomes not only me but also my Father who sent me."

Here we have Jesus teaching a kind of Sunday School class in God's Arithmetic. There is a great deal to be said at this point regarding how God views greatness. (As you know, this was the main point of the last chapter: "No One Wants To Be Last.") Our topic of focus though here, is on Jesus' identification of this little child with Himself and His Father. Understanding this identification, is a necessary part of gleaning the principles Jesus is about to teach. It is also essential for us to grasp that it is not simply or exclusively "small children", which Jesus exhorts us to welcome and receive. The little child here also represents the spiritual children of God. Now we are prepared for v.38, where John is speaking to Jesus. By saying "we", John appears to be speaking on behalf of all the disciples. As Jesus began to discourse about greatness and set the little child before them, there were many things that began to roll around in John's mind, which were likely typical of all of them. John no doubt was starting to have pangs of conscience about wanting to be prominent. He also recognized (as we must), the close intimate relationship that Jesus portrayed between Himself and His followers in v.37. As he struggles for understanding and wrestles with his pride, he recalls an incident with all the disciples that had likely taken place recently. So John speaks up, and confesses it to Jesus. Whether this was a prideful statement to protect their prestige, or a mild attempt to show Jesus how zealous they were for his good name and reputation, we cannot be certain. In any case, Jesus again seizes the moment, and provided them with some powerful essentials for vibrant Kingdom living. The first of these is found in vv.38-40:

38 "Teacher," said John, "we saw someone driving out demons in your name and we told him to stop, because he was not one of us." 39 "Do not stop him," Jesus said. "For no one who does a miracle in my name can in the next moment say anything bad about me, 40 for whoever is not against us is for us."

From this, we learn that **we must be tolerant of those who work to advance the Kingdom of God, even if they are not just like us.** John has just protested that this unnamed exorcist was not part of 'their' group. Perhaps the disciples were like many of us who take such pride in our church or denomination - that we resent anyone else succeeding. I have witnessed Christians many times - refuse to support the work of God, because a particular ministry did not adhere exactly to their entire creed or statement of faith.

We are not talking here about ministry that is *not* truly Christian in nature and character. Examples of this can be found in Acts 19 and Matthew 7. In Acts 19, we find in Ephesus, seven sons of Sceva, a Jewish priest, attempting to perform exorcism by imitating what they assumed to be Paul's scheme - using the name of Jesus. They failed epically, but it's worthy of note that God magnified the name of Jesus, and used the situation to bring many new believers to faith in Christ - even where false ministry was performed! In Matthew 7:21-23, we read of the pretense and performance of those who claimed to be speaking, driving out demons, and doing miracles in Jesus' name. Jesus rebukes them with a harsh, *"Get away from me, you who do evil. I never knew you."* (Matthew 7:23 NCV). There is also the example in Acts 8:9-25 of Simon Magus, whose falsehood and attempt to buy spiritual power with money - elicited a scathing rebuke from the Apostle Peter. There is no doubt then, that we ought to oppose those who attempt to falsely represent our Lord. Such false teachers pervert the gospel, and fail to exhibit Jesus' character.

This however is not the case, here in Mark 9, with John and the rest of the disciples. Jesus said of this unnamed exorcist, *"Don't stop him!"* — he's actually participating in our mission! Jesus affirmed this man's work, and the miracle that was done in His name – a miracle wrought by His own power, and with the approval of God. Those who advance the Kingdom of God in the power of the Holy Spirit, and in the name of Jesus, are truly for us. They are on our team, one of our own - whether or not they are part of our group. The sectarian spirit that so many of our churches display when it comes to Christian ministry, is a direct hindrance to all that Jesus wants to do in the world, and to the cooperation that is necessary to bring the gospel to the ends of the earth. <u>Whenever the good news about Christ is faithfully proclaimed, we need to rejoice - no matter who is doing it.</u> A beautiful example of this, is found in Philippians 1:15-21 MSG. Here we find Paul imprisoned in Rome for his faithfulness to Christ. He was rejoicing because the believers there had gained confidence and boldness in their proclamation of the gospel, due to his imprisonment. There were some however, who were spreading the good news with less than the purest of motives. But listen to what Paul says:

It's true that some here preach Christ because with me out of the way, they think they'll step right into the spotlight. But the others do it with the best heart in the world. One group is motivated by pure love, knowing that I am here defending the Message, wanting to help. The others, now that I'm out of the picture, are merely greedy, hoping to get something out of it for themselves. Their motives are bad. They see me as their competition, and so the worse it goes for me, the better — they think — for them. So how am I to respond? I've decided that I really don't care about their motives, whether mixed, bad, or indifferent. Every time one of them opens his mouth, Christ is proclaimed, so I just cheer them on!

I pray to God - that we might all be more like Paul. As long as Christ is proclaimed, we should eagerly cheer them on. The Kingdom of God consists of much diversity, but it is the same gospel, and the same cause.

Look now at Mark 9:41 NIV:

"Truly I tell you, anyone who gives you a cup of water in my name because you belong to the Messiah will certainly not lose their reward."

With one simple sentence, Jesus lays down several precepts that can greatly energize our service to God. It doesn't seem like there's much here, does it? A simple cup of water to a fellow believer. Such a little thing. Why is a cup of water significant? It's significant because of who is really receiving the water. *Even the smallest service done for our fellow Christians, such as the giving of a cup of water, is being done for Jesus - who lives in them.* The water is given in His name, because that person belongs to the Messiah. The simple and undeniable truth we have to grasp; is that Christ comes to us in other believers. Whatever we do for them because they are a Christian - we do for Jesus. The little child in vv.36-37 is us - all of us - who belong to Jesus. I suspect that there are many Christians who really don't believe this. We look at the brother or sister in front of us, and we think, 'they are not much'. This is a very worldly way of thinking, and does not line up at all in God's Arithmetic. Learn to see in every believer - the face of Jesus. God does — and as we will see here shortly, He takes this matter very seriously. When you realize that even the smallest service to one of God's little ones is done to Jesus — it will transform the way you interact will all of your fellow believers. A new joy will take hold of you, when you become aware of how meaningful even your smallest acts of service can be.

Looking further at v.41, we find another source of encouragement. *Faithful service to God is not beyond our power. We are asked to give only what is within the power of anyone to give.*

One of my very favorite people in the whole world - is my brother Ken. He's always been there for me, and has always loved me, even when we were children. I enjoy Ken very much, and he always makes me laugh. One of the things I admire about him, is that he is a very generous man. Ken is always thinking of ways he can give to those he cares about, placing their needs before his own. When we are together, he will often muse aloud about what he would do for everyone if he won the lottery. He will go on at length about the costly gifts he would give us, and all the money that will be at our disposal. I am always amused when he does this, because each time he brings it up, he comes up with entirely new ways to spend the money! What Ken doesn't realize - is how great the gifts are that he has already given. He will often give family members small amounts of money. In his eyes, these gifts are inconsequential and don't amount to much. In my eyes, his kindness is very great, because he gives generously what is within his ability to give. He really is giving sacrificially to us, although to him, it is a pleasant thing done from a heart of love. He is to me - a great example of giving what you can. God does not ask us to give great amounts of money. We do not need to win the lottery to be able to provide for the saints. A cup of water may not seem like much, but anyone can give it. Jesus makes it clear that God is pleased when we give the simple things that are readily available for us to share. It may be the gift of time that perhaps we had planned for something else. It can take the form of money, clothes, food, household items, a ride in your car, a handwritten note, a book, a light bulb, or anything and everything that God has resourced you. Whatever is close at hand, can be used to meet the needs of our fellow believers. Nothing is too small; and even the least thing you can imagine - be it even a cup of water - may mean more to someone than you can possibly know.

Closely akin to giving only what is within the power of anyone to give — is the thought that *no act of service toward other believers - which is done out of love for Jesus - is trivial in God's eyes.* This is really quite revolutionary, and not at all how we are accustomed to seeing things. <u>God's Arithmetic is not complicated, but it can be hard to grasp.</u> To the western mind, value and significance are often measured in terms of size. The larger and more costly an undertaking for God and its results, the more important we imagine it must be to Him. Christians are not immune to this way of thinking. A large church must obviously be blessed by God; a small church, not so much. A missionary who has many converts must be blessed by God; a missionary who has struggled for years with only a few converts, not so much. A large ministry that impacts thousands or even millions of people must be blessed by God; a small ministry that only makes a difference in the lives of a few people, not so much. If you think about it, the news media has caused our minds to become accustomed to this way of assigning merit to people and events. Great weight is often attached to someone's opinion on a matter - simply because they are famous. When a prominent person performs an act of charity, it is made out to be a very great thing, because somehow this "important" person has condescended to do something nice for a "nobody." It is the great and broad sweeping events that impact people locally, nationally, and world wide, which make the news. Earthquakes, revolutions, hurricanes, tsunamis, fires, killings, scandals, politics, economic upheaval, sports, health care, controversies - are all paraded before us daily - as what is most important in our society. When everyday people do everyday things, they are seen as ordinary, or possessing little value. It is easy for us to allow the images from the wide variety of news media to shape our values, instead of allowing the Word of God to do so. The issue is not whether all these occurrences in the daily news are really important or not — of course they are. The point is, that when it comes to the Kingdom of God, a totally different way of assigning value to "ordinary" acts of service is called for. This is difficult for us to accept. We are so used to categorizing acts of spiritual service to believers into "small" and "great." Everything that affects God's Kingdom is significant to Him, when it is done for His children out of love for Jesus. All the acts of ministry we do for our brothers and sisters in Christ, are part of an interconnected whole, which is wider in scope than we can possibly imagine. Every person, place, and thing involved in God's enterprise, is seen in His eyes as contributing to His work for time and eternity. God Himself is at work in the world; so all service that is truly done in His name - and for His glory - is consequential to Him. All such acts of service are valued by Him; not based on size, but on faithfulness, motive, and intent. The Spirit means for us to recognize this; for as we do, we become more and more free to give spontaneously to our fellow believers. There can be great joy even in the smallest help we give to God's children, because we know that it is pleasing and valued in His eyes. Perhaps an illustration will help. Although I am the author of the book I am writing, there are many people who are contributing to its production. The work needs to be edited, reviewed, and corrected several times, and in different ways. A variety of skilled individuals will be required to properly format and finally publish the book. Each of these people is making a contribution by participating in the overall completion of my book. I greatly esteem each person who does so, because regardless of the size of their task, their actions are all essential to the success of the final outcome of what

I hope to accomplish. In a similar way, God is writing a book. Only His book is a much larger story; it is the Book of Life. This book is the story of the salvation of His children - written across all of human history. To bless God's children, even in the most trivial manner, is important to Him. The reason is because the future of His Kingdom is established on the building blocks of countless "small" decisions. These decisions help to build the great temple of believers He is creating, to show forth His glory for all eternity. The simplest things we do for His children, though perhaps small in our own eyes, are far from trivial in His limitless sight.

This leads us naturally to our last point in v.41. *All genuine acts of service for the Kingdom of God, no matter how small, are noticed by Him, and will be rewarded.* Have you ever taken one of those tests where you were asked to look at a photograph of a scene for a specific number of seconds — and then answer questions based on what you observed? Most of us are surprised when we take those tests, at how many details we fail to notice - which might be essential for someone testifying as to what they really saw. Two of the wonderful attributes of our God, are that He is all knowing, and is present everywhere. <u>He doesn't ever miss anything we do.</u> While this truth will be a frightening reality for those who will face God's judgment without Christ, it is also a great comfort for those of us who know Him. When we remember that we all must stand before the judgment seat of Christ to answer for the things we have done in this earthly body (2 Corinthians 5:10), we are often worried that God is going to kind of "pick on us." We imagine that He will remind us of all the terrible mistakes we ever made, and of all our failures. I personally find it much more helpful to realize that God took notice of every good action I ever took for Him, whether I thought it was good or not. Not only did He notice, but He will reward me for it! It is always needful at this point, to remind ourselves that we do not obtain God's reward on the basis of our own righteous acts. It is only through Christ that we stand acceptable to God. The reward spoken of here, is bestowed by God in His grace, to those of His children who have acted in faith and obedience to Him. All that is involved in this, we cannot say. What we do know, is that God has promised us that in Christ, our genuine acts of service will receive their reward. Who among us would not one day be overjoyed to hear Christ say, *"Well done, my good and faithful servant. Enter into the joy of your Lord."* As we think upon these grand lessons that Jesus was imparting to His disciples, we can't help but see the irony in what He tells them here. For we recall that it was not long before this, that they were arguing about which of them was the greatest. In their pride, they reasoned that their closeness to Jesus should elevate them to a status above others. Thus, they would rank ahead of Jesus' other followers, and be entitled to a place where those others would be under obligation to serve them. This they felt, was the reward due them. Jesus places before them a small child; helpless, insignificant, unimportant. He tells them that true greatness lies not in self elevation, but in love and kindness shown in humility toward even the least of His followers. For it is in serving them, that they truly serve Him. The one who would be genuinely most important, must take last place, and be the servant of everyone. Then in v.41 He makes clear that it is the simplest act of humble kindness, which brings the reward that their pride could not. A well expressed commentary on the kind of thinking that Jesus is advocating, can be found in Philippians 2. Here Paul exhorts the Philippian church to have the attitude of Christ.

"Is there any encouragement from belonging to Christ? Any comfort from his love? Any fellowship together in the Spirit? Are your hearts tender and compassionate? Then make me truly happy by agreeing wholeheartedly with each other, loving one another, and working together with one mind

and purpose. *Don't be selfish; don't try to impress others. Be humble, thinking of others as better than yourselves. Don't look out only for your own interests, but take an interest in others, too. You must have the same attitude that Christ Jesus had.*

Though he was God,
he did not think of equality with God
as something to cling to.
Instead, he gave up his divine privileges;
he took the humble position of a slave
and was born as a human being.
When he appeared in human form,
he humbled himself in obedience to God
and died a criminal's death on a cross.
Therefore, God elevated him to the place of highest honor
and gave him the name above all other names,
that at the name of Jesus every knee should bow,
in heaven and on earth and under the earth,
and every tongue confess that Jesus Christ is Lord,
to the glory of God the Father." (Philippians 2:1-11 NLT)

Before we leave this particular class that Jesus has been holding in God's Arithmetic, there is one further point to consider. It is found in v.42 NLT:

"If anyone causes one of these little ones — those who believe in me — to stumble, it would be better for them if a large millstone were hung around their neck and they were thrown into the sea."

Here we have Jesus saying that <u>it is a very serious matter in the eyes of God - to cause even the least of His children to fall into sin or to do damage to their faith.</u> I find myself almost wishing Jesus hadn't said this. No matter to whom

143

this is applied, or how we attempt to explain its meaning, the seriousness of His intention is unmistakable. In case you are wondering why Jesus said it, it is the converse of v.41. Jesus has made it clear that He identifies Himself closely with each of His children, since He and the Father have made their home in each heart belonging to Him (see v.37 and cp. John 14:23). If the kindness shown to Him personally through His children will not fail to be rewarded, then cruelty to His children will not fail to be punished. This is a warning of the terrible consequences for those who cause a weak or struggling believer to stumble in their faith. To be the cause of temptation for such believers; to trip them up and cause them to sin; or to be a willing participant in bringing harm to those for whom Christ died and tenderly cares for. . . Well, Jesus says you'd be better off dead before you ever did this! Honestly, I can't tell you what this would mean that God will do in the life of a person who does harm to those in whom His presence dwells. I do know however, that I wouldn't want it to be me. The parallel passage in Matthew 18 adds these words:

"What sorrow awaits the world, because it tempts people to sin. Temptations are inevitable, but what sorrow awaits the person who does the tempting." (Matthew 18:7 NIV)

If we understand the "anyone" of v.42 to mean "the people of the world" (those who do not belong to Christ, and are not God's spiritual children), then the passage makes good sense to us. Certainly Matthew 18:7 presents that possibility. We who belong to the Church of Jesus Christ, would surely say a hearty 'amen' to this. After all, we sense immediately, how deserving of punishment it is, to cause damage to the tender faith of a believer struggling to find their way through the confusion and perplexity that often confronts us, in this life on earth. But before we get too carried away applauding the just judgment of the world — perhaps some self examination is in order. What if Jesus is directing this warning to believers? What if it is you and I, who must be forewarned against the danger of causing our fellow believers to stumble in their faith? You may think this unlikely, but I am ashamed to tell you on how many occasions I have had needless disputes and arguments with my fellow Christians. This kind of fighting with our brothers and sisters in Christ due to pride - and a dispute over which of us is greater - is not limited to only Jesus' original disciples. Sad to say, the New Testament is filled with similar warnings for us. Although it is the words of Jesus here - which are the most disciplinary in their tone. That alone tells me how important this is to God, who lovingly cares for each believer as Christ is formed in their hearts. In my own personal growth in grace, I have become increasingly aware of how hurtful it is, to get into nasty disputes with my fellow Christians over doubtful issues. By nature, we want everything spelled out for us in an easy to understand way. Kind of like the ten commandments. Black and white; no room for argument. Unfortunately, when it comes to Christian freedom, there are many matters where we all have our own opinions. The Lord is well aware of this, and has not left us without guidance. Through the Apostle Paul, God addressed many such questions crucial to believers of that time. In doing so, He also left us the underlying principles that are needed in our day, to prevent us from similarly causing harm to each other. It is beyond the scope of my topic here, to write about this at length. A few key examples are sufficient to help us think soberly about Jesus' warning — and to remind us of the love that must be paramount, as we relate to other believers. In Paul's day, Christians were arguing about issues such as: what to eat, or not to eat; and whether or not one day was more important than another day. There were disputes over matters of individual conscience. Some of these disagreements involved whether or not it was permissible to eat meat offered to idols. To those who may have been unnecessarily critical of their brothers and sisters in Christ, Paul had this to say:

"Accept other believers who are weak in faith, and don't argue with them about what they think is right or wrong. For instance, one person believes it's all right to eat anything. But another believer with a sensitive conscience will eat only vegetables. Those who feel free to eat anything must not look down on those who don't. And those who don't eat certain foods must not condemn those who do, for God has accepted them. Who are you to condemn someone else's servants? They are responsible to the Lord, so let him judge whether they are right or wrong. And with the Lord's help, they will do what is right and will receive his approval.

In the same way, some think one day is more holy than another day, while others think every day is alike. You should each be fully convinced that whichever day you choose is acceptable. Those who worship the Lord on a special day do it to honor him. Those who eat any kind of food do so to honor the Lord, since they give thanks to God before eating. And those who refuse to eat certain foods also want to please the Lord and give thanks to God. For we don't live for ourselves or die for ourselves. If we live, it's to honor the Lord. And if we die, it's to honor the Lord. So whether we live or die, we belong to the Lord. Christ died and rose again for this very purpose — to be Lord both of the living and of the dead.

So why do you condemn another believer? Why do you look down on another believer? Remember, we will all stand before the judgment seat of God. For the Scriptures say,

"'As surely as I live,' says the LORD,
'every knee will bend to me,

146

and every tongue will confess and give praise to God.'"

Yes, each of us will give a personal account to God. So let's stop condemning each other. <u>Decide instead to live in such a way that you will not cause another believer to stumble and fall.</u>

I know and am convinced on the authority of the Lord Jesus that no food, in and of itself, is wrong to eat. But if someone believes it is wrong, then for that person it is wrong. And if another believer is distressed by what you eat, you are not acting in love if you eat it. Don't let your eating ruin someone for whom Christ died. Then you will not be criticized for doing something you believe is good. For the Kingdom of God is not a matter of what we eat or drink, but of living a life of goodness and peace and joy in the Holy Spirit. If you serve Christ with this attitude, you will please God, and others will approve of you, too. <u>So then, let us aim for harmony in the church and try to build each other up.</u>

Don't tear apart the work of God over what you eat. Remember, all foods are acceptable, but it is wrong to eat something if it makes another person stumble. <u>It is better not to eat meat or drink wine or do anything else if it might cause another believer to stumble.</u> You may believe there's nothing wrong with what you are doing, but keep it between yourself and God. Blessed are those who don't feel guilty for doing something they have decided is right. But if you have doubts about whether or not you should eat something, you are sinning if you go ahead and do it. For you are not following your convictions. If you do anything you believe is not right, you are sinning." (Romans 14:1-23 NLT underlines mine)

<u>It is clear from this that God wants each of us to act in love, and to live in such a way that we will not cause another believer to stumble and fall.</u> Our aim must be harmony in

the church, and acting in ways that will build each other up. We must not tear apart the work of God by trampling over the sensitive conscience of others. This responsibility for our freedom, was also emphasized by Paul in his first letter to the Corinthians. In chapter 8, where he discusses the issue of eating food offered to idols, he says:

"But you must be careful so that your freedom does not cause others with a weaker conscience to stumble. For if others see you — with your "superior knowledge" — eating in the temple of an idol, won't they be encouraged to violate their conscience by eating food that has been offered to an idol? So because of your superior knowledge, a weak believer for whom Christ died will be destroyed. <u>And when you sin against other believers by encouraging them to do something they believe is wrong, you are sinning against Christ.</u> So if what I eat causes another believer to sin, I will never eat meat again as long as I live — for I don't want to cause another believer to stumble." (1 Corinthians 8:9-13 NLT underline mine)

Note again Paul's emphasis, that when we cause another believer to stumble, we are sinning against Christ. Later in 1 Corinthians, Paul addresses the question that arose over meat sold in the market place which may have been offered to an idol. Once again, we find the key to the proper use of Christian freedom:

"You say, "I am allowed to do anything" — but not everything is good for you. You say, "I am allowed to do anything" — but not everything is beneficial. Don't be concerned for your own good but for the good of others.

So you may eat any meat that is sold in the marketplace without raising questions of conscience. For "the earth is the LORD's, and everything in it."

If someone who isn't a believer asks you home for dinner, accept the invitation if you want to. Eat whatever is offered to you without raising questions of conscience. (But suppose someone tells you, "This meat was offered to an idol." Don't eat it, out of consideration for the conscience of the one who told you. It might not be a matter of conscience for you, but it is for the other person.) For why should my freedom be limited by what someone else thinks? If I can thank God for the food and enjoy it, why should I be condemned for eating it?

So whether you eat or drink, or whatever you do, do it all for the glory of God. Don't give offense to Jews or Gentiles or the church of God. I, too, try to please everyone in everything I do. I don't just do what is best for me; I do what is best for others so that many may be saved." 1 Corinthians 10:23-33 NLT

Here again, we are exhorted to be concerned for the good of others. Any inconsiderate action on our part that hinders the saving work of God in another believer, must be avoided. In the exercise of Christian freedom, our highest aim must always be the glory of God. On the back of one of my personal electronic devices, I have etched this scripture verse by Paul; also written in the context of the way we are to treat our fellow believers:

"And whatever you do or say, do it as a representative of the Lord Jesus, giving thanks through him to God the Father." Colossians 3:17 NLT

Perhaps you have heard the expression used of caring church leaders, "They have a pastor's heart." We mean by this; a Pastor has a heart that is sympathetic, tender, and sensitive to the struggles, hurts, and pains in the lives of those under their charge. They are protective of them, and would sacrifice anything to see that their little flock is not harmed in their relationship with God. When Jesus says, *"If anyone causes one of these little ones — those who believe in me — to stumble, it would be better for them if a large millstone were hung around their neck and they were thrown into the sea."* — what we are really seeing, is the infinite tenderness of the heart of God. A tenderness that reaches out in a very personal and protective love toward each and every one of His little children. Peter puts forth this pastoral love of Jesus when he says:

"He personally carried our sins
in his body on the cross
so that we can be dead to sin
and live for what is right.
By his wounds
you are healed.
Once you were like sheep
who wandered away.
But now you have turned to your Shepherd,
the Guardian of your souls." (1 Peter 2:24-25 NLT)

The insights we've gained thus far from Mark 9:38-42, have been helpful. When we began this study, I mentioned that there was a second passage to help us understand God's Arithmetic. There are great things happening in the world all the time - through the smallest actions of His children. The next words of Jesus we will explore, are found in Matthew 10:40-42. From them, we can discover additional compelling reasons to find joy in the simple ways that God has resourced us to participate in advancing His Kingdom. There are nuances in these considerations which may slightly overlap with those we've just reviewed. They are different enough however, that we will find a thorough accounting of them, well worth our effort. The gospel of Matthew is divided into several segments of narrative and discourse. We follow Jesus throughout His various ministry activities to the people of Israel; then we sit at His feet to listen as He teaches us about life in the Kingdom of God. In many modern Bibles, the difference is often easily recognizable due to 'red letter editions'. All you have to do is look for large sections of red letters, and you know that Jesus Himself is speaking. One such section begins at the end of chapter 9. As Jesus ministered throughout Galilee, He taught in the synagogues, and proclaimed the good news about the Kingdom. He also went about healing every kind of disease and illness among the people. As He observed the great crowds that gathered around Him, He saw that they were hurting and helpless - like sheep without a shepherd. In words that are still used today to marshal us to prayer, Jesus said to the disciples:

"Ask the Lord of the harvest, therefore, to send out workers into his harvest field." Matt. 9:38 NIV

He then called the twelve apostles together, and sent them out with His authority, as agents of healing and grace among the people. This is not unlike us today, who are sent out among the great hurting masses of humanity, to bring to them the gospel of God's grace and forgiveness in Jesus Christ. The apostles were not sent out aimlessly. They were given instructions by Jesus as to where they were to go; how they were to prepare; how they were to behave; and what they could expect as they went. These instructions are found in Matthew 10:5-42. In them, we not only have specific guid-

151

ance to the disciples for this occasion, but also Matthew's collection of Jesus' warnings regarding persecution that all His followers would need, after he rose from the dead. In these timeless words of encouragement, He exhorts the disciples (and us) not to fear opposition:

"Don't be afraid of those who want to kill your body; they cannot touch your soul. Fear only God, who can destroy both soul and body in hell. What is the price of two sparrows — one copper coin? But not a single sparrow can fall to the ground without your Father knowing it. And the very hairs on your head are all numbered. So don't be afraid; you are more valuable to God than a whole flock of sparrows." Matthew 10:28-31 NLT

Then, after confirming the reward for loyalty in vv.32-33, He reminds us in very pointed words (vv.34-39), that His message will divide people. Some will believe, and some will not. We are called to a loyalty and love to Jesus that is higher than even the relationships within our own family. We must take up our cross and follow Him; give up our life for Him to truly find it. (A more detailed discussion of this, is found in the chapter, "Losing Life to Keep It.") Finally, Jesus concludes the instructions for ministry in His name, with these simple words:

40 "Anyone who welcomes you welcomes me, and anyone who welcomes me welcomes the one who sent me. 41 Whoever welcomes a prophet as a prophet will receive a prophet's reward, and whoever welcomes a righteous person as a righteous person will receive a righteous person's reward. 42 And if anyone gives even a cup of cold water to one of these little ones who is my disciple, truly I tell you, that person will certainly not lose their reward." Matthew 10:40-42 NIV

Simple words indeed; but to most of us, they sound as if Jesus is being cryptic. I was very surprised and reassured to uncover the rich gems of truth that came forth, as I meditated on these verses. I believe you will be encouraged and strengthened as well. Let's begin in v.40 with what is most obvious. These words are an echo of what we heard Jesus say in Mark 9:37. There, our emphasis was on how even the smallest service done for our fellow Christians - is being done for Jesus, who lives in them. Here in this similar verse, we broaden our scope just a bit, and learn that **when we welcome anyone who is involved in working for the spread of God's Kingdom, we are directly welcoming Jesus and the Father.** Think of it! What an encouragement this is for us! A brother or sister in Christ is serving God. We receive them, we welcome them, we take them to ourselves in any number of ways. How? We listen to them, and we learn from their words and example to us. We esteem them and their service. We love them. We treat them with kindness, and we help them in their time of need. We speak words of encouragement. We feed, clothe, and comfort them. They see Christ in us through our warm personal reception, and the support we give to their ministry. We share what we can. We do what we can. The smallest ministration, done out of love for Jesus, we provide to them.

We learned previously, that none of this is trivial to God. We welcome their *person,* and in doing so, we have welcomed the person of Jesus and the Father. When God sends us forth with His message in Jesus' name, to do His work, we are His very 'red letter' representatives. We may have not seen Jesus bodily as the Apostles did, but we have the selfsame spiritual privileges they had. Each of God's servants has in their heart 'the Spirit of Jesus and the Father' (see Rom.8:9; John 14:15-21, 23). How closely our Lord has identified with us! How circumspect our lives ought to be - and how eager to welcome even the most humble of His children. We welcome them, and God says we welcome Him and His Son. Step back and think on this - the next time you are about to criticize one of God's faithful servants because everything is not being done your way. I'm not saying we are above criticism, but I am saying that there is an attitude - a posture - we should have, towards God's faithful ones. This attitude recognizes that God lives in His people; and how we treat them, is how we are treating Jesus and the Father. This is why Paul says:

"Since God chose you to be the holy people he loves, you must clothe yourselves with tenderhearted mercy, kindness, humility, gentleness, and patience. Make allowance for each other's faults, and forgive anyone who offends you. Remember, the Lord forgave you, so you must forgive others. Above all, clothe yourselves with love, which binds us all together in perfect harmony. And let the peace that comes from Christ rule in your hearts. For as members of one body you are called to live in peace. And always be thankful." Colossians 3:12-15 NLT

There is a close association between God and His people! This should be seen especially in our service and ministry together. We all have a part to play in God's enterprise, and each of us is important. In vv.41-42 we see from Jesus' instructions, the chain of people in the great work of salvation. Let's see if we can identify them all. What we have here, is a very Jewish way of speaking. To welcome a prophet or righteous man as (or because they are) a prophet or righteous man, is to say that we accept them because they belong to God, and are doing His work. A prophet speaks for God, and is His messenger. A righteous man lives for God, and is an example for others to follow. A disciple follows Jesus, and is living to work in His Master's service. Keep in mind, that Jesus' point is not to create categories. It is to group together all

His followers, who serve in different ways in the Kingdom of God. Taking this all together - the great chain of salvation is represented thus: God; Jesus; God's messenger; a good man who is an example; the disciple who receives them and learns; and the believer who provides even the smallest ministration to any of Jesus' servants. What we have here, is a kind of miniature picture of the body of Christ as Paul would later describe it (see Rom.12:3-8; 1Cor.12:12-27). The first idea I take from Jesus here, is that *whether we serve other believers or receive their service - the Kingdom of God is advanced.* Jesus sends us forth to labor together. When we each exercise our spiritual gifts in His service, it is obvious that God is at work to effectively build up Christ's body, and call people to salvation. What is not always obvious, is that just as we are called upon to exercise our gifts, we are also called to be recipients of the gifts of others. The labor of each of us individually - and all of us collectively - is of no value, if there is no one to actually reap the benefit from our work and service. Both giving and receiving are critically important. When my pastor preaches, it is to no avail if I am not a willing respondent. When I teach a Bible study class, what use is it if no one is willing to learn and grow. When our worship leaders guide us in worship, how can anyone benefit if we refuse to take up a posture of worship before God? When I am offered wise godly counsel, what is the point if I refuse to put it to use? If I have a practical need; and my gifted brother or sister reaches out to meet that need; and I in turn refuse their help; then their kindness is stymied, and we both lose a blessing. This is a tremendous thought. <u>Part of our service to God, is to allow our fellow disciples to share their gifts with us. To receive them - to welcome them - is to share in both their blessing and reward.</u> As these personal interactions take place, the body of Christ grows and God's Kingdom is advanced. We should never think it a small matter, to be willing to receive from others. Our failure to do so, may put a roadblock in the way of what God is trying to accomplish - both in their life and in ours. Also, by refusing to welcome them (thus failing to follow their good example as they exercise their gifts in faith), we may lose out on a multiplied blessing — the grace that God desired to extend from us to others - through what we might have gained - had we listened to what He was trying to teach us through their ministry. So, share your gifts in Christ's service, and welcome those whom He has sent to share their gifts with you.

Along these same lines, we learn from v.41 that *while we cannot all exercise great spiritual gifts - we can all support those who do*. The prophet and the righteous man both, must have those who will welcome them. The Spirit of God in His transcendent wisdom, has dispersed many prominent spiritual gifts among His people. The Church needs its powerful evangelists, masterful preachers, brilliant teachers, and successful church planters. We must have qualified missionaries, effectual givers, and skilled administrators. Where would we be without talented musicians and singers, as well as gifted engaging writers? Yet there's not a single one of those people who can go it alone. None of them could minister effectively, without the help and support of others in the Church. Each of them depends on all of us to support their efforts through our prayer, obedience, financial contributions, and encouragement. In truth, there are countless ways that we can show our support to others in ministry. The point here, is that all of us can support fruitful ministries. There are none among us who can say, "There is nothing I can do." Each of us can throw our "mite" into the treasury of Kingdom service; knowing that the least act of support to His servants will be noticed, valued, and rewarded by King Jesus.

Before we move to v.42, I would like to slide along a small tangent suggested by the thought that we cannot all exercise great spiritual gifts. Part of what we have been doing here, is making the point that **in God's Arithmetic, those things that seem small to us, may appear quite large to Him.** It is helpful to remember that while man looks on the outward appearance, God looks on the heart (1 Samuel 16:7). With that in mind, let's take a short detour into the writings of Paul. Along this byway, I would like us to see that *while we cannot all exercise great spiritual gifts, we can all exercise love, and employ in God's service - those gifts that Christ has given us.* We turn our attention to the local church at Corinth. Among the matters that were causing conflict and disunity in the church, was the question of the proper use and value of spiritual gifts. In 1 Corinthians 12:1-14:40, Paul addresses this issue. Our purpose here, is not to list and define spiritual gifts - or to specifically discuss the gifts of tongues and prophecy. Rather, I would like to point out Paul's emphasis on the kind of spiritual outlook God wants us to take towards each other. It should be easy for us to identify the connection between what Paul is saying, and what Jesus was impressing upon us. We begin with 1 Corinthians 12:4-7 NLT:

"There are different kinds of spiritual gifts, *but the same Spirit is the source* of them all. There are different kinds of service, but *we serve the same Lord.* God works in different ways, but *it is the same God who does the work in all of us.*

A spiritual gift is given to each of us so we can help each other." *(italics mine)*

Paul wants us to see our unity, just as Jesus did. <u>All our service is for the same Lord, empowered by the same Spirit, and is for the common good. It is God in fact, who is working through all of us. We are a unified body, and there is no place for jealousy among us.</u> Our gifts are not for our personal benefit, but have been given so that we can help each other (cp. 1 Peter 4:10-11). God in His wisdom, knows what is best for all of us:

"It is the one and only Spirit who distributes all these gifts. He alone decides which gift each person should have." 1 Corinthians 12:11 NLT

There is a gift and a place of service for each of us, and God has given you a part that only you can fill. So then, who are we to overvalue or devalue ourselves or others? There is no room to boast of our ministry, or to make light of the ministry of others. In vv.12-13, Paul makes clear to us that even ethnic and social differences - have no significance in the church:

"The human body has many parts, but the many parts make up one whole body. So it is with the body of Christ. Some of us are Jews, some are Gentiles, some are slaves, and some are free. But we have all been baptized into one body by one Spirit, and we all share the same Spirit."

The church is one unified body. Our care for one another is an essential part of the unity. Each of us is a vital part; and all of us together are one spiritual body with Christ as our head:

"This makes for harmony among the members, so that all the members care for each other. If one part suffers, all the parts suffer with it, and if one part is honored, all the parts are glad.

All of you together are Christ's body, and each of you is a part of it." 1 Corinthians 12:25-27 NLT

It is clear to anyone reading chapters 12-14 of 1 Corinthians — the value Paul places on using our gifts to help and strengthen the church; as well as employing them to bring those who do not believe into a saving relationship with Jesus Christ. Consider these verses from chapter 14 NLT:

"A person who speaks in tongues is strengthened personally, but one who speaks a word of prophecy strengthens the entire church. I wish you could all speak in tongues, but even more I wish you could all prophesy. For prophecy is greater than speaking in tongues, unless someone interprets what you are saying so that the whole church will be strengthened." (vv.4-5)

"And the same is true for you. Since you are so eager to have the special abilities the Spirit gives, seek those that will strengthen the whole church." (v.12)

"You will be giving thanks very well, but it won't strengthen the people who hear you." (v.17)

"But if all of you are prophesying, and unbelievers or people who don't understand these things come into your meeting, they will be convicted of sin and judged by what you say. As they listen, their secret thoughts will be exposed, and they will fall to their knees and worship God, declaring, "God is truly here among you.""

"Well, my brothers and sisters, let's summarize. When you meet together, one will sing, another will teach, another will tell some special revelation God has given, one will speak in tongues, and another will interpret what is said. But everything that is done must strengthen all of you." (vv.24-26)

From all of this, we conclude that <u>it is very important</u> <u>that we all identify our spiritual gifts - and put them to use</u>. In fact, Paul makes a point of saying that together, we should have an earnest desire to discover these gifts for ourselves, and to put them into action. For while there is no place for 'showoffs' in the church — there most certainly is a place for us to 'show off' these gifts; for they are meant to be on display among us - to show forth God's glory - and to build His Church. This is what Paul means when he says in 12:31 NLT:

"So you should earnestly desire the most helpful gifts. But now let me show you a way of life that is best of all."

And in 14:1 NLT:

"Let love be your highest goal! But you should also desire the special abilities the Spirit gives — especially the ability to prophesy."

Prophesy of course - the special ability to speak effectively for God - should be sought by all of us because of its great benefit to both the church and to unbelievers. But did you notice those short phrases that actually bracket chapter 13?! Here they are:

But now let me show you a way of life that is best of all.

Let love be your highest goal!

Between those brackets - is one of the most well known chapters in the entire Bible. In 1 Corinthians 13, Paul purposely connects chapters 12 and 14, in order to emphasize the importance of Christian love. He places chapter 13 where it is, to highlight that spiritual gifts must be used and displayed in love. As we live and work together in the service of King Jesus, all our gifts have no value apart from the expression of love. We noted earlier how God is not concerned with the size of our service or the greatness of our gifts - but with our faithfulness, motives, and intention. Love is more important than any of our spiritual gifts. Love alone gives meaning to our acts of sacrificial service. Love seeks not only its own interests, but also the interests of others. The benefits of love have no limits. When we are guided by love, it allows us to put all of our actions in their proper perspective. Love casts out fear (1Jn.4:17-18). It binds us all together in perfect harmony (Col.3:14). Love gives meaning to our lives, and marks us as true disciples of Jesus (John 13:34-35). Love is the moral center of our faith, and is essential to any claim of a genuine experience with God (1Jn.3:11-18; 4:7-21). There can be no question for the Christian, of the importance of seeking to become a person like Jesus - through whom God's love can be shared with others. *We cannot all exercise great spiritual gifts, but we can all exercise love, and employ in God's service - those gifts Christ has given us.*

We return now from our brief detour, and resume our look at Matthew 10:42 NIV:

"And if anyone gives even a cup of cold water to one of these little ones who is my disciple, truly I tell you, that person will certainly not lose their reward."

If you were to read this verse out of context - not knowing who said it or why - it would still have a sense of profoundness to it. As you listen to it spoken, you hear a ring of truth that creates a desire in you - to know what it really means. I don't know if this is caused by the simplicity of the cup of cold water, the image evoked by the little ones, or the promise of the certainty of reward. In any case, it is very instructive for us to learn its lessons, and to discover how profound it really is. In Jesus' briefing to his disciples before He sent them out, we have observed the great chain of salvation. Thus far in v.41, we have seen notable servants of God — a prophet, a righteous man, and the disciple who welcomes them. Here in v.42, we come to a believer who provides to even the least of Jesus' disciples, what appears to be the slightest of charity — a cup of cold water. The beauty of this does lie in its simplicity, and in the picture it paints for us. We must step back for just a moment, and think about all the Christians we encounter. Our fellow believers come in all types, stripes, and varieties. There are the well known and the unknown; the weak and the strong; the joyful and the morose; the brave and the fearful; the highly gifted and the lesser gifted. We see the sold out; the worn out; and the drop out. Not everyone who we encounter in the service of Jesus, is bearing some great message from God. They are not all prophets or teachers with deep and weighty things to say. Certainly, they are not all Christian teachers. In fact James tells us:

"Not many of you should become teachers, my fellow believers, because you know that we who teach will be judged more strictly." James 3:1 NIV

This however, does not mean that we have nothing to teach other Christians, or that they have nothing to teach us. *While we cannot all be teachers — we can all teach our fellow believers through our life and example.* One of Jesus' little ones comes to another of Jesus' little ones in the course of their service for Him. Nothing spectacular takes place. They simply minister to one another the little things that make up the necessities of life — such as a cup of cold water. In doing so, they observe one another in their Master's service. They strengthen and encourage each other through their common commitment to honor Jesus, and they do whatever they can to participate in His work. I am so thankful that God brings Christians into my life who are not like me. They help me in my weaknesses, and they serve as God's change agents. As I watch them share and employ their gifts in His service, I am prodded in my spirit to ask God to add their strengths to my own. I do not have the gift of hospitality, but I can learn to be more hospitable. I am not an evangelist, but I can learn how to better share my faith. I do not have a gift for generosity, but I can learn to be more giving. I do not have a gift of helps, but I can learn to be more helpful. I am not a gifted intercessor, but I can learn to improve my prayer life. I do not have a gift of faith, but I can learn to better exercise the faith I do have. I am not musically inclined, but those with gifts of worship and song have much to teach me - in my approach to God. I love the phrase Jesus uses — his *"little ones."* Even the least of His children. The 'nobody' Christians. They aren't lion-like in their service, and they may be totally unknown. No great gifts to speak of; nothing that makes them stand out. But what is this really? Jesus is not saying He has disciples who are of lesser value to God than other disciples. We have already seen that none of us has any reason to boast; for it is God who is working through all of us. What then shall we say? No more than we have already said — that Christ comes to us in other believers; and that we all learn from each other, through seeing God at work in our life and example. I believe that God places other believers in our path for a reason. If we will stay alert to it, <u>there is something that He can teach us through every believer</u>. How about you? Would you like to be a good example for others? "Sure I would", you say, "But no one's going to look at my life and think there's anything great about my example." Remember that Jesus said true greatness would be shown by being the servant of everyone (Mk.9:35). Even the giving of a cup of cold water to the least disciple - is an act of faithfulness.

Our tendency to misjudge others as well as ourselves - is so evident at this point. We are so conditioned to think that if we are to be good Christians, that we must be doing something "great" for Jesus. I want to be careful here. I think that all of us who love Jesus will want to do something "great" for Him - in the sense that our service will bring high honor and praise to Him. I think we all can pray that our actions will result in many souls coming into God's Kingdom, and for the glory and honor that this would bring to God. The problem we have is twofold. First, are we asking to do something great for Jesus — or are we really asking to be great ourselves? (This takes us back to the disciples problem with pride; their contention among themselves to be first.) Second, and perhaps more to the point — we misunderstand how God views greatness. Jesus uses the welcoming of little children and the giving of a cup of cold water - to set greatness before our eyes. I seriously doubt we would use either of these things to explain greatness to anyone. Therefore, it's easy to view our own simple acts of service (and the acts of others) as being far from "great." So we fail to esteem the opportunities to do good that we have each day; never realizing how important they are, in the sight of God. We misjudge ourselves and others, by failing to see the greatness that lies in giving even a cup of cold water to an 'ordinary' disciple, who comes to us in Jesus' name. <u>We fail to see the 'greatness' in our life and example, because we are not placing the same value on our actions that God does</u>. God is so amazing, powerful, and immense, that we reason that a cup of cold water means nothing to Him; it must be beneath His notice. Little do we realize, that the greatest work of our life may have been viewed by God by its quality - not by its quantity. What seemed to us as a small act of mercy or compassion toward one of God's beloved children, may have been to Him - more highly regarded than we would ever dream of. Learn to live in the moment. Ask God to give you the eyes of Jesus - toward everyone you meet. Let the Holy Spirit teach you how to listen with your spirit and with your heart - beyond just the words that you hear. When you begin to see Jesus and the Father coming to you in every believer, you will come to properly esteem even the smallest acts of kindness - both given and received. I am reminded so pointedly here, of something Paul said while addressing the premature mistaken judgments of some in the Corinthian church:

"So don't get ahead of the Master and jump to conclusions with your judgments before all the evidence is in. When he comes, he will bring out in the open and place in evidence all kinds of things we never even dreamed of — inner motives and purposes and prayers. Only then will any one of us get to hear the "Well done!" of God." 1 Corinthians 4:5 MSG

Another conclusion that comes directly from changing our view of greatness, is that **true discipleship does not involve doing what we think is great - but is shown by doing what we can.** Here again is the beauty in a cup of cold water. The point is not that giving a cup of cold water "does not take much effort." Really, it's almost just the opposite. We are to do whatever we can in service to Christ, by giving our best effort. The idea here, is that whatever the best you have is - that's enough. Earlier we saw Jesus say - by using a cup of water as an example - that we are to give only what is within anyone's power to give. Here, a similar emphasis is that if the best we can do in the moment is to give a cup of cold water - then that is pleasing to God. We come back again to motive and intent. <u>We can't allow the limits of our resources and abilities to prevent us from doing all we can. Nor should we feel guilty when we have done the best we can do.</u> Each of us individually, and all of us collectively as a church, can and will make a difference for the Kingdom, by doing what we are able to do. The Lord is not asking us to do the impossible — that's His job! Our own efforts may seem meager to ourselves - but our offering is acceptable to God; not on the basis of what is beyond our capability - but on the faithful use of the resources and abilities given to each of us. The Bible is filled with examples of God multiplying the most simple offering given to Him from a pure heart. A few notable ones should suffice. Remember the young boy who offered Jesus his 5 small barley loaves and 2 little fish? Not much - maybe a very light meal. But Jesus took the boy's contribution, and used it miraculously to feed a crowd of about 5,000 men, in addition to all the women and children (see Matt.14:13-21; Mark 6:3-44; Luke 9:1-17; John 6:1-13). There is also the story in 1 Kings 17:8-15 (NLT) of Elijah and the widow of Zarephath:

"Then the LORD said to Elijah, "Go and live in the village of Zarephath, near the city of Sidon. I have instructed a widow there to feed you."

So he went to Zarephath. As he arrived at the gates of the village, he saw a widow gathering sticks, and he asked her, "Would you please bring me a little water in a cup?" As she was going to get it, he called to her, "Bring me a bite of bread, too."

But she said, "I swear by the LORD your God that I don't have a single piece of bread in the house. And I have only a handful of flour left in the jar and a little cooking oil in the bottom of the jug. I was just gathering a few sticks to cook this last meal, and then my son and I will die."

But Elijah said to her, "Don't be afraid! Go ahead and do just what you've said, but make a little bread for me first. Then use what's left to prepare a meal for yourself and your son.

For this is what the LORD, the God of Israel, says: There will always be flour and olive oil left in your containers until the time when the LORD sends rain and the crops grow again!"

So she did as Elijah said, and she and Elijah and her son continued to eat for many days. There was always enough flour and olive oil left in the containers, just as the LORD had promised through Elijah."

Even though this poor widow knew that she and her young son might die, she gave what she could - which was all she was able to give - a handful of flour and a tiny bit of cooking oil. Her faith in God was rewarded; and for some three and a half years, there was ample flour and oil in her containers, until God sent the rain again (cp. James 5:17). Perhaps the most significant example of how God values not the size or cost of the gift - but the heart and love of the giver - is found in Luke 21:1-4 NIV:

"As Jesus looked up, he saw the rich putting their gifts into the temple treasury. He also saw a poor widow put in two very small copper coins. "Truly I tell you," he said, "this poor widow has put in more than all the others. All these people gave their gifts out of their wealth; but she out of her poverty put in all she had to live on.""

If there was ever a picture of how God measures gifts offered to Him - this is it! It's easy to criticize the rich folks in this story; but in truth, they are like most of us. We give out of our surplus, and it really costs us nothing. I am reminded of King David; who, when given an opportunity to take what belonged to someone else and offer it to God (at no cost to him) said:

"No, I insist on paying the full price. I will not take for the LORD what is yours, or sacrifice a burnt offering that costs me nothing." 1 Chronicles 21:24 NIV

It is heart sacrifice that is God's coin. Are we doing what we can? Are we trusting in God's promise and provision? Are we giving as God's beloved children from a heart of love to our Heavenly Father? There is no guilt, pressure, or slavery in this; no oppressive sense of duty. We live in a relationship of love and grace with the most generous being in the universe. Do what you can, and you will find the reward of a peaceful and satisfied heart. There is no joy like the joy of sharing together with God in the wonderful work of salvation.

It's possible that you are reading this, and you are feeling overwhelmed at the thought of giving sacrificially to God and His people. You want to serve Christ and return His love in some way, but you don't know where to begin. It's a struggle for you, and you worry that if you aren't doing all you can, God will turn His face from you, and refuse to bless you. You think of His displeasure, and you hesitate to seek Him, because you are not yet ready to do more. You have a little grain of faith, but it seems so unworthy - in light of all He has done for you. You are tired of feeling guilty, but are unsure of what to do next. If this is your dilemma, I have good news for you! You've got your Lord all wrong! You need not fear that God will be harsh with you. The eyes of your Father look tenderly upon you. His love for you is far greater than you can imagine. The point of all this, is that God looks on the heart. He sees your intentions and the struggle within. It is His desire to encourage and cultivate your good intentions - not to censure them. As we realize this, we find another comforting truth that Matthew 10:42 teaches us. **Our desire to serve Christ faithfully need not overwhelm us. <u>We can all start small</u>.** Forget all those notions about what a hard taskmaster God is! He will have no grudging servants! He will make your heart sing, and His love will flow through you freely and unhindered. A cup of cold water is a great place to begin. I know it's only a small thing - but it won't stay that way for long. It is well said, that you can't out-give God. Begin where you spiritually are today. Give to God and your fellow believers - all that your faith will bear. What you will discover, is that the more you give, the more you will have of the *desire* to give. Faith and generosity will grow with use; and God will provide all you need for yourself and others.

A magnificent picture of God's promise of this, is found in 2 Corinthians 9. The Apostle Paul had initiated the collection of a monetary gift for the poor Jewish believers in Jerusalem. Those giving this money were the gentile Christians throughout the world, from all the churches Paul established and worked with. It was Paul's hope that this generous offering would have several positive results: It would relieve the suffering of the Jewish believers in Jerusalem; it would advance the unity of the Jewish and non Jewish elements of the church; and it would bring glory to God through the obedience of His people (and the prayers of thanksgiving and gratitude that would be offered to Him). When we meet with Paul in 2 Corinthians 9, he is in the midst of collecting this offering from the churches in the northern and southern provinces of Greece. He writes to the Corinthians in advance of his visit to them, to ensure that the gift offering they had been promising for a year, would be ready for him when he arrived to pick it up. Paul then sends some of his coworkers ahead of him, to make sure everything is ready for his visit. His reason for doing this, is that he wants to give everyone a chance to give from their hearts - and not feel pressured, guilty, or rushed when he arrives. Listen carefully to what he says to these Christians, to foster their generosity. Look especially for God's promises, and the gentle spirit by which

He evokes in them a greater capacity and readiness for generous giving:

"5 So I thought I should ask these brothers to go to you before we do. They will finish getting in order the generous gift you promised so it will be ready when we come. And it will be a generous gift — not one that you did not want to give.

6 Remember this: The person who plants a little will have a small harvest, but the person who plants a lot will have a big harvest. 7 Each of you should give as you have decided in your heart to give. You should not be sad when you give, and you should not give because you feel forced to give. God loves the person who gives happily. 8 And God can give you more blessings than you need. Then you will always have plenty of everything — enough to give to every good work. 9 It is written in the Scriptures:

"He gives freely to the poor.
The things he does are right and will continue forever." —
Psalm 112:9

10 God is the One who gives seed to the farmer and bread for food. He will give you all the seed you need and make it grow so there will be a great harvest from your goodness. 11 He will make you rich in every way so that you can always give freely. And your giving through us will cause many to give thanks to God. 12 This service you do not only helps the needs of God's people, it also brings many more thanks to God. 13 It is a proof of your faith. Many people will praise God because you obey the Good News of Christ — the gospel you say you believe — and because you freely share with them and with all others. 14 And when they pray, they will wish they could be with you because of the great grace that

God has given you.15 Thanks be to God for his gift that is too wonderful for words." 2 Corinthians 9:5-15 NCV

We see from this how God desires his grace to work in our lives. We are reminded that it is a principle of spiritual life - that generosity is always rewarded. We learn that it is not God's desire that our giving be compulsory - but that it come from the heart. We are encouraged to trust the teaching of scripture - that when the support of God's work is first in our hearts - He will supply us with all we need for ourselves and for others (cp. Matthew 6:33). Our capacity to live robust spiritual lives, will grow as we continue to serve the needs of God's people. I love verse 11. I don't believe that Paul is speaking there exclusively about money. A rich experience of God's grace, awaits those who are willing to cheerfully give their all to Him. It is instructive that we are told in v.7 that God loves the person who gives happily. Most Bible translations make that, "God loves a cheerful giver." Many Bible students will tell you that the word for 'cheerful' can also mean 'hilarious'. What does that mean? It doesn't mean that our giving is funny. It means that God delights in giving that is uninhibitedly enthusiastic and joyous. This kind of giving is irrepressible, excited, bubbling right out of us. I have often heard this taught as if we should feel guilty that we do not feel this way when we give. That is the opposite of what God intends. Feeling guilty would put us back to giving with a motive that does not please Him. The idea is to learn to live by God's grace through the power of His Spirit - in a loving relationship with Him. It is to trust that if we really give ourselves without reservation to Him, He will begin to transform us into His likeness. It is to know that your Father is at work in your life - and that faithful obedience in small things (even a cup of cold water), will lead you on a spiritual path that ends with a heart that has learned to give as God does — hilariously. This brings us back to our cup of cold water. It's such a powerful symbol to me. Every time I think of it, I am reminded that *all Christians can have a rich experience in God's grace, without being rich in the eyes of the world. God is more concerned with our motives than our means.* This has been evident in each of our illustrations. We have the believer who gave the cup of cold water to the least of Jesus' disciples, out of love for their Master. We saw the young boy with his 5 small barley loaves and 2 little fish. We looked at the widow of Zarephath with a handful of flour and a little cooking oil. We watched Jesus observe a poor widow as she put 2 tiny copper coins into the massive temple treasury. We noted David - who would not give to God that which cost him nothing. Lastly, we looked at the Corinthians, who gave what they could, and were learning from God - the loving obedience in the grace of giving. In all these cases, as well as our own, God's Arithmetic is on display in a way that the world can neither know nor understand. It has always been of great comfort to me that God shows no favoritism (Rom.2:11; Gal.2:6; Acts 10:34; Eph.6:9; Col.3:25). The fullness of spiritual life is available to every believer, regardless of their bank account. A deeper spiritual walk in God's grace - is there for the asking. Nowhere does any scripture say, "Okay, you want to live more like Jesus — how much money do you have?" We laugh at such a thought; but the truth is that we often get our values mixed up. The world bombards us constantly with the idea that success = money. It's easy to carry that into the spiritual realm, and falsely conclude that if we are poor money-wise, then we must be poor spiritually as well. I have no issue at all with the accumulation of material wealth. The Bible has a great deal to say to Christians who are materially wealthy — but that is a separate discussion. The danger we have to watch out for, is that we don't allow money to take over our lives. It's all too easy to give to wealth and material things - the place in our heart that belongs to God alone. To caution us against such idolatry and greed, Jesus put it this way:

"Don't store up treasures here on earth, where moths eat them and rust destroys them, and where thieves break in and steal. Store your treasures in heaven, where moths and rust cannot destroy, and thieves do not break in and steal. Wherever your treasure is, there the desires of your heart will also be.

Your eye is a lamp that provides light for your body. When your eye is good, your whole body is filled with light. But when your eye is bad, your whole body is filled with darkness. And if the light you think you have is actually darkness, how deep that darkness is!

No one can serve two masters. For you will hate one and love the other; you will be devoted to one and despise the other. You cannot serve both God and money." Matthew 6:19-24 NLT

I don't think we can stress this enough. There is a really fascinating verse in Luke which makes this point. On one occasion when Jesus was teaching about wealth, He used the same words we just saw in Matthew 6:24. Among those listening to Him teach, were a group of Pharisees. The Pharisees were a sect of Judaism that were learned in the Jewish Law - and zealous in its observation. To all outward appearance, they were the most holy and religious of God's chosen people. After hearing Jesus teach that you cannot serve both God and money - it provoked them. Listen to their reaction and Jesus' response to it:

The Pharisees, who dearly loved their money, heard all this and scoffed at him. Then he said to them, "You like to appear righteous in public, but God knows your hearts. What this world honors is detestable in the sight of God." Luke 16:14-15 NLT

I'm afraid that even now, there are modern-day counterparts to these Pharisees, even among believers. We must guard ourselves always, against allowing the love of money to take root in our hearts. Speaking to Timothy, the Apostle Paul had some sober words of warning for certain false teachers - who thought that serving God was a way to get rich. In these telling words, he reminds us of the value of true riches; and warns us against the love of money:

"Yet true godliness with contentment is itself great wealth. After all, we brought nothing with us when we came into the world, and we can't take anything with us when we leave it. So if we have enough food and clothing, let us be content.

But people who long to be rich fall into temptation and are trapped by many foolish and harmful desires that plunge them into ruin and destruction. For the love of money is the root of all kinds of evil. And some people, craving money, have wandered from the true faith and pierced themselves with many sorrows." 1 Timothy 6:6-10 NLT

Getting back to the point at hand; no believer has any advantage over another in terms of access to God's grace, and living by the power of the Holy Spirit. These gifts are ours by inheritance - as God's children in Christ (cp. Lk.11:11-13; Rom.8:32). Whether we are rich or poor - has no bearing whatsoever on the quality of spiritual life we may enjoy. **In God's Arithmetic, success *is not equal to* money. In God's eyes, success = faithfulness** — and you can take that to the bank!! Since God is concerned with our faithfulness; it is our motives that matter to Him - and not our means. We who serve in God's churches, must learn to value our brothers and sisters in Christ as God does, and to recognize the presence of Jesus in every believer. It simply will not do - to apply the world's standards of respect to the members of our church. When discussing this kind of discrimination and improper motive, James said:

"Listen to me, dear brothers and sisters. Hasn't God chosen the poor in this world to be rich in faith? Aren't they the ones who will inherit the Kingdom he promised to those who love him? But you dishonor the poor!" James 2:5-6a NLT

Let us honor God by taking courage from the fact that Jesus Christ belongs to all of us. God's love for us does not depend in the least - on how much money we have or don't have. Let this comfort you in all your trials. You can make as large an impact for the Kingdom of God as anyone. God has no favorites - and you are his well loved child in Jesus Christ.

Before we leave these excellent lessons Jesus gave us in Matthew 10:40-42, it is necessary to address the matter of rewards. Three times in vv.41-42, Jesus declares the promise of reward. The first thing we can take to heart, is that *the support we provide for even the least of Jesus' disciples as they work for the advancement of His Kingdom - will be rewarded by God.* A prophet, a righteous man, or any disciple who comes to us in the King's name, and on the King's mission, is worthy of our support. By providing such support, we undergird the ministry and mission of our Master, in every place He is at work. In the eyes of our Heavenly Father, when we welcome and receive His workers, it is deserving of reward. Why would God tell us this? What is the value in us knowing that God will reward even the least service given out of love and faithfulness to Him? It isn't because God wants us to serve Him for reward (as if we could merit such a thing by our own goodness anyway). That kind of spirit serves God only because of what we can get out of it. It isn't much different from those who supposed that godliness was a means to financial gain. No, God wants us to serve Him out of love; from a heart of gratitude for all He has done for us in Christ; and as a result of the bonds of intimacy we realize from His presence in our lives. We are not like Judas who followed Christ for his money bag. We are those who gladly serve Him because of the felicity and fulfillment it brings to our hearts, and for the joy we find as people come to know Jesus as their Lord and Savior. Nothing in this world can match the satisfaction that comes to us through serving Jesus. Let me briefly then suggest three reasons why God wants us to know that He will reward our service.

First, it reminds us that our labor for the Lord is not in vain. Encouraging the Corinthians with their heavenly hope, Paul assures them:

"So, my dear brothers and sisters, be strong and immovable. Always work enthusiastically for the Lord, for you know that nothing you do for the Lord is ever useless." 1 Corinthians 15:58 NLT

Unlike earthly treasure, <u>service to Christ has value that can never fade away</u>. Think about this the next time you are tempted to ask yourself, "What's the point?" God will make use of your faithfulness. We have no idea how everything ties together in the grand scheme of things — but our Father does! There is indeed a reward for our efforts - they are not for nothing.

Second, the promise of reward is an incentive to even greater effort. It is an incentive not because we are thinking merely of personal gain, but because we know that there is a harvest of blessing assured if we persevere:

"Don't be misled — you cannot mock the justice of God. You will always harvest what you plant. Those who live only to satisfy their own sinful nature will harvest decay and death from that sinful nature. But those who live to please the Spirit will harvest everlasting life from the Spirit. So let's not get tired of doing what is good. At just the right time we will reap a harvest of blessing if we don't give up. Therefore, whenever we have the opportunity, we should do good to everyone — especially to those in the family of faith." Galatians 6:7-10 NLT

Since our service to God will ultimately yield great blessing to both ourselves and our fellow believers, we are motivated to give to Him our very best. Sow life *in* the Spirit, and reap life *from* the Spirit. The reward or 'happy consequence' of doing good to everyone - is beyond our imagining. There is a sense that God's rewards are personal gain; but as we will see - it's not in a purely selfish sense. We gain personally from the knowledge that obedience to God is rewarded; and those who reject Him are not. Those who are slaves to sin, have their own harvest — decay and death. It is only right, that God reward His faithful servants. Since this is so, we strive to take advantage of every opportunity to serve Him. In this we rejoice, and we continue to rejoice.

The third reason God wants us to know He will reward our service, is that it gives joy to our labor. Serving God is not always easy. There are times when great personal sacrifice is required. I find it interesting and inspiring that those who surrender the most in obedience to the will of God, never seem to see it that way. I have some dear friends, Cliff and Beverly Vick, who serve God faithfully as missionaries to South Africa. During their long years of service, they have had to make a great many sacrifices. Were I to try and list them all — I could go on for a long while. If you were to ask them about the things they had to give up to serve the Lord, or the opportunities here in America they lost or missed out on, their answer would surprise you. The last thing they want is pity or sympathy. 'Oh, woe to us in the service of Christ.' No. They will speak only of what a joy and privilege it is to serve Christ in this way; and not at all of what they have given up to do so. It isn't that my friends don't realize their "losses." They are very astute and sensitive people, and they know all too well the heartache that can sometimes come their way. *But*, they are also well versed in God's Arithmetic. They know full well how to weigh these things in the proper balance. In the words of Paul:

"For our present troubles are small and won't last very long. Yet they produce for us a glory that vastly outweighs them and will last forever! So we don't look at the troubles we can see now; rather, we fix our gaze on things that cannot be seen. For the things we see now will soon be gone, but the things we cannot see will last forever." 2 Corinthians 4:17-18 NLT

My faithful friends know not only the joy that awaits them, but the joy that belongs to them now. They will be the first to tell you that obedience to the will of God is not drudgery – and that they have made no 'real' sacrifice, but instead what they have done brings with it a joy that the world cannot give or take away. Their joy gives their labor wings! They have taken up the cross, and will not set it aside. I have no doubt that they wouldn't trade their service to Christ for anything this world might give. The loss of joy and blessing in doing so, would be incalculable. The most obedient Christians always seem to see it that way. God will reward their faithfulness. Anticipating this - having God's smile - is a reward that only the faithful can know.

We see then that Jesus has affirmed that God will reward our faithful service. We looked briefly at why God thought it important to tell us this. It only remains now - to look at the rewards themselves. What are they? What should we expect? Primarily, *the rewards God gives - are spiritual in nature. They are received both now and in the life to come.* I believe that the New Testament looks at the idea of rewards in different ways. One prospect, is the affirmation of a personal heavenly reward that God will give to the obedient. In the following passage, Paul is speaking to the Corinthians about God's house (i.e. His Church), and all those who labor in it. God is building His Kingdom through His Church. Paul, as a master builder, has laid the proper foundation. Jesus Christ is the only foundation, and anyone who builds on that foundation must be careful.

"Anyone who builds on that foundation may use a variety of materials — gold, silver, jewels, wood, hay, or straw. But on the judgment day, fire will reveal what kind of work each builder has done. The fire will show if a person's work has any value. If the work survives, that builder will receive a reward. But if the work is burned up, the builder will suffer great loss. The builder will be saved, but like someone barely escaping through a wall of flames." 1 Corinthians 3:12-15 NLT

Anyone whose work is deemed by God as having lasting value - will receive a reward. What that reward will be - who can say? It's enough for us to know that God in His grace - will reward those who faithfully join Him in the great enterprise of building His church in the world. When we work in the name of Jesus, as His representative, and by the power of His Spirit, it makes glad the heart of God. As a side note, do you remember our discussion earlier from Mark 9:42, where Jesus said that you'd be better off dead than causing one of the little ones who believe in Him to stumble? Look here at 1 Corinthians 3:16-17 NLT, which immediately follows the promise of reward. Just as in Mark, we have the converse expressed as a caution - that we must not do damage to God's Church:

"Don't you realize that all of you together are the temple of God and that the Spirit of God lives in you? God will destroy anyone who destroys this temple. For God's temple is holy, and you are that temple."

This is every bit as stern as Jesus' earlier warning. It is a timely reminder to us - that although we serve our Father in a relationship of intimacy - we also must be aware, with a holy reverence, of the danger in doing harm to the people that He loves.

When we speak of personal heavenly reward, I can almost hear someone say that God has promised us various "crowns." There are several passages that speak of this. (e.g. 2 Timothy 4:8; Rev.2:10, 3:11; James 1:12; 1 Peter 5:4; Phil.4:1; 1Thess.2:19) The crowns spoken of in these scriptures are quite real — but not literal crowns. Crowns, as they pertain to the reward of faithful Christian living, are a figure of speech. Look at Philippians 4:1 (NLT) and 1 Thessalonians 2:19 (NLT):

"Therefore, my dear brothers and sisters, stay true to the Lord. I love you and long to see you, dear friends, for you are my joy and the crown I receive for my work."

"After all, what gives us hope and joy, and what will be our proud reward and crown as we stand before our Lord Jesus when he returns? It is you!"

It is immediately evident that the crown spoken of in these instances - refers to the godly pride that Paul took in those people for whom he had labored so hard in the Lord.

Their faithful lives in Christ and their salvation — would be Paul's joy and great reward. The other verses referenced, often use *"crown"* in the sense of the distinction and honor that comes from an achievement; the inner dignity that comes from the satisfaction of a life well lived. It's an expression of the final beauty of one's spirit; the consummation of Eternal Life; the everlasting joy that will be revealed in us when we receive God's *"well done."* Such crowns are our eternal reward. Should we receive such a reward, we gladly return all glory and praise to God - for the surpassing grace that made our lives possible. These "crown" passages that are listed, refer to a *'crown of life'*, a *'crown of righteousness'*, a *'crown of glory'*, and *'a crown that will last forever'*. All of these are expressions that describe this end result of a life of faithfulness. The character we ultimately reap by living according to the Spirit of God - is one that will be distinguished by the qualities of glory, righteousness, and life. It is also said to be a *'crown that will last forever'*. This style of speech is really communicating to us in various ways - the Biblical concept of Eternal Life. At the consummation of all things, on that great Resurrection Day, our new bodies will reflect the glory of God (1 Corinthians 15:42-58). The quality of life implanted in us - God's kind of life (Eternal Life) - will be fully revealed to the waiting universe. It is then that we will be fully crowned — invested with all the honor and dignity of the glorious qualities of life befitting the children of God. Finally we will be like Jesus; for we will see Him as He really is (1 John 3:2). Then, those who live in Jesus will receive their final reward.

As we conclude our look at rewards, we return to Matthew 10:41-42. Jesus tells us that the prophet, the righteous man, all faithful disciples, and those who welcome them - will all receive their reward. In saying this, we find the sense of reward both now and in the life to come. Our last considerations have been of the life to come. But what about life now? In what ways are the faithful workers in God's field rewarded — even as they serve Him here and now? To see this in a practical way, let's follow one of these missionaries of Jesus, as they go about their ministry. The prophet of Jesus, who speaks in His name, goes forth each day on his mission. As he goes, he sows the seed of the gospel message to anyone who will listen. Some people will reject his message. Others, whose hearts God has touched, will welcome him, and embrace the Savior he has placed before them. Jesus said (v.41) that this prophet would receive a prophets reward; and the one who accepts him and his message - would also receive the same reward. What precisely is it that they will receive? The most fundamental meaning we must see - is that these rewards are *spiritual*. It's tempting at this point to digress, and point out the grave error of those who believe that God wants us all to be healthy and wealthy. However, to avoid wandering too far afield — let me just affirm that spiritual service yields spiritual reward. If you should find yourself the recipient of material blessings from the Lord in the course of serving Him, remember this: We are all stewards of everything that God has resourced us with. It all belongs to Him. Never make the mistake of assuming that materially wealthy Christians are blessed by God - and poor Christians are not. Back to the point that the reward of v.41 is spiritual; it may help us to think of reward in the sense of blessing. Spiritual rewards are the blessings that God gives by His grace to those who faithfully work in His harvest field. Foremost among these blessings, is that when we honor God as growing disciples in the path of obedience — He receives the glory, honor, and praise that are due His name (cp. John 15:8). For our faithful prophet, I would like to divide the blessings he receives into two categories. There are blessings (rewards) that come *to him directly,* and blessings that come *by him to others.* My intention is that the following lists are suggestive. I hope you will be able to add to these lists; your own biblical thoughts and personal experiences - of the kind of rewards that God has bestowed upon your life while serving Him. Some of the blessings that come to God's prophet directly, are these:

• Rewarding answers to prayer. How wonderful it is for us, when we entreat the Lord for fruit that will last - and the result is new souls added to His Kingdom. There are so many matters to pray about, in support of God's work. The prophet rejoices to see his many petitions come to pass — and so do we.

• Confident assurance of full access to the cornucopia of God's promises in His Word. The faithful believer has an ever growing confidence that all the promises of God belong to him (cp. 2 Corinthians 1:20). While these promises belong to all Christians by inheritance — a growing assurance of how to apply them, is the reward of walking daily in step with Jesus. The faithful prophet will never fail to see God's promises come to fruition as part of his experience.

• Joy that comes from partnering with God in the salvation of lost souls. Anyone who has had the privilege of introducing another person to Christ — knows a joy that is like no other in the world. I can think of no greater reward than having a part in the eternal salvation of another human being. A "prophet's reward" indeed!

• Deepening confidence in personal faith, as we see the Spirit at work through our gifts and ministry. Paul said of those who serve well as Deacons, *"Those who do well as deacons will be rewarded with respect from others, and will have increased confidence in their faith in Christ Jesus."* 1 Timothy 3:13 NLT. I believe the same thing applies to all who serve well in ministry. We grow in our boldness, and we acquire a good standing for ourselves among God's people. Truly a rich blessing for anyone who desires to increasingly serve the Lord.

• A growing capability and capacity in the Lord's work and service. As we discover and use our spiritual gifts, we enhance our ability to serve God in more effective ways. Our gifts and abilities are refined as we use them. Our usefulness in the Kingdom grows, and God is able to entrust to us - a broader scope of ministry opportunities.

• A clearer sense of our life's calling and purpose - of who we are in Jesus. The prophet who serves well as a prophet (the Christian who serves well at whatever their calling may be), will recognize more and more with each passing year, how God plans to use their life. They will have greater insight into where they are most effective in ministry, which in turn will help guide them into those opportunities that the Lord will gradually place before them.

As if the kind of rewards that come directly to the faithful prophet weren't enough — there are further rewards that God brings by the prophet to others. Again, let me propose a few:

• The opportunity to support the prophet in his ministry. We may not all be on the front lines of ministry, but we can all give support to those who are. For example, when we provide for the needs of our faithful Pastor, we join him in ministry, and we enable him to do all that God has called him to do. Thus, we receive his reward. Remember v.42. If we provide even a cup of cold water - we will not lose our reward. God sees us all as being in this work together. What we do for one - we do for Him - and we all share the reward He gives for taking part in His Kingdom's work.

• We grow in loving fellowship with each other, and we acquire a growing sense of our shared mission. Those who share together in Kingdom ministry - form bonds of spiritual love - which provide added strength to their resolve and commitment. Working together with other believers, helps us to persevere. We are reminded that we are not in this work alone, and that the mission we are on is much greater than our own individual needs and differences. When God's people are busy working hand in hand to spread the gospel, there is far less opportunity for the Devil to work mischief, and disrupt the fellowship of the church. The faithful prophet strengthens the church, and calls us by example to the same dedicated service to the Lord as his own. Hence, we receive his reward.

• God can multiply the fruit in the prophet's life through the lives of those who learn from his ministry. The simplest example of this - is a Pastor's sermons. When we follow God's direction for our lives as our Pastor shares the Word of God (with us), we too become more faithful and obedient servants. The Pastor's good example and effective ministry to his flock, is extended through us as we follow him; as he follows Jesus. Truly, all of us can bring reward to our fellow Christians in this way. As we follow Jesus, others follow along with us - and we all share in the blessing of bearing fruit for the glory of God. That, surely, is a very great reward.

• We are encouraged to grow and persevere in our faith, as we observe God at work through the prophet's ministry. I am reminded of the exhortation to us in Hebrews 13:7 NLT, *"Remember your leaders who taught you the word of God. Think of all the good that has come from their lives, and follow the example of their faith."* While this is certainly true of the challenge and encouragement provided by the example of our leaders — it is also true of the example set by all of God's faithful children. The committed prophet, righteous man, or disciple, sets an example that enlivens each of us. As we look at other believers with all of their weaknesses, problems, struggles, and hurts, we see God's sustaining power at work in their lives. This encourages us, even as we go through the same difficulties - because God comforts us with the same comfort that He has given to them (2 Corinthians 1:4).

We have looked at some of the rewards that the prophet has received — those that come to him directly, and those that come by him to others. Jesus declares that the person who welcomes the prophet, the righteous man, or the disciple that comes in His name - will receive a reward like theirs. Even by providing a cup of cold water — those who engage in the giving and receiving of blessing - exchanged with all those sent forth by Christ - will not lose their reward. The sum and substance of Jesus' assurance to us is this: *the ultimate reward we receive - is Jesus himself.* All the reward and all the blessing - is one and the same. The prophet, the righteous man, and all faithful disciples, partake of the salvation that is ours in Christ. We all enjoy the same privileges; a personal relationship with God that consists of peace, forgiveness, prayer, and fellowship. Faith, hope, and love, are our possessions now and forever. We all have the Holy Spirit living in us; freeing us from the power of sin; sealing us for the day of redemption; guaranteeing to us the promise of salvation; and holding us firm until the end. We have God as our Father, Christ as our brother, and the Church as our family. As citizens of heaven, we share with all the saints in the inheritance of God's people in the kingdom of light, and in the full assurance of our resurrection. Our reward is no less than what God - by His infinite grace - has promised us freely in His Son, Jesus Christ our Lord. In the words of Paul:

"What shall we say about such wonderful things as these? If God is for us, who can ever be against us? Since he did not spare even his own Son but gave him up for us all, won't he also give us everything else?" Romans 8:31-32 NLT

And:

"So don't boast about following a particular human leader. For everything belongs to you — whether Paul or Apollos or Peter, or the world, or life and death, or the present and the future. Everything belongs to you, and you belong to Christ, and Christ belongs to God." 1 Corinthians 3:20-23 NLT

The Surprising Color of Joy

"2 Consider it pure joy, my brothers and sisters, whenever you face trials of many kinds, 3 because you know that the testing of your faith produces perseverance. 4 Let perseverance finish its work so that you may be mature and complete, not lacking anything. 5 If any of you lacks wisdom, you should ask God, who gives generously to all without finding fault, and it will be given to you. 6 But when you ask, you must believe and not doubt, because the one who doubts is like a wave of the sea, blown and tossed by the wind. 7 That person should not expect to receive anything from the Lord. 8 Such a person is double-minded and unstable in all they do." James 1:2-8 NIV

*N*o matter who we are, at some time during our childhood, we very likely played with crayons. If you're like me - the larger the box of crayons, the more fun it was. I particularly enjoyed the box with 64 colors, because I had so many to choose from. Depending on my mood or feelings at the time, I would choose a color to use that felt just right for whatever object I was coloring or drawing. Many of us live out our spiritual lives in a similar manner. At any given time, we experience the "color" of our attitude, based on our moods and feelings. There isn't anything wrong with this, since our emotional states vary quite often, and this is just part of what it means to be human. However, in God's Arithmetic, there is no need for us to be bound or limited by our emotional state, when it comes to dealing with the tests and challenges of life. In our life in Christ, we have a choice. We can actually choose the "color" of our attitude toward our circumstances.

As a young Christian, some of the strongest influences on my spiritual life were the people and training materials from Campus Crusade for Christ. In fact, their small booklet, "The Four Spiritual Laws", has helped me to share the gospel with others on many occasions. It has also made it easier to help point people in the right direction for 'next steps', after their initial decision to trust in Christ. Near the back of this booklet, is a small diagram of a train with 3 cars.[4]

The first train (or engine) represents FACT - the truth of God and His Word. The second car represents FAITH - our trust in God and His Word. The third car (or caboose) represents FEELING - the result of our trust in God and His Word. This simple diagram is an attempt to introduce the new believer to the concept that "in our spiritual life, we live by faith - and not by feelings." Our lives are to be directed by the truth of God's character and the expressions of Scripture - not by the feelings and emotions we experience. Our feelings and emotions change almost continually, but God does not change. He is forever the same, and can be relied on completely (Malachi 3:6; Hebrews 13:8). The Bible - God's Word - cannot and will not fail - to be a totally dependable and trustworthy guide for our lives. This remains true in any and all situations and circumstances. While this fact is extremely helpful for the new believer, it is also profoundly powerful and necessary, for even the most experienced of believers. This simple diagram reminds us that when hardships come our way, we have a "color" of attitude we can choose from God's coloring box. This color is dependent on God's Word, and not on our uncertain feelings and emotions. It is a color that brings us the steadfastness and stability we need, for the practical steps we must take in a given situation. This color also speaks to the inner state of our mind and heart, during times of pain and distress. Our choice color; the most desirable color of attitude in the midst of all our struggles — is the color of JOY. The apostles James, Peter, and Paul, all have something vital to say to us about our joy as believers. Can we really choose to have joy in the midst of our difficulties? What reasons are there for doing so? Join me as we discover together — the Surprising Color of Joy.

We begin in chapter one, verses two through eight of the book of James (above). James opens his letter to believers with a statement that takes us completely by surprise. He says that when troubles come our way, we should consider it pure joy (v.2). In other words, our trials and difficulties actually create for us 'an opportunity to embrace an attitude of joy'. Finding a way to color my attitude with joy - has been a great challenge. I wish I could say that I've always been successful at doing so, but that is not the case. Maintaining a joyful attitude in every situation, is a vibrant goal that the Word of God has set before us. What's more, God provides us with a great many opportunities for choosing how we will face the hardships that confront our lives.

Sometimes I feel that I am a very slow learner in the ways of God. Despite the many opportunities for progress, my successes are slow to come - and they have often come in baby steps. Nevertheless, my natural disposition toward negativity, often coupled with an occasional lack of faith, has been transformed by God. As the years pass, He continues to move me toward a more determined outlook of joy. I have come to realize that I can *choose* to pull the needed color of my 'mental approach' to circumstances, out of God's Coloring box. When I do so, my hardships become my servants. They are actually used by God to train me. I am learning how to determine the appropriate spiritual color of attitude that will brace me to face anything that life throws my way. When I consider some of the various struggles I have experienced, I can look back and see how my attitude affected their outcomes. As I meditate on the past, it allows me to see how my attitude has affected my daily feelings and moods, during times of suffering. Thus, after careful reflection on past experience, I am reminded of two important considerations. First, is the need for us to choose the color of joy in the face of life's hardships. Second, is determining how we can make progress in God's grace, and pursue a more focused spiritual outlook during our times of adversity.

I am currently in my late 50's. About 26 years ago, I moved into a small apartment in Mesa, Arizona, with my wife and young child. I found a job teaching in a small Christian school, run by a local Baptist church. I had a falling out with the school administrator, over his lack of support for student discipline. He felt we could not afford to alienate the parents who provided support for the school - by insisting that the students be held accountable to classroom rules. I, on the other hand, was not able to effectively teach or maintain a stable classroom environment while the school was unwilling to enforce even the most simple disciplinary procedures. When we could not resolve the matter, I was forced to leave. My wife was working, but I was unable to find another job for the next few months. This period of unemployment put us behind on our bills. At the worst point, we were 3 months behind on our rent! The apartment manager wanted us evicted. I wrote a letter to the apartment owners, and asked for their patience. Through the Lord's intervention, they did allow us to stay. I promised we would pay them all that we owed, and then stay current on the rent. I eventually found another job, and we were able to pay back every cent of the overdue rent. It was several months before I actually saw any of my paychecks, since they all went directly toward paying our debt. *My attitude during these months was not one of joy.* I spent a good deal of time complaining to God about the unfairness of it all. I kept wondering why my service to the Lord, and my good intentions, had to be mixed with such a bitter struggle. As I look back, I view this time as one of the milestones of my spiritual education. God was helping me to learn the proper color of attitude to pick out of His coloring box. I would have saved myself a great deal of misery through this struggle, had I chosen the best colors of joy and trust. Instead, I allowed my outlook to be strongly tainted with colors from the devil's coloring box - bitterness, doubt, grumbling, and despondency. If I had chosen the better color of joy, the struggle itself would still have been difficult and painful — but facing each day with joy, would have made it possible for me to see more clearly - the kindness of God in allowing this hardship. It would have enabled me to pass through this period of time with a song in my heart, and a deeper experience of the daily power and presence of God. Instead, I limped through - only gradually seeing the light at the end of the tunnel. By choosing joy, I could have had all the light I needed along the way, while passing through the tunnel.

Another such learning experience occurred for me, at a time early in my last employment. For more than 23 years, I worked in state government, serving in large welfare offices. Most of those years, I was a Supervisor in charge of groups of employees who were responsible for the issuance of various types of benefits to those in need. God was very wise in selecting the venue for my "coloring box" training. A 'welfare office' can offer a person a great many opportunities to choose their attitude, in response to difficult people and demanding situations. As a Supervisor, customer complaints were a regular part of my job. There were long stretches of time when every single day, someone was angry with me, regarding the decisions that our staff made on their benefit determinations. I also faced continuous pressure from completion deadlines, written reports, managing staff performance, employee training, and other similar job responsibilities. My workload could often result in a great deal of distress. I had daily opportunities to choose the color of joy, rather than several much darker colors. With practice, I could occasionally turn my mental swampland into a garden of roses, but I was not always successful at this. Sometimes, choosing the right color of attitude took me a long while. Have you ever had a difficult boss? In my line of work, I would often have a new manager. Anytime the new manager was especially overbearing, it made a demanding job even more so. I remember reading somewhere, that troublesome bosses are the number one reason people quit their jobs. I'm not surprised at this. For several years, I had one boss in particular, who made my work days very difficult. This was due to an autocratic attitude, and a lack of sympathy for the daily workload. The pressure I was under was unrelenting, and there were no excuses for anything. As long as the job got done, it didn't seem to matter who became emotionally damaged or physically exhausted — sink or swim, as it were. Now there are always people who like that kind of boss; a hard nosed 'by the book' kind of person, who will stop at nothing to succeed. Their mindset is, "It you can't cut it — too bad." For me however, this created an atmosphere that made it miserable to come to work every day. I never felt appreciated or encouraged in what I was doing. For a period of time, I harbored a very deep resentment toward this manager. The ill-will and sense of indignation I was carrying, was as strong as any I have ever felt in my life. As a result of the grace of Jesus, I have always been able to demonstrate the love of God to everyone, even toward those with whom I did not get along. In this instance, it was a constant struggle for me to extend God's love toward this individual. Eventually, I did choose the 'color of forgiveness' out of God's coloring box, and was able to love this person as God desired. However, due to the resentment I had been carrying, there was a joy that was absent from my life during this period of time. For nearly a year, I allowed the behavior of my boss to color my attitude toward all of life. Everything beyond the workplace became tinged with the dark-shaded colors of anger and resentment. As a result, all of the other problems I experienced at that time, seemed much larger than they actually were. They became more difficult to face and to deal with, due to my agitated emotional state. I experienced a great deal of unnecessary distress, because I could not bring myself to see God's love at work in the midst of my situation. Therefore, I did not consider the situation as His gift to me, or as an opportunity for joy. Had I determined to pull the 'color of joy' out of God's coloring box, all my burdens would have seemed lighter. Love and forgiveness would have come more easily, and my anger and resentment would have vanished like the morning mist.

Something I read and taught in a Sunday School class years ago, has never left me. When we do not trust God in any given situation, it's the result of doubting one of three traits of God's character. We do not trust (or we doubt): His wisdom, His love, or His power. By reminding ourselves of these three vital attributes of God, along with the regular discipline of studying His Word, we can "sharpen our crayon of joy". We learn to fix our spiritual eyes on Jesus (Hebrews 12:2). He can transform our thoughts and attitudes into those that conform with His own. We can discover how to rise above our problems; not by making them go away, but by becoming "more than conquerors through Him who loved us" (Romans 8:37). We become able to triumph in Christ by learning to trust God in all circumstances. Then as our trust grows, we are better able to pull the color of joy from God's crayon box. We can then employ it to add a bright hue to our dark circumstance. Choosing the color of joy, allows God to open our eyes to the depth of His love toward us - even in the most unpromising situations.

This is something that James wants us to understand - right off the bat. Namely that we can learn to see in our trials, an opportunity for joy. As we choose joy, and allow it to color our lives, it becomes part of God's way of helping us grow in our faith. Joy leads us to a deeper and more rewarding experience of His love. James is not saying to us in this passage, that 'choosing the color of joy simply places rose colored glasses on our situation'. The essence of his inspiration, is that we can consider it pure joy when trials come our way; because there are significant and substantial spiritual benefits that advance in our lives through God's grace.

The first of these spiritual benefits, is 'endurance or perseverance' (v.3). The Greek word that James uses for perseverance is *hupomone*'. I have always thought this to be a magnificent word, although it's quite difficult to capture its meaning in English. Perhaps the best translation I have seen of this word for endurance, is "triumphant fortitude". The testing of our faith - produces triumphant fortitude. The idea is that we do not have to simply 'grit our teeth and endure our trials' - as if we were at a dentist visit - just glad to get it over with. Rather, our hardships are infusing into our character 'spiritual strength', which enables us to be better prepared for the challenge of each new situation. An 'unswerving constancy' develops in our faith. This constancy allows us to march through life, and to take hold of each difficulty, using it as a step forward in learning to trust in God. James tells us that this quality of character comes from the testing of our faith (v.3). This testing is like a purging process - such as one which purifies heated metals by removing the dross.

Through trial, the flaws in our character are melted away. We are transformed toward a healthier and more single minded spiritual outlook. This kind of endurance in trial, can also be likened to the training of an athlete. An athlete's workout regimen adds new strength to their body, and serves to improve their performance in the next competition. For us then - perseverance is an actual drawing of strength through the trial itself. By the transforming power of the grace of God, we are given the inner fortitude to press on, toward the highest spiritual outcome for our souls. The Bible paraphrase, "The Message", expresses this well by saying:

"You know that under pressure, your faith-life is forced into the open and shows its true colors. So don't try to get out of anything prematurely. Let it do its work so you become mature and well-developed, not deficient in any way." (vv.2-4).

As we relate to people in the daily orbit of our lives, they observe the way we react to life's pressures. Although those around us may not see it, our 'inner faith life' is in the process of transformation. We are compelled by the pressure of each trial - to face the true color of the way we are responding to God, ourselves, and others. If we choose the best color out of God's coloring box, we will become mature and well developed disciples of Christ. We will also move steadily forward in preparation for more fruitful service in the Kingdom of God, and our fellow man. Another way to say this, is that the wonderful byproduct of choosing the color of joy in our trials - will surprise us. It will be a growth in grace, which makes it easier in each successive trial to fully trust in God; and to have our attitude of joy made more and more real in our daily experience. Joy will increasingly become not just a disposition of mind, but a rich, deep, spiritual power in our heart. As we learn how to choose and receive this joy, it is

God's delight to bring each of us more and more into conformity with the image of His Son. He is able to do this, through the same power that raised Jesus from the dead. The power that is at work in all of us who believe in Jesus (Ephesians 1:19-20; 3:20).

As James reveals to us the benefits of choosing the color of joy, it leads him naturally into addressing a vital practical dilemma which quickly comes to mind. James realizes that when we are facing a stressful or pressure filled situation, we are going to need wisdom. 'Spiritual wisdom' is the ability to think and act using the knowledge, experience, understanding, awareness, and insight, consistent with the Word of God. Such Godly wisdom is made available to us by the Holy Spirit. So James says, *"If any of you lacks wisdom, you should ask God."* (v.5). Here is the situation: We find ourselves facing a new challenge, and trying to consider it joy. So we say to ourselves, "Okay, here I go". Then we pause, and we realize that we don't really know what to do next. The questions we ask ourselves while deciding on our next step, are as varied as our individual experience. We face questions like, "What do I say to that difficult person?", "How will I determine what is right and what is wrong?", "Where is the money going to come from?", "Which of the choices before me is the best one?", "How should a Christian handle this problem?", "I'm so confused - what do I do next?" James tells us that we can in fact be certain, that God will provide us with the practical insight we need; insight necessary to plot the best course of action in our situation. James plainly states, *"Ask God. . . and it will be given to you."* (v.5). This is a clear echo of Jesus' promise to us in Matthew 7:7 NLT:

"Keep on asking, and you will receive what you ask for. Keep on seeking, and you will find. Keep on knocking, and the door will be opened to you."

It is also a good reminder that we must sometimes persevere in prayer - when requesting wisdom. A situation may call for varying course corrections as we walk through it and observe events transpiring. God may need to prepare us for the next step of action — or He may need to prepare the situation so we are able to take that step. We may also need to carefully evaluate the behavior of others - before the full scope of God's direction is made clear to our minds. This calls for vigilance and continuance in prayer, on our part. God will certainly lead us - but He will not reveal to us all at once, the next ten steps we must take. His leading will be made plain, one step at a time. As we follow Him step by step, the fulness of wisdom we seek will be revealed.

There is also something very beautiful in the additional aspects of this promise - that James now asks us to consider. He invites us to ponder the way or manner in which God grants this wisdom we so urgently need. God provides His wisdom generously, graciously, and without rebuke (v.5). In addition, He does not act condescendingly toward us when we ask. These brief insights can be easily overlooked. However, we should not pass them by, because they provide us with an amazing insight into God's character. They also reveal to us, one of the ways that our Heavenly Father encourages us to come into an even deeper intimacy with His person. As Christians, we have been born again, and have entered into a personal relationship with God. It is part of human nature to respond eagerly and receptively toward those who treat us with generosity and an open hand. The kindness and charity shown to us by special people in our lives, is even more meaningful when we know it comes from a heart of pure love, and the sincere desire to give - without expecting anything in return. It is our Heavenly Father's delight to do good to His children. When we grow in our relationship with Him to the place where we have come to know - by long and deep personal experience - how good, kind, and generous

He is — it endears Him to us in a very special way. Through the kindhearted manner that our Father bestows His gifts, we are drawn into an ever deepening relationship with Him - with the bond of love between us growing progressively stronger. This happens for us almost imperceptibly, as we receive from His grace the 'observed tokens of his acts of compassion' in our daily experience. This growing bond of love between God and us, is enhanced by the other aspect James reveals, of how His wisdom is bestowed upon us; God gives this precious gift without rebuke or condescension.

Most of us have had the experience of receiving a generous gift from someone. But. . . have you ever received such a gift - and been annoyed or even mildly angered - due to the *manner* with which it was given? You received the gift, but it was either given with strings attached, or given in such a way that it made you feel guilty or even belittled for have even taken it? Such "gifts" are instances of someone forcibly trying to exercise power or control over you in a certain way; to manipulate you into behaving in a manner that seems suitable or necessary to them. This is indeed a kind of giving, but it is of a nature that does not necessarily build up or encourage the one receiving the gift. It also does not endear the recipient to the giver, nor strengthen the bond of their relationship in a positive or healthy way. Let me give you a small example. Many years ago, I allowed some friends to persuade me to attend a presentation on time sharing. In exchange for my attendance, I would receive a free gift. You know the ploy; you listen to their pitch for an hour or more, while high pressure sales people attempt to convince you of the wonderful benefits of making monthly payments to share time in a house or condo at some exotic location. After I had listened to the presentation, I was presented with a voucher that could be redeemed for a two night stay at a fancy resort, including plane fare. The company selling this time share did indeed give me a nice gift. However, they did not give

me this voucher because they cared about me in any meaningful way. Their motive, as you know, was to convince me
to purchase their time share. So not only did their gift have a
string attached, but they also tried to make me feel guilty and
uncomfortable when I chose to decline their offer. The color
of joy is revealed to our minds and hearts, when we see that
our wondrous God does not give to us in that kind of calculating manner. God's grant of wisdom - never makes us feel
small, belittled, manipulated, demeaned, scorned, or contemptible. Our heart's and lives are always enriched, whenever we receive anything from God's hand. The blessings
He gives, are not only for our certain good, but are given in
a manner that brings about feelings of gratitude and a sense
of our unworthiness. This is not because we are made to feel
badly about His mercy. Rather, it is because His generous
love elicits a response from the depth of our soul. In this
response, we experience a real sense of how generous God
is, and how precious and well loved we must be to Him, to
receive such very special personal attention from the Lord
of all creation.

At this point, James is compelled to remind us of the
one thing necessary on our part, to enjoy the real and satisfying experience of receiving wisdom from God. Often,
the problem with obtaining the mercy of God, stems from
an unwillingness on our part to fully trust Him. Underlying
our distrust, is the fact that we don't really want to give a
matter over entirely to the Lord, and truly find *His* guidance.
Instead, when we ask for wisdom, our intent is to work out
the options for ourselves, in a manner of our own choosing.
This is a subtle point, but an important one. I believe that
finding the will of God in a situation, is 90% our *willingness* to obey Him, and only 10% the actual spiritual wisdom
we seek. James says that our loyalties must not be divided
between God and the world (v.6, 8). It's as if we are trying
to seek God with two different minds. One mind wants to

know His will and guidance as to how to act and proceed in our situation. The other mind is saying, "Well, I do want to maybe hear God's *opinion,* but I also want to keep my options open. Then I can do what I think is best, regardless of what God may say to me". For some people, praying for wisdom from God in this way – can be almost superstitious. It's as if they are saying, "I don't really believe that God will answer me, but just in case He does, I am going to ask." James is clear that such people should not expect to receive anything from the Lord (v.7). We must ask God for His wisdom without doubt, and without divided loyalties. The Message puts it well by saying, *"Ask boldly, believingly, and without a second thought."* It is our Heavenly Father's prerogative to grant us our requests on His own terms. Faith in Him is always central in receiving answers to prayer. As the writer of Hebrews tells us in Chapter 11, verse 6:

"It's impossible to please God apart from faith. And why? Because anyone who wants to approach God must believe both that he exists and that he cares enough to respond to those who seek him." MSG

We must ask in faith, because God has made us a promise. To ask Him for wisdom - and at the same time doubt that He will grant it - is to cast aspersion on His character. It is to hold Him in disrespect. In addition, to ask without faith, is to deprive ourselves of a settled frame of mind, and the peace of God. For as we receive God's wisdom in our trials, one of the ways we will know that God has spoken to us - is through the peace He gives. The pressures of life can leave our minds troubled and confused. When God speaks to our situation, the distress in our heart is replaced by the peace that only God can give. This peace rests on our soul, and the world cannot take it away (see John 14:27). Such peace cannot be our possession, if we do not ask believingly, trusting in His promises, and recognizing His love. In fact, James states that if we ask in doubt, "worrying our prayers" (MSG), the result will not be an experience of peace. Rather, our minds will be "as unsettled as a wave of the sea that is blown and tossed by the wind" (v.6 NLT). The broader picture for us, is that if we attempt to look to God while harboring divided loyalties, the framework of spiritual stability that reinforces our entire life cannot be established. Our life will appear to us as being tossed around like the waves of the sea. We will not be able to experience the spiritual clarity and focus that brings us into harmony with all that our Father wants to work out in our experience.

The bar that James sets for us in this passage, is very high indeed. We cannot achieve such a spiritual attitude in our own strength. We must acknowledge, as with all God's Arithmetic, that Jesus is the vine, and we are the branches. We must remain joined with Him in an intimate living relationship. If we live our lives apart from Him, through disobedience to His commands, we can not produce any spiritual fruit (John 15:5). While we realize this, we must also recognize that spiritual growth is not always easy. Some of the best spiritual fruit in our lives - that will be to God's glory - may take a very long time to ripen. <u>Learning how to habitually choose the 'color of joy' out of God's coloring box, will take a lifetime of cultivation</u>. It is *hard* to view a situation with joy, when everything within us cries pain, and everything around us is in chaos. It is absolutely necessary at such times, to arrive at the awareness that *the color of joy is not a feeling - but a belief. It's not something we suppose - but something we can count on. It's not something we suspect - but something we can have and know as our own.* When we learn to cultivate the color of joy in our lives, we will discover how fulfilling it is to live as a friend and child of God. This way of thinking is not for those who want to live simply as casual Christians. It is for those who want to learn to grow spiritual wings to soar above life's hardships - with a joyful confident trust in God (cp. Isa.40:31).

When we are truly seeking the Lord, yet our struggle leaves us feeling that we have arrived at our wit's end, it is there that God will meet us, and there that we will learn His joy. The Surprising Color of Joy takes root — and then ripens through hardship and pain.

Psalm 107:27-28 NIV:

"They reeled and staggered like drunkards; they were at their wits' end. Then they cried out to the LORD in their trouble, and He brought them out of their distress."

Are you standing at "Wit's End Corner"
Christian with troubled brow?
Are you thinking of what is before you,
And all you are bearing now?
Does all the world seem against you,
And you in the battle alone?
Remember — at "Wit's End Corner"
Is just where God's power is shown.

Are you standing at "Wit's End Corner"
Blinded with wearying pain,
Feeling you cannot endure it,
You cannot bear the strain,
Bruised through the constant suffering,
Dizzy, and dazed, and numb?
Remember — at "Wit's End Corner"
Is where Jesus loves to come.

Are you standing at "Wit's End Corner"?
Your work before you spread,
All lying begun, unfinished,

And pressing on heart and head,
Longing for strength to do it,
Stretching out trembling hands?
Remember — at "Wit's End Corner"
The Burden-bearer stands.

Are you standing at "Wit's End Corner"?
Then you're just in the very spot
To learn the wondrous resources
Of Him who faileth not:
No doubt to a brighter pathway
Your footsteps will soon be moved,
But only at "Wit's End Corner"
Is the "God who is able" proved.

                              -Antoinette Wilson[5]

We have seen from James, that the surprising color of joy is all about learning to choose the best attitude that God wants us to take toward our circumstances. When we choose to face our problems with joy — we are not pretending they are not really there. We are also not pasting a false smile on our face, to try to convince the people in our lives that everything is fine, when it is not. Through James, God reveals to us that we can consider it *'pure joy'* when trials come our way; because there are rich spiritual blessings that are advanced in our lives through His grace. When we choose the color of joy, our inner spiritual strength is caused to grow. Our trials produce for us an endurance, or triumphant fortitude, that allows us to become mature and fully developed believers. We may still struggle to work out our problems, but we do so armed with the strength of God. We become confident that He who has brought us through 999 trials — will bring us safely through 1,000 as well. In every situation, our faith in God secures for us His wisdom. We need never find ourselves without the clear direction that will guide us every step of the way. This is God's promise to us. Since we have this assurance that our trials will help us grow, and the promise of God's wisdom to direct our way – we have every reason to count it all "joy." **This is God's Arithmetic. We can learn to count as He does.** Yet, as encouraging as this is, it does leave us with an obvious two-part question. Are there other spiritual blessings that God brings into our lives through our hardships? And; Is there more we can add to the list of benefits we may obtain — by the way we learn to face our problems? Every spiritual blessing we discover in our trials, will powerfully reinforce the color of joy that can permeate our lives. James is not the only Apostle who speaks of why we may face our trials with joy. Peter and Paul provide us with such encouragement as well. Let's see if we can determine from their words, those additional spiritual blessings that will sustain our spirit of joy during times of trial. . .

The letter of First Peter was written to Christians who were in need of encouragement. Several congregations in Asia Minor were undergoing persecution from the neighbors in their communities. There are references to this throughout the letter. We read that they are in the midst of various trials (1:6). They are likely to be accused as evil-doers (3:16). A fiery ordeal is going to try them (4:12). They are sharing in the sufferings that Christians throughout the world are called upon to endure (5:9). This was not an official persecution of the Roman government, nor did it have their sanction. The Neronian persecution did not begin until A.D. 64. That period of oppression was limited to Rome anyway, and Peter does not mention it. The widespread persecutions under the Emperors Domitian and Trajan took place much later - well after the time of Peter's death. This persecution was probably the result of the natural dislike people felt for those who followed a new religion. It may also have been due to persistent rumors regarding Christian beliefs and practices. Only Christians and Jews held a belief in the one true God.

But Christians were also accused of cannibalism (the Lord's Supper), and of being haters of mankind; a result of their teaching the doctrine of hell - and a terrible end to the world. Additionally, some members of a family may have become Christians - while others did not. Since their commitment to Christ may have caused discord within the home, the believers were accused of breaking up families. Then there was the offense that came as Christians referred to Jesus as their King. This created suspicion of disloyalty to the Roman Government, because only Caesar or other designated officials were to be spoken of in this way. So, Peter wrote to these churches because he knew they needed encouragement. They faced an uncertain future, and were under the constant threat of harm. So he begins his letter by emphasizing the security they had as believers. They could be sure that God had chosen them in Christ. The world around them may reject them, but God would not! The Father, Son, and Holy Spirit, were all at work to secure their salvation (1:2). In 1:3-5, Peter reminds them of several choice blessings they have received from God. They have been born again to a living hope (v.3); a hope that cannot die. This hope - a great expectation of future blessing that even now has already begun - is secured by the resurrection of Jesus from the dead. This future holds the hope of heaven, the hope of seeing Jesus, the hope of eternal reward, and the hope of a heavenly home. Christians have also been born into an inheritance that can never be destroyed (v.4). For God who gave birth to them - has planned that they will receive their promised inheritance. It will never spoil or be corrupted in any way. It can never tarnish, rot, wither, or waste away. It is beyond the reach of change or decay (cp. Matthew 6:19-21). Best of all, this inheritance is reserved by God in heaven for them. God placed it in His own safekeeping (v.4). Nothing can touch it, and nothing can overcome their certain hope of receiving it.

No suffering or persecution can rob them of their salvation. As Paul said:

"Who shall separate us from the love of Christ? Shall trouble or hardship or persecution or famine or nakedness or danger or sword? As it is written:

"For your sake we face death all day long;
we are considered as sheep to be slaughtered."

No, in all these things we are more than conquerors through him who loved us." Romans 8:35-37 NIV

Through their faith, given and preserved by God, they are protected by His power; safe until that salvation is fully revealed at the end of time when Jesus comes again (v.5). Some of these believers may have been anxious - as we are - that their faith would fail. What if they faced actual physical abuse or even death? What if they were thrown in prison? Would their faith stand the test? The Bible teaches that there is no need for us to fear this will happen. God, who has given us our faith, has promised to preserve it, and to ensure our perseverance. Our faith is an inseparable part of our salvation — the provision of the covenant promise God has made to us in His Son. Peter says we are "guarded" or "protected" by God's power. The word he uses for "guarded" is the same word Paul uses in Philippians 4:7 when he says, "God's peace will guard your hearts and minds in Christ Jesus." It is a military word used of a garrison. God has set a protective garrison around us that guards us against the loss of our salvation in any way - and from every enemy. Our inheritance has been secured for us, and we have been secured for our inheritance. It is ours, in the last time, when Jesus comes for us (v.5). Nothing can prevent our receiving what God Himself has promised. By means of God's great mercy, everything bequeathed and granted to us in Christ - is secure and certain. God has given all believers to Christ, as the reward for the travail of His soul - and nothing can take them from Him (see John 6:39; 10:27-30).

Peter understood God's Arithmetic; and he wanted these believers to understand it too. He wanted them to see their trials as purifying tests that would strengthen their faith - not weaken it. He hoped to show them that their persecution could focus their minds on the certainties of their faith — and not on the tension in their lives. With this in view, Peter now reminds them of the color of joy they maintain, and the reasons this joy will sustain them during their time of testing and mistreatment:

"6 In all this you greatly rejoice, though now for a little while you may have had to suffer grief in all kinds of trials. 7 These have come so that the proven genuineness of your faith — of greater worth than gold, which perishes even though refined by fire — may result in praise, glory and honor when Jesus Christ is revealed. 8 Though you have not seen him, you love him; and even though you do not see him now, you believe in him and are filled with an inexpressible and glorious joy, 9 for you are receiving the end result of your faith, the salvation of your souls." 1 Peter 1:6-9 NIV

In v.6, Peter affirms the great daily joy they take in their salvation. A joy that remains undiminished despite any grief or distress they are suffering. When he says their grief is only for a little while or a short time, he is speaking comparatively. Any suffering on earth, short or long, is short in comparison with eternity. No matter what griefs we experience here, they are only really for *"a little while."* Peter, who has a Pastor's heart, understands that Christians undergo all kinds of trials. The word he uses for *"all kinds"*, is a word that means "many colored." Our trials take many forms.

They vary in intensity, type, and kind. Each one of us as a Christian, is on a unique spiritual journey. Our faithful Lord permits for each of us, only those trials that He knows will work the special blessing that we personally need. Nevertheless, there is something we all have in common when it comes to any type of persecution that we may face for our faith. We can all face it with joy, because of the great inheritance that lies ahead, and the security of a relationship with Christ from which nothing can separate us.

As if that were not enough — we have additional reasons to face our trials with joy. They are found in v.7:

"These have come so that the proven genuineness of your faith — of greater worth than gold, which perishes even though refined by fire — may result in praise, glory and honor when Jesus Christ is revealed."

These "many colored" trials would produce two results. First, they would demonstrate the genuineness of the believers' faith. Peter likens this to the process of heating gold to a high temperature to rid it of any impurities. That is what James said, when he spoke of *"the testing of our faith."* Another way to say this, is that when you place gold in the fire, that which is pure gold will be shown to be so. It is proved to be pure by the fire that has tested and refined it. In the same way, when our faith is put through suffering, it is proved to be authentic and genuine. How does this help us? Well, God not only desires to strengthen our faith, but He wants *us* to be certain and fully assured that it is genuine. In order for God to do this for us, He must allow us to suffer. If life were easy, our faith would have no opportunity to grow. We would have no assurance that it was the real thing; or that God was able to sustain and keep us, when we go through trials. It is because God loves us, that He sets life before us as an antagonist to overcome. When we come through a trial and are still trusting the Lord, we see that our faith is like refined gold. It is pure and genuine. Our faith, our love, and our confidence in the Lord, grows stronger. We learn through experience that *"God is our refuge and strength, an ever-present help in trouble."* (Psalm 46:1 NIV). Peter also reminds us that our faith is far more precious and valuable than gold. Even gold can be ruined by fire — but our faith will only grow and be strengthened through our 'fiery trials'.

I love that Peter says that we greatly rejoice in this. That is God's Arithmetic. The world does not advise us to take joy in severe trials. We are told that nothing good can come from them. Even many Christian preachers today, falsely teach that God only wants us to be happy and prosperous. Such teaching can be very dangerous for believers, because when a fiery trial comes, we may be tempted to doubt God's involvement or care. This can hinder us from realizing and experiencing the blessing that God has imbedded into our painful circumstance. We may also be misled into thinking that since we are suffering, our faith must be weak, or that we must have sinned in some way. Jesus was clear that 'in this world, we will face troubles, trials, and sorrows' (John 16:33). If we expect otherwise, we will be greatly disappointed. Expecting too much out of this life, will rob us of our joy. Instead, if we expect little from this world, but remain grateful for every small benefit, and live in the light of the life to come, then this life can steal nothing of our joy (see also Colossians 3:1-4). Furthermore, our prayer lives are also affected by such teaching. Oftentimes, our first prayer is that God would remove our suffering, because we suppose that it does us only harm. We never stop to think how God may be using our problems to our benefit. If we did, we might learn to pray differently. The way we intercede in prayer for ourselves and others, would be transformed. Instead of asking the Lord to remove the trial and suffering — we should ask Him *to bless the suffering to us* — to cause it to effect the good in our lives that He desires to bring about. We should ask Him not to take us from the trial — but to take us safely through it, and to help us find the attitude that will allow Him to further His work in our lives - and maximize our joy. This kind of praying would sound strange to many of us. Our tendency is to think that the best thing for someone - is that God would immediately stop their pain. We might even think such prayer as I'm suggesting, to be unsympathetic or uncaring toward the person who is suffering. Nothing could be further from the truth. To see this, all we have to do is imagine ourselves with Jesus in the garden of Gethsemane. "Father, if you are willing, please take this cup of suffering away from me. Yet I want your will to be done, not mine." (Luke 22:42 NLT). If the cup of suffering is removed prematurely - who knows what damage would be done, or what opportunity for growth and blessing would be forever lost. Yes, we should always surely work and pray for the relief of human suffering; but we must always do so with the deepest conviction that God's will be done. We must trust our Father's wisdom - and more than that, we must learn to rely unflinchingly upon His love. For; "We know that in all things God works for the good of those who love him, who have been called according to his purpose." (Romans 8:28 NIV). So Peter declares, "in our grief under many trials, we greatly rejoice." We rejoice because these tests prove the character of our faith. If our faith were self manufactured, it would surely fail. It would never stand the test. But because our faith originates from God, and is sustained by Him, we recognize its divine origin, and we are assured that it will last. Do you remember what Jesus said when he interpreted the parable of the sower? Matthew 13:20-21 NIV:

"The seed on the rocky soil represents those who hear the message and immediately receive it with joy. But since they don't have deep roots, they don't last long. They fall away as

soon as they have problems or are persecuted for believing God's word."

So our trials strengthen our faith, and they reveal its genuineness. Every time we go through a trial, we see the nature of our faith — what it's really made of. Our trials become a joy to us, because we see what they produce. We saw in James that their gift to us is maturity and endurance. Peter tells us that their gift is a growing assurance of faith in the power and salvation of God. Peter, by the way, also knew this from personal experience. On one occasion, in Acts chapter 5, the apostles are dragged before the Jewish High Council - the Sanhedrin. This is at least the second time that this occurred (see Acts 4:1-22; 5:12-42). No less than the 'Jewish High Priest', demanded that the apostles cease their teaching and preaching in the name of Jesus. Peter and all the apostles, answered him:

"We must obey God rather than human beings! The God of our ancestors raised Jesus from the dead — whom you killed by hanging him on a cross. God exalted him to his own right hand as Prince and Savior that he might bring Israel to repentance and forgive their sins. We are witnesses of these things, and so is the Holy Spirit, whom God has given to those who obey him." Acts 5:29-32 NIV

The Council was enraged at this and wanted to kill them (5:33). Ultimately, they had them all brutally flogged, and ordered them not to speak anymore in the name of Jesus (5:40). We might expect the apostles to leave from there, with heads hanging in disgrace, while being totally discouraged about what had just happened. Instead, we read:

"The apostles left the Sanhedrin, *rejoicing* because they had been counted worthy of suffering disgrace for the Name. Day after day, in the temple courts and from house to house, they never stopped teaching and proclaiming the good news that Jesus is the Messiah." Acts 5:41-42 NIV (italics mine).

So here were Peter and the other apostles; beaten, bleeding, and humiliated - but rejoicing. Rejoicing! Imagine that. Abused for Jesus' sake — yet full of joy! Honored — that God gave them the privilege of suffering for His name. The result was that the gospel flourished, and the number of disciples in Jerusalem multiplied greatly. What could the Council do? Nothing. For even if they brought them in again, the apostles would be strengthened even more. The apostles knew, from the Holy Spirit, that what they had was real. As a result, their persecution made them even bolder than they had been before. We see then, that Peter knew from his own experience — the value of rejoicing in all kinds of trials.

In a sense, our trials actually protect us — and God uses them to keep us safe. They strengthen us, and they keep us from drifting away from the faith. I have been a Christian now for nearly four decades. My life has had its share of challenges and heartaches. Yet I can say with joy — that the Word of God is sure. As a result of my experience with God, through every circumstance of the years, I am more certain of my salvation now, than when I first believed. Has it been easy? No. But I have learned the truth of Hebrews 12:11 NIV:

"No discipline seems pleasant at the time, but painful. Later on, however, it produces a harvest of righteousness and peace for those who have been trained by it."

The dross is being consumed, and my faith is being refined; I am learning that even through painful experiences — I can live with an attitude of joy.

The first result of our many colored trials, is to demonstrate the genuineness of our faith. The second result (v.7), is that they will result in praise, glory, and honor, when

213

Jesus Christ returns. Peter doesn't say who would receive the praise, glory, and honor. This praise may well be what God will give to us as believers. Thus we are the recipients; and God is the one that bestows on His faithful people - all the honor heaven can afford. Or, it could be the praise, glory, and honor, that flows from us to God - as a result of our faithfulness as His people. While I think the context favors the former — the two are certainly bound together. This is because God Himself is also glorified when He honors His people for remaining faithful. When Jesus is revealed to the world at His return, it will be a time of great praise, glory, and honor, for those who have believed. The persecution they endured, has never put their salvation in doubt. The faith they demonstrated under suffering - will shine in the full robed beauty of its proven genuineness - when Jesus comes to fulfill all His promises. God's "well done" - will be the praise to all His faithful servants. The glory and honor of eternal life will ravish His children - who will forever share in His joy.

What more could Peter possibly add to all of this? Is there yet a further blessing to foster our joy? V.8:

"Though you have not seen him, you love him; and even though you do not see him now, you believe in him and are filled with an inexpressible and glorious joy."

The believers to whom Peter writes, were trusting in Jesus in the midst of persecution. Though they had not physically seen Him, their trust showed that they loved Him. They didn't see Him now — but one day they would. Yet, even now, they knew Jesus as a living person; not just someone they had heard or read about. There comes to us 'a joy' in our daily fellowship with Jesus. A joy that the world cannot give or take away. We walk with Jesus, and we love Him. Because we love Him, we experience an inexpressible and glorious joy, even in our suffering. This is not what we would expect. In the world's arithmetic, we would expect suffering to produce self pity, despondency, hopelessness, and despair. In God's Arithmetic, we possess an inexpressible joy. Our joy is inexpressible because we can't put it into words. It isn't found in normal human consciousness. It's a joy of a different kind; spiritual, heavenly, humanly impossible, and transcending all expected human experience. It's a glorious joy; infused with the radiance that belongs to God's character and essential nature. It is the joy of Jesus; energized and endowed with a divine glory. Why can believers sing songs of joy when they are persecuted? Peter has already told us that we rejoice because our salvation is so great - in comparison to what we now suffer for a little while. Here, he goes beyond even that! We have inexpressible joy even under persecution, because we love Jesus. There is nothing in this world that motivates us, fulfills us, satisfies us, and inspires us - like the love of Jesus. We love Him because He first loved us. A personal relationship with Jesus - one where He loves us and we love Him - is totally life transforming. Through our love for Him, we find the power to endure, and a joy that a sense of duty and obligation alone could never provide.

In 1975, I went on a mission trip to Israel for 6 weeks. At the time, I had only known Jesus for just over a year. I grew up in a Jewish home and community. As a child, I was schooled in the Hebrew language, as well as Jewish customs and traditions. I was familiar with the stories of the Bible and the history of ancient Israel; and I have always loved the Jewish people. Here was an opportunity for me to share my new found faith with the people God has used to give so much to the world. Jesus had brought a rebirth of meaning and purpose to my life, and made it possible for me to have a personal relationship with God; something I had earnestly longed for, but was never able to find — despite the rich heritage my parents had provided me. Now, on this trip to

Israel, I would be able to have a part in sharing with other Jewish people - the joy I found through Jesus Christ. Our missionary group consisted of about 12 people — made up of both Jewish believers in Christ and non-Jewish believers. We traveled throughout the entire country, and shared the gospel wherever and whenever we could. On one occasion, we were in the city of Gaza by the sea. Our group stationed itself on a busy street corner, and was attempting to witness for Christ to all who passed by. We spoke with every person who would listen - about what Jesus had done for us — and we distributed gospel literature in both the Hebrew and Arabic languages. Someone must have taken offense to what we were doing, because we soon found ourselves approached by some local police officers. We were taken to a small building not far away, and placed behind bars in a large jail cell. Now you might think we would be terrified at this point — not knowing what would happen to us. But let me tell you — every one of us was completely filled with joy. Speaking for myself, I may have been naive - too young and inexperienced to understand all the possible consequences that might have occurred — but the Spirit's joy was unmistakable. As it turned out, we were set free after about an hour or so. Nevertheless, I have never forgotten the joy we all experienced that day, and on similar occasions during our travels. I am convinced that we had this joy - simply because we loved Jesus. The honor we felt while we were locked up in that cell, could not have come from any sense of duty or obligation. It was love for Jesus alone, born of His Spirit, that accounts for what we experienced on that day. Do you remember the story of Paul and Silas in the city of Philippi? As a result of preaching the gospel, they were mobbed, beaten with rods, thrown in jail, and put into the inner prison with their feet secured in stocks. Then we read:

"About midnight Paul and Silas were praying and singing hymns to God, and the other prisoners were listening to them." Acts 16:25 NIV

How could Paul and Silas sing hymns of praise while they were imprisoned in stocks? What could possibly motivate a response like that, under these most terrible conditions? They loved Jesus. They trusted in Him. They knew how much Jesus loved them, and thus they were filled with a glorious and inexpressible joy. I noted earlier how our joy and praise allow God to work out His purposes - in and through us - in the most wonderful ways. Look at the result here. The apostles are set free by an earthquake! The doors were opened; everyone's chains came loose; and the jailer was spared suicide - because God made sure that none of the prisoners sought to escape. The jailer and his whole household believed in the Lord — and the Kingdom of God was advanced. What if Paul and Silas had not chosen the color of joy? What if instead, they had allowed their unjust treatment to make them bitter and resentful? Would any of those other events have happened? I do not believe so. It is through our joy - born of love for Jesus - that God works in the moment to magnify His grace through our lives — as He did with Paul and Silas. A close personal daily walk with Jesus — and a heart filled with love for Him — secures for us the highest readiness for the inexpressible joy that is our spiritual birthright in Christ — even when we experience those many colored trials.

Peter wraps up this section of his letter in v.9, by giving us one more reason we can face our trials with joy. He says that we possess this joy, because we are receiving the end result of our faith — the salvation of our souls. Peter says that even now, we are receiving the salvation of our souls. In what way can we say that we are receiving salvation now? Well, for one thing, we are being delivered from the sin that so easily entangles us, to a life vibrant with faith, love, and hope. To take in all that Peter is saying, we must remember that salvation has three tenses. We *have been* saved — we *are being* saved — and we *will be* saved. *We were saved* when we first trusted in Jesus, and received Him as our Lord and Savior. *We are being saved now,* as we are made more like Jesus – with our lives being progressively set apart to God. The Holy Spirit is empowering us, and we are no longer under the dominion of sin. *We will be saved* when Jesus Christ returns, and we receive the resurrection body that God has promised us. Thus, our salvation continues to be received now, and we will receive its final consummation in the future. We possess it now — yet it is still to come. We are presently enjoying Christ's ongoing blessings in our lives. Salvation is God's work in us - from its beginning to its end (see Philippians 1:6). Our faith does have an end result (or goal), but we can speak of having received that goal in our lives even now; because when Jesus saved us - He saved us forever. Although we individually experience God's salvation over segments of time, it was granted to us by Him, as an already completed whole. God does not save us piecemeal. We are saved once, for all time, by the death and resurrection of Jesus Christ (see Hebrews 7:25, 9:26-28, 10:10-18). Once we receive salvation, it is bestowed by God in all its entirety. We are already fully saved — even though God is working it out in our experience now, and we have yet to come into its ultimate fulfillment. That is why Paul can say:

"And those he predestined, he also called; those he called, he also justified; those he justified, he also glorified." Romans 8:30 NIV

There is really only one salvation. It is already ours in full possession. We take joy because we are experiencing it now, and we will soon be endowed with all its fulness. To assure us of this, the Holy Spirit dwells in us as a fore-taste of future glory. All His wonderful ministries to us, are part of our present salvation. We are empowered to live holy lives, and to overcome our tendency to sin. We enjoy those Christ-like traits of character that are the fruit of following Jesus (Galatians 5:22-23). We have God living in us to teach us, to guide us, and to equip us to live out His purposes for our lives. Here especially in 1 Peter; we have the Spirit to comfort us when we are persecuted for our faith in Jesus. All the rich spiritual blessing that God gives to us now — is our source of joy — even under fiery trial. The Spirit reminds us that through it all — we possess the salvation of our souls. Even under threat of death, we know our souls are safe. The body may die for now, but remember that in Biblical thought, we don't just *have* a soul — we *are* a soul. Jesus died to save us — body, mind, and spirit — all we are as a person. This is why the resurrection of the body is so important (see 1 Cor-inthians 15:35-58; Philippians 3:20-21). When He warned the disciples of persecution, Jesus said, *". . . not a hair of your head will perish! By standing firm, you will win your souls."* (See Luke 21:12-19 NLT). By saying this, Jesus did not mean that they would never die for their faith. What He told them is, that in the end, their bodies will be raised from the dead; and nothing of all they are as a person will ever truly be lost.

All Peter has told us; serves to remind us that joy is not limited by our circumstances. Our joy is connected with our salvation. Since even suffering under persecution is a blessing to our faith — we have reason for a 'supernatural joy'. No one who lives without Christ, can pull that color out of God's coloring box. Peter's words also fix our hope on the final consummation of salvation when Christ returns. This too is a source for our joy. It is not uncommon for us to endure a great many hardships if we have something to look forward to. Most of us know someone who has undergone a surgical procedure to restore their good health. For example, I know friends who have had knee replacement or hip replacement surgery. Although they needed lengthy and painful physical therapy — they were eager to do it because of the comfortable pain-free walking that would result from their efforts. In my own life; I worked hard for many years so that I could enjoy the benefits of retirement. I persevered through difficult times, so that I would have a permanent income and health benefits. I was strengthened to endure, because I had something to look forward to. Even Jesus experienced this. He is both our example and our source of strength:

"And let us run with endurance the race God has set before us. We do this by keeping our eyes on Jesus, the champion who initiates and perfects our faith. <u>Because of the joy awaiting him</u>, he endured the cross, disregarding its shame. Now he is seated in the place of honor beside God's throne. Think of all the hostility he endured from sinful people; then you won't become weary and give up. After all, you have not yet given your lives in your struggle against sin." Hebrews 12:1b-4 (NLT) (underline mine)

Later in his letter, Peter picks up this same theme of following Christ's example as we face hostility for our faith:

"For God called you to do good, even if it means suffering, just as Christ suffered for you. He is your example, and you must follow in his steps.

He never sinned, nor ever deceived anyone.
He did not retaliate when he was insulted,
nor threaten revenge when he suffered.
He left his case in the hands of God,

who always judges fairly.
He personally carried our sins
in his body on the cross
so that we can be dead to sin
and live for what is right.
By his wounds you are healed.
Once you were like sheep
who wandered away.
But now you have turned to your Shepherd,
the Guardian of your souls." 1 Peter 2:21-25 NLT

Then once more, Peter encourages us to rejoice under trial, as we think of Christ's example, and anticipate His future glory. When we suffer for Jesus' name, we find joy in God's abundant blessing:

"Dear friends, do not be surprised at the fiery ordeal that has come on you to test you, as though something strange were happening to you. But rejoice inasmuch as you partici-pate in the sufferings of Christ, so that you may be overjoyed when his glory is revealed. If you are insulted because of the name of Christ, you are blessed, for the Spirit of glory and of God rests on you." 1 Peter 4:12-14 NIV

As we conclude our look at Peter's insights, let's recap what he said. What are the reasons that joy will sustain us when our faith is tested and we are mistreated?

- Our hope is so great - compared to what we suffer now for "a little while."

- We have an eternal inheritance from God - that can never perish, spoil, or fade.

- We enjoy the security of a relationship with Christ from which nothing can separate us.

- Our trials actually serve to refine our faith, prove it's character, and assure us it is genuine.

- Our tried and proven faith - which God values so highly - will result in praise, glory, and honor for us, when Jesus Christ returns.

- Jesus loves us, and we love Him. We have His living presence with us — and we value our fellowship and communion with Him, each and every day. This relationship fills us with an inexpressible and glorious joy.

- Even while undergoing persecution — we are now receiving and experiencing all the spiritual blessings of our salvation. The certain hope of our final redemption - springs up into a fountain of joy - that we may drink from today.

The 'Surprising Color of Joy' is our journey to understand that every spiritual blessing we discover in our trials, will powerfully reinforce the spirit of joy that can permeate our lives. We have listened to James and Peter as they encouraged us with several reasons we can cultivate a life of joy while under affliction. Now, let's listen to Paul, as he adds to our awareness of why we should rejoice when we run into problems and trials.

Unlike Peter, Paul did not write his letter to the church in Rome due to any specific persecution they were undergoing. Paul was in Corinth at the end of his third missionary journey, about A.D. 56 or 57. He was preparing to travel to Jerusalem to deliver an offering to the poor and persecuted Jewish Christians in the region. After that, he intended to visit Rome to minister to the church there. He hoped that he could encourage their faith, and that they in turn would be an encouragement to his faith (see Romans 1:11-12). Ultimately, Paul was looking toward a missionary journey to Spain. He hoped that the believers in Rome would partner with him by supporting that challenging undertaking (see Romans 15:22-33). Paul had never visited the church in Rome, nor was he the one who founded it. So the Holy Spirit directed him to write to these believers before he went to see them. Through his letter to the Romans, Paul set forth at length - the gospel that he believed and preached. He also set forth some facts about himself that might answer any questions they had about him.

When we pick up the portion of Romans relevant to our discussion — Paul has already established that salvation comes through faith in Christ, and not by works. In chapter 5, Paul begins to consider the benefits of the life of faith. The chapter breaks down into three parts. The first part, verses 1-5, is where we want to focus our attention. Peace, hope, and love from God, are benefits that we presently possess. Every day, we can count on these blessings of God's grace. We have not been left alone to live by our own power. God's sustaining grace is given to help us stand strong now - and on that future day when Christ returns. In these verses, Paul is going to remind us that Christians in every age endure trouble. Our troubles do not mean that we need to live defeated lives. We can rejoice in God, because our afflictions actually begin a process of character building that produces even more hope in our lives. Essentially, this is the same message we have heard from Peter and James. So now, let us begin our exploration of Romans 5:1-5 NIV:

"1 Therefore, since we have been justified through faith, we have peace with God through our Lord Jesus Christ, 2 through whom we have gained access by faith into this

grace in which we now stand. And we boast in the hope of the glory of God. 3 Not only so, but we also glory in our sufferings, because we know that suffering produces perseverance; 4 perseverance, character; and character, hope. 5 And hope does not put us to shame, because God's love has been poured out into our hearts through the Holy Spirit, who has been given to us."

Paul picks up right where he leaves off at the end of chapter 4. He starts by proclaiming God's peace that comes by faith in Christ - as a major benefit of salvation (v.1). Since God has put us into a right relationship with Him through our faith in the Lord Jesus Christ, we have peace with Him. When we are made right with God (i.e. justified), it opens the way for a great flow of blessing to us. These blessings strengthen our sense of security in this new relationship. The first of these ongoing blessings is peace. The peace Paul speaks of, is not the feeling or sense of peace that God gives us to calm our minds and hearts when we are troubled. This peace has to do with being justified - or made right - with God. It means that through Christ, we no longer face divine wrath because of our sins. We have no fear of standing before God in the final judgment. Another way to express this — is that our peace through Christ refers to the complete restoration of a loving relationship with our Heavenly Father. Due to the sin in our lives, no relationship with God was possible. Through faith in Christ's atoning sacrifice, we are restored to a place of favor and fellowship with our Creator. Once again, *God's* purpose for our lives *becomes our purpose.* We have obtained a new position before God as His children, and it is a position of peace. This peace — our new standing and fellowship with God — enables us as believers to rejoice in the midst of the problems of daily living, and in the hope of a secure future.

Our peace comes through faith in the Lord Jesus Christ. Through Him, we have been permanently placed into this position of grace in which we stand (v.2). Paul says we have gained *access* into this grace. This word "access" was used to refer to the way a normal citizen could approach a king, or someone of importance. Say you wanted to have a chat with the President of the United States. You couldn't just walk into the oval office. Either the President himself would have to call you in — or someone who had immediate access to him would have to introduce you. Otherwise, you would have no access to him at all. Jesus Christ has given us complete access to God's grace. That is — we can boldly enter His presence, and enjoy the salvation He offers. We have entered into the realm of God's grace — and that is now our home. The tense of the word for *"gained access"*, means that we were restored to a right relationship with God when we first trusted in Jesus — and we remain permanently and securely in that position. This reminds me of the words of assurance spoken to us in the book of Hebrews. Here we have a beautiful picture of this access into grace:

For our high priest is able to understand our weaknesses. He was tempted in every way that we are, but he did not sin. Let us, then, feel very sure that we can come before God's throne where there is grace. There we can receive mercy and grace to help us when we need it." Hebrews 4:15-16 NCV

As if to cement this confidence of the grace we enjoy — Paul says that we stand in it (v.2). Here we have another word in the perfect tense that assures us that our peace - and God's presence in our lives - is abiding, protected, and sure. This is just like our protected inheritance that Peter spoke of. Everything has been made right between us and God, through Jesus Christ. We now have full access into all the rich blessings that our relationship to God brings our way.

Because of our favored position, we boast in the hope of the glory of God (v.2). It may sound a bit strange that Paul states that we as Christians can boast about anything. However, that isn't the case if we take a moment to look at what he means by this word for 'boast'. The NIV translates this word as "boast." The Holman Christian Standard Bible renders it as "rejoice." The NAS version has "exult." We do indeed 'boast' in these rich blessings — but not in a prideful bragging kind of way. In context, the word has the sense of rejoice and exult. It carries the idea of having a lively and triumphant joy. It is to rejoice exceedingly; especially due to the triumph and victory that was won by the Lord Jesus Christ. His victory has become our victory. We have great cause for celebration. The closest I can get to fittingly describing this kind of spiritual rejoicing or exulting, is to use an example of what happens when we are in church, and we hear the Word of God proclaimed. Have you ever listened to a preacher who has declared the truths of the gospel so beautifully, that you just wanted to cheer and shout out loud? In fact some people do, when they shout "Hallelujah" (or "Amen") so loudly that everyone can hear it. It is a celebration in our spirit of the triumph of Christ, and of our assurance that we personally partake in His victory. That is what the word "boast" means here. This is joy at the highest level. It is a rejoicing that expresses our confidence of being justified - at peace with God - possessing a place and standing forever in the fulness of God's grace. Specifically, Paul says that we boast (rejoice) in *"the hope of the glory of God."* This refers to the hope we have of sharing God's glory. It means that we are looking forward to our final standing before God in heaven - when we will be made like Christ. In our resurrection body - as the living temple of God - we will live without sin, and we will shine forth His glory forever. This is our living hope (as Peter put it). Such hope, in the biblical sense, has a very distinct meaning. It does not mean mere wishful thinking - as is commonly used in everyday conversation; as in, "I hope it doesn't rain today." 'Christian hope' has no element of uncertainty or doubt. It is a divine assurance that what God has promised — He is able also to perform. It is our confident expectation, or future certainty, that what God has declared - is already a 'fait accompli'. This ongoing hope of the glory of God, and our rejoicing in it, has a very practical application for us as well.

It is here that we come to the heart of how God's grace helps us 'when we are up against it'. Like Peter and James, Paul is going to tell us why we can rejoice in our sufferings and troubles. I love the way he introduces us to these blessings. He says, *"not only so.."* (v.3). Not only have we been justified by faith; not only do we have peace with God; not only has Jesus introduced us into a permanent state of grace in which we stand; not only do we *rejoice* in the hope of sharing in God's glory; but we also glory in our sufferings (v.3 NIV). The word Paul uses for "glory" (in our sufferings), is the very same word we just looked at in v.2 (where it was translated as) - boast, exult, or *rejoice*. There, he said, we rejoice in the hope of the glory of God. Here in v.3, we rejoice in our sufferings. In the same way that we 'rejoice in the triumph of Christ' as we eagerly anticipate our future blessings; we are to also rejoice in our present suffering. Before we look at why in God's Arithmetic 'we can take joy in our sufferings' — there are two ideas I must clarify.

First; is the meaning of the word used here for 'sufferings'. The Greek word is *thlipsis*. It means 'pressure'. My college Greek professor, Dr. J. Niles Puckett (who is now at home with the Lord), had a mantra he would recite when describing the meaning of this word. He would say it means, "pressure, stress, tribulation, distress." It is the word Jesus uses in John 16:33 (NIV) where He says:

"I have told you these things, so that in me you may have peace. In this world you will have *trouble*. But take heart! I have overcome the world." (italics mine)

In this verse from John, the word "trouble" is used to describe the various pressures and stresses that living in this world brings. It is alternately translated as "suffering", "trials and sorrows", "difficulties", and "afflictions." This word certainly has undertones of the persecution we suffer because of our faith in Christ, as we saw in Peter's writing. Here in Romans however, Paul was not writing to a church that was currently under any direct persecution that we know of. Paul is referring to a broad range of problems to which Christians particularly may be subjected. It may involve persecution; for even today it is not uncommon to be reproached, harassed, and mistreated for professing faith in Christ. Yet none of us as Christians are strangers to trial, suffering, and pressure. I think that for Paul, any type of problem in the Christian life, can lead to a positive process of spiritual growth. We're going to see that any of these pressures may produce something for us — which in turn contributes to our ability to take joy in the midst of them.

The second idea I want to make clear - is another aspect of the word for "rejoice." I don't wish to be overly grammatical here, but there is a nuance that we must address. In both v.2 and v.3, Bible translators have to decide whether Paul is making a statement - "we are rejoicing" - or if he is giving us an exhortation - "let us rejoice" (for you grammar types — the first is a present indicative; the second a subjunctive middle). Most translators and commentators seem to favor the indicative, "we are also rejoicing in our sufferings." However, I tend toward the subjunctive — especially in v.3. I don't believe that we automatically rejoice in our sufferings. I have been contending from James and Peter, that 'taking joy under trial' - is a spiritual attitude (or color) we may learn and experience with divine help. So even if this is an indicative statement here, it's clear that there is an element of exhortation as well. Paul is encouraging us to choose to take joy under pressure — not simply declaring that joy is ours, just because we face problems. He had learned to take joy in his afflictions - and we can also. He is now about to give us the reasons why we may have joy in our trials. So even if he is saying, "we are rejoicing" (in our sufferings) — what he means, is that we have reason to glory in them - if only we stop to consider how they are benefiting us.

Paul starts by saying that we can have a triumphant joy under affliction, *"because we know that suffering produces perseverance"* (v.3). When he says *"we know"*, he isn't saying that we simply have a 'head knowledge' of what life's pressures produce. He means that when we live out our hard experiences with faith, we learn the meaning of perseverance, and we grow spiritually by what we go through. The life of the Spirit within us - is actually producing change; it's causing us to mature in our understanding of how He is continually at work in our lives. This is a very important truth - and is central to what the apostles are trying to communicate. In the world's arithmetic, no one would expect life's problems to have a very positive result in our lives. Our suffering appears to be a totally negative matter — and certainly not a cause for us to rejoice! In God's Arithmetic, it is crucial to understand that He is working out something wonderful in our experience, in the midst of what appear to be totally negative circumstances. This is important to every Christian, because when we understand it, God can bring about the highest spiritual outcome for the trials that He permits to come into our lives.

Our exulting begins by learning that suffering produces *perseverance*. Not surprisingly, this is the very same word that James used in James 1:3; where he says that the testing of our faith produces perseverance (please refer to my earlier explanation of the Greek word *hupomone'*). By way of reminder, this word means more than just to persevere or endure through a situation. It is a triumphant fortitude - an unswerving constancy that develops through experience. Hupomone' allows us to march through life - and take hold of each difficulty - using it as a step forward in learning to trust in God. It infuses into our character - 'new strength'. A kind of 'spiritual muscle building' that enables us to face each new circumstance better spiritually prepared for the next one. It is a quality that looks trial in the face — and makes it a stepping stone to victory.

This growth process continues as our developing fortitude in turn produces character (v.4). Alternate translations express this better as "proven character" (HCSB) or "strength of character" (NLT). What is this character that our fortitude produces — and in what way is it proven or strengthened? Generally speaking, character refers to the moral qualities, ethical standards, and principles, that together distinguish a persons nature — 'what they are like inside that leads them to act as they do'. In context, we are speaking of the development of Christian character, as opposed to the character that all people develop. Everyone is having their character formed, as they live through the pressures of life. How we respond to those pressures, determines the kind of character that is produced. As believers, when we go through hardships with a steady faith and trust in God, there is a spiritual transformation that is taking place. Qualities and traits are forming in our renewed nature, which distinguish us as belonging to God in Christ. We are learning to live morally, ethically, and with a spiritual integrity that is based on the Word of God and the example of Christ. This is the kind of character - that a faith-driven fortitude produces in believers - in contrast to everyone else. As Christians, there is a standard and model for character, that God is using to shape our lives — and that standard is Christ.

Now in what way does this character develop? Our fortitude grows while our faith passes successfully through each trial. Thus our spiritual integrity is "proven" or "strengthened." The image here is of a valuable metal that is being purified by fire (much as Peter described the genuineness of our faith being refined by fire). As God works through each trial to brace us for the next one — our spiritual mettle is being established and fixed in place. Our ability to walk with God, and to live like Christ, is becoming increasingly steadfast and immovable. God is making us into Christians whom he can count on; people who will be reliable and trustworthy in all He directs them to do. Certainly this does not happen all at once. 'Proven character' is a life long process that comes only through experience. We see in every trial - how God meets us in our pain and suffering. By faith, we are helped to see it through tough times by trusting in God - and our fortitude grows. As our fortitude grows, we see our Christian character gradually established and fixed in our nature. So it is, that through our sufferings, we find reason to exult and rejoice. God is teaching us that Jesus has overcome the world. Our afflictions can not ultimately hurt us. They can only move us further along the path of our experience in God's grace. As we grow older and more assured in our walk with the Lord, these truths become etched into our minds and hearts. Our capacity to take joy in suffering is increased, and we praise God for everything. His love is greater than all our sin. Even our failures become monuments to His power to work out our salvation. Truly, we have reason to rejoice!

It is worthy of mention again here, that learning to exult in God during times of suffering - is not automatic. The problems we face as Christians, in a world pervaded by sin, can make us bitter and resentful. Sometimes we choose to blame God for everything, and we get angry with Him. We may be disappointed that things did not turn out the way we had hoped or prayed for. Our dreams are shattered, and our life hurts - but God just doesn't seem to care. Our faith is weakened, and we become discouraged, despondent, and lose hope. If you are at such a place in your life, allow me to encourage you. God has not left you, nor has He let you down. Dare to trust Him. Take Him at His word. For he has said:

*""I will never fail you. I will never abandon you." So we can say with confidence, "The L*ORD *is my helper, so I will have no fear. What can mere people do to me?"" Hebrews 13:5-6 NLT*

It was during the darkest days of my life (during a divorce) that I felt most strongly - the pull of Christ's right hand. I did not want a divorce and yet I could not stop it. Thus, there was pain and many tears. But God brought me safely through it all - with my faith intact. Just when I thought I would never again experience a happy day — Jesus made my heart sing for joy once more. I took hold of this promise:

"The Spirit of the Sovereign LORD is on me,
because the LORD has anointed me
to proclaim good news to the poor.
He has sent me to bind up the brokenhearted,
to proclaim freedom for the captives
and release from darkness for the prisoners,
to proclaim the year of the LORD's favor
and the day of vengeance of our God,
to comfort all who mourn,
and provide for those who grieve in Zion —
to bestow on them a crown of beauty
instead of ashes,
the oil of joy
instead of mourning,
and a garment of praise

instead of a spirit of despair.
They will be called oaks of righteousness,
a planting of the LORD
for the display of his splendor." Isaiah 61:1-3 NIV

It may not seem like it now, but Jesus can bind up your broken heart; turn your mourning to joy; and give you a heart full of praise - instead of a spirit of despair. Even though you now live in a prison of darkness — the Lord can set you free. From a place of weakness, we can be turned into oaks of righteousness. Remember, the trial of your faith is precious to God. When He has brought you through this trying time, your faith will endure and be strengthened. God will establish your character. Even your pain will be blessed to you, and give you reason for joy. Listen again to Peter:

"And the God of all grace, who called you to his eternal glory in Christ, after you have suffered a little while, will himself restore you and make you strong, firm and steadfast." 1 Peter 5:10 NIV

So far, we have seen that we can rejoice in our sufferings, because we know that suffering produces perseverance (fortitude), and perseverance produces proven character. Paul completes his thought by telling us that proven character in turn - produces hope. In v.2, he told us that we rejoice in the hope of the glory of God. The reason we rejoice in hope, is because God has given us His Word of promise. We possess a confident assurance, a future certainty, that we will receive (and in fact have already received!) all that God has reserved for us in Christ. Paul began with hope - then told us what God is working out in our lives through suffering - and he returns to hope. Only now, our hope is even stronger than before. For even as the trial of our faith - proves it to be genuine - and increases our assurance of the relationship and confidence we have in God — so also our hope grows in the same way. Through every trial, we see how God is at work in our hearts - and how faithful He is. We learn from experience how God supplies all our needs in Christ Jesus, and how He is sufficient for every situation. We are growing in grace, and in the knowledge of Jesus. As we make our way down life's road, we can look back and see all that God has brought us through, and how He provided along the way. As we head forward, we are better equipped for what lies ahead, and we are confident that God can bring us safely through. This is hope in the 'present' sense. We are more deeply assured that no matter what circumstance we might face - there is no need to doubt God's faithfulness to us, or the sure expectation that He is working out His good purposes in our lives. This is the hope that 'proven character' produces. A hope that allowed Paul to face every situation with contentment, as he expressed by saying:

"For I can do everything through Christ, who gives me strength." Philippians 4:13 NLT

Paul is a great example for us of how this hope is put on display, even when facing the most perilous situations. Despite all he suffered for the sake of Christ — hope gave him courage as he boldly faced each new crisis. In 2 Corinthians 11:22-28, there is a catalog of the many painful cruelties Paul endured in his ministry. When we read about his imprisonments, beatings, floggings, and hardships, it is enough to make us cringe. We would expect that someone who has been through this kind of pain - would want to avoid further persecution at all costs. Instead, Paul's 'hope in Christ' never allowed this to be his first consideration. For example, after Paul's missionary journeys, he traveled to Jerusalem to deliver the large monetary offering gathered from many of the gentile churches. On the way, he and his party stopped for a time in Caesarea, and stayed at the home of Philip the evangelist. We pick up the narrative at Acts 21:10-14 NIV:

"After we had been there a number of days, a prophet named Agabus came down from Judea. Coming over to us, he took Paul's belt, tied his own hands and feet with it and said, "The Holy Spirit says, 'In this way the Jewish leaders in Jerusalem will bind the owner of this belt and will hand him over to the Gentiles.'"

When we heard this, we and the people there pleaded with Paul not to go up to Jerusalem. Then Paul answered, "Why are you weeping and breaking my heart? I am ready not only to be bound, but also to die in Jerusalem for the name of the Lord Jesus." When he would not be dissuaded, we gave up and said, "The Lord's will be done.""

Jesus had sustained Paul through every conceivable situation. When faced with the prospect of imminent death, his hope propelled him forward, despite even the pleading of his friends that he avoid the danger. It was not long after this, that Paul arrived in Jerusalem. While he was there, he was attacked by a mob, and was being brutally beaten when Roman soldiers arrived and rescued him. The violence and threats of the mob were so severe, that Paul had to be carried by the soldiers down the temple steps to get to the military barracks (Acts 21:35). At this point, we might expect that Paul is happy to escape the mob. Instead, he asks the commander of the soldiers for permission to address them! (Acts 21:37-39). At even greater peril to himself, Paul then spoke boldly about Christ - to those who were seeking his life. His hope once again gave him courage, because he knew from experience that God was working out His purpose for him, even in this volatile situation. Some two years later, we find Paul a prisoner on a cargo ship heading for Rome. While at sea, the ship was caught in a severe storm. It was being badly battered by the winds, and for many days all those on board could not see the sun or the stars. There were 276 people on this ship, and they all finally gave up any hope of being saved. . . All except one, that is. We pick up the story at Acts 27:21-26 NIV:

"After they had gone a long time without food, Paul stood up before them and said: "Men, you should have taken my advice not to sail from Crete; then you would have spared yourselves this damage and loss. But now I urge you to keep up your courage, because not one of you will be lost; only the ship will be destroyed. Last night an angel of the God to whom I belong and whom I serve stood beside me and said, 'Do not be afraid, Paul. You must stand trial before Caesar; and God has graciously given you the lives of all who sail with you.' So keep up your courage, men, for I have faith in God that it will happen just as he told me. Nevertheless, we must run aground on some island.""

A short time later, Paul addresses everyone again (Acts 27:33-36 NIV):

"Just before dawn Paul urged them all to eat. "For the last fourteen days," he said, "you have been in constant suspense and have gone without food — you haven't eaten anything. Now I urge you to take some food. You need it to survive. Not one of you will lose a single hair from his head." After he said this, he took some bread and gave thanks to God in front of them all. Then he broke it and began to eat. They were all encouraged and ate some food themselves."

How could Paul display such hope in these perilous situations? It is because he had learned that no matter what circumstance he faced — there was no need to doubt God's faithfulness to him. Paul carried the expectation that the Lord was continually working out His good purposes in his life. This is the hope that 'proven character' produces. It is because God had infused this hope into Paul's spirit - that he could declare to us that *"we also glory in our sufferings, because we know that suffering produces perseverance; perseverance, character; and character, hope."*

So far, we have seen from Romans 5, that we are justified by faith, and we have peace with God. We stand in grace, and we rejoice in our sufferings - which produce fortitude, strength of character, and hope. We rejoice in our hope for a promised glory. But what if, after all our trials, our hope should lead us to disappointment or shame? Paul makes it clear in v.5 - that this hope will never disappoint us:

"This hope does not disappoint, because God's love has been poured out in our hearts through the Holy Spirit who was given to us." HCSB

Because our hope is grounded in God's character and His covenant engagements — we need never doubt His faithfulness. Our hope is like an anchor for our souls:

"God also bound himself with an oath, so that those who received the promise could be perfectly sure that he would never change his mind. So God has given both his promise and his oath. These two things are unchangeable because it is impossible for God to lie. Therefore, we who have fled to him for refuge can have great confidence as we hold to the hope that lies before us. This hope is a strong and trustworthy anchor for our souls. It leads us through the curtain into God's inner sanctuary. Jesus has already gone in there for us. He has become our eternal High Priest in the order of Melchizedek." Hebrews 6:17-20 NLT

The grounds for our rejoicing can never be shaken. No matter what we have to face in life — our hope can never be defeated. We need never fear that our hope will ever put us to shame (the literal meaning of disappoint). Paul used this same word in Romans 1:16 NIV:

"For I am not ashamed of the gospel, because it is the power of God that brings salvation to everyone who believes: first to the Jew, then to the Gentile."

Paul means here, that the gospel is dependable. It can never disappoint us or let us down. So it is - with our hope. Because our hope is so sure and certain, it becomes a powerful motivational force in our lives. No matter what our affliction; hope draws back the curtain of our pain, and provides the certainty that God is still with us. Hope urges us to look beyond the surface of our circumstances, and to realize the all seeing eye of God is ever watching over His own. As Christians, we experience a reality - the people of the world cannot. Apart from Christ, the world lives without hope (Ephesians 2:12). What hope they do have - is a deception. When the godless die, all their expectation comes to nothing (Proverbs 11:7). We all know people who have placed their hope in the wrong things. Many people hope in wealth - but wealth cannot save them. Some look for answers in other people, but they too will disappoint. Some seek fame to achieve immortality, while others try to find it in their careers or their legacy; they think all is well, because they left the world a better place. Today, there are those who believe that fate, or the universe, will somehow make everything turn out alright. Saddest of all, are those who place their hope in *religion*. Religion cannot save — no matter how dedicated or sincere a person's beliefs might be. Only Jesus Christ can give true hope:

"Salvation is found in no one else, for there is no other name under heaven given to mankind by which we must be saved."
Acts 4:12 NIV

The hope He imparts - will never disappoint us or let us down. We will never be put to shame - because our hope is sure; built on the foundation of the apostles and prophets with Jesus Christ Himself being the chief cornerstone. We turn now again - to the surprising color of joy. We want it to fill our lives, yet we constantly struggle to find it. How can we acquire it? How do we choose 'joy' when the pressures of life are weighing us down so heavily? The answer lies in God's love (v.5). The 'certainty of hope' finds its expression in our experience of God's love. His love abides in our lives, because God Himself dwells in us. There are times when our suffering seems to have no present value. Sometimes we don't see any good come from it, until we look back later in our lives. There are even situations when life here on earth comes to an end, and we still don't see any benefit from certain pains we had to endure. For example, why does God allow our loved ones to linger for so long, while suffering from a painful disease? Why does He allow those with Alzheimer's or other debilitating illnesses to remain on earth so long - in a condition that makes no sense to us? It is during those times — that we must hold fast to God's love. We rest in His Word that declares, "love never fails" (1 Corinthians 13:8). Like Paul, we become certain that nothing can separate us from the love of Christ:

"Who shall separate us from the love of Christ? Shall trouble or hardship or persecution or famine or nakedness or danger or sword? As it is written:

"For your sake we face death all day long;
we are considered as sheep to be slaughtered."

No, in all these things we are more than conquerors through him who loved us. For I am convinced that neither death nor life, neither angels nor demons, neither the present nor the future, nor any powers, neither height nor depth, nor anything else in all creation, will be able to separate us from the love of God that is in Christ Jesus our Lord." Romans 8:35-39 NIV

Even when we don't understand our suffering, we experience the love of Christ in a very real way. Paul states this in v.5 as cited above; *"God's love has been poured out in our hearts through the Holy Spirit who was given to us."* We were touched by His love at our conversion, and that love remains with us, all the days of our lives. God lives in us through the Holy Spirit. His love is not just words on a page or a promise in a book. His love is a present overflowing experience in our lives. It is lavished on us as His children (see Ephesians 1:7-8; 1 John 3:1). Paul says His love has been poured out in our hearts. This metaphor of God's love 'completely poured out on us', carries the idea of abundant and continual spiritual refreshment. In Jesus' words, the Spirit becomes in us, "rivers of living water":

"Anyone who is thirsty may come to me! Anyone who believes in me may come and drink! For the Scriptures declare, 'Rivers of living water will flow from his heart.'" *(When he said "living water," he was speaking of the Spirit, who would be given to everyone believing in him. . .)"* John 7:37-39 NLT

The Holy Spirit continually communicates God's love to our hearts. He takes the vast riches of Jesus, and all the wonderful gifts of God's love and salvation, and makes them known to us (John 16:14; 1 Corinthians 2:12). In fact, the

Holy Spirit is Himself the guarantee of God's love, and His promise of all that is to come:

"When you believed, you were marked in him with a seal, the promised Holy Spirit, who is a deposit guaranteeing our inheritance until the redemption of those who are God's possession — to the praise of his glory." Ephesians 1:13-14 NIV

"Now it is God who makes both us and you stand firm in Christ. He anointed us, set his seal of ownership on us, and put his Spirit in our hearts as a deposit, guaranteeing what is to come." 2 Corinthians 1:21-22 NIV

The Greek word Paul uses to describe the Holy Spirit in both of these passages is *arrabon*. The Holy Spirit is the *arrabon* of our promised inheritance. When I bought my car, the dealer required a portion of the total purchase price up front. This earnest money - or down payment - was given in advance, as a pledge of what was to follow. It indicated my promise or commitment that the full obligation I had undertaken - would eventually be paid. Now in my case, I may have the best intentions of fulfilling this commitment — I always do my best to satisfy my obligations. However, circumstances may arise which hinder me from completing what I promised to do. With God, there are no such limitations. When He gives His word and makes a promise, there is no possible doubt of its fulfillment. A sure word from God - is the most certain reality in all existence. We have received the promise of eternal life (John 3:16). The Holy Spirit is God's pledge to us - that He will fulfill His promise. The Spirit is the down payment - the first installment of all that is to follow. When the Spirit takes up residence in us, He becomes God's guarantee that we will receive all that He has promised us; everything encompassed by our bodily resurrection and future glory. If we don't have the Holy Spirit, we are not Christians (Romans 8:9). Because He lives in us, we are God's temple, His dwelling place (1 Corinthians 6:19). As He lives in our hearts, He testifies to us that we are God's children:

"So you have not received a spirit that makes you fearful slaves. Instead, you received God's Spirit when he adopted you as his own children. Now we call him, "Abba, Father." For his Spirit joins with our spirit to affirm that we are God's children. And since we are his children, we are his heirs. In fact, together with Christ we are heirs of God's glory. But if we are to share his glory, we must also share his suffering." Romans 8:15-17 NLT

So it is - that our hope will never disappoint us. God's love has been poured into our hearts through the Holy Spirit who resides within us. He is God's guarantee of our inheritance, and of our adoption as His children. Every day, we are aware of His presence, and we experience the continual refreshment of His overflowing love. This is how we choose joy when life's pressures weigh us down so heavily. The pressure may weigh us down — but God's love in our hearts lifts us up!

We have listened to James, Peter, and Paul. They have each told us how we can rejoice in our sufferings - if we will only consider the ways that our trials benefit us. We have learned to understand how, in God's Arithmetic, life's problems have come to bring a very positive benefit to our lives. God is working out something wonderful in our experience - in the midst of what appear to be totally negative circumstances. James says, *"Consider it pure joy, my brothers and sisters, whenever you face trials of many kinds."* Peter says, *"In all this you greatly rejoice, though now for a little while you may have had to suffer grief in all kinds of trials. . . you believe in Him and are filled with an inexpressible and glo-*

rious joy." Paul says, *".. we confidently and joyfully look forward to sharing God's glory. We can also rejoice, when we run into problems and trials."*

Choose the surprising color of joy. There is never a reason for the Christian to give in to hopelessness or despair. Give all your worries and cares to God, for He cares about you (1 Peter 5:7 NLT). We must not allow the enemy to deceive us. He will do anything to rob us of our joy. But Jesus has saved us, and it is He who will have the final word. We conclude with this word of encouragement from the wise and tender heart of Peter (1 Peter 5:8-11 NLT):

"Stay alert! Watch out for your great enemy, the devil. He prowls around like a roaring lion, looking for someone to devour. Stand firm against him, and be strong in your faith. Remember that your Christian brothers and sisters all over the world are going through the same kind of suffering you are.

In his kindness God called you to share in his eternal glory by means of Christ Jesus. So after you have suffered a little while, he will restore, support, and strengthen you, and he will place you on a firm foundation. All power to him forever! Amen."

"He sat by a fire of seven-fold heat,
As He watched by the precious ore,
And closer He bent with a searching gaze
As He heated it more and more.
He knew He had ore that could stand the test,
And He wanted the finest gold
To mold as a crown for the King to wear,
Set with gems with a pride untold.
So He laid our gold in the burning fire,
Tho' we fain would have said Him 'Nay',
And He watched the dross that we had not seen,

And it melted and passed away.
And the gold grew brighter and yet more bright,
But our eyes were so dim with tears,
We saw but the fire — not the Master's hand,
And questioned with anxious fears.
Yet our gold shown out with a richer glow,
As it mirrored a Form above,
That bent o'er the fire, tho' unseen by us,
With a look of ineffable love.
Can we think that it pleases His loving heart
To cause us a moment's pain?
Ah, no! but He saw through the present cross
The bliss of eternal gain.
So He waited there with a watchful eye,
With a love that is strong and sure,
And His gold did not suffer a bit more heat,
Than was needed to make it pure." (Author unknown)

One For Good Measure

It's a bright clear December day, as you leave your car and walk toward the grocery store. With the ringing of the Salvation Army bell still sounding in your ears, you pick up your cart and enter the store. As you walk the aisles selecting your groceries, you start thinking about the spirit of the season. The lights, the decorations, and the music of Christmas, have caused you to think about the whole spirit of giving. As a Christian, you start to wonder if the same spirit of generous goodwill you are feeling now, could possibly carry over throughout the entire year. While you wait in line to pay for your groceries, you notice that a woman standing two people in front of you is having difficulty. The card she has used at the register to pay for her large cart of groceries is not working. You overhear the cashier telling her that her card has been declined. The woman starts to cry, and it becomes one of those awkward moments in life when no one knows quite what to do. Suddenly, the man in front of you says to the cashier that he would like pay for the woman's groceries. After he does so, the woman thanks him profusely, and he wishes her a merry Christmas as she leaves the store with a smile on her face and joy in her heart. The cashier says to the man, "That was really nice of you." The man replies, "Well, it's good Karma." An elderly gentleman who has been bagging everyone's groceries, asks the man, "What do you mean it's good Karma?" The man replies, "You know, what goes around comes around, the golden rule and all that. I'm just being a good person and creating good vibes for myself. It always seems to come back to me." As you listen to this, you can't help but admire the man's generosity, but it makes you think. . . You say to yourself, "That was indeed a very 'Christian' act, but the man made no mention of God. I wonder whether or not what he said is Biblical? It sure sounds like it." Various Bible verses play through your mind, as you ponder the man's words. "Do not be deceived: God cannot be mocked. A man reaps what he sows." (Galatians 6:7) "Remember this: Whoever sows sparingly will also reap sparingly, and whoever sows generously will also reap generously." (2 Corinthians 10:6) "Give, and it will be given to you. A good measure, pressed down, shaken together and running over, will be poured into your lap. For with the measure you use, it will be measured to you." (Luke 6:38) And of course, the golden rule in Luke 6:31, "Do to others as you would have them do to you." You finish paying for your groceries, and head out into the parking lot to load your car.

Walking down the parking aisle, you run into the man who paid for the woman's groceries. It occurs to you that this might be an opportunity to talk about Christ with the man, so you stop and ask him about what just happened. "That was pretty cool what you did in there.", you say to him. "Do you believe in God?" "Not really.", the man says. "But I do believe in Karma." "Exactly what do you mean by Karma?", you reply. "Hmm.", the man says. "Well, Karma is what happens when I do good deeds. It's a kind of force in the universe that brings me luck and good fortune when I'm generous to others. The good things I do for others have a way of coming back to me." Curious about this, you ask him, "Is the opposite also true? If you do bad things to others, will bad things happen to you?" "Yes", he replies, "It always seems to work like that. If I do harm to others, then somewhere down the line, I can expect a harmful result. But if I try and do good, it will return to me somehow." "You see,", he continues, "I'm creating a kind of 'cache' in positive energy. The more I take advantage of my opportunities to do good, the more of them I will have. This way, I keep attracting good Karma to myself." By now, your mental wheels are really turning — so you ask him, "Well, what does it mean then, when your circumstances are difficult? Does it mean that you did something bad to deserve it?" "No.", he replies, "Sometimes it just means that people made poor choices. Or it may mean that I have to take a positive attitude toward my problems. That way everything will improve. It's kind of a 'mental Karma'. If I learn what life has to teach me through my hardships, I won't have to go through something even worse to learn my lesson. "So..", you reply, "You also believe in the power of positive thinking?" "Pretty much.", he says. "When I have positive thoughts, it encourages me to have a positive attitude. Then I feel good throughout the day, and it helps prepare me to do good things for others, which in turn brings me positive rewards. It's simple really. My positive thoughts initiate positive actions, which bring on positive Karma. It surrounds me with a kind of positive energy that brings good things into my life." "Well, what do you do about your sin?", you ask. "When you make poor moral choices, don't you feel guilty or troubled?" "I don't believe in sin.", he says. "I don't think there's a God who will judge me. Besides, even if there were, a 'just' God would know that I tried really hard, and I did more good things than bad. So even God would reward me - just to keep things in balance. Who knows, maybe I'll even get rewarded in my next life." "Like in reincarnation.", you say. "Yes.", he replies. "Well, its been nice talking with you." And with that, the man gets into his car and heads off.

On your way home, you start really thinking about what the man said. He was actually a decent sort, and generous at that; but he was not a Christian, and was way out in left field in his thinking. You ponder on his philosophy, which in one form or another, seems to be quite popular these days in western culture. Then you think about the Bible, and the truths you've been taught; which are distinctly and unmistakably different from what you just heard. You start rehearsing those truths in your mind: Christians serve the Living God - the one revealed in the Bible alone. He isn't Karma, or an impersonal force that balances cosmic accounts, but He is the great *I am* — the one and only true God who created the universe, and is guiding history toward His own purpose. He is a God who loves us individually and personally, and who made us living souls created in His image. He is the Holy God, who hates sin, declares all human righteousness to be as filthy rags, and who will one day call every person before Him to give account of themselves at the final judgment. He is the God and Father of our Lord Jesus Christ - who gave His only Son to die on the cross as a sacrifice for our sins. And He is the God who has promised to one day raise the dead; some to eternal death, and some to everlasting life, according to their faith in Jesus.

These thoughts of our loving God cause you to feel very sorry for this man, since you know from the Bible that not all the Karma, good deeds, or positive energy in the whole world, can save his soul from the wrath to come. Nevertheless, there is something still bothering you. Seeing his kind actions in the grocery store, and hearing his words, has left you a little confused. Some of what he said sounded very Biblical; so questions start to form in your mind. When he spoke of Karma, and how it ties into the golden rule and the law of sowing and reaping — isn't that the same as what the Bible teaches? Should the follower of Christ strive to be generous because we tap into an impersonal force that brings a generous return? Is there a difference between Christian generosity and the generosity that ungodly people demonstrate? If Karma isn't actually a Bible concept, then what is the *Christian* idea of giving really all about? If I'm a disciple of Jesus Christ, then what should my motive for giving be — if not to get something in return? In other words, why does God say I should be a generous person? Should I even ask the question, "What's in it for me?"

This chapter isn't about Karma. Karma itself, as perceived by Hinduism, Buddhism, Sikhism, and Jainism, is a complicated study that is not part of our Biblical theme. While Karma is distinctly unchristian, its form in western culture has led to ideas that have taken root in our society. These ideas have helped us to generate a conversation about the meaning of Christian generosity. In our discussion, I hope to answer those questions just raised, and also to consider these: Why should a Christian strive to live with an open hand and an open heart to others? Is generosity of any benefit to us? What does the spirit of generous giving look like in our lives? In order to discover these answers, we will first look at the gospel of Luke, to see what Jesus teaches about generosity. Then, from Paul's second letter to the Corinthians, we will look at what the apostle teaches the Church about generous giving, and why it is important. Finally, we will look at select passages from the Old Testament, to show how God's grace underlies His Law, and how the Bible is in harmony from start to finish, in its teaching about the meaning of Christian giving.

We begin our discussion in Luke chapter 6, where we find several of Jesus' well known sayings about giving. Along with the golden rule, one of the most popular of these sayings is Luke 6:38 NIV:

"Give, and it will be given to you. A good measure, pressed down, shaken together and running over, will be poured into

your lap. For with the measure you use, it will be measured to you."

While this verse makes sense to us if we take it at face value; its meaning comes into a much sharper and surprising focus when it's framed in its proper context. Most Christians have heard this verse used to encourage generosity; but few if any could tell you what Jesus was talking about when He said it. To arrive at the kernel of meaning for this catchy aphorism, we must review all of Luke chapter 6. There we will find the emphasis Jesus placed on the needs of people, as He shares with us the proper way to understand God's law. Building from His focus on human need, Jesus will highlight God's love for everyone, as He teaches His disciples how they are to behave in the world. To set the stage for the sermon Jesus preaches in chapter 6, we must look briefly at some emphases from chapter 5. Luke's gospel sets before us the consistent claim that Jesus is the Son of God. As we come to chapter 5, we find Jesus forgiving sins on His own authority (v.20,24), and befriending people who were considered disreputable sinners (vv.27-32). Although He was severely criticized by the religious authorities, Jesus was actually revealing God's heart of love, and His offer of forgiveness toward everyone who was willing to receive it. In a parable about new wine and new wineskins (vv.36-39), Jesus pointedly told the fault-finding Pharisees that the joy and new life that He was bringing, could not be contained by the rules and ritualistic religion of the old Jewish legalism. Something greater than Moses and the prophets had come. The new life that He was offering, would involve the kind of love and acceptance of others that the Pharisees were not willing to receive. As chapter 6 opens, Luke follows up Jesus' admonition to the Pharisees about new wine and old wineskins, by relating two incidents that took place on Sabbath days (vv.1-11). On both of these occasions, the Pharisees criticize

Jesus and His disciples for their failure to observe certain Sabbath regulations. While *they* are unwilling to receive the 'new wine' of Jesus teachings, *He* declares Himself Lord of the Sabbath. By His healing power, He validates His claim to rightfully interpret the Law. Then, in two stunning questions put to the Pharisees and teachers of religious law, Jesus asks, "Does the law permit good deeds on the Sabbath, or is it a day for doing evil? Is this a day to save life, or to destroy it?" (Luke 6:9 NLT). The Pharisees were concerned with protecting their Sabbath traditions. Jesus was far more concerned with protecting people. Essentially, He declared that trying to do good by observing Sabbath rules - at the expense of people who are hurting - is to do evil, not good. He tries to help them see that the true meaning of the 'Sabbath law' was meant to help people. Traditional religious rules about the Sabbath - which harm people or leave them suffering - are evil — even when such rules were made in an attempt to safeguard God's law. So, when the Pharisees ask Jesus, "Does the law permit a person to work by healing on the Sabbath?" (Matthew 12:10 NLT); Jesus refutes their duplicity, and makes the law's meaning plain:

And he answered, "If you had a sheep that fell into a well on the Sabbath, wouldn't you work to pull it out? Of course you would. And how much more valuable is a person than a sheep! Yes, the law permits a person to do good on the Sabbath." Matthew 12:11-12 NLT

The events just described, portray Jesus as the Son of God - the Lord of the Sabbath, and the one who can authoritatively interpret scripture. They serve as a compelling introduction to what is commonly known as His Sermon on the Plain. Jesus is about to teach His disciples how to live as children of God; in contrast to those who reject Him and persecute them. Before this discourse begins, Luke briefly mentions two other events that also prepare us to receive Jesus' teachings in the sermon that follows. First is Jesus naming His twelve apostles — thereby showing His authority to guide our lives and choose our calling (Luke 6:12-16). The fact that He chose twelve, may highlight that He was establishing a new Israel. As Moses led twelve tribes — Jesus would lead twelve apostles. Perhaps this is also indicative of the new wine He had just spoken of, in 5:36-39. The second event is in Luke 6:17-19. There, Jesus has attracted a large crowd of His disciples and a great number of people from Judea, Jerusalem, and the coastal regions of Tyre and Sidon. Luke tells us:

"They had come to hear him and to be healed of their diseases; and those troubled by evil spirits were healed. Everyone tried to touch him, because healing power went out from him, and he healed everyone." Luke 6:18-19 NLT

It is important to understand that Jesus' healing ministry emphasizes His authority to lay out for us - the character of a life that is blessed by God. To help us get ready to grasp the full meaning of Luke 6:38, we must now take hold of the message of Jesus' sermon — a message that culminates with a call to build our lives on the foundation of listening to His words and putting them into practice. Jesus is about to teach us that as His followers, the way we demonstrate our relationship with God - is through our interaction with other people.

The entire text of Jesus' sermon is found in Luke 6:20-49. In vv.20-26, Jesus begins His message with a series of contrasts. He pronounces four blessings on those who follow Him, and four woes (sorrows, troubles, warnings to anticipate heartache) on those who oppose Him - and persecute His disciples. The 'blessings and the woes' oppose and correspond to each other. Thus we have:

The poor (v.20) versus the rich (v.24).

Those who hunger now (v.21a) versus those who are now well fed (v.25a).

Those who weep now (v.21b) versus those who laugh now (v.25b).

Those who are persecuted now (v.22) versus those who everyone praises now (v.26).

The "poor" (as spoken of here in v.20), carries a more spiritual sense than an economic significance (cp. Matthew 5:3); although the sacrifices involved in following Jesus - can result in economic poverty. It is clear that Jesus is not blessing poverty itself, nor any particular social class (as if the Kingdom of God belonged only to poor people). Yet those who are 'materially poor' must understand that their poverty is not a hindrance to entering the Kingdom of God. Biblically speaking — the poor are those righteous people who live in complete dependence on God. In terms of material wealth, they may have little - or they may have much. But they realize spiritually - that they can do nothing on their own (John 15:5), and only God can provide meaning in life and satisfy their deepest needs (John 6:35). If a person is poor materially, they can find God's blessing in the sense that their poverty has led them to discover their total dependence on God. Anyone, rich or poor, who will fully trust God's provision of grace in Jesus Christ alone, will find that the Kingdom of God belongs to them.

Following Jesus can also result in hunger or weeping. While this hunger and weeping may be literal; it may also refer to spiritual hunger and sorrowful weeping over sin (one's own sins or the sins of others). Either way, Jesus said that God's hungry people would be fully satisfied, and those who weep would one day laugh. Ultimately, under God's reign, His children would know complete satisfaction and joy.

All who live godly lives in Christ can expect to suffer persecution (2 Timothy 3:12). Jesus' followers are blessed when they are hated, excluded by others, insulted, and slandered as evil for His sake (6:22). When this happens, we can literally leap for joy, because there is a great eternal reward awaiting us in heaven, and even God's prophets were treated that way.

In contrast to those who wholeheartedly follow Christ, are those who oppose Him and His followers. Jesus speaks of those 'rich people' who find meaning only in material possessions. Apart from God, comfort in this life is all they can ever expect (6:24), and they have no anticipation of future blessing. There are those who are now well fed - who by rejecting Christ, will come to a state of emptiness, and find nothing to bring them satisfaction. There are those who laugh now - scorning their need for God, and rejoicing in their self sufficiency. These people have nothing to look forward to but the realization of the emptiness and futility of what they based their lives on, and supposed that life was all about. Mourning and weeping will ultimately be their lot (see Luke 16:19-31 for a good example of this). Finally, there are those who enjoy the approval of society now (v.26). They have lived only for the approval of others - and not for the approval of God. Their falsehood and appeal to that which ingratiatingly pleases others, will lead them only to the destruction that was the lot of all the false prophets of the past.

Having established a context of blessing for His disciples - and woes for those who reject and oppose Him - Jesus now gives His followers God's guidelines for behavior toward those who would so cruelly persecute them:

"27 But to you who are listening I say: Love your enemies, do good to those who hate you, 28 bless those who curse you, pray for those who mistreat you. 29 If someone slaps

you on one cheek, turn to them the other also. If someone takes your coat, do not withhold your shirt from them. 30 Give to everyone who asks you, and if anyone takes what belongs to you, do not demand it back. 31 Do to others as you would have them do to you." Luke 6:27-31 NIV

To those who are ready to fully follow Him - even though mistreated for their faith - Jesus says that although you are being treated this way — you are not to retaliate. God has a higher standard for you. By nature, we love those who love us, and we hate those who hate us. By grace, we can love those who hate us (v.27). We cannot for a moment suppose that this is a matter of feeling. We might not hold loving feelings for those who do evil toward us. Jesus is speaking of God's kind of love. A love that chooses by a decisive commitment of faith — that we will act in a person's best interest, regardless of how they treat us. Such love is an act of the will. It is made possible for us by the power and Spirit of God at work in our lives - after we have come to saving faith in Christ. Jesus goes on to give us several practical examples of how this love will show itself in action (vv.27-28). We must - whenever possible - direct our energy toward doing what good we can for our enemy. This means that we will seek ways to promote their welfare and best interests. Though they may speak hurtful words to us — we will speak only words full of blessing and kindness to them; for our words have genuine power through the grace of God - to help and to heal. Though our enemy may mistreat us — we will pray for them; for God may grant them repentance that will lead them unto life. When we follow Jesus in this way, we break the cycle of hate, and we prevent the devil from gaining a foothold.

Now, beginning in v.29, Jesus gives us some concrete examples of what this love requires. By turning the other cheek and offering the shirt (inner garment) when our persecutor has taken the coat (outer garment) — the faithful disciple overcomes evil with good. Thus, what may appear from an outside perspective to be our loss, is - on a higher level - the active power of God's love permeating our situation. When someone asks for our goods or assets, even with intent to take advantage of us - or they take them from us outright - we are not to retaliate to get them back (v.30). For it is as we suffer loss graciously that we show God's love - by making it obvious that we value 'people' over 'things'. By showing that material things are not what matter most, we are also demonstrating that our trust is placed fully in God. This is not to say that we should just give everyone anything they ask. There are often times when love is best served by withholding rather than giving. This is also not a prohibition against the proper use of societal laws that protect ourselves and others; for the Bible exhorts us to work for social justice and the protection of the innocent and helpless. The underlying truth in Jesus' teaching, is His mandate for our attitude and motive as His disciples. We are not to retaliate against our persecutors; but rather to live out God's higher standard of love toward those who mistreat us. We are to cultivate the kind of character that does not allow a love for material things to keep us from giving to others. Our hearts should hold a charity that is always ready to do good to others, without requiring anything in return.

Jesus has been teaching us the ultimate meaning of God's law. In v.31, He now sums up what He has taught us, in a timeless statement that we have come to call the golden rule:

"Do to others as you would have them do to you."

The parallel verse in Matthew 7:12 adds:

"for this sums up the Law and the Prophets"

Most books I have studied on this matter — point out that this rule appears in negative forms in other ancient literature; e.g. "Do *not* do to others what you would *not* have them do to you." This is basically the principle or philosophy of reciprocity. If someone does something nice for you — do something nice for them. If they do something hurtful to you, return their act in kind — 'an eye for an eye' as it were. If you don't want a person to be mean to you — then don't be mean to them. Give everyone what their actions deserve. That is reciprocity, and it is exactly the *opposite* of what Jesus has been saying! Rather than giving others what they deserve — we are to give them what they do not deserve: Love, acceptance, forgiveness, and kindness. We are to behave this way, even when others do not. We are to treat our enemies as though they are our friends. So instead of stating this in a negative way, Jesus puts it positively: "*Do* to others what you would want them to *do* to you." God's Arithmetic isn't about refraining from doing hurtful things to others because you don't want them doing hurtful things to you. That is simple self preservation, and not a life of sharing God's love; a life that distinguishes us as followers of Christ. Instead, Jesus says to take the initiative in showing God's love. Don't wait for someone to show it to you. Take His love to them first, and continue to show it whether they return it or not. By doing so, we are acting as God acts, and we will know the blessedness that comes from giving His love away. We are learning to live with an open hand and an open heart. In vv.32-36, Jesus makes this clear:

"32 If you love those who love you, what credit is that to you? Even sinners love those who love them. 33 And if you do good to those who are good to you, what credit is that to you? Even sinners do that. 34 And if you lend to those from whom you expect repayment, what credit is that to you? Even sinners lend to sinners, expecting to be repaid in full.

35 But love your enemies, do good to them, and lend to them without expecting to get anything back. Then your reward will be great, and you will be children of the Most High, because he is kind to the ungrateful and wicked. 36 Be merciful, just as your Father is merciful."

When Jesus speaks of "sinners" here, He is referring to people who do not follow God's way. It's only human nature to 'love those who love us'. Most of us are like that, and we usually feel pretty good about it. We pat ourselves on the back, because we treat others as they deserve. We show love to those who show it to us; and we do good to people who do good to us. Sensible and wise, we loan to those who we know can pay us back; and we think, "What a good banker am I." Reciprocity — a judicious way to live! Surely God must be pleased, and we must be worthy of His special commendation. Well, not exactly. If you are a "sinner", sure; that's all that can be expected of you. However, if you want to follow Jesus, He expects us to move beyond that. We are called to move beyond justice, and into God's realm of mercy and grace. There is no special merit or commendation from God for acting like everyone else. The Kingdom standard in v.27, is repeated again here in v.35. It isn't that we 'shouldn't love those who love us'; but we must also 'love those who do not love us' — and in fact are actively hostile toward us. It isn't that we shouldn't do good to those who do good to us — but we must also do good to those who treat us quite the opposite. Even to those who are not kindly disposed toward us, and who cannot pay us back — we must offer to help and give - without expecting a return. Well that's crazy, you're thinking. Love others and not presume to get something back? Do you know what would happen if I lived by such a principle? People might take advantage of me! Imagine the loss I could suffer! That's true; but think of the gain (vv.35-36):

Then your reward will be great, and you will be children of the Most High, because he is kind to the ungrateful and wicked. Be merciful, just as your Father is merciful.

When we live and act as God does, we show ourselves to be His children. Our Heavenly Father is gracious to everyone, whether they deserve it or not. He is kind to those who have no gratitude for His benevolence — even to those who are wicked and sinful. I have heard people say that they wish that God would give everyone in this 'evil world' exactly what they deserve. It's a good thing that is not what happens; for if it were so, then none of us would escape God's wrath! As followers of Jesus, we are declaring ourselves publicly to be God's children. As such, we must conduct ourselves as our Father does, and share His character with everyone. If we live by the golden rule, and thereby suffer loss; isn't it worth it to know we are children of God and that we have His smile? If we have a good conscience and the joy that comes when we suffer for Jesus' sake — isn't that more than all this world can offer? (cp. 1 Peter 3:8-17) If we know that we have done what is right and pleasing in the sight of God — isn't that reward enough? Jesus says that when we act like the Most High, our reward will be very great. We will be recognized and approved as His children. This doesn't mean that we love our enemies for the sake of 'personal gain' or something we will 'immediately get out of it' from God. That is simply another kind of reciprocity; waiting for God to give us what we "deserve." What Jesus is teaching us - is that we are to walk in such a close relationship to God - that He loves others through us — without our totaling up the reward. We love others because He first loved us, and His approval is all we seek. If anyone is reading these words and this still doesn't make sense — remember that Jesus said that if we love in this way - our reward will be great. Leave the arithmetic to God. Our reward is not always seen just now.

To follow Christ - is to partake of eternal life in heaven; and although we don't deserve it — this is the reward God gives to all those who trust in Jesus, and who follow Him along the narrow way.

Just as our Father is compassionate and merciful to everyone - whether they deserve it or not - so we must act the same way, for we are His children (v.36). Moreover, although it is not specifically stated, it is most certainly implied that we must extend tender mercy to all; *because we ourselves have been the recipients of that mercy from God.* It is ungracious in the extreme - to expect God to show mercy to us - if we are unwilling to extend that mercy to others. In Christ, God has taken us into His family. As His children, it is 'our mission in this world' to take the message of the gospel, in word and deed, to the very ends of the earth (Matthew 28:18-20). Inherent in that mandate - is taking the *love* of God and Christ to a lost and dying world. Always be ready to do good — without asking for anything in return. Do to others as you would have them do to you. Take the initiative. Learn to live with an open hand and an open heart. Love your enemies. Love freely; without expecting anything in return. The reward of fellowship with Jesus is very great; and you will be called the children of the Most High.

The golden rule isn't just a demand on our lives. It is not merely words on a page that must be slavishly obeyed. It is a living thing; spiritual. As Jesus said:

"The words that I have spoken to you are spirit and are life."
John 6:63b HCSB

To live the golden rule - is not something superficial or religious that we strive for, in order to be a good person. It is part of our spiritual inheritance in the covenant of grace; written onto the tablet of our heart through Jesus Christ. The Holy Spirit is at work to weave the golden rule into the essence of who we are; part of the warp and woof of our being. It is not something we will feel compelled to do for fear of punishment, but rather the very beating of our heart - the very fiber of who we are. Therefore, while the golden rule will show itself in our actions - it originates in our heart. It is what animates and motivates us at the core of who we are in Christ; and it is part of the transformation that is ours as a new creation (2 Corinthians 5:17). So listen now as Jesus addresses the conduct that comes from the attitudes of our heart..

"Do not judge, and you will not be judged. Do not condemn, and you will not be condemned. Forgive, and you will be forgiven." **(6:37)**

As we attempt to demonstrate mercy and compassion to others, there are certain attitudes that hinder our efforts. Our efforts may be frustrated by our natural tendency to build ourselves up - by tearing others down. For instance; it's easy to find fault with others, and to criticize them. It makes us feel good to do so - as if that somehow made us better than they are. That is what is meant here by "judging." When we attempt to show our moral superiority by pointing out the shortcomings of others - whether in our own mind or spoken aloud - we hinder our own efforts to exercise God's love for that person. It is difficult to love our enemies - or anyone else for that matter - if we choose to dwell on their faults. Also, how are we to help someone, if in our hearts we continue to condemn a person and pass sentence on them as if we were God? How can we love those who do us harm — if we will not forgive them? Forgiveness sets us free to love. By cherishing the memory of our injuries with the hope of revenge, we prevent the flow of God's love through us toward another individual. It is only as we pardon them - setting them free in our heart from the sin that has wounded us - that we are free to love them. Not only so, *but we ourselves are set free;* free to heal from our pain; free from the bonds of resentment and bitterness; and free to love each individual as God desires. In addition, as we forgive others their sins, we are likely to experience the forgiveness of both God and others flowing back to us. It will flow from God, because our unwillingness to forgive is no longer acting in our lives to impede the free grace of His forgiveness in Christ; and it will flow from others, because as they experience God's love and forgiveness through us, they are set free from that terrible cycle of hate, revenge, and bitterness. As they see God's love in us, they may discover His grace - and choose to forgive our sins as well. This is what Jesus means when He says that we will not be judged or condemned - that we will be forgiven. Our hurtful attitudes no longer act as a barrier to what the Lord wants to work into our lives (see also Matt.6:9-15, 18:23-35). God's grace transforms us. We are made new in Christ. From the inside out, God is at work in our experience to make us into the kind of Kingdom citizens that Jesus sets before us - those who have tasted for themselves that the Lord is good; and having received the heavenly manna - are willing to share it with others - without the hindrance of a judgmental and unforgiving spirit.

We come now to Luke 6:38. We are now ready to see the fullness of what Jesus means, and the spiritual riches that God desires us to possess.

"Give, and it will be given to you. A good measure, pressed down, shaken together and running over, will be poured into your lap. For with the measure you use, it will be measured to you."

All too often, this saying of Jesus' has been taken as a promise of financial prosperity - based on our generosity toward others. The idea being put forth is that we are taught to 'give' in order that we might 'gain' from others. That thought is essentially a selfish one; almost an appeal to greed — and it takes us back again to the idea of reciprocity. 'Tit for tat' as it were. You give, and voila, you will get back; and the more you give, the more you will get back. If this were true, then everyone would want to be generous - because of what's in it for themselves!

This kind of false teaching is still popular today, but it originated years ago. There was a well known preacher who taught about "seed faith." His idea was that if by faith - you would generously give financially to support his ministry - then God would prosper you financially in return. This is essentially a form of manipulation, but he didn't say it that way. What he was claiming to his followers, is that by giving to his ministry, they were really giving to God. Since you can't 'out-give' God — He would give you more in return than you were giving to Him. Kind of like you were in a competition with the Lord, to see which of you could 'out-give' the other. You give the preacher your money — and God would keep giving money into your bank account. This interpretation of Jesus' words in v.38, is not at all in accord with the spirit of the passage. It is in fact - to misrepresent to Christians - what giving is all about. We will come to understand that God does indeed bless faithful giving. But nowhere in the Bible does God promise us material wealth in return for giving money to Christian causes — or any other causes for that matter. When we give, even to God, while calculating the dollar return on our investment - is to miss the point. What Jesus is actually teaching us in Luke 6:38, is an entirely new way of thinking. God does desire to bless and reward generosity; but it is our own unwillingness to be loving and merciful toward the undeserving - that obstructs the flow of His *spiritual riches* into our lives. Jesus is teaching us simply to give. To allow God to make us into the kind of person who freely loves others as He does - without thought of what we will receive in return; even to our enemies and to those who despitefully use and persecute us. Loving and giving, can take many forms. We can give financially to those in need, but that is not the only way. The needs of our fellow man can vary greatly. There are needs for food, clothing, and shelter to be sure; but there are many others as well. People are very complex; and the needs of no two people are alike. We can offer friendship to those who are lonely, and a human touch to those who feel unloved. We can offer time, talent, and labor to those who need help in their hour of need. We can provide opportunity to those who have made mistakes, and ongoing personal encouragement to those who have experienced failure. And if nothing else, we can always offer a kind word, a listening ear, and an understanding heart, to everyone we meet. As Jesus spoke of the righteous who would inherit the Father's kingdom, He said:

"For I was hungry and you gave me something to eat, I was thirsty and you gave me something to drink, I was a stranger and you invited me in, I needed clothes and you clothed me, I was sick and you looked after me, I was in prison and you came to visit me." Matthew 25:35-36 NIV

What is striking about this are Jesus' next words in vv.37-39:

"Then the righteous will answer him, 'Lord, when did we see you hungry and feed you, or thirsty and give you something to drink? When did we see you a stranger and invite you in, or needing clothes and clothe you? When did we see you sick or in prison and go to visit you?'"

Those blessed of God, didn't even realize that by giving to those who were overlooked and ignored - they had done this to Jesus. In other words, they *gave without trying to merit a reward.* They gave because it was their nature to do so. They loved Jesus, and they allowed God to make them like their Master. They were merciful because their Father is merciful; and they did to others as they would have others do to them.

While we know that a 'generous giving spirit and life-style' must be nurtured and cultivated without thought of reward — we must not think for a moment that *there is no reward.* That is the wonder of God's Arithmetic. For while we are not to give only for reward — God does reward generous giving. In Luke 6:38, Jesus does in fact emphasize the blessing God grants to those who are generous with others:

"Give, and it will be given to you. A good measure, pressed down, shaken together and running over, will be poured into your lap. For with the measure you use, it will be measured to you."

What does this mean? If it isn't a promise of financial prosperity, then what is being promised? What is the image that Jesus is conveying to us? I read a story that explained how a merchant would sell corn in Jerusalem, during the time of Jesus. The seller would place their legs around a large basket, and fill it part way. Then they would give the basket a good shake, so that the grain would settle and fill up all the excess space. The basket would then be filled to the top, and the shaking repeated. This process would include pressing the corn down firmly with both hands to ensure that the basket was fully packed as much as it could be. Then the seller would form a cone at the top with additional grain, and bore a hole in the center of it. As the mass of grain was carefully pressed and continued to settle, more and more would be placed in the hole, until absolutely nothing more could be added - or it would spill over. That is the good measure Jesus is talking about. It is a picture for us of something measured out and packed down, until it completely overflows. It is a 'fullness of blessing' with nothing missing - and then some. The concurrent idea of an overflow being poured in your lap, has to do with the outer robe that people wore at that time. It was a long loose robe that went down to the feet - with additional material that formed a belt about the waist. The robe could be pulled up through the belt - to form a kind of 'outside pocket' in which things could be carried. Today, we might describe this as having your pockets overflowing. Let's see now if we can put together what Jesus is saying. When we learn to give freely from the heart, we will find the blessing of God measured back to us from His riches - far in excess of what we gave, and of anything we might imagine. God in His grace will provide for our needs; He will add to our ability to give, in a way that will make it clear to us that 'generosity carries with it its own reward'. Remember what Paul said to the Philippians in response to their generous giving?

"I have received full payment and have more than enough. I am amply supplied, now that I have received from Epaphroditus the gifts you sent. They are a fragrant offering, an acceptable sacrifice, pleasing to God. *And my God will meet all your needs according to the riches of His glory in Christ Jesus.*" Philippians 4:18-19 NIV (italics mine)

God will bless and reward our generosity. In Second Corinthians chapter nine, Paul exhorts the Corinthian church to give generously toward the offering for the poor believers in Jerusalem. Look carefully at how God responds to generous giving, as Paul speaks to the church about the best way to give:

"Remember this: Whoever sows sparingly will also reap sparingly, and whoever sows generously will also reap generously. Each of you should give what you have decided in your heart to give, not reluctantly or under compulsion, for

God loves a cheerful giver. And God is able to bless you abundantly, so that in all things at all times, having all that you need, you will abound in every good work. As it is written:

"They have freely scattered their gifts to the poor; their righteousness endures forever."

Now he who supplies seed to the sower and bread for food will also supply and increase your store of seed and will enlarge the harvest of your righteousness. You will be enriched in every way so that you can be generous on every occasion, and through us your generosity will result in thanksgiving to God." 2 Corinthians 9:6-11 NIV

Paul wants God's people to understand that when they plant seeds of generosity, they will reap a harvest of God's grace. The reward for their generosity is an 'abundance of blessing' from God. As they give cheerfully from the heart, their capacity to give - and their resources to do so - will be enriched from God's own limitless store.

As Jesus said, *"For with the measure you use, it will be measured to you."* Or as the New Century Version puts it, *"The way you give to others - is the way God will give to you."* It isn't that God is stingy with His blessings; for He is generous to all, whether they deserve it or not. The idea is that by our unwillingness to be generous, we 'check the flow of blessing' that God in His grace desires for us to experience through our generosity. When we give to others with an open hand, God is free to give to us with an open hand; for we are then in a state of spiritual readiness to obtain and perceive His bounty. The 'overflowing riches of God's grace' are not given to us to be hoarded - but to be shared. The better we understand this, the more we are fit to be a channel for the rivers of living water that God desires to flow through our lives. It is only our own hardness of heart, and selfish parsimony, which keep His grace from enlarging our harvest of righteousness. There is plenteous provision on God's part; if only we will cease acting like a cistern - that only hoards and never gives - and start acting like a spring — whose very purpose is to share its abundance with everyone.

Before we leave Jesus' sermon on the plain, it's in our spiritual interest to briefly review the rest of His message; as it rounds out our understanding of the nature of discipleship. The section that remains, is generally divided into three segments. The first of Jesus' thoughts is found in Luke 6:39-42 NIV:

"39 He also told them this parable: "Can the blind lead the blind? Will they not both fall into a pit? 40 The student is not above the teacher, but everyone who is fully trained will be like their teacher.

41 Why do you look at the speck of sawdust in your brother's eye and pay no attention to the plank in your own eye? 42 How can you say to your brother, 'Brother, let me take the speck out of your eye,' when you yourself fail to see the plank in your own eye? You hypocrite, first take the plank out of your eye, and then you will see clearly to remove the speck from your brother's eye." "

This simple parable reminds us that it is not the job of the disciple to be critical and fault-finding of others. There are times however, when 'living for the glory of God' requires keen discernment on our part - especially when we are involved with 'speaking the truth in love' - into the lives of our brothers and sisters in Christ. For the disciple who would love others like Jesus did, it is very important to focus on our own faults first — before we can see clearly enough to offer God's guidance to another. If we are not willing to address our own spiritual blindness, how can we hope to be a guide to our fellow Christians? (Or to anyone else for that matter?) We will never be more mature than Jesus who is our teacher. If He was persecuted, we will be also. If He loved His enemies, then we can learn to love our enemies too. Yet only if we are willing to humble ourselves and learn from Him - will we able to channel His generous love through a life filled with mercy and forgiveness. Like our teacher, we can live by the golden rule, if we will follow His example and obey His training (v.40). Jesus goes on to tell us; if we as believers want to help other people with their problems, we must first get right with God, regarding our own personal sins. Jesus uses hyperbole, and perhaps a bit of humor, to make His point. If a person has a small matter in their life that needs to be addressed (which Jesus likens to a speck of dust in their eye) — how can we be ready to help them, while there are much greater faults in our own lives (which Jesus likens to a huge log in our eye). If we're not careful; it's too easy for us to avoid and excuse the prominent faults in our own lives - and focus on much lesser sins in someone else's life. There is a word for this kind of behavior; when we act like we are faithful disciples who have got their lives right with God in all respects - but we are actually only pretending; when we want to present ourselves as qualified spiritual counselors - but we refuse to take God's counsel and deal with our own sins. Jesus says we are *hypocrites*, play actors - purporting ourselves to be true disciples, while our relationship with God is far from what He intends it to be. It is not until we have addressed the sins in our own lives - that we are ready to be used by God to help others. We cannot live generously, and effectively represent the Lord, while our sins remain unconfessed, and suppress His work in our hearts.

The next segment of the sermon for us to consider is Luke 6:43-45 NIV:

43 "No good tree bears bad fruit, nor does a bad tree bear good fruit. 44 Each tree is recognized by its own fruit. People do not pick figs from thornbushes, or grapes from briers. 45 A good man brings good things out of the good stored up in his heart, and an evil man brings evil things out of the evil stored up in his heart. For the mouth speaks what the heart is full of."

These verses point back to the preceding segment - and forward to the next. Each tree is recognized by its own fruit. True discipleship cannot be lived in hypocrisy - so we must look well to our own hearts. People will recognize a 'real disciple' by the way they live their lives and act toward others. A thornbush will not yield figs. A tangled mass of briers will not yield grapes. A true Christian will be known 'when their life looks like their Lord's.' Like trees - people act according to their nature. What we really are on the inside - will inevitably show itself on the outside - in both words and deeds. As we observe and listen carefully to those who live in the orbit of our lives — we can tell what occupies their thoughts and affections: What do they speak about in their unguarded moments? What do they do with their free time? What is it that motivates them each day to relate to others as they do? What do they do with their resources? How do they react when Jesus Christ is the topic of conversation? To put matters simply; if we really abide in relationship with Jesus, our lives will bear much fruit (John 15:5), and everyone will see that we belong to Him. As we read in v.45 about the things stored up in the heart, and how our heart governs our speech, we hear an echo of Proverbs 4:23 NIV:

"Above all else, guard your heart, for everything you do flows from it."

If we will nurture our spiritual life, and receive the grace of God, our light will shine before all men, and they will glorify our Father in heaven. To be Jesus' disciple, His words must remain in our hearts, and they must be obeyed - as the final thoughts of His sermon teach us:

46 "Why do you call me, 'Lord, Lord,' and do not do what I say? 47 As for everyone who comes to me and hears my words and puts them into practice, I will show you what they are like. 48 They are like a man building a house, who dug down deep and laid the foundation on rock. When a flood came, the torrent struck that house but could not shake it, because it was well built. 49 But the one who hears my words and does not put them into practice is like a man who built a house on the ground without a foundation. The moment the torrent struck that house, it collapsed and its destruction was complete." Luke 6:46-49 NIV

As Jesus spoke of trees bearing fruit - and the way our actions and speech flow from the heart - He prepares us for this final invitation at the end of His sermon. His entire message has been about discipleship; how a brand new quality of life is ours 'when we cast our lot completely with the Son of Man'. Living in relationship with Him — we are learning to love others with the same open-hearted mercy as our Heavenly Father. When we call Jesus our Lord, it is simply not possible to establish a life built on this relationship - without doing what He says. Lordship is not shown by simply doing good works, with no consideration for what God desires - but by obedience to the will of the Father (cp. Matthew 7:21-23). To enter the Kingdom of God - we come to Jesus. Not to a religion, a church, an organization, a philosophy, a tradition, or even to any good works - but to Jesus Himself. If He is to be our Lord, we must listen to His words, and put them into practice — that is what Lordship means.

When Jesus speaks of *"my words"*, He is not only referring to the immediate teaching of this sermon, but to more. Since discipleship is a matter that covers all His teachings — we can safely say that our obedience to His words 'extends to the totality of Biblical teaching' - as the foundation for our lives. To follow Jesus - is to build our lives upon the Word of God; for He is the sum and substance of its pages, and in Himself, is embodied all the purpose God has for man (see John 1:1-18).

As we look at vv.48-49, Jesus compares those who hear His words and put them into practice, with those who do not. He likens each group to a man building a house. One man builds his house on a proper foundation, and one does not. It is not necessary for us to enter into a lengthy discussion on carpentry or masonry - to understand Jesus' meaning. The dramatic contrast between the two builders is apparent. One accepts Jesus' words and builds his life on them. It wasn't easy, but the foundation is deep, firm, and secure. The other rejects Jesus' words, and chooses a way of life with no foundation — rejecting the narrow way of committed discipleship. Both men's lives are inevitably tested by the setbacks and vicissitudes of life, and the judgment of God. One stands; one falls. The difference is the foundation.

One last thought. What does Jesus mean 'that those who build their lives on Him will remain unshaken by life's torrents?' It's clear enough that the Christian will stand safe and unharmed at the final judgment; for Jesus is his surety - and has paid the penalty for all his sins. But what about the 'here and now'? How can it be said that the follower of Christ will not be shaken - when battered about by life's storms? It can't be our emotions that stay settled; for we are subject to the same distress as everyone else. It isn't our finances or possessions; for in following Christ we may lose everything. Nor is it our health; for we have no promise that will we escape the ills of this world. What is it then that the Christian possesses

- that nothing in this life can shake? Let me suggest at least *three* unshakeable possessions that belong to those who have built their lives on the gospel of Christ. . .

First is our salvation; for nothing can separate us from the safety of God's hand, or the embrace of His love. The passages that speak of this are many. A good example is Romans 8:30-39; which assures us that nothing in all creation can separate us from the love of Christ. None of life's hardships can change God's love for us. Moreover, there is no power in all the universe that can pull us from His mighty hand:

"My sheep listen to my voice; I know them, and they follow me. I give them eternal life, and they shall never perish; no one will snatch them out of my hand. My Father, who has given them to me, is greater than all; no one can snatch them out of my Father's hand." John 10:27-29 NIV

Second; there is nothing that can shake the foundation of our hope. This is because our hope is built on the Word of God that endures forever (1 Peter 1:23-25). It is built further on the great and precious promises of God - which are more sure than any other kind of evidence. God gave us His promises, so that by grace through faith, they may be made certain and guaranteed to all who believe (2 Peter 1:3-4; Romans 4:16). Also, the foundation of our hope is built on the resurrection of Jesus Christ (1 Peter 1:3; Revelation 1:17-18; 1 Corinthians 15:12-20). It is God's promises to us, and the resurrection of Jesus Christ, that establish the validity and permanency of the new covenant; a covenant ratified by His blood, and which serves as a sure anchor for our souls (Hebrews 6:17-20).

Third; the very Kingdom that we hope for, and has been promised by God - is itself unshakeable:

Therefore, since we are receiving a kingdom that cannot be shaken, let us be thankful, and so worship God acceptably with reverence and awe, for our "God is a consuming fire." Hebrews 12:28-29 NIV

The faithful disciple of Christ has a firm foundation; one which will ultimately stand - despite all the raging torrents of life. Surely it was the words of Jesus in Luke 6:46-49 and Matthew 7:24-27 - that inspired Edward Mote to pen the famous hymn, "The Solid Rock":

My hope is built on nothing less
Than Jesus' blood and righteousness;
I dare not trust the sweetest frame,
But wholly lean on Jesus' name.

When darkness veils His lovely face,
I rest on His unchanging grace;
In every high and stormy gale,
My anchor holds within the veil.

His oath, His covenant, His blood
Support me in the whelming flood;
When all around my soul gives way,
He then is all my hope and stay.

When He shall come with trumpet sound,
Oh, may I then in Him be found;
Dressed in His righteousness alone,
Faultless to stand before the throne.

Refrain:
On Christ, the solid Rock, I stand;
All other ground is sinking sand,
All other ground is sinking sand.

As we looked at Luke 6:38, we focused on the idea that generous givers will find themselves enriched by God. To give an example of this, we mentioned briefly the church at Corinth, whose seeds of generosity would reap a harvest of blessing from God. In order to get a better understanding of the attitudes that should underlie our giving — we need to take a more in-depth look at Paul's assurances to this church; assurances that would be realized as a result of cheerful giving. To understand the need for Paul's words of encouragement, we must recall the situation that inspired them.

The first time Paul visited Corinth (on his second missionary journey), he established the church there. During his lengthy stay, he told them about the desperate poverty of the Jewish believers in Jerusalem. The church responded to this with a pledge that they would 'contribute generously to a relief fund' Paul had started, for those brothers in Christ that were having such a rough go of it (see 1 Corinthians 16:1-3). When Paul visited Corinth for the second time, it was a very painful visit, and not at all the right time to collect what they had pledged. Later when Paul wrote 2 Corinthians — many of the previous problems had been resolved, and he was preparing to visit the church again. Among other things he planned to do when he arrived, was to secure the money they had promised to give for the relief fund. In order to get the offering ready, Paul was going to send a delegation ahead of him to collect the funds. This delegation would consist of Titus and two other well known brothers who were trusted and well respected by all the churches. Then, Paul himself would come to visit and wrap matters up (2 Corinthians 8:18-24; 9:4-5).

In 2 Corinthians chapters 8 and 9, Paul exhorts the church as to why it was important that they fulfill their promise 'that the offering would be a generous one'. In the process of prompting them about this, Paul gives us some valuable reminders concerning the grace of giving. It's important to mention at this time - that although we are discussing giving here in terms of money — money is not our ultimate focus. Our focus is on learning 'how and why' we are to become people who live generously from the inside out. We must keep that foremost in our minds - as it always was for Paul. Paul's intention was never to coerce people to give. For him, it was always about grace and inner transformation. So, as chapter 8 opens, he first reminds the Corinthian church about how the Macedonian churches had determined to give. The Macedonians gave sacrificially, joyfully, and eagerly, even though they were poor, and had severe troubles of their own. They counted giving as a privilege, because they realized it was a reflection of who they were in relationship to the Lord (8:1-4). The faithfulness they showed with their money - was not enacted with a sense of guilt - but with a knowledge that they had first given themselves totally to God — and then to Paul in accordance with God's will. The bonds of love in their relationship with God - affected every aspect of their lives including their finances (v.5). Since the Corinthians excelled in their experience of God's grace in so many ways - such as faith, speech, knowledge, enthusiasm, and love; Paul encouraged them to excel in the grace of giving as well (v.7). Under that same framework of grace, Paul was not commanding the Corinthians to give; but he wanted to draw out the sincerity of their love by comparing it with the generosity of others (v.8). Then, to drive the point home, he points out that the foremost example of sacrificial love and giving - is the Lord Jesus Christ (v.9):

"For you know the grace of our Lord Jesus Christ, that though he was rich, yet for your sake he became poor, so that you through his poverty might become rich."

By reminding the Corinthians of the indescribable grace of Jesus — he is reminding us all that 'giving is not something a Christian does because he feels obligated'. Rather; a Christian gives as an expression of God's grace at work in his life, and in response to that grace. The spirit of giving comes from Christ living in our hearts, and not from the weight of a burden; as if someone were trying to deprive us of our livelihood through heavy taxation. God is not some kind of tyrant who doesn't care about what we have or do not have. He regards our giving in proportion to what we have, and the willingness or eagerness we bring to it (vv.11-12):

"11 Now finish the work, so that your eager willingness to do it may be matched by your completion of it, according to your means. 12 For if the willingness is there, the gift is acceptable according to what one has, not according to what one does not have."

As always; giving is about our attitude and motive - which God alone can see.

After Paul's words commending Titus and his companions to the church (vv.16-24), we come to chapter 9. Paul continues his appeal to the Corinthians to have their funds ready when his delegation arrives. To begin with, Paul lets them know that the Macedonian churches had already contributed very generously to this offering. One reason they had done so, was because he told the Macedonians that the Corinthians had been ready to give for a year. That 'earlier enthusiasm on the part of the Corinthians' had then inspired many of the Macedonians to begin giving. So (now) it was important that the Corinthians be as ready as they said they would be. Therefore, Paul urges them to prepare the offering they had already promised (9:1-3). It was now time for the church to fulfill its pledge to give generously. Paul was going to have some of the Macedonians with him when he eventually arrived. If the Corinthians were unprepared and their offering was small; or if it seemed to the Macedonians that

Paul was pressuring the Corinthians to do something grudg-ingly — then the whole situation would be an embarrass-ment to everyone. To avoid this, Paul sends his delegation ahead - leaving plenty of time for the collection to be pre-pared (vv.4-5). This situation is a good reminder for us - of how important it is to keep our promises and commitments to God. The reputation we develop before believers and unbelievers - is often based on the effort we make to keep our word. If we keep our promises — we gain a reputation as reliable and responsible people. If we break our promises — we obtain for ourselves a bad reputation; and we may do irreparable harm to our witness and influence for Christ.

Now we come to the heart of Paul's motivation in verses 6-11. Paul continues to encourage the church's generosity - by sharing with them God's promises to generous givers. We begin with v.6, where we hear an echo of God's message of the flow of grace that we saw in Luke 6:38:

"Remember this: Whoever sows sparingly will also reap sparingly, and whoever sows generously will also reap gen-erously."

Here we have an agricultural illustration where Paul likens 'us as Christians' to 'farmers who sow seed'. A farmer casts seed - in the hope that there will be a harvest of valu-able crops. For a farmer to sow with an eye toward economy - is to guarantee himself an unfruitful harvest. The same thing is true in the spiritual realm. When we give to God's work, we do so because we are looking to God to bless our investment, and to make His work fruitful. If we scrimp and are miserly in our giving to the Lord — we cannot hope to see a rich harvest of blessing for ourselves or for others. If we give generously in our service to the Lord and to the needs of others — we can expect a generous return from our Heavenly Father. We must emphasize again - that this is not a promise to us of financial prosperity in response to our giving. We do not give 'to become rich in the things of the world'. The treasure we seek, is of an entirely different kind (Matthew 6:19-21). When we give, we are not placing God under an obligation to us for a specific kind of reward. He alone determines the time and manner in which He will reward our generosity. It is enough for us that He has promised to do so. There is no shortage in God's storehouse of grace - to bestow blessing upon us; both now and in the world to come. Generous Christians will find themselves rich in love, rich in friends, rich in help, and rich toward God. When we give from the heart - it carries its own reward with it. As Jesus taught in Luke 6:38; when we allow the grace of God working in our hearts to flow freely through our generosity - we open a channel for that same wonderful grace to flood our lives in ways we can't begin to imagine. God will always see to it that no one is ever 'the loser' because they are generous. Also, Paul is reminding us once again that it is not the 'quantity' of what we give - but the 'quality' that matters most. As we saw in 2 Corinthians 8:11-12; sowing generously does not necessarily mean large amounts of money. It has to do with our eagerness to give in proportion to what we have. God is concerned with the motive and attitude of the heart.

The importance to God of our attitude in giving, is stated in the most memorable way by the contrast Paul draws in v.7:

"Each of you should give what you have decided in your heart to give, not reluctantly or under compulsion, for God loves a cheerful giver."

The first part of this contrast makes it clear that our giving is to come from the heart. Paul doesn't want the Corinthians to wait until Titus and the others get there - and then decide at the last minute what to give. He wants them to decide ahead of time what they will give, and have it ready when the delegation arrives. This way, their giving will come from the heart - and not be done under pressure. Paul did not command everyone to give a certain percentage, nor did he tell them how much they were to give. Anyone honest with the scripture will see that he wanted them to give from a generous heart — and not as if their gift was being extorted from them. (Later we will talk about tithing - and how it fits in with the whole grace of giving.) Here we can see the importance of thoughtful prayer and consideration; as we prepare to give to God's work through our local church. Under God's guidance and grace, we are to determine *ahead of time* how much we will give to the church offering. Giving impulsively or sentimentally in response to what happens in a worship service - is no way to base our practice of giving. While there may be occasions when God touches our hearts in response to a sudden or special need; we are to base 'our ongoing giving to the Lord's work' on the faithful stewardship He deserves; in gratitude for our life in Christ. Grace is our motivator; love - the dynamic; and joy - the reward — for giving to God's work.

In contrast to the importance of giving generously from the heart, Paul cautions us how *not* to give. Again, motivation is the key. We are not to give to God or others reluctantly. The word *reluctantly* literally means "out of grief". When we give, it is not to be a sad or grudging thing. If it grieves us to give - there is something very wrong in our spirit. We are also not to give under compulsion. Our giving is not to be generated because someone is pressuring us to do so; or as if it were being forced out of us. Giving is not something we do out of necessity; as if we had no choice, or there was no way to avoid it. Giving is what we do because it is our nature in Christ to do so, and because we have learned the blessedness that comes to us through generosity. By the way — all of this serves as a caution to church leaders - that using high-pressure tactics to obtain better offerings - is not pleasing to God. To put it another way; it is always grace, not guilt, that will foster in believers 'the growth of a generous spirit'. Thumping people on the head with the Bible - will not promote consistent giving. Teaching people faithfully about Jesus - and showing them from 'God's Word' the riches of His grace - is the only way to cultivate a lasting spirit of generosity. Yes, we are to teach faithful giving — but always in a manner that nurtures believers to give for the right reasons. It is only as we give willingly - that we accurately reflect Jesus' presence in our lives. It is only when our motives are right - that we can expect the blessings that God has promised to those who give generously.

Consistent with the thought that 'it is our motives that are pleasing to God' — Paul tells us that God loves a cheerful giver. The idea isn't that God only loves cheerful givers 'and no one else' — for God loves everyone. What he is saying, is that it is especially pleasing and delightful to our Heavenly Father, when His children show cheerfulness in their giving. The word Paul uses for *cheerful,* is derived from the word for *hilarious.* The idea is that we learn to seek the joy that comes from a willingness to give. When it becomes a pleasure and a delight for us to give — it is God's pleasure and delight to bless us. We become a reflection of His own generous goodness. Thus we are sharing what we can of ourselves eagerly — without the motive or demonstration of selfishness, self-advancement, or self-promotion. Our Father desires to help us discover the thrill of giving; to truly relish and take hold of the goodness inherent in reaching out beyond ourselves; to sense the depth of what Jesus meant when He said, "It is more blessed to give than to receive" (Acts 20:35). When we learn to give with that kind of cheerfulness — God takes notice and assures us of His blessing.

There are times when we hesitate to give, for reasons that seem very convincing to us. We suppose that we are not being so much 'ungenerous', as we are being careful and prudent. We counsel ourselves that if we give too generously, we will not have enough left to take care of our own wants and legitimate needs. That is not an unconvincing argument; and while we are not to be foolish with what God has entrusted to us — many of us use this thinking to justify our lack of faith and trust in God. For those of us who are sometimes reluctant to give for this reason — Paul shares some additional assurances from God, beginning with vv.8-9:

8 And God is able to bless you abundantly, so that in all things at all times, having all that you need, you will abound in every good work. 9 As it is written:

"They have freely scattered their gifts to the poor; their righteousness endures forever."

As beautiful and poetic as this sounds — it really gets down to the spiritual nitty-gritty. God is promising us that no one who has a generous heart will be unable to give, because He will provide all that we need. There is no need for us to fear that through our generosity, we will be impoverished. God has already told us that generous sowing will yield generous reaping. Here, He reminds us that He is *able;* able to provide us with abundant blessing. There is no lack of supply and resources on God's part. We need not be afraid to give. What this says literally — is that He is able to provide us with *all grace*. In other words; He will provide for us generously and abundantly anything we might need, so that we can give in the generous way we desire. Not only will He place the grace in our hearts to motivate our giving, but He will provide us with the 'resources we need' to give. So, if we really want to give — we can! The emphasis that follows this in the Greek text, can be seen in English by the word *all*. *All* things, at *all* times, having *all* that you need. God's grace - in response to our willingness to give - is absolutely sufficient for us. We will have enough for every good work that needs to be done. <u>There is no limit to God's resources to bless the good deeds He inspires in His people</u>. His heart is fully committed to provide what is necessary for those who desire to be generous givers, and to share in His compassion. That is not to say we will have everything we want. We may in fact choose to do with less than we might want - in order to give generously to others for Jesus sake. But God will see to it that not only are we content with less than we might have had — but there is an overflow of blessing from Him in our giving, which will more than make up for any so called "loss" we may perceive. Put simply; if you have a heart to give, then God will provide for you. He will not let us fail in our desire to be generous. A great example of this, is the Macedonian churches we mentioned earlier. Remember what Paul said about them in 8:2-4. . .?

"In the midst of a very severe trial, their overflowing joy and their extreme poverty welled up in rich generosity. For I testify that they gave as much as they were able, and even beyond their ability. Entirely on their own, they urgently pleaded with us for the privilege of sharing in this service to the Lord's people."

These Christians gave more than anyone thought possible. Not only did they give sacrificially, but *joyfully*; and they actually begged Paul for the privilege of sharing in the offering for the Lord's needy people. What an outstanding example of *hilarious* giving. Hearts filled with joy in giving — even when they had little materially to speak of. Such a spirit cannot fail to know the fullness of God's blessings.

In v.9, Paul quotes Psalm 112:9; to illustrate and support God's promise of blessing for the faithful giver. It is a picture for us 'of the good person who sows generously'. Such are they who give to the poor; their actions are a credit and joy to them forever. The deeds of a generous person have lasting value.

Verses 10-11 give us further assurance of God's ability and desire to bless the generosity of His people. Here, Paul returns to the farming imagery of v.6; where he likens Christians to farmers who sow seed:

"10 Now he who supplies seed to the sower and bread for food will also supply and increase your store of seed and will enlarge the harvest of your righteousness. 11 You will be enriched in every way so that you can be generous on every occasion, and through us your generosity will result in thanksgiving to God."

An astute Bible student might notice in Paul's words - undertones of Isaiah 55:10 and Hosea 10:12. Just as God provides seed for the farmer, and then bread to eat; so He will provide us the resources we need so that we can share with others, and then reap a great harvest of righteousness. All that we possess in this world belongs to God. They are His resources; given to us not to hoard - but to share. Our generosity releases the flow of God's blessing into our lives. Through His grace to us in Christ, He enlarges our harvest of righteousness. What does this mean that God enlarges our harvest of righteousness? It may have the sense of God enlarging the harvest *produced* by our righteous acts; meaning that we will be enabled to do more and more benevolent deeds. Or it may mean that God will increase the harvest of spiritual fruit *in our* lives; thus the blessings that God promises us as a result of our generous giving. Such blessing would include the aforementioned spiritual resources that will ensure we have enough for ourselves and others - allowing us to continue to plant seeds of giving. When we look at v.11; it seems that either of these nuances for our *harvest of righteousness* may apply. Either way, I believe there is even more. What we have is ultimately a promise — that if we allow God's generous grace to flow through our lives to others, He will be free to transform us more and more readily into the image of Christ. Then we will be fully mature Christians; rich in the grace of God, and ready to continue living lives of generosity on every occasion. That is exactly what v.11 says. As we sow generously, God will enrich us in every way. Nothing that we require spiritually will be denied us. Everything we need 'to continue living generously' - will be provided for us. God will bless, enlarge, and enrich, all He is doing in our hearts to make us complete in Christ.

Paul concludes his words of assurance by telling the Corinthians that the result of their generosity will be *'thanksgiving to God'*. The believers in Jerusalem - and everyone who heard of the generous gift from these gentile churches - would raise their voices in gratitude to God. It is God alone who gives us the desire to give - and the resources to do so. While we should always express our personal gratitude to those who show us kindness — our hearts must be filled first and foremost - with gratitude to God. For it is He alone who is the source of every generous act and every perfect gift (James 1:17).

Generous giving provides an abundance of blessing. The needs in people's lives are met, and joyful thanksgiving is expressed to God (9:12). Our Father is glorified as our generosity reflects His love. Our profession of faith in Christ is shown to be genuine as we freely share of ourselves with others (9:13). The expression of Christian love promotes unity in the church and the healing of strained relationships, as well as prompting and stimulating the prayers of believers for the needy and for one another (9:14). What can we say then, to the surpassing grace of God in our lives through Jesus Christ? We join Paul in almost speechless admiration, as he speaks his final words (9:15):

Thanks be to God for his indescribable gift!

Thus far, we have looked at what the New Testament teaches about the grace of giving. We have listened to both Jesus and Paul, as they spoke of the importance of our attitudes and motives as we give to others. We have learned about the transforming grace of our Heavenly Father - as He works in our hearts through Jesus Christ - to make us into the kind of people that reflect His compassionate love. In order to embrace an understanding of God's grace that encompasses the entire Bible — we need to look now at the heartbeat of the Old Testament. What do the Law, the Prophets, and the Writings, say about the matter of generosity? Is it different from the grace of God in Jesus Christ? Is there any underlying discrepancy between what God said to Israel, and what He says to the Church - with regard to giving to others? To find out, we begin with what may be the most frequently preached Old Testament passage to call forth obedient faithful giving. It is found in the third chapter of the book of Malachi:

"I the LORD do not change. So you, the descendants of Jacob, are not destroyed. Ever since the time of your ancestors you have turned away from my decrees and have not kept them. Return to me, and I will return to you," says the LORD Almighty.

"But you ask, 'How are we to return?' "

"Will a mere mortal rob God? Yet you rob me."

"But you ask, 'How are we robbing you?'"

"In tithes and offerings. You are under a curse — your whole nation — because you are robbing me. Bring the whole tithe into the storehouse, that there may be food in my house. Test me in this," says the LORD Almighty, "and see if I will not throw open the floodgates of heaven and pour out so much blessing that there will not be room enough to store it. I will prevent pests from devouring your crops, and the vines in your fields will not drop their fruit before it is ripe," says the LORD Almighty. "Then all the nations will call you blessed, for yours will be a delightful land," says the LORD Almighty. Malachi 3:6-12 NIV

The prophet Malachi delivered his message to Israel sometime between the building of the second temple (516 B.C.), and the governorship of Nehemiah (444 B.C.). This period of Israel's history was a time of discouragement and disillusionment. The hopes that were stirred by the fall of Babylon and the return from exile there, had not been realized. The prophets Haggai and Zechariah had promised many blessings from God when the temple was completed; under the leadership of Zerubbabel and Joshua the High Priest. But it is likely that by the 'time of Malachi', these men had died, and nothing significant had occurred in the land; other than the completion of the temple. There were no miracles taking place, and the small Jewish community in Jerusalem and Judea was living under very difficult conditions. The soil was unproductive, rainfall was minimal and unpredictable, and the harvests were poor. The residents even had to contend with swarms of locusts and the ruin they brought, along with famine and drought. From the words of prophets past, the people were looking with hope and expectation for the great things God had promised them. These included a king from David's line (Ezekiel 34:11-16, 23-24), prosperity (Haggai

2:7, 18-19; Zechariah 2:4-5; 8:1-12), and the new covenant promised through Jeremiah (Jeremiah 31: 31-34). We also learn from Malachi, that while God's people were carrying out their religious duties, they were doing so without enthusiasm. This is not surprising, since in the minds of many, God had failed His people. Because His promises of blessing had not yet been fulfilled, even the faithful were tempted to doubt. People were starting to become skeptical and cynical, and were questioning traditional spiritual beliefs. Using a series of six short messages, Malachi shares with us 'some of their doubts and contemptuous actions' toward the Lord. As he displays a unique prophetic style, Malachi writes these messages in the form of questions and answers. It was as if he put into writing 'the verbal arguments he was having with his opponents' - who were rebelling against God. By presenting God's word in this way, he effectively communicates with us 'the mood of the times'; where the covenant people were losing faith, and could not find their way back to God from the strain and disenchantment of everyday life. God desired to bless His people; but He could not do so while they remained in this state of mind, and lived in disobedience to their covenant obligations. He was seeking appropriate worship from them, in every aspect of daily life - but was receiving instead only contempt from priests and people alike; as we see from some of their dialogue:

"I have always loved you," says the LORD.
But you retort, "Really? How have you loved us?"
Malachi 1:2 NLT

"The LORD of Heaven's Armies says to the priests: "A son honors his father, and a servant respects his master. If I am your father and master, where are the honor and respect I deserve? You have shown contempt for my name!"

"But you ask, 'How have we ever shown contempt for your name?'"

"You have shown contempt by offering defiled sacrifices on my altar."

"Then you ask, 'How have we defiled the sacrifices?'"

"You defile them by saying the altar of the LORD deserves no respect. When you give blind animals as sacrifices, isn't that wrong? And isn't it wrong to offer animals that are crippled and diseased? Try giving gifts like that to your governor, and see how pleased he is!" says the LORD of Heaven's Armies."
Malachi 2:6-8 NLT

"But you dishonor my name with your actions. By bringing contemptible food, you are saying it's all right to defile the Lord's table. You say, 'It's too hard to serve the LORD,' and you turn up your noses at my commands," says the LORD of Heaven's Armies. **Malachi 2:12-13a NLT**

"Here is another thing you do. You cover the LORD's altar with tears, weeping and groaning because he pays no attention to your offerings and doesn't accept them with pleasure. You cry out, "Why doesn't the LORD accept my worship?" I'll tell you why! Because the LORD witnessed the vows you and your wife made when you were young. But you have been unfaithful to her, though she remained your faithful partner, the wife of your marriage vows." **Malachi 2:13-14 NLT**

"You have wearied the LORD with your words.
"How have we wearied him?" you ask.
You have wearied him by saying that all who do evil are good in the LORD's sight, and he is pleased with them. You have wearied him by asking, "Where is the God of justice?""
Malachi 2:17 NLT

"You have said terrible things about me," says the LORD.

"But you say, 'What do you mean? What have we said against you?'"

"You have said, 'What's the use of serving God? What have we gained by obeying his commands or by trying to show the LORD of Heaven's Armies that we are sorry for our sins? From now on we will call the arrogant blessed. For those who do evil get rich, and those who dare God to punish them suffer no harm.'" **Malachi 3:13-15**

Now, as we prepare to look at the matter of tithing as an act of worship, we would do well to reflect a moment on the dialogue above. Before we criticize the people and priests of Israel for their attitudes — we may want to consider our own. Are we really that different from those in Israel during Malachi's day? Are our times really that different from theirs? Even as I write these words, there are millions in America who are unemployed. Jobs are scarce, home foreclosures are still out of control, federal debt is rising, and the threat of more war is on the horizon. Our nation faces issues that ancient Israel never dreamed of; such as health care, immigration, abortion, entitlements, gun control, terrorism, global warming, education, and the role of government. While the issues are different for us — the mood of the times may be very much alike. We face an uncertain future, just as they did. Faith in the integrity of our national leaders - is not exactly at an all-time high; and the corruption in financial markets and the banking industry, has left us in the throes of widespread cynicism about tomorrow. Even in the Church, this uncertainty and financial hardship, has caused many Christians to cease giving to the Lord's work - believing that they have to hoard every penny, just to survive. Faith in God's provision has been lost in many hearts. This makes Malachi's message to Israel on the need to worship God through faithful giving - more urgent than ever. As we look now at the prophet's dialogue on this concern, we want to pay careful attention to God's invitation and the promise of His grace:

6 "I the LORD do not change. So you, the descendants of Jacob, are not destroyed. 7 Ever since the time of your ancestors you have turned away from my decrees and have not kept them. Return to me, and I will return to you," says the LORD Almighty.

"But you ask, 'How are we to return?' "

Malachi's thoughts here, come between two messages concerning God's justice (2:17-3:5; 3:13-15). Even as the nation questioned God's justice, they needed to realize that the only reason they could even do so, is that He is unchanging in His patience (v.6). By His grace, He continues to give His people the opportunity to repent (v.7). They in turn, want to know what they are to do. The action God has in mind - is going to touch their checkbooks. This will show each individual that their repentance will be costly; and therefore genuine. However, their return to the Lord would not be in vain. God's gracious response to such repentance, will be to provide tangible evidence of His blessing (v.11). Moreover, He will prove to the trusting heart, that the person who puts all their resources at His disposal - will know His blessing in a far greater way than they can imagine (v.10). The nation had broken the bonds of the covenant. God was offering them a way back to restored fellowship with Him; and into a place where they could experience the fullness of His blessings.

8 "Will a mere mortal rob God? Yet you rob me.
But you ask, 'How are we robbing you?'"
"In tithes and offerings."

Through Malachi, God accuses His people of robbing Him. They were failing to give the tithes and offerings required under the Mosaic law. The word tithe means 'tenths'. The practice of giving a tenth of one's 'gain or increase' - to God - predates even Moses. We see it practiced in the life of the patriarch Abraham, when he gave a tenth of his spoil to Melchizedik, priest of God Most High (Genesis 14:18-20). We see it again during Jacob's life, when he made a vow to God at Bethel (Genesis 28:20-24). The 'covenant under Moses' decreed that a tenth of all produce and livestock was 'holy to the Lord' (Leviticus 27:30), and was intended for the Levites (Numbers 18:24) — who in turn gave a tithe to the priests (Numbers 18:25-28). From Moses' sermons in Deuteronomy, we learn that others also benefited from the tithe. Every three years, a community feast was held at the time when the tithes were offered. To this feast, the needy were invited; as well as the Levites (Deuteronomy 14:28-29; cp. 12:5-7, 11-12, 17-18). When the tithes were not given, the needy would suffer. This may have been of particular concern to Malachi, who notes the oppression of the widows, the fatherless, and the foreigner among the people (Malachi 3:5). No matter how we understand the frequency and extent of all that was involved in the giving of 'tithes and offerings' in Malachi's day, it is clear that the nation was failing to give God 'all that the law required of them'. God was calling upon His people - to repent of this sin.

Like many Christians today; the people of Israel in Malachi's generation - were using the hardness of the times as an excuse for their lack of giving to the Lord. The prophet confronts them by telling them that their unwillingness to give - was in fact a reflection of an inner contempt for the Lord. He wants them to understand that the lack of God's provision they were experiencing - was directly tied to their lack of giving. In other words, they would not experience the Lord's blessings - while they were living in disobedience. Their own 'hardness of heart' was preventing God from granting the covenant blessings He desired to give them. While we as followers of Christ are not under the law; the underlying principle here is the same. As we saw with both Jesus and Paul, there are generous blessings that God desires to impart to the giving heart; blessings we cannot receive when we act with parsimony toward Him and to others. Under grace, in our relationship with Jesus Christ, it is not so much that we are robbing God, as we are robbing ourselves — by refusing to give as the Holy Spirit directs and prompts us. By withholding *at least* the legal standard of the tithe from the Lord — we are walking as 'ungrateful disobedient children' who are not breaking God's law - but breaking His heart. There is so much that our loving Father desires for us to possess of our inheritance in Christ. As we close our hearts to giving and generosity, we are forfeiting some of the richness of our spiritual inheritance that God has prepared for us to enjoy.

9 You are under a curse — your whole nation — because you are robbing me.

Under the terms of the old covenant, God had placed a curse on the land as a result of their failure to give Him His due. If the people gave a proper tithe and offering in cheerful obedience, they would be blessed. As long as they refused, this curse would be the result. Their failure to tithe, showed a disrespect and contempt for the Lord - that went beyond their external acts alone. They were robbing *Him,* as the Hebrew emphasizes. This lack of 'grateful obedience' began in their hearts, and was a reflection of their want of trust in God's faithfulness, power, and love - as promised through the covenant. 'Obedience to God' is more than only what is seen on the outside — because the Lord looks on the heart. Our attitudes and motives in a life of worship, are always the key. Jesus made this clear when He rebuked the

Pharisees who were faithful in their tithing — but neglected the weightier matters of the law; matters that deal with the way we are to treat others, and with having a faithful trust in God (Matthew 23:23). (Our focus in Malachi precludes us from discussing at length — the many times in Israel's history when outward religion was thriving, but God completely rejected their worship.) Prophets such as Jeremiah and Isaiah, had to address this kind of religious hypocrisy on many occasions. In fact, Jesus quotes Isaiah, as he rebuked those who 'put on a show of pious worship' - while their hearts weren't in it:

He replied, "Isaiah was right when he prophesied about you hypocrites; as it is written:

'These people honor me with their lips,
but their hearts are far from me.
They worship me in vain;
their teachings are merely human rules.'
You have let go of the commands of God and are holding on to human traditions." Mark 7:6-8 NIV

As followers of Christ — we should tithe and live generously. But we must always remember that the only worship God accepts and blesses — is what comes from the heart, and is born in gratitude for His own grace. Anything else is self serving - and is an attempt 'to use religion or giving for one's own ends'. Such giving may benefit others, but it will not be the kind of giving that is an acceptable sacrifice to God.

As we consider God's curse on those who treated Him with a closed hand; it is a good time for us to look at what 'traditional Hebrew wisdom' has to say about the matter. How would this curse on the 'tightfisted giver' work itself out, in the life of an individual? To put the matter in a positive way — what benefit is there to the generous person; and how does it affect someone when they act miserly? To see the answer, and to confirm our understanding of God's grace, we turn to the book of Proverbs:

One person gives freely, yet gains even more;
another withholds unduly, but comes to poverty.
A generous person will prosper;
whoever refreshes others will be refreshed. Proverbs 11:24-25 NIV

Although various modern Bible translations give us a few different nuances of the Hebrew - the meaning is clear throughout. The person who gives freely - is enriched through their giving. The person who withholds what they should give - finds themselves impoverished. The overtones to Jesus' words in Luke 6:38 are unmistakable. <u>God's blessing is upon the generous giver.</u> Accordingly, He cannot bless the individual, church, or nation that can spare nothing for Him; as their own stinginess blocks the flow of blessing. I have written elsewhere, that God identifies Himself intimately with His children. Therefore, to withhold from His servants - is to withhold from Him — so much so, that in Malachi, to withhold from those who serve Him in worship - is to *rob* Him. Here in Proverbs, what we have are 'general truths to live by' - that apply to everyone. Anyone can profit by applying to their lives 'these words of divine wisdom'. Even the person who is living apart from God - and outside of a relationship with Jesus Christ - will benefit from listening to God's wisdom, and living as He directs. But there is most certainly a distinction between how such virtuous practical living 'benefits the godly' - in contrast to the ungodly. Anyone may benefit materially through their generosity, but *the believer* will benefit *spiritually*. The Christian can be aware and assured that *it is God* who blesses His generosity;

not Karma or an impersonal universe. As we saw from Paul, God has promised an abundance of grace to support our generosity, as He continues to transform us into people like Jesus. His grace and resources will be totally sufficient for every good work He inspires in us. He will make us content with what we have; and He will not let us fail in our desire to be generous. The Lord has at His disposal 'infinite ways and means' - to bring His grace into our lives. He is limited only by our refusal to allow this grace to flow through us to others. As we give freely — we are freely given. The Lord's hand and heart are wide open to those who will joyfully channel His love to all people - whether they are deserving or not - thereby showing compassion just as He does. While those who live apart from God may experience temporal blessings for their generosity; there are spiritual riches that are available only in Jesus Christ. To wit: Will the ungodly 'love their enemies', pray for them, bless them, forgive them, and do good to them? Will they know what it means to receive the smile of their Heavenly Father? Can they know the kind of joy that comes from doing God's will - or taste what it's like to know that Jesus lives in them, and is giving them the privilege of being co-workers in ministry with Him? Can they share in the hope of eternal life that God has promised to those who love Him? Is there any way they will see the hand of God in their prosperity; or recognize His providential care in what has been provided for them? All this and more - is the Christian's by inheritance. So, while the Proverbs teach the universal blessings of generosity; only the believer can take hold of the treasures of God's grace 'that are the possession of those who have faith in Jesus'.

The 'inclusive blessings of generosity' are laid out for us throughout the book of Proverbs. In the proverbs below, we can see the similarity to what we have been saying. Notice especially 'God's identification with the needy'; His curse on the hardhearted and ungenerous; and His blessing upon those who live with an open heart toward Him, and an open hand toward others. All of the following quotations are from the NIV:

Honor the LORD with your wealth,
with the firstfruits of all your crops;
then your barns will be filled to overflowing,
and your vats will brim over with new wine. Proverbs 3:9-10

Whoever is kind to the poor lends to the LORD,
and he will reward them for what they have done. Proverbs 19:17

One who oppresses the poor to increase his wealth
and one who gives gifts to the rich — both come to poverty.
Proverbs 22:16

Those who give to the poor will lack nothing,
but those who close their eyes to them receive many curses.
Proverbs 28:27

The message is the same throughout the Hebrew Writings. The person who gives freely is enriched through their giving. The person who withholds what they should give - finds themselves impoverished.

We return now to Malachi 3:10, where God not only offers His people a way back to Him, but issues one of the most amazing challenges to faith and blessing in all of scripture. As we read it, we cannot help but hear the resounding call of *grace*.

10 "Bring the whole tithe into the storehouse, that there may be food in my house. Test me in this," says the LORD Almighty, "and see if I will not throw open the floodgates of heaven and pour out so much blessing that there will not be room enough to store it."

It was time for 'those who were accusing God of being unjust' to face up to their own responsibility for what was happening to them. To help His people see the truth of the situation, God essentially calls their bluff! He does this by issuing them a challenge to authentic commitment. In reality, He is reaching out to them in the most positive and constructive way possible. He is trying to help them understand that the problem isn't on His part - but on theirs. So He issues this challenge. If the people will trust Him by bringing in the whole tithe in obedience to the covenant — God will bless them beyond their ability to take it all in! In modern parlance, we might say that God was inviting them to put their money where their mouth is! They were saying hard things about God, as we referenced above (2:13a, 17; 3:13-15). God said to them that if they really believed all those harsh things they were saying about Him, then here was their chance to prove it. They could prove to God, as it were, that there was no use in serving Him (3:14). He invites them to test Him. It's as if He said to them, "I'm going to prove to you that it is not *my arm* that is too short or has lost its power, but it is *your refusal to trust me* that is causing your distress." It was time to quit playing games in their relationship with God. Were they going to trust Him - or not? Did they really want to start living the life He meant for them - or not? Would they follow the Lord with all their hearts — or would they resign themselves to living out their years in the kind of life always prone to accepting less than it could be; always longing for more, and blaming God for what they didn't have; instead of trusting His love, and learning what their spiritual inheritance was meant to be. God invites His people to an act of trusting faith. If they will change their attitude, and give as an act of joyful worship, He will show them that their faith is justified, and they do not worship God in vain (see 3:14). They will not find the Lord's service hard (2:13), if they will simply allow God to show them that by following His lead in everything, they will experience all the spiritual richness He desires for them. Contrary to what we might think — this is as far from forced obedience and 'legalistic giving' as it can be. By comparing this with the words of Jesus in Matthew 11:28-30 MSG, we will see that even under the old covenant, it is truly *grace* that the Lord was inviting His people to:

"Are you tired? Worn out? Burned out on religion? Come to me. Get away with me and you'll recover your life. I'll show you how to take a real rest. Walk with me and work with me — watch how I do it. Learn the unforced rhythms of grace. I won't lay anything heavy or ill-fitting on you. Keep company with me and you'll learn to live freely and lightly."

We must not miss the connection here. God was not trying to burden His people. He wanted to set them free! They were burned out on empty religion, but God's heart ran out to them. He wanted to help them understand that obedience is grace; giving is grace; worship is grace; and that all of it was intended for their good. His commandments and instructions were not given to make them tired of serving Him. They were given to free them to serve Him; with a joy and enthusiasm that comes from the discovery that living for Him - is the best life possible. Such is God's Arithmetic. So gentle is the Most High — that He condescends to the desperate needs in the troubled hearts of His children, by inviting them to test Him in this matter. Why would God do this? Because, *"As a father has compassion on his children, so the LORD has compassion on those who fear Him." Psalm 103:13.* We shouldn't see God's 'invitation to test Him' as something out of character, as many have. True, this is the only place in the

Bible where God specifically invites us to test Him (i.e., to prove He will keep His word); but this is really only one of a thousand ways that God reaches out to us when we are in need of Him. And even here, He does not dismiss the need for faith on the part of His people. God took the initiative to reach out. He offers them blessing if they will trust Him. But this is really not any different as it applies to us — when we lay hold of any of the promises of God. As we begin to trust in God's promises, He may not have said the words "test me in this" - but the end result is still the same. His invitation, while not spoken, is always understood. We are not 'putting God to the test' in the sense of trying to force His hand into doing what we want done. What we are doing, whenever we take hold of a promise from God, is aligning ourselves with His will - by trusting in a provision He has already made available to us. Every one of God's promises is an invitation, spoken in tones of grace. If we will step out in faith on His promises, He will *always show Himself true*. God is calling us to spiritual growth and maturity. Here to Israel, God is not 'pandering to their doubt' by allowing them to force Him into something He never intended to do. He is trying to 'awaken their faith' by offering to show them first-hand — why faithfulness is its own reward. In gentle tenderness, He invites them back to Him, by encouraging their weak faith with a promise of abundant provision. If they will only take this step of faith - guided and motivated by His hand of grace - they will find themselves led back by that hand into the sphere of blessing. What a good, gracious, and generous God we serve!

See now how the Almighty describes the blessing He will give:

"*. . . and see if I will not throw open the floodgates of heaven and pour out so much blessing that there will not be room enough to store it.*"

The floodgates (or windows) of heaven, bring to mind the flood in the time of Noah (Genesis 7:11). There, God's judgment was poured out on mankind. Here, we find flood-gates of blessing. What an amazing picture this is! "Flood-gates in heaven" that can be opened to pour out blessing. It's as if there is a great rushing river of blessing stored in heaven for us - just bursting to overflow - which is being held back by floodgates. These floodgates (or windows, as in the KJV) open from heaven to earth. If God will just throw the gates open — the blessings will pour out in a deluge - in a torrential surge - that will flood our lives to the point where we will not be able to comprehend them all, or take them all in. It is to say, that there will be so much blessing that we can't stop it from surrounding us! Our lives will be so flooded with blessing that we won't know what to do with all of it. Well out of proportion to what we gave - is what we will receive from God's own hand — far more than anything we deserve. Such is grace; and such is the nature of God's response to our faithful giving — that in Christ, we have a return far greater than anything we can imagine. Remember Jesus' words:

"Truly I tell you," Jesus replied, "no one who has left home or brothers or sisters or mother or father or children or fields for me and the gospel will fail to receive a hundred times as much in this present age: homes, brothers, sisters, mothers, children and fields — along with persecutions — and in the age to come eternal life." Mark 10:29-30 NIV

Living for Jesus, giving to God, and living generously with an open hand; all are channels of grace into our lives. Grace received not by any merit of our own — but freely through the covenant God has made with us through Christ Jesus. Who would not want to be a generous giver, if they could only see the truth; that no one is truly poor who gives themselves away. Such is the way of God; and of every true follower of Jesus Christ.

11 "I will prevent pests from devouring your crops, and the vines in your fields will not drop their fruit before it is ripe," says the LORD Almighty. 12 "Then all the nations will call you blessed, for yours will be a delightful land," says the LORD Almighty.

If the people would trust and obey — the Lord would make the land abundant once again. The blessing God would pour out in response to the nation's obedience - would be obvious to all. Other nations would recognize that God's hand of favor rested on His people. They would receive blessings both material and spiritual, and theirs would be *a delightful land*. The Message states this beautifully in v.12 by saying:

"You'll be voted 'Happiest Nation.' You'll experience what it's like to be a country of grace."

Whether it's a nation or an individual; <u>liberal giving will always enrich the personality of the giver</u> (Proverbs 11:25). As we express our love to God through generous giving, without a selfish expectation of return, we will experience an abundance of grace, and a life that is truly rich in all that God has promised. As Christians, we do not have laws about giving. What we do have - is an invitation. An invitation of grace. An invitation to a deeper richer life than we have ever known. An invitation to follow Jesus; and to learn that when God asks anything of a person, they can only be enriched through their obedience. So God sets the challenge before us now. Each Lord's Day (or as it is fitting), we are to give to our local church in proportion to our income (1 Corinthians 16:1-2). We do not give because we are afraid that "God will get us" if we don't — but because we discover the treasures of grace when we do. There are many good reasons to present our tithes and offerings: To support the ministry of the church; to relieve the needs of others; and to advance the gospel mission in all the world. But the best reason of all — is to give out of overflowing gratitude for Jesus Christ — God's gift too wonderful for words.

We have been looking at what the Law, the Prophets, and the Writings have to say about this matter of generosity. We have started to see how both the Old and New Covenant are rooted in a foundation of grace. To drive this home, and to establish it firmly in our minds — we turn now directly to the Law of Moses.

In our discussion of Malachi 3:8 above, we noted the purpose and requirement of tithes and offerings in the law. A tithe of all the produce and livestock, was holy to the Lord. It was used to support the Levites, who in turn gave a tithe to the priests. The tithe was brought annually to the place where He chose to be worshiped (in the presence of the Lord). There, the people would celebrate before the Lord; and every third year, the tithe would be used to care for the needy as well as the Levites. The question of whether there were three separate tithes - or one tithe used in different ways - is not the subject of our present discussion. What we want to emphasize, is that just as in Malachi, God's people were to 'give a portion of their increase' to support the Lord's worship and work, and in gratitude for His blessings. In Deuteronomy 14:23 NIV, while giving direction for the annual tithe, Moses says this:

"Eat the tithe of your grain, new wine and olive oil, and the firstborn of your herds and flocks in the presence of the LORD your God at the place he will choose as a dwelling for his Name, *so that you may learn to revere the LORD your God always*." (italics mine)

All of these commodities were eaten in a ritual meal that was symbolically shared with the Lord. God was present at the meal. This idea is similar in all of Israel's annual celebrations. As everyone participated in the meal, they would increase their awareness that the Lord was near to them, and that they were always living life in His presence. They would learn to revere Him, because worshiping in this way would remind them of His holiness - and of the Lord's choice of them as His special possession. In addition, this reverence would help increase their faith — since their worship would also remind them that the credit for the entire harvest and all the livestock - belonged to God. He was the source of all their blessing. The faithful Israelite would realize that not only did God provide for the tithe, but that He would also provide for the needs that the designated tithe could have been used to meet. Thus, at these communal celebrations, they would remember God not only as their redeemer - but as their provider.

As Christians, all of this reminds us of the Lord's Supper — a ritual meal through which we remember what God has done for us in Christ, and how His grace is sufficient for all our needs. When we celebrate communion during our time of worship, and as we also bring our tithes and offerings, we see how the grace of the New Covenant is related with the grace that was the foundation of the Old. For just as Israel learned through faithful giving that this holy God was their savior, redeemer, Father, and provider — so we are reminded of the same. When Jesus said, *"Do this in remembrance of me"* — it was not only to keep His great sacrifice at the forefront of our thinking. It was also to teach us by way of reminder, that *everything* we have received by God's grace - is ours through the covenant He has established by His blood. We, like Israel, celebrate in God's presence as we bring our tithes and offerings. They were not celebrating 'a burden of religious duty and obligation', but rather their freedom from slavery - and their joy at being the people of God. And while the Lord's Supper relates primarily to their celebration of the Passover — it is God's love and grace that underlie all our celebrations - Old and New Testament alike. The people of Israel were not in bondage when they tithed. In God's Arithmetic, they were celebrating their freedom. They were given an opportunity to participate with God in the support of His work. By placing Him first, they were promised in return that He would provide for all their needs (cp. Matthew 6:33). When we join with God, and allow Him to bring our hearts into harmony with the grace of generous giving, we discover that law and grace are part of the same interconnected whole. Underlying both, is God's desire for us to become generous people - filled with the joy of eternal life. To the extent that grace makes us more like Jesus — will we understand the essence of the law as He did:

Jesus replied, "'You must love the LORD your God with all your heart, all your soul, and all your mind.' This is the first and greatest commandment. A second is equally important: 'Love your neighbor as yourself.' The entire law and all the demands of the prophets are based on these two commandments." Matthew 22:37-40 NLT

Tithing, giving, and generosity — are all matters of the heart. They come to us not as commandments written on tablets of stone, but as the law of God 'written on the tablets of our hearts'. All of it now made possible through the covenant of grace — that is our inheritance in Christ.

As Jesus united the importance of 'loving one's neighbor' with 'the love we have for God' — so did Moses in his commands to Israel. Immediately after the instructions for the tithe in Deuteronomy 14, chapter 15 reminds God's people of the importance of a generous heart. Under grace, we are taught, "freely you have received, (and so) freely give." Here we will see that the law says the same:

7 If anyone is poor among your fellow Israelites in any of the towns of the land the LORD your God is giving you, do not be hardhearted or tightfisted toward them. 8 Rather, be openhanded and freely lend them whatever they need. 9 Be careful not to harbor this wicked thought: "The seventh year, the year for canceling debts, is near," so that you do not show ill will toward the needy among your fellow Israelites and give them nothing. They may then appeal to the LORD against you, and you will be found guilty of sin. 10 Give generously to them and do so without a grudging heart; then because of this the LORD your God will bless you in all your work and in everything you put your hand to. 11 There will always be poor people in the land. Therefore I command you to be openhanded toward your fellow Israelites who are poor and needy in your land. Deuteronomy 15:7-11 NIV

Moses instructs God's people to be compassionate toward those who have become poor. We have already seen that one of the reasons for the tithe - was to support the needy. Here, we go even further, and we discover God's intention that His people have a generous heart. We see again that tithing and giving are ultimately about attitude — and not about grudgingly fulfilling a requirement. God cautions His people "not to become hardhearted or tightfisted" toward the poor. When an Israelite needed a loan, they were to give with an open heart and an open hand. Now we must not suppose here that the loans in ancient Israel were like the loans we think of today. When a person became poor, debt was their last recourse. An Israelite could only incur debt for life's necessities - not for luxuries. Because of this, God decreed that every seventh year, all debts must be canceled (Deuteronomy 15:1-6). This created a problem for the person who was asked to loan to the poor. It would be very tempting to be hardhearted toward the fellow Israelite who needed help. Here's the scene: A poor brother comes to you and asks for a friendly loan. You realize that the time for canceling all such debts is close at hand. So you say to yourself, "If I make this loan, it is almost certain that I will not be paid back, because in short time, I will have to cancel the debt!." With this in mind, you might not choose to extend the loan to your needy brother — as it would then amount to a gift. God's response to this is that it is wicked thinking, and reflects ill-will toward your brother. The poor brother may then cry to the Lord about the matter — and your lack of compassion will be considered sin by God; who identifies Himself closely with the needy. God says, "*Give generously to them and do so without a grudging heart*" *(v.10)*. In these words, we hear an echo of Paul's words to the Corinthians, as he appealed to them to contribute to the offering for their poor brothers in Judea: "*Each of you should give what you have decided in your heart to give, not reluctantly or under compulsion, for God loves a cheerful giver.*" (2 Corinthians 9:7). Both cases are not an attempt at forced giving, but an appeal by God to learn to be the kind of people He wants us to be; those who will experience the flow of His grace and blessing if we will love others as He has loved us. One might argue that in Moses day, the people didn't have Christ living in them to empower and motivate their giving in that way. But God's gracious intention was the same. <u>As His people, the love He showed to them must be allowed to flow to others, if they hoped to experience His blessings.</u> The fact that we as Christians have the transforming power of Jesus within us, only serves to highlight the greater obligation we have to grace, and the help we have available to overcome our selfishness and become compassionate individuals. God's promise to the generous Israelite was that, "*the LORD your God will bless you in all your work and in everything you put your hand to."* (v.10). Again we see that generosity carries its own reward with it — and the generous giver will themselves be refreshed. In v.11 there is the sad statement echoed by Jesus (Matthew 26:11), that there would always be poor people in the land. This is a sober reminder to us of the condition of a world lost in sin. Until Jesus comes again — we will never lack the opportunity to show compassion to others through our generosity.

There are two powerful lessons here for us, which bring to mind what we heard Jesus teach in the sermon on the plain. First, generous giving was not to be done for profit. The challenge for the Israelite to loan to his needy brother 'as the time of canceling debt approached' - was a deeply spiritual one. He had to decide if he would totally trust in the Lord to provide for him - should he suffer loss through his generosity. This is the same challenge that Jesus presents us with today. The second and closely related lesson, is that the cost of this generosity toward the poor was irrelevant. It did not matter that the creditor might have to take a loss. Even if the loan to a brother amounted to a gift — God said it was not an excuse to be hardhearted. Jesus taught us to do to others as we would want them to do to us. If we desire to be distinguished as His followers — we must love in this way. We are to take the initiative to love, whether it is returned or not. By doing so, we will learn the blessedness that comes to us 'when we give His love away'. God will be pleased; our reward will be great; our joy will be full; and we will be called the children of the Most High.

Throughout our study, we have been making the case that the best way to live as a Christian - is with an open hand and an open heart. Such a life is also the most felicitous way to live, since we find the blessing of God measured back to us from His riches in Jesus - to be far in excess of anything we might deserve or imagine. If this is true, we must ask ourselves what we can do to foster a generous spirit in ourselves and others. Let me suggest three actions we can readily take, which will hasten our progress in experiencing the grace of generosity.

First, **learn as much as you can about Jesus.** Make the study of God's Word a priority in your life. Read the gospels often, and observe how Jesus responded to all those who were placed in His daily path. Note especially how He was never too busy to help someone, and how He never treated the needy as a nuisance. Also, be mindful of how carefully He listened to people and observed them; so that He would always know how to respond to their deepest needs. Try to discover as much as you can from His teachings - about the way that citizens of the Kingdom of God are to live; for much of His time with the disciples was spent teaching just that. Also, as you study the rest of the Bible, pay careful attention to 'those attitudes and motives that God designs to develop and cultivate in our hearts' as we follow His commands — and not just to the commands themselves. That way, your religion will never degenerate into a set of rules to follow; but will remain a vital growing relationship with a living Savior who is bringing your heart into harmony with His own.

Learning as much as we can about Jesus — is only possible as we feed upon the Word of God. Let me urge you to make Bible reading 'an indispensable part of your daily life'. There are many effective plans available to guide us in this exercise. Devoting only a few minutes a day to Bible reading - we can read it through in its entirety - in only a year. Many churches offer printed material for reading through the Bible. Ask your Pastor or church office if such a guide is available. There are also many good online sources that offer plenty of these Bible reading guides for free. In addition to Bible reading, I would encourage you to take advantage of every opportunity to participate in group Bible study. No matter what size your church is, chances are there are Bible study groups available that will fit your schedule. There is no substitute for 'the group dynamic' in Bible study. Together, Christians share insights into God's Word, and are guided by the Holy Spirit into a deeper understanding of its meaning. In this same vein — if we want to be challenged to attain the generous attitude of Jesus, we must not neglect meeting together with God's people. Corporate worship is vital to our growth as believers; for it is 'in community' that God allows us to discover our gifts of service, and to employ them in the growth of His church and the advancement of His Kingdom. Also, as we worship together, we hear the voice of God speaking to us — reminding us that there is more to life than our own concerns.

Along with Bible study and worship, the most effective way we have to learn as much as we can about Jesus - is to spend time with Him in prayer. If we desire Jesus to impress upon our spirit 'the image of His own generosity' - and to make it real in our lives - then there is no substitute for spending time alone with Him. The influence of His personality will inexorably become our possession as a matter of course, as we involve Him in all of our thinking, decisions, and priorities. No matter how far we are spiritually from where we want to be — the time we spend in private prayer with Jesus - will not be barren. In the course of time, and as the years pass — 'sincere consistent believing prayer' will yield the fruit of right living; just as surely as the branch will bear fruit - as it remains in the vine. 'Intimacy with the Lord' is not the privilege of a few special saints, but is the inheritance of all God's children. While our prayer life can always grow - just as our generosity can always grow - direct access to the throne of God is within the reach of the most humble believer. It doesn't matter whether or not you are very good at praying. God does not give us bonus blessing for eloquence. It is our heart that matters — not our exact words. Our attitude and motives are what God sees when He looks upon us. We can be certain when we ask God to make us more like Jesus and to share in His Spirit of generosity — that God will do just that. Luke affirms this, as he shares with us an occasion when Jesus was teaching His disciples how to pray. As Jesus taught 'the importance of perseverance in prayer' as essential to spiritual growth, he spoke these words:

"Which of you fathers, if your son asks for a fish, will give him a snake instead? Or if he asks for an egg, will give him a scorpion? If you then, though you are evil, know how to give good gifts to your children, how much more will your Father in heaven give the Holy Spirit to those who ask him!" Luke 11:11-13 NIV

As we spend time with Jesus, we will become more like Him. It is the Father's delight and the Spirit's gift, to conform us to His image. In this way, we will always be ready to enjoy the good gifts that have been laid in store for those who do the will of God.

The second action **we can take right away 'to grow in the grace of generosity' — is to start where we are.** There are many ways to do this. Let me give you some examples. As you go about your daily routine, watch and listen carefully for anyone who mentions a specific need that is within your power to meet. For the next week, ask God to make you sensitive and aware of the needs around you - both spoken and unspoken. These needs do not have to be financial. A person may simply need someone to talk to. Perhaps there is a mention of a needed household item; a need for transportation; or a service within your ability to perform. If we are willing to give — God will surprise us with opportunities.

Another way to start to give, is to ask yourself if there is anyone in your life right now that is acting unkindly toward you, or with open hostility. If the Lord has brought someone to mind — commit to Him that during the next week, you will pray for that person; speak a good word about them; and do a kind act for them. As you pray for the person, ask God to put His love for them into your heart. Then, as the Spirit leads you, find some way during this week to put your intention into action. Right at this moment, you may suppose that this is too difficult for you - if not impossible. But if you will determine to faithfully pray for that individual, you will discover that God is gradually changing your heart toward them. Be patient, for in time the Lord will indeed give you the grace to put His love into action. Your kind acts do not need to be great; they only need to be genuine. Do as God bids you, and leave the rest to Him. In a thousand such situations, God will work on your behalf nine hundred ninety nine times - and one besides.

One of the most purposeful ways to set in motion the transforming power of generosity - is by giving to your local church. If you really desire God to make you into a more generous person — you must ask yourself where you are at in the matter of stewardship. If you are not currently giving at least a full tithe of your income to the church, then where is your heart set? Is it set on the Kingdom of God, or only on your own concerns? If you are currently in the same place as those in Malachi's day - who were afraid to give to God out of fear of additional financial hardship - then it's time to take the first step back. Ideally, I would recommend that you take a step of faith in full obedience to God — and start tithing immediately. God has invited each of us personally to test Him in this, and has promised to prove Himself true; unmistakably and beyond doubt. However, if your heart is willing, but you can't quite overcome your fear, then start where you can, and God will help you. Begin with 3%, 5%,

7%, or whatever your faith will allow. Ask God to show you through His word of promise - that He can be trusted. Pray that He will increase your faith. Have Him assist you in laying out a plan in your mind, so that you will gradually increase your giving to the level it needs to be. Speak with other believers 'who are faithfully giving to the Lord's work' about their experience with tithing — and you will find great encouragement. Their faith will aid your own commitment; and your readiness to give will be more easily achieved.

We have looked at length through various scriptures - at the meaning of grace in giving. What we have found, is that for God — it's all about our attitude and motive. On the one hand, if we have in our heart 'a willingness to obey Him' and 'a desire to give' - but we are struggling in our faith - God will accept our offering, bless it, and enable us to trust Him more. On the other hand, if all we are willing to give to the Lord are our "leftovers" — that is not an offering He will accept. Also, as we have already seen from Paul — we cannot expect God's blessing if we give 'reluctantly or under compulsion' (giving because we feel *forced to* rather than because we *want to*). This manner of giving will never help us grow into the kind of generosity that is a delight to God. It is our motive that counts — and God knows our hearts all too well. If your heart is not right in this matter — tell the Lord. He will not condemn you for it, but will provide the grace needed to transform your mind, and teach you the true joy and meaning of giving. I recognize that there are some pastors and teachers who will say that this is all wrong. They will declare that tithing is a fundamental obedience to our faith, and must be done fully — and to do otherwise is to rob God; as Malachi states. They believe that anything less than 'the whole tithe' is not acceptable to God at all — and that partial obedience is really no obedience. However, we have already made the case that even in Malachi — compulsory giving is not the kind that pleases God. Our Heavenly

Father is in the business of accepting us as we are, and then moving us 'by grace' to where we need to be - in every part of our lives. In our relationship with Christ — giving is no different. God doesn't need our money. It is the spiritual growth of our soul that concerns Him the most. If we are willing and sincere, then God will come to our aid and gently move us from 'where we are' in our giving - to 'where we need to be'. He seeks open-hearted givers who do so cheerfully, joyfully, and in a way that shows we understand the blessedness of a giving heart. We do not live under the law - as did the Israel of Malachi's day; a law that said, "do this and you will live." We live under a new covenant — a covenant of grace; wherein we are already fully accepted by God in Jesus Christ. God is patiently writing His law on the tablets of our hearts. He is growing us into 'gratefully obedient children' who will give not because we have to — but because we want to; not because we are paying a debt — but because we are free from debt. As we grow in our giving, we are starting to walk at liberty as God's children; children who are learning that everything belongs to God anyway. His resources are unlimited — and therefore as we have freely received - we can also freely give.

For those of you who by His grace are already giving the full tithe; I suggest you gradually increase your offering, and see what God will do. You may want to set a goal for yourself to increase your giving by a certain percentage each year, or as the Spirit leads you. There are always greater heights for us to reach; and there is greater grace to receive. Wherever you are 'in this grace of giving' - take the next step of faith - and you will soon find yourself running willingly along the path of His commandments; rejoicing in blessing along the way.

***Finally, the third action* we can take 'to grow in the grace of generosity'** — **is to practice random acts of**

kindness. Many of us have seen this expression on posters, or heard it used as a buzzword in pop culture. Even on the surface, it sounds to us like a good way to live; but have you ever thought about why that is so? Most of us probably understand that 'practicing random acts of kindness' is simply helpful to others; but I want to suggest that there is more to it than that. Through spontaneous unplanned acts of kindness - done purely with an attitude of giving - we experience spiritual fruitfulness in three ways.

First, it blesses the giver. Giving is one of those virtues that the more we do it, the more we want to do it. This is because we experience in our hearts the satisfaction inherent in generosity. It brings happiness to us and joy to others. As we make 'generous giving' a way of life, we find an increase in our capacity to recognize and experience the many ways God rewards it. We also become more aware of how God is at work in the world around us, and of the spiritual hunger that exists in society - which we may not have sensed before. Through our acts of kindness, our bond with humanity grows; as our giving brings us more into harmony with the reason God has put us here in the first place. By giving generously, we become more sensitive to our place in this world, and to God's purpose for our lives. We have all heard it said that 'practice makes perfect'. The practice of 'random acts of kindness' actually serves to fix generosity as part of our new nature. The desire to give generously becomes habitual, easier, and more natural, the more we do it. As our habit of generosity grows, we become more capable of hearing the gentle whispers of the Holy Spirit as He guides us toward the opportunities to do the good works that God has planned for us. Perhaps even to our own surprise — we will find ourselves excited about opportunities to give. We will have discovered how truly rich it makes us - not in dollars and cents - but in the only life that will last forever.

The second way our 'random acts of kindness' bear spiritual fruit — is that they are a blessing to others. Not only will the people we help 'thank God' for what they received, but they in turn will be motivated and inspired toward generosity to others. One of our many exhortations to godliness is found is Hebrews 10:24 NLT:

"Let us think of ways to motivate one another to acts of love and good works."

Certainly, one way to motivate such acts — is to do them ourselves. By following in the footsteps of our Savior, who went about doing good (Acts 10:38), we are bound to have an influence on the lives we touch. Once each year, the Pastor of my church takes the time to rehearse the good works our church body has done during the past year; prior to sharing God's vision for the year ahead. One reason for his public review of what we have collectively accomplished — is to spur us on to further acts of love and good deeds in the days ahead. He desires that the good deeds some of us have done - will inspire all of us to live out our faith in the same spirit of love and generosity. If the generosity of other believers inspires us - when we are not even the ones who have received their kindness – then how much more do you suppose 'will people be inspired to give of themselves' — when they are the recipients of our kind acts in Jesus' name? Moreover, 'living with a generous heart' may well be the best gospel preaching we can do. Through our acts of kindness, Jesus may open the hearts of sinners to His word; He may be giving us the opportunity to share with them - all that He has done for us. I can think of no greater blessing to others — than that 'a random act of kindness' would lead them to a personal knowledge of our Savior. Generous giving enriches everyone it touches - as we become the hands and feet of

Jesus - who is still going about doing good through the lives of His faithful people.

The third way our 'random acts of kindness' bear spiritual fruit — is that they are pleasing to God.

"And do not forget to do good and to share with others, for with such sacrifices God is pleased." Hebrews 13:16 NIV

When we live in this way, our whole life becomes an act of worship to God 'in spirit and in truth' — and He is well-pleased. Speaking to the Samaritan woman at the well (who wanted to take issue with Jesus as to the proper place to worship God), Jesus said this:

"Yet a time is coming and has now come when the true worshipers will worship the Father in the Spirit and in truth, for they are the kind of worshipers the Father seeks. God is spirit, and his worshipers must worship in the Spirit and in truth." John 4:23-24 NIV

The *place* we worship God - is not as important as the *place* we give Him in our heart - and the *way* we act toward others. The kind of worship that is pleasing to God — can take place anywhere. Our 'random acts of kindness' are not limited to the church, to "respectable" people, nor to any other place. The verse from Hebrews quoted above, comes alive in The Message:

"Make sure you don't take things for granted and go slack in working for the common good; share what you have with others. God takes particular pleasure in acts of worship — a different kind of "sacrifice" — that take place in kitchen and workplace and on the streets."

The kitchen, the workplace, and on the streets — are all places where the kindness of God may be extended to others. Any believer can 'live the golden rule' in any place - and at all times. As you give — give a little extra. . . One for good measure. Let God surprise you with His joy. Ask Him to help you "become a disciple of Jesus who lives with an open hand and an open heart." Together, let us pursue a life of true blessedness; as we discover the deeper meaning of Jesus' words:

"Give, and it will be given to you. A good measure, pressed down, shaken together and running over, will be poured into your lap. For with the measure you use, it will be measured to you."

Be Weak To Be Strong

Limitation: noun: A condition which limits something; an impairment or restriction; a lack of capability or
capacity; a handicap or disability. *(e.g., I know my limitations as an author!)*

*L*imitations. We all have them, and they take many forms
in our lives. Our *age* could limit us from the kinds of
activities we enjoyed when we were younger. Or perhaps
an illness or physical infirmity limits the common activities
of daily life. All of us in some way, are limited genetically
from pursuing certain kinds of goals or career paths. For
example, since I can't carry a tune, it's very unlikely that
I will ever be a successful singer! At 5'7" tall and 150 lbs.,
there is little chance I will play professional football either.
Because we each have certain kinds of limitations, some
doors are closed to us, while others are not. Learning what
our personal limitations are, can therefore be helpful. We can
gain a unique insight into who we are, and into the ways we
may best serve God and our fellow man. On the other hand,
if we are not careful, we can allow our limitations to keep us
from being all that God intends for us to be. I have met gifted
public speakers who started out afraid to talk to an audience;
or whose early attempts at speaking did not turn out very

319

well. You may have seen videos of President Obama giving a speech as a much younger man. Listening to them, you might never imagine that he would be the kind of speaker he is today. I recently watched a documentary on the life of pop singer Billy Joel. As a struggling young musician, he had signed a contract with a production company; a contract that he described as "onerous". Because he was so young and weighed down by the conditions of this agreement, he decided to run away. He left New York, and he moved all the way to California. There, out of work and penniless, he was forced to take any job he could find just to survive. However, convinced of his abilities and holding on to his dreams, he persevered, and was gradually able to make a living as a singer. Ultimately, he was discovered by the owner of a large recording company, and given the opportunity to allow his talent to shine. We see then, that despite our personal limitations, we can achieve our goals. Nowhere is this more certain than in our spiritual lives. As we live in daily fellowship with Jesus Christ, we are still subject to the same kinds of limitations as everyone else. What we find though, is that God is not bound by our limitations. By faith, there is no limit to what He can accomplish in our lives. This is what Paul means when he says:

"Now to him who is able to do immeasurably more than all we ask or imagine, according to his power that is at work within us" Ephesians 3:20 NIV

In God's Arithmetic, there is a clear path to spiritual strength and power. What we're going to find, is that this path is not impeded by our limitations and weaknesses. In fact, it is by discovering that *God's power is perfected in our limitations*, that we learn how to see it most clearly on display in our lives. How do we get on this path to spiritual power? What attitudes must we adopt to allow God to work most effectively in our lives? To find the answers to these questions, we will be looking at a very personal struggle that takes place in the life of the Apostle Paul. (Our special attention will be focused on what he shares with us in 2 Corinthians 12:7-10.) But before we examine the situation that leads us there — I would like to introduce you to an extraordinary person. If there was ever a man other than Paul who exemplifies the truth of this scripture for me, it is Nick Vujicic. The following biography is taken directly from one of Nick's websites[6]:

"Imagine being born without arms. No arms to wrap around someone, no hands to experience touch, or to hold another hand with. Or what about being born without legs? Having no ability to dance, walk, run, or even stand on two feet. Now put both of those scenarios together: no arms and no legs.

What would you do? How would that effect your everyday life?

Meet Nick Vujicic. . . Born in 1982 in Melbourne, Australia, without any medical explanation or warning, Nicholas Vujicic (pronounced Voy-a-chich) came into the world with neither arms nor legs. Having had an uneventful pregnancy and no family history to expect this condition, imagine the shock his parents felt when they saw their first born, brand new baby boy, only to find he was what the world would consider imperfect and abnormal. A limbless son was not what nurse Dushka Vujicic, and her husband Pastor Borris Vujicic had been expecting. How would their son live a normal happy life? What could he ever do or become when living with what the world would see as such a massive disability? Little did they know that this beautiful limbless baby would one day be someone who would inspire and motivate people from all walks of life, touching lives all over the world.

Throughout his childhood Nick dealt not only with the typical challenges of school and adolescence such as bullying and self-esteem issues; he also struggled with depression and loneliness as he questioned why he was different to all the other kids surrounding him; why he was the one born without arms and legs. He wondered what was the purpose behind his life, or if he even had a purpose. After a lot of frustration and feeling like the odd one out in school, at seven years of age Nick tried out some specially designed electronic arms and hands, in hopes that he would be more like the other kids. During the short trial period of the electronic arms, Nick realized that even with them, he was still unlike his peers at school, and they turned out to be much too heavy for Nick to operate, effecting his general mobility quite significantly.

As Nick grew up he learned to deal with his disability and started to be able to do more and more things on his own. He adapted to his situation and found ways to accomplish tasks that most people could only do by using their limbs, such as cleaning teeth, brushing hair, typing on a computer, swimming, playing sports, and much more. As time went by, Nick began to embrace his situation and achieve greater things. In grade seven, Nick was elected captain of his school and worked with the student council on various fund-raising events for local charities and disability campaigns.

According to Nick, the victory over his struggles throughout his journey, as well as his passion for life, can be credited to his faith, his family, his friends, and the many people he's encountered during his life who have encouraged him along the way.

After school Nick went on with further study and obtained a double bachelor degree, majoring in accounting and financial planning. By the age of 19, Nick had started to fulfill his dream of encouraging others by sharing his story through motivational speaking. He found the purpose of his existence, and also the purpose in his circumstance. Nick wholeheartedly believes that there is a purpose in each of the struggles we encounter in our lives, and that our attitude towards those struggles that can be the single most effective factor in overcoming them.

In 2005, Nick was nominated for the "Young Australian of the Year" Award, which is a large honor in Australia. The award honors a young person for their excellence and service to their local community and the nation, as well as their own personal accomplishments. Nominations for this award are only given to truly inspirational people.

Now at 27 years old, this limbless young man has accomplished more than most people even twice his age. Nick recently made the massive move from Brisbane, Australia to California, USA, where he is the president of an international non-profit organization, and also has his own motivational speaking company; Attitude Is Altitude. Since his first motivational speaking engagement back when he was 19, Nick has traveled around the world, sharing his story with millions of people, speaking to a range of different groups such as students, teachers, youth, business men and women, entrepreneurs, and church congregations of all sizes. He has also told his story and been interviewed on various televised programs worldwide. However, Nick's speaking engagements have gone beyond purely motivational speaking. He has had the opportunity to speak with several leaders, including the vice president of Kenya. This year alone Nick is set to speak in over 20 countries.

People ask Nick, "How can you smile?" Then they realize there's got to be something more to life than meets the eye, if a guy without arms and legs is living a fuller life.

Nick shares with his audiences the importance of vision and dreaming big. Using his own experiences in worldwide outreach as examples, he challenges others to examine their perspective and look beyond their circumstances. He shares his view of ceasing to see obstacles as problems, but instead begin to see them as opportunities to grow and reach out to others. He stresses the importance of how attitude can be the most powerful tool we have at our disposal, and illustrates how the choices we make can have a profound effect on our lives and the lives of those around us. Nick shows through his own life that the major keys in fulfilling our biggest dreams are persistence and choosing to embrace failure as a learning experience, rather than allowing the guilt and fear of failure to paralyze us.

How does Nick Vujicic feel about his disability now? He accepts it, embraces it, and oftentimes pokes fun at his own circumstance, as he shows off his many tricks. He meets challenges with his special blend of humor, perseverance, and faith always encouraging those around him to examine their perspective as they develop and define their vision. Using those new definitions he challenges each person he meets to make changes in their lives so that they can begin the path to fulfilling their biggest dreams. Through his amazing ability to connect with people from all walks of life, and his incredible sense of humor, he captivates children, teens, and adults alike. Nick is a true inspirational and motivational speaker."

This brief biography of Nick's life does not begin to do him justice. Let me encourage you to visit one of Nick's web sites (lifewithoutlimbs.org, attitudeisaltitude.com). There you will find just some of the compelling pictures and videos of this remarkable man. He is also on YouTube, where one video with him has over 33 million hits! I first encountered Nick around 2002, not too long after he began his speaking engagements. He spoke at my church in Mesa, Arizona, and was already quite well known at that time. His vibrant attitude toward life, and his love for Jesus, deeply touched the hearts of everyone present. When I asked the Lord about how to introduce this chapter, Nick came prominently to mind. Nick has also written a book, <u>Life Without Limits: Inspiration for a Ridiculously Good Life</u>. As of August 2011, the book has sold 350,000 copies worldwide, and has been translated into 14 languages. A film he made, <u>Butterfly Circus,</u> has won awards as a *short* film, and is in process of being produced into a *feature* film. There is a line of dialogue in the film which I think exemplifies the message Nick brings into people's lives. Nick plays the part of Will; a circus side show freak who is constantly mocked, while onlookers are told that God has abandoned him. A kindly circus director later takes Will under his wing and makes him part of his troupe. As the story progresses, we learn that Will badly lacks any self confidence or self esteem. One day, he is observing the other circus performers; who all have overcome various adversities in their lives. When the director challenges Will to do the same, Will says to him that the others have an advantage that he does not (he has no limbs). The director responds, "You do have an advantage. The greater the struggle, the more glorious the triumph." That is the message of Nick Vujicic. Our struggles can actually be an advantage, since they give God an opportunity to show Himself powerful on our behalf. It's all about faith in God, and the attitude we choose to take toward our limitations. With this in mind, we are going to look at a passage of scripture that can be truly life changing — if we are willing to take hold of its message. We will discover from God's Arithmetic, found in the words of Paul

- the way to spiritual strength and power - no matter what limitations we might face.

The Apostle Paul was facing a very troubling situation that had arisen in the church at Corinth (a church he had founded). A serious breach of trust in his relationship with some of the members of the church, had taken hold. This disaffection was entirely on the part of the Corinthians, and was in no way caused by Paul. Paul faced criticism and accusations from some who doubted him as a leader. Compelled to defend himself, he wrote the letter we have now as "Second (2) Corinthians". In the letter, he opens his heart to this congregation; to a degree not found in his other letters. Paul had faced many dangers and a great deal of physical pain - from the persecution he suffered while taking the gospel throughout the Roman empire. Yet when he was falsely accused of being a phony - by the Christians whom he had won to Christ - it was one of the most emotionally painful trials he faced. What he wrote to them to deal with this situation, has become a source of encouragement and hope for us. It speaks to Christian leaders who are having their leadership challenged; as well as to congregations who can see from Paul's example - how Christ loves His church.

At the time Paul wrote Second Corinthians, he had already made two trips to Corinth. The first trip was when he planted the church, as described in Acts 18. Sometime after this, he wrote the letter of First Corinthians while ministering in Ephesus. Not long after the letter was delivered, he learned from Timothy that the church was in something of an uproar. So he interrupted his ministry in Ephesus, and made a second visit to Corinth - which he called a "painful visit" (2 Corinthians 2:1). After he returned to Ephesus, Paul wrote a letter of rebuke to the Corinthians, which is now lost to us. He desired to be reconciled with them, and was anxious to learn what was going on. Ultimately, his friend Titus (who had delivered the letter for him) brought good news, when they met up somewhere in Macedonia. The majority of the Corinthians had repented, and were deeply concerned for Paul - longing to see him again (2 Corinthians 7:5-7). Paul was then ready to announce another visit to them (2 Corinthians 12:14; 13:1); yet there were still those who opposed him. Somewhat relieved, but still feeling it necessary to address those who remained unrepentant — he wrote the letter of Second Corinthians while in Macedonia, around A.D. 56.

The letter as we have it, has been divided into 13 chapters. The first 7 chapters deal with Paul's ministry and itinerary. Chapters 8-9 contain Paul's appeal for generous giving. Then, beginning with chapter 10, Bible students often note a distinct change in Paul's tone. Up to that point, the letter reads as warm and friendly. After that, the rest of the letter sounds much more harsh and critical. The reason for this abrupt shift in tone is widely debated. Yet however we view these chapters, it's clear that Paul is addressing those within the congregation who had not yet reconciled with him. It's also likely that a new situation had arisen since Paul received the good report from Titus. It seems that there were some "anti-Paul" missionaries who had arrived in Corinth, and they had launched a malignant campaign against his presentation of the gospel. They also made many false claims against Paul, in an attempt to undermine him and his ministry coworkers. We must remember from Acts 18, that Paul spent nearly two years ministering in Corinth. Many people were won to faith in Christ, and Paul invested himself heavily in their lives. He labored for them, prayed for them, taught them, and later wrote extensively to them. So in order to undermine Paul's work, these false apostles would have to mount a very serious attack against him. Unfortunately, a detailed list of all the slanderous things they said about him does not exist. All we have is Paul's response to the cruel things of which he was accused. But from his defense - we can get some idea of what was being said. He was being painted as cringing and wishy-washy when he was with the church, but harsh and demanding when at a safe distance writing letters (10:1 MSG). His accusers said he lived by worldly motives as an unprincipled opportunist (10:2). They claimed he was not a real apostle or even a true Christian (10:7), and that he was barging in on their territory, taking credit for work that wasn't his own (10:15-16). On his part, Paul states these men were preaching a different Jesus, a different Holy Spirit, and a different gospel than he preached (11:4). He sarcastically calls them "super apostles", because they thought him to be inferior, and his message to be inferior to theirs (11:5). They regarded Paul as an untrained public speaker who lacked the proper dignified eloquence (11:6). Paul in turn identifies them as false apostles, deceitful workers who were in ministry only to take advantage of the church. He says that they are really Satan's servants, masquerading as apostles of Christ. In the end, they will be punished as their wicked deeds deserve (11:12-15). These men boasted about their human achievements, and all the while were trying to enslave, exploit, and take advantage of the church members, even slapping some in the face (11:20). Their campaign against Paul got so ugly, that they even had the audacity to attack his personal appearance. We see from 10:9-10, that they said Paul was trying to scare people with his letter writing, but that when he was there in person, he was actually a weakling, and his preaching was despicable, worthless, contemptible, and added up to nothing. Sadly, some of the Corinthians that Paul loved so dearly were actually buying into this nonsense. So Paul, speaking with Christ's authority in the sight of God, determined that it was necessary to write as he did. He appeared to be defending himself, when all the while he was really writing to build up and strengthen the church, and to prepare them for his next visit (12:19-21).

As we read the letter, it is obvious that Paul loathed having to speak like he did - appearing to defend and promote himself. He makes it clear that he was engaging in a form of writing that was distasteful to him (11:1, 16-17; 12:1). However, it was necessary that he do so, because the truth of his message was at stake. He could not allow his critics to undermine the Word of God, or to damage the tender faith of his new converts. Paul had to set the record straight. So in 11:21-12:21, this is exactly what he does. The thing is, he takes a completely different approach to demonstrating his integrity and devotion to Christ (than the method of self promotion which his detractors used). First, rather than calling attention to his knowledge, abilities, and experience, Paul recounts his hardships as the evidence of the genuineness of his ministry. He does this because, as we will see, he had learned that God's power is seen most plainly in the midst of human weakness — not in the self aggrandizement of his opponents. Second, Paul establishes the issues involved in the conflict. He will make it evident that he has done nothing for monetary gain (as they had), but has acted only in the best interest of the church. His only desire is to build up the believers, and to keep them from all forms of sin.

As we continue to set the stage for our look at the path to spiritual strength and power - we need to narrow down our focus. How exactly does Paul defend his 'integrity and calling' as an apostle of Christ? In 11:21-29, he tells us of his personal background and heritage, as well as the variety of persecutions and hardships he suffered for the cause of Christ. As we read his account of suffering while serving Christ, we see the evidence of his love for Him. It is very important to understand as we read this passage of scripture - that Paul is using *satire* when he boasts of his sufferings and achievements for Christ. He is employing irony, sarcasm, and ridicule, to expose and denounce his opponents, and to help the Corinthians see the foolishness of their behavior. In other words, when Paul talks about himself, he is not really acting in the same self-seeking manner as his adversaries. By the power of Christ, he is using every literary device at his command to defend the truth, and to build up his spiritual children. With this in mind, we look at his account in 11:21-29 NIV:

"Whatever anyone else dares to boast about — I am speaking as a fool — I also dare to boast about. 22 Are they Hebrews? So am I. Are they Israelites? So am I. Are they Abraham's descendants? So am I. 23 Are they servants of Christ? (I am out of my mind to talk like this.) I am more. I have worked much harder, been in prison more frequently, been flogged more severely, and been exposed to death again and again. 24 Five times I received from the Jews the forty lashes minus one. 25 Three times I was beaten with rods, once I was pelted with stones, three times I was shipwrecked, I spent a night and a day in the open sea, 26 I have been constantly on the move. I have been in danger from rivers, in danger from bandits, in danger from my fellow Jews, in danger from Gentiles; in danger in the city, in danger in the country, in danger at sea; and in danger from false believers. 27 I have labored and toiled and have often gone without sleep; I have known hunger and thirst and have often gone without food; I have been cold and naked. 28 Besides everything else, I face daily the pressure of my concern for all the churches. 29 Who is weak, and I do not feel weak? Who is led into sin, and I do not inwardly burn?"

Now Paul is about to continue his so called "foolish boasting" as the passage goes on. But at this point, in verse 30 NLT, he says something profound:

"If I must boast, I would rather boast about the things that show how weak I am."

As we gain insight into Paul's approach to the criticism he faced, it's here that we really begin to see it. His opponents were boasting of their Jewish ancestry and accomplishments. Paul certainly could have boasted pridefully about his own ancestry and accomplishments for Christ. Instead, he uses the word "boast" ironically - to mock the prideful attitudes of the false teachers. What he really wants to do, is to speak only of his weaknesses, in order to show that the power at work in his life is truly from God. So in 11:31-33 NLT, he gives us the first example of his own weakness:

"31 God, the Father of our Lord Jesus, who is worthy of eternal praise, knows I am not lying. 32 When I was in Damascus, the governor under King Aretas kept guards at the city gates to catch me. 33 I had to be lowered in a basket through a window in the city wall to escape from him."

Calling on God as his witness, Paul relates the nerve-wracking and humiliating escape from his Jewish enemies in Damascus (see Acts 9:22-25). Luke's account in Acts - does not mention the involvement of the governor under Aretas. Aretas was an Arabian king who ruled in Damascus at that time. Here, Paul gives this example of looking ridiculous and foolish - to make it clear that he is only really boasting about God's work - even though he should appear weak. He is going to return to this idea in the latter part of 12:5. But first, he reluctantly continues his so called "boasting", by moving from the account of his trials, to "visions and revelations from the Lord" (12:1). In this verse, he's really telling us that there is normally nothing to be gained from this kind of "bragging" about such extraordinary spiritual experiences. He is doing so, only because the circumstances have compelled him to; since his critics were boasting of visions and ecstatic experiences they claimed to have. Paul, by contrast, is telling us about a genuine vision or revelation; and also unlike them - he gives all the glory to God.

It's somewhat of a temptation here - to go into a long discussion about Paul's exalted, ecstatic trip to heaven, described in 12:2-4. We as Christians have a very natural curiosity about what heaven will be like. Paul was caught up to Paradise, and heard things so astounding that they can not even be expressed in words (v.4). I would love to have all the details of this heavenly visit — wouldn't you? But that was not Paul's purpose here. He only wanted to affirm the genuineness of his apostleship, in contrast to the false claims of the "super apostles" - as he called them. Also, there are certainly very legitimate matters of spiritual interest we could discuss regarding these verses; matters concerning the afterlife and final judgment - but that is not our purpose here either. Suffice to say, we should not allow our natural curiosity to lead us into the realm of foolish questions and disputes; the kind Paul cautions us of, in principle, in Titus 3:9. The sad truth is that by ignoring the Word of God, and focusing on the appeal of 'ecstatic experiences', many believers have lost their way. Because of the danger this presents, I offer these brief words of admonition concerning the best way to weigh claims of special revelation:

There are many people today who sell a lot of books by claiming to have an experience such as Paul had. Some say "they have died and been to heaven and back". Others say that they have not only been to heaven - but to hell as well. I know there are some Christians who would doubt the scriptural validity of all such non-apostolic-era experiences. But regarding these claims of such special revelation, let me just say this: First, it is useless to argue about 'life after death' beyond the truth of what the Bible itself teaches us. Studying about heaven and hell can be profitable; but we must always distinguish between what the Bible actually says - and our own speculation. Had God wanted to give us all the exciting details of the next life - he would have done so. Second, the Bible is our only authority on the matter. Any claim of revelatory experience that contradicts the Word of God is to be summarily rejected. This is especially true of those who claim to have been given *new revelation* from their ecstatic experience — Revelation which *adds to* or *takes away from* - clear Biblical teaching and sound doctrine. Third, we ought to look carefully at the life and witness of anyone claiming such experiences and profiting by them. Paul spoke of his unique experience reluctantly; only to authenticate his message and apostleship. Why is the one writing or boasting of their experience doing so? Are they exalting Jesus Christ or themselves? Is the message of the gospel being advanced by the person's words and ministry? Are they giving all the glory to God — or is it really just about self-promotion? I am not willing (as some are) to censure any believer who claims to have had such divine revelations. I would however advise extreme caution with all such books, and/or any such claims to possessing special knowledge. History is replete with examples of Christians led astray by unscrupulous individuals and groups that have made such claims — especially when it involves an assertion of divine authority for their words and actions.

Our focus now returns to Paul, who truly had the kind of experience that really was worth boasting about; yet preferred to boast only about his weaknesses (v.5). Again, he wants to make it clear that this is all about God, and not about himself. Paul admits that even if he were really boasting, he would be telling the truth. Nevertheless, he refused to boast of his private spiritual experiences. He deliberately chose not to boast, because others might credit him with something special; more than was warranted by his life and message. Had that been the case, it would have been easier for someone to focus attention on Paul instead of the Lord. It was Jesus alone that Paul desired to place in the spotlight.

Also, Paul did not want others to base their evaluation of him on unverifiable spiritual experiences; but only on what could be seen in his daily life and heard in his message (v.6-7a). Paul's desire is to boast only in his weaknesses; in order to show that 'the power at work in his life' is truly from God. He does share with us the fact that 'he received this unique revelation', so as to help us affirm his apostleship — but he also has another reason for doing so. By sharing such an unparalleled experience, he now has a select opportunity to give us a very personal glimpse at one of his most distressing weaknesses. As he does, we are going to gain a profound insight into God's Arithmetic as it pertains to our path to spiritual strength and power - despite the many limitations we may face.

We have now in Paul's own words, an account of how he wrestled in prayer to God over a very painful physical problem he had. As we examine what he has to say, not only will we see how he continues to magnify the work of God in his life, but we will also discover several key principles. These principles will teach us how to find the most satis-fying experience of God's power and strength at work in our hearts:

"6 Even if I should choose to boast, I would not be a fool, because I would be speaking the truth. But I refrain, so no one will think more of me than is warranted by what I do or say, 7 or because of these surpassingly great revelations. Therefore, in order to keep me from becoming conceited, I was given a thorn in my flesh, a messenger of Satan, to tor-ment me. 8 Three times I pleaded with the Lord to take it away from me. 9 But he said to me, "My grace is sufficient for you, for my power is made perfect in weakness." There-fore I will boast all the more gladly about my weaknesses, so that Christ's power may rest on me. 10 That is why, for Christ's sake, I delight in weaknesses, in insults, in hard-

ships, in persecutions, in difficulties. For when I am weak, then I am strong." 2 Corinthians 12:6-10 NIV

The first principle we come to, has been touched on already from verse 6. *A true experience of spiritual strength and power comes only by giving all glory to God.* We noted that Paul was "boasting" only to highlight God's work in his life; unlike his opponents who were boasting entirely for self promotion. He has already begun to speak of his weaknesses, contrasting himself with the false apostles. This was to help the Corinthians see how the power at work in his life was solely from God (11:31-33). In v.6 (and up to the word "therefore" in v.7), he wanted everyone to understand that any evaluation of his true spirituality - should only be based on observation of his life, ministry, and message - not on unverifiable claims of lofty spiritual experiences (which might only serve to make *him* sound great). Anyone can claim to be a spiritual person with an exclusive pipeline to God. This is part of what the false "super apostles" were about. They wanted everyone to be in subjection to them - based on their unsubstantiated claims to possessing God's spiritual authority. They made themselves out to be super spiritual people, but they did not live and act as a genuinely spiritual person would. Paul said that if you were going to evaluate him as an apostle, it must be based on what he was doing and saying — not on the basis of something that happened to him fourteen years ago that he couldn't prove. Paul lived as Jesus lived. He acted as Jesus would act, and treated people the way Jesus did. His daily life was marked by a Christlike love for others. Thus, his character spoke for itself. The way he lived among the Corinthians (and their very salvation in Christ) was all he needed - to attest that he was the true Apostle of Jesus. Everything he did and said was meant to point people to Christ, and to build up their faith in Him. It was never all about Paul — it was always all about Jesus.

Everywhere we look today, there are so called "great spiritual leaders" with large followings. Having a large following does not make anyone truly spiritual — in the same way that truth is not determined by the majority. Biblical truth remains valid, regardless of how many people believe it. Those who have a large following are not necessarily walking in the truth. A person who is genuinely spiritual, is identifiable in specific ways — not just based on their personal claims to have a special message from God. One of the chief characteristics of authentic spiritual power, is that the individual always gives all glory and credit to God. Such people do so not in word only, but by a life that consistently reflects the love of Jesus. In his first letter to the church at Corinth, Paul was already trying to make it clear that the Spirit's power is most evidenced when Christ is magnified, and faith is centered on Him alone. God, not man, must be the focal point of our attention. Listen carefully to the emphasis Paul places on God and Christ, rather than on himself, in 1 Corinthians 2:1-5 NIV:

"1 And so it was with me, brothers and sisters. When I came to you, I did not come with eloquence or human wisdom as I proclaimed to you the testimony about God. 2 For I resolved to know nothing while I was with you except Jesus Christ and him crucified. 3 I came to you in weakness with great fear and trembling. 4 My message and my preaching were not with wise and persuasive words, but with a demonstration of the Spirit's power, 5 so that your faith might not rest on human wisdom, but on God's power."

Many people came to believe in Christ through Paul's ministry in Corinth. Paul is clearly aware that God used him to share the gospel. However, it couldn't be more plain that Paul wanted them to understand that all the power and all the praise - belongs to God alone. Right after this, Paul addresses some in the church who were acting like spiritual babies. They were jealous of one another, and were quarreling amongst themselves. They had divided into little camps; arguing over who was the best spiritual leader and teacher. Some said Paul was the best. Others said Apollos was the one to follow. Paul tells them that they were acting infantile. Truly spiritual people do not compare one leader to another, and fight over who is greater. Leaders are all just servants of God, and it's all about Him - not about His servants. Listen again to how Paul identifies where our focus ought to be:

"5 Is Apollos important? No! Is Paul important? No! We are only servants of God who helped you believe. Each one of us did the work God gave us to do. 6 I planted the seed, and Apollos watered it. But God is the One who made it grow. 7 So the one who plants is not important, and the one who waters is not important. Only God, who makes things grow, is important. 8 The one who plants and the one who waters have the same purpose, and each will be rewarded for his own work. 9 We are God's workers, working together; you are like God's farm, God's house." 1 Corinthians 3:5-9 NCV

Here once again, Paul - who is certainly a true spiritual leader - is making sure that our eyes are fixed on God. It is God, and He alone, who is worthy of all honor and praise. Those who would place themselves and their own spirituality as the center of attention - are nowhere near the zone of genuine spiritual power. Whether they appear on television, write best selling books, or draw large crowds to hear them speak — only those who give all the glory to God - are the true ambassadors of Christ. We will also see them reflect God's glory by their sincere love for others, and by demonstrating the kind of spiritual outlook that Paul is about to share with us - an outlook of total trust in God and His grace. True spiritual leaders will not hesitate to confess their own weaknesses — because they know that it is through their weaknesses that the power of Christ will be made most fully known as they minister in His name.

Paul had received what he called *"surpassingly great revelations"* (see 1 Corinthians 12:7 above). Not only did Paul receive a unique glimpse of heaven; but God gave him a great deal more as well. After his conversion, he received from Jesus a full revelation of the gospel (cp. Galatians 1:11-12). He also received the revelation of the 13 New Testament epistles; which were unfolding to him during those years of his life. In addition, the Lord Jesus Christ had appeared to Paul personally. By my count, the book of Acts has four occasions of such appearances (Acts 9:3-6; 18:9-10; 22:17-21; 23:11); not to mention other visions and special messages from angels (e.g., Acts 16:9; 27:23-24). I don't know about you — but if any one of these things had happened to me — it would be very easy to think that I was someone pretty special. Knowing how prideful poor human nature is; it isn't hard to imagine how I might think of myself, were I to receive this kind of favor from God. I'd want to tell everyone that "I saw Jesus personally", and that He gave me special revelations. People would say to me, "Well, what did he tell you?" I would tell them what He said, of course, and they would look at me and think, "Wow, you must be pretty special if Jesus singled you out for a personal visit." Perhaps I would even try to act humbly, as if it were nothing at all — but in my head I'd be thinking, "Yes, I'm the man!". At any rate — the temptations of pride, conceit, and self exaltation - even to someone with Paul's integrity - must have been overwhelming. So in order to prevent this from happening, God gave Paul a very special gift. We read what this gift was, as we pick up our narrative again from 2 Corinthians 12:7. . .

"Therefore, in order to keep me from becoming conceited, I was given a thorn in my flesh, a messenger of Satan, to torment me."

On the surface, this doesn't sound like very much of a gift at all. However, in God's Arithmetic, that's exactly what it was. In order for us to understand this gift, we need to talk a little about the nature of it. Let me say at the outset — that it really doesn't matter exactly what it was that Paul went through. Whatever his "thorn in the flesh" really was - does not change the meaning of what God, through Paul, is trying to tell us. Even so, that hasn't affected the mountain of speculation by Bible commentators - as to what Paul was suffering from. I'm not going to join them here in a full analysis of Paul's thorn — but we do need to briefly highlight the severe nature of the thorn. By making clear how severe it was, we can better understand God's grace in giving it; and the way it speaks to the experience of God's power in our lives.

The Greek word used here for "thorn", can also mean "stake", "a splinter", or "the pointed end of a fishhook". That the thorn was in the "flesh", can be understood to mean his physical body — or it could mean our sinful human nature apart from God - as Paul often used it in Romans. The choice an interpreter makes as to how to understand these words, will determine what they think Paul is referring to. Some of the main theories are that his *"thorn in the flesh"* refers to a physical affliction, a besetting temptation, or severe persecution. Other ideas are that it refers figuratively to self crucifixion (Galatians 2:20), or to a demonic individual opponent - who was like a thorn in his side. All of these ideas have their champions. My own belief is that it was likely a physical affliction - most probably the one Paul refers to in Galatians 4:13-15 (and cp. Galatians 6:11). Even when we adopt this view, it only initiates another round of speculation as to what the affliction might be! The most popular theories I'm familiar with — are that Paul suffered from poor eyesight, epilepsy, or a form of malaria. Any of these could have caused him the savage intermittent pain he experienced, perhaps in the form of severe headaches, as some interpreters and early tradition have suggested. Whatever it was, the reference in Galatians suggests that it affected the dignity of his outward appearance, and it was evident to those who observed him. It is also entirely possible that Paul deliberately did not identify his problem. This makes good sense (as noted above), since the insight he shares is unaffected by our exact identification of what the thorn in the flesh might be. Paul goes on to say that the thorn in the flesh was *"a messenger of Satan, to torment me"*. "Torment" here is in the present tense, indicating to us that Paul's affliction was ongoing in his life. While the word "torment" is used (quite correctly) in most Bible translations — this word is also found elsewhere in the New Testament. These usages give us an added perception of what Paul was trying to express. The word is used in Matthew 26:67 and Mark 14:65 - of the soldiers beating Christ in the face with their fists. In 1 Corinthians 4:11, the word is translated "brutally treated" or "beaten". So Paul felt like Satan was beating him up; tormenting him by this affliction which was acting as a messenger to him from the enemy. The question naturally comes up now, as to why this was given to Paul by God. That it came from God is clear — because no matter what Bible translation you choose to review - this is what Paul said. It is not enough to simply say that God *permitted* it, but that Satan was *responsible* for it — that much is evident. Whatever Satan may have had in view with this, God had something wonderful wrapped up in it. Thus Paul, reflecting on his affliction as he wrote to us, says that it was *given* to him; given, I believe, by God, in the sense of a blessing or a gift. Such an act of God is not without precedent in the Bible (cp. Job 1-2). Other notable examples of God's plan for someone that encompasses their suffering - and overrides the intentions of evil - are Jacob's son Joseph, and Jesus. Joseph was sold into slavery by his brothers - who intended to harm him. But when Joseph rose to power in Egypt, and later revealed himself to his brothers, he told them, *"You planned evil against me; God planned it for good to bring about the present result — the survival of many people."* Genesis 50:20 HCSB. The greatest example of God's sovereign wisdom in permitting suffering at the hands of evil, is seen in the death of our Lord Jesus Christ. Jesus' suffering was necessary to accomplish our salvation. Consider these words Paul spoke to the Corinthians in his first letter to them:

"6 Yet when I am among mature believers, I do speak with words of wisdom, but not the kind of wisdom that belongs to this world or to the rulers of this world, who are soon forgotten. 7 No, the wisdom we speak of is the mystery of God — his plan that was previously hidden, even though he made it for our ultimate glory before the world began. 8 But the rulers of this world have not understood it; if they had, they would not have crucified our glorious Lord." *1 Corinthians 2:6-8 NLT*

Whatever the intention of evil may be — it cannot change God's plans, or defeat his purposes. So here in 2 Corinthians 12:7, Paul has come to see the terrible affliction he suffered as a gift of God— but this was not his first reaction to it. His actual response to the painful torment he was going through, was to beg and plead with God to remove it. Paul apparently knew that God had a purpose in this affliction, because he tells us that God did not want him to become too proud, due to the surpassingly great revelations he had received. Nevertheless, Paul begged God to remove it. I imagine his prayer was something like this: "Okay Lord, I get it, I really do! You want me to stay humble. But Lord — is this suffering really necessary? Must I continue to endure this awful agony — when all I want is to keep proclaiming your glory — and to tell those who have never heard about you how they can know you and have their sins forgiven?" There must have been occasions like this when Paul had about as much pain as he could bear, on top of everything else that weighed upon him. We must not imagine that these were casual prayers. If you've ever personally suffered some terrible physical, mental, or emotional pain - and poured out your heart to God about it - you have some idea of the urgency of Paul's prayers. He tells us that he entreated the Lord about this three times. It's not perfectly clear whether God answered Paul the same way each time he prayed; or whether God finally answered him after he had prayed about it for the third time. Either way, it is instructive for us. If God answered him the same way each of the three times he prayed, then Paul persisted in prayer until he was certain that he was hearing God correctly. If God answered him after he had prayed about the matter for the third time, then Paul was demonstrating the wisdom of importunate prayer (which resolutely persists until it knows an answer has been received). Both of these possibilities illustrate for us what Christians mean when we speak of "praying through" a matter, to seek the will of God. This concern of 'persevering in prayer while seeking the will of God', is closely related to any experience of genuine spiritual power. Thus, a few brief words on finding God's will for our lives, may be helpful at this point:

When we pray to God about the burden on our hearts, we must be absolutely determined to trust and obey Him — whatever we discover His will for us may be. For whenever we are fully prepared in our hearts to do God's will, most of the difficulty in finding it has already been overcome. Discovering God's will is also not a matter of simple impressions and feelings. To seek God's will in this way, is to leave ourselves open to great delusion and deception from the enemy. As we pray, we must seek God's mind through purposeful study and reflection upon the Word of God, under the guidance of the Holy Spirit. The Word of God and the Spirit of God are always in one accord as God speaks to His people. The Holy Spirit will guide us, but He will always do so according to the Scriptures - never contrary to them. While we continue in prayer, we should also take into account providential circumstances which can often indicate God's will in connection with His Word and His Spirit. Thus through persistent prayer, the study of God's Word, and careful consideration, we will come to a deliberate judgment according to the best of our ability and knowledge. If our mind continues at peace after reviewing the matter with the Lord two or three times - we may proceed accordingly. This way of seeking the will of God is fruitful for us whether the issue is great or small, pressing or trivial.

For a young or inexperienced believer, it is usually a good idea to seek the counsel of a more mature believer when you are uncertain regarding God's answer. A Pastor, or a more mature brother or sister in Christ, can help affirm that you are on the right track and understanding the Word of God correctly. As we lift our petitions to God, it may happen (as in Paul's case) that the matter at hand is one upon which there is no specific scriptural instruction. When that occurs, we have many promises from God that He will faithfully guide us. One such promise is found in James 1:5-6, and is discussed at length in the chapter "The Surprising Color of Joy". It is also often a source of frustration for many believers, when they petition the Lord upon a matter once or twice - and do not immediately receive an answer. One of the keys to a successful prayer life is *importunity*. On some occasions, I have received an answer to a prayer after the first request. On other occasions, I have had to pray about a matter a great many times; often more than I can count. There are Christians who may think it is foolish to pray over and over about a matter. However, apart from a clear word from God in Scripture, "praying through" our requests and concerns may call for determined and steadfast perseverance on our part. We must continue to pray and not give up. A good example of the need for such importunity - is prayer for the salvation of a soul that needs Jesus. We may need to pray persistently and tenaciously for many years — before we see an answer from God. I believe we should continue in prayer about our concerns, great or small, until God has given us a clear "Yes", "No", or "Not yet". Until then, we should persevere no matter how long it takes. God is infinitely wise in all His ways with us, and even His delays are part of the blessing in His answer. He always knows when the time is right to bestow His gifts — and when it is best to withhold them. We must also remember that while God responds to our petitions with an unparalleled generosity, He also has a right royal heart - and will not be dictated to by anyone. While there are no restrictions on the kinds of petitions we may make — the Lord is not a magic genie - there to grant us three wishes. He is our God and King, to whom our wishes must always remain subordinate. Ultimately, prayer is not just about getting things we want. Prayer is a privileged intimacy with God, whereby we are learning to partake of the infinite riches of Jesus - in a manner that advances His will and purpose in our lives. This is what it means to pray in Jesus' name. We learn to want what He wants, and to desire what He desires. So when Paul besought the Lord three times for the removal of his painful thorn in the flesh, we can be sure that his highest goal remained the glory of God. Paul would accept God's will for his life - and embrace it - as we will soon discover. What is truly inspiring to me — is that he did so even though God answered him with a resounding _No_.

We have been moving through this passage toward the goal of learning how to find spiritual strength and power in our lives, despite our limitations. The first principle we observed from Paul, was that a true experience of spiritual strength and power comes only by giving all glory to God. Our next observation, is that when faced with a serious weakness or limitation, *the first thing Paul did is to bring his problem straight to God.* I learned early on - that life is not always fair. I had no choice as to who my parents would be, where I would be born, or how I would be raised. I was not consulted as to what my physical appearance and limitations would be, or whether I would be rich or poor. No one asked me to choose my native intelligence, early educational opportunities, or social environment. I came into this world with particular opportunities and handicaps, just as all of us did. As a young man, I had to come to terms with who I was. This involved learning both my gifts and my limitations. Yet the world is a big place - and life isn't always fair. How was I to learn where I fit into the scheme of things? Moreover, where would I find meaning and purpose when I had setbacks, and when I had to face bitter and unpleasant experiences? Like many people, I could have just lived by the axiom "hang in there, and it will all work out" — as if there was some kind of magic karma in the universe that would somehow make everything okay. Or I could have adopted the mantra of self-help gurus; that if I would take a positive attitude about my problems, then there is nothing I couldn't accomplish. The problem is — life can be filled with serious pain. Times when there is nowhere to go, no one to turn to, no magic bullet to relieve your suffering, and give meaning to your heartache and grief. As Christians, we know there is someone to whom we can turn when the pain doesn't make sense. Our heavenly Father, who made us, and who placed us into this world for a purpose - is the only one who can provide those answers. I am not trying to be glib or simplistic about this. There is terrible pain and suffering in this world for which there simply is no answer; an awful mystery to some events, which in this life, will never be solved. But for each of us personally, there is a God who cares, a Savior who brings meaning, and a Spirit who gives comfort and strength.

The first place Paul went with his pain - was to God. Where do you go first when life hands you more than you can bear? Your spouse? Parents? Friends? A therapist? Your Pastor? All of these persons may provide some comfort; but no one can speak healing as deeply into your spirit as God can. If it is real spiritual strength that you seek — go first to God. "Cast all your anxiety on Him because He cares for you" (1 Peter 5:7 NIV). There is no guarantee that your suffering will be removed — but there is every guarantee that God loves you, that he cares, and that in Jesus Christ, all your needs have been anticipated and provided for. If you would know spiritual power, then take your pain first to God.

We come now to verse 9, where we find God's answer to Paul's plea for the removal of his thorn in the flesh:

"My grace is sufficient for you, for my power is made perfect in weakness."

In other words — God said no. Before we review what he *did* say — we must be honest with the fact that God said, "No, I am not going to remove your pain." It is here we find the first of the next two closely related principles on our path to spiritual power. *Our experience of spiritual power deepens as we learn to trust God's "No's".* On the surface, God's refusal to remove Paul's thorn - may seem very unfair to us. Paul had done so much in his service to God. He had endured terrible suffering and persecution for Jesus sake; more than most of us would ever want to face. (We looked at some of his ordeals in 11:21-29.) God's refusal wasn't due to a lack of faith — Paul had plenty of that. It wasn't that he was arrogant — for the New Testament paints the portrait of a man with the deepest humility (cp. 1 Corinthians 15:9-10). The fact is, God had something for Paul - even better than removing the thorn. God's love for us is unimaginably great. It is so great - that His purpose for us may allow our pain - because there is an infinitely precious gift embedded in it for us. God will not always remove our suffering in answer to prayer. Yet His refusal is itself an expression of His love and grace toward us. God is always working out in our lives *a different kind of blessing* than the one that comes from the immediate removal of our suffering. There is a larger blessing in store — if we are only willing to trust Him. Learning to trust God when He says "no", extends into every aspect of our lives. We sometimes encounter difficult people. People who mistreat us, and try our patience. We pray to God that they be removed from our lives, but He says no. All of us face unpleasant circumstances at one time or another. The pressure mounts, and we entreat the Lord to take swift action on our behalf, but He says no. It may be an unpleasant occupation or a difficult coworker that discourage us. Problems in our home or with our family that exasperate us. Frustrations over our finances or the necessities we lack that drive us to our knees. We may desire a larger sphere of influence, or maybe even the removal of a problem that hinders our service to Christ. Sometimes we want more. Sometimes we want less. Some things we want added, and some we want removed. But no matter what the reason for our petitions before God, there are times when He says "no". If we ever want to grow spiritually, we must move past a childish adulthood where we get upset with God every time He refuses to give us what we want. Not only does the Lord love His children too much to spoil them; but that same love knows exactly what we need, and the right time to bestow it. Do God the honor of trusting Him as you pray. When He says "no", it is always because He is looking well beyond the immediate need that is pressing upon you. His ways are higher than our ways (Isaiah 55:8-10), and He needs no one to counsel Him (Romans 11:34; 1 Corinthians 2:16; Isaiah 40:13). Look for the gift that is always wrapped up in God's refusals. Watch and wait. Sooner or later, you will most certainly find it. Believe that the refusal itself is a confirmation of His promise for something even better than what you asked

When God says "no", it doesn't mean He has abandoned us, or that He is not active on our behalf. As we come back to v.9, it is here that we, like Paul, find another principle on our path to spiritual power. *Our spiritual life grows as we learn the total sufficiency of God's grace.* In so many words, the Lord said to Paul, "I'm not going to remove your thorn, but I am going to give you all the grace you need. It will always be enough — for you will never have a need that is greater than my resources and provision for you."

We must pause for a moment here, to reflect on what God's grace actually is. Grace is a word we throw around without really understanding it. If we were pressed to define it, most of us would say that grace is God's undeserved or unmerited favor. That sounds very Christian — but what does it mean? In the New Testament sense, grace is a generous benefit given, a favor bestowed, on someone who could never earn it. This grace is of a very practical nature. It is not only God's loving disposition toward us — it is His love and mercy in action. <u>Grace is what God *does* for us that we could never do for ourselves.</u> It is a covenant word; a word that declares that when God accepts us in Christ, He does so solely on the basis of His own goodness and nature, and not on the basis of anything deserving in us. Grace describes the loving actions of God that are operating in our lives (see 2 Corinthians 9:14). It is the God-given practical inner power that works every spiritual blessing in our lives (Ephesians 1:3). Many of these blessings are in fact recounted by Paul in the first chapter of Ephesians. He says that in Christ - we are chosen, predestined, adopted, redeemed, forgiven, and lavished with grace - along with all wisdom and understanding. We are saved and sealed with the Holy Spirit. He even goes on to say that our entire salvation, including our faith, is an act of God's grace to us in Jesus Christ (Ephesians 2:4-10). So, we are saved by the work of God's Spirit - as an act of grace on His part. We are caused to grow spiritually (sanctified) by the Spirit - as an act of God's grace. We will be glorified by the same Spirit - also by God's grace. Paul even states that in all future ages, we will continue to experience the immeasurable riches of His grace (Ephesians 2:7). In the Christian life, this grace abounds to us. Through the active power of grace, we are enabled to understand the Word of God, and to apply it to our lives. It is grace that helps us to overcome sin and temptation. It is grace that helps us to obey and serve God. It is grace that manifests all the spiritual gifts that God channels through us for the benefit of others. It is also grace that gives us the inner strength to endure heartache, disappointment, and pain. Grace is the active expression of God's undeserved favor at work in our lives. John says that out of the fullness of Christ, we have received grace upon grace, or one blessing after another (John 1:16). Luke tells us that this grace was powerfully at work in all the early Christians (Acts 4:33). Peter exhorts all of us to be faithful to serve others, using whatever spiritual gift we have received; because together, these gifts express the wide variety of all the facets and colors of God's grace (1 Peter 4:10). Earlier in 2 Corinthians (9:8), while encouraging cheerful giving, Paul tells us that God can make His grace overflow to us - so that in every way and at all times - we might have all that we need to excel in every good work to others. God tells Paul that this all-sufficient grace will always be available; more than enough to allow him to triumph over his thorn in the flesh.

Now that we know what grace is, we are ready to understand why God told Paul that He had something better prepared for him than the removal of his thorn.

"My grace is sufficient for you, *for my power is made perfect in weakness.*" (v.9 italics mine)

This sentence should be emblazoned on our church walls, and on the secret chambers of our hearts. If we ever hope to have God's power on display in our lives, then it is absolutely essential to understand what it means for God's power to be made perfect in our weakness. The words *"made perfect"* mean: to be brought to an intended or desired goal; to bring to completion or finish what was started. Paul realized God had an intended goal that He would bring about through his weaknesses and limitations. In some way, God's power was able to work to its fullest extent in Paul's life through his weakness. It would show itself most effective when he was weak. Paul's weakness opened the way for God's power to flow through him. <u>We might think that just doesn't add up. How can God show Himself strong when we are weak?</u> **<u>This is God's Arithmetic. Our limitations allow God's power to work - without us getting in the way.</u>** Our weakness creates the clearest contrast between the human and the divine. The false apostles were boasting in their own strength. Paul boasted in his weaknesses — because then the power of Christ would be most undeniably on display. God's glory - His presence and action in our lives - is most evident when we are unable to produce or perform something on our own without divine aid. The more that is accomplished despite our limitations, the more it becomes apparent to ourselves and to others that it is the mighty power of God at work through our lives. All that God brings about through us - is then shown to be from His power alone. We are indeed the instruments through whom He works, but we are not the cause of the results. From this, we see again how important it is to learn to trust God's "No's". When the Lord does not grant us relief from our suffering, it does not mean we have been abandoned. We must understand that His refusal is itself a promise that His all-sufficient grace will always be available to see us through to a place of triumph and victory. What throws so many of us for a loop — is our failure to understand another aspect of God's Arithmetic. <u>God is more concerned with our character than our comfort</u>. This is one of those aspects of our walk with Christ that we seem to know with our minds, but not with our hearts. Unless we are fully convinced of the truth of this — we will never know spiritual power, or why we can be certain of the sufficiency of God's grace. If we believe that our comfort is God's highest concern for us — we will either be very disappointed Christians - or very flabby ones.

On one side of this, is that for most of us, life is not always comfortable and easy. People are not always agreeable. What we need is not always convenient to obtain. Daily life is not always enjoyable. We are not always in good health or well rested. Our labors are not always satisfying, and our paths are filled with trouble. We are not well off, we can't keep up with the Joneses, and we don't have many of the things that our hearts desire. The result of all this, is that we come to believe that God doesn't care. We are sad and disappointed at our lot in life, and we feel that God has short-changed us. Our culture has so affected our minds, that our values have been turned upside down. This is because our understanding of what God purposes for us - is in opposition to His. The Bible is clear that God's priority is to work through the entire tapestry of our lives, to conform our character to the likeness of Christ. The Lord isn't striving with all His mighty power in us - to make our lives easy. We are His masterpiece in Christ. Day by day, year by year, we are being molded and shaped into living stones that God is building into His spiritual temple (1 Peter 2:5). When this life is over, all we will take with us is our character. God has promised to always be with us, and to take care of our basic needs. Our concern is to set our hearts on spiritual matters; making God's Kingdom and His righteousness our top priority (see e.g., Matthew 6:24-34; 28:18-20; Hebrews 13:5-6).

On the other side of this kind of thinking — are those who believe that our comfort is God's highest concern for us; so they fashion a life that has become quite complacent. The danger here - is of becoming spiritually flabby. We find ourselves living in a state where there is no iron in our soul, no fortitude being developed, and no spiritual fruit in our life. This is not to say that we cannot be fruitful Christians and also be materially wealthy. God does have select children with whom He has entrusted much wealth, as a stewardship for the work of His Kingdom and the good of many people. These are Christians who have remained faithful to Him, and have not allowed their possessions to turn their hearts to the world. Unfortunately, it's all to easy when we are in that position - to think we are somebody special, and that we don't need God as much as our poorer brothers and sisters. We fail to remember our weaknesses, and to nourish our relationship with Christ. The result is plenty of monetary clout — but little evidence of spiritual power or influence in our lives. A very poor trade-off indeed.

Truly, God is more concerned with our character than our comfort. Unless we recognize this, God's grace will appear weak to us instead of strong. We will be more concerned with promoting our own glory than with God's power being made perfect through our weakness. It will seem that God doesn't care about us - because He is addressing the higher concern of character - while we are fixated on the lesser concern of comfort. If we desire an experience of genuine spiritual power, these are truths we must understand. Our weaknesses and limitations are not a cause for discouragement. Instead, they are God's opportunity to show Himself strong on our behalf. They are also our opportunity to allow

God's power to work to the fullest extent in our lives, and to make His glory known.

We have been listening to Paul as he has opened his heart to the Corinthian church. He has resorted to *"foolish boasting"* to help his beloved church see the true from the false. Everything he has shared was ultimately to help build up their faith in Christ. He has even gone so far as to share his private prayer to God over a very painful personal affliction - which he calls "a thorn in the flesh". This was done to teach the believers the total sufficiency of God's grace, and how God's power expresses itself to the fullest extent through our weakness. Paul had come to understand how even such a 'prolonged condition of infirmity' was a necessary part of God's plan for him. Now that he has shared with us the answer God gave to his prayers about the thorn, he tells us the lesson God taught him through his painful experience. As we look at the last part of v.9 and all of v.10, we see that lesson - and the outlook Paul adopted toward all his limitations. From this, we will find the final principle which allows us to begin experiencing spiritual power in our own lives. Paul writes:

"Therefore I will boast all the more gladly about my weaknesses, so that Christ's power may rest on me. 10 That is why, for Christ's sake, I delight in weaknesses, in insults, in hardships, in persecutions, in difficulties. For when I am weak, then I am strong."

Here, Paul picks up again on the thought he began in 11:30 and 12:5. He would not boast except in regard to his weaknesses. Noteworthy here — is that he speaks of his weaknesses *gladly*. We should not understand "gladly" to mean that he is simply *very willing* to do this (as in the sentence: *"I'll be glad to speak to you."*). What he is saying, as we see in verse 10, is that he *delights* in speaking and experiencing such things. He actually took pleasure in them. They put him in good cheer. This is a most amazing attitude. Most of us have not learned to take any delight whatsoever in our limitations. Our focus always seems to be on our handicaps. Paul had learned to see his handicaps as gifts. Pause for a moment to really consider this. You might feel (as most of us do) that an outlook such as this, is too high a goal. How can we ever attain to it? Well, the only way of course, is by grace. Grace that is ours only when we learn the same lesson that Paul had to learn. He states this lesson two ways. *When I am weakest, Christ's power rests on me. When I am weak, then I am strong.* Paul goes well beyond his 'thorn in the flesh' when he speaks here about being weak. This lesson extends to all the limitations in his life (v.10). It extends to insults, hardships, persecutions, and difficulties. In other words — everything that humbled him. All his seeming disadvantages. Every problem and pressure that *he thought* limited him from being his best for God. Whenever he came to the place that all he could see about himself was weakness — the power of Christ showed up! It didn't just show up, it *rested on him, dwelled with him, pitched its tent with him, and made its home there.* In the midst of Paul's natural weakness - when he knew the task was well beyond his own abilities - the power of Christ shows up to facilitate and effect the accomplishment of God's will. So, for example, as Paul preached the gospel to the Corinthians in a state of personal weakness, the dynamic life giving energy of Christ set about working in the hearts of those present - to minister life to them. We can easily see this principle at work in Paul's own account of his ministry among them, from a passage we quoted earlier:

"1 And so it was with me, brothers and sisters. When I came to you, I did not come with eloquence or human wisdom as I proclaimed to you the testimony about God. 2 For I resolved

to know nothing while I was with you except Jesus Christ and him crucified. 3 I came to you in weakness with great fear and trembling. 4 My message and my preaching were not with wise and persuasive words, but with a demonstration of the Spirit's power, 5 so that your faith might not rest on human wisdom, but on God's power." 1 Corinthians 2:1-5 NIV

We hear Paul declare this very same principle again, right after the current passage. As he anticipates his third visit to the church, he tells them:

"1 This will be my third visit to you. "Every matter must be established by the testimony of two or three witnesses." 2 I already gave you a warning when I was with you the second time. I now repeat it while absent: On my return I will not spare those who sinned earlier or any of the others, 3 since you are demanding proof that Christ is speaking through me. He is not weak in dealing with you, but is powerful among you. 4 For to be sure, he was crucified in weakness, yet he lives by God's power. Likewise, we are weak in him, yet by God's power we will live with him in our dealing with you." 2 Corinthians 13:1-4 NIV

In Paul's very weakness, he was undeniably the most strong spiritually; in the sense that God's power was most vibrantly seen as belonging not to Paul - but to Christ. God will not share His power with those who think themselves strong. Paul was used by God to plant churches in cities all over the Roman Empire. There are probably few Christians today who (if we could trace all of holy history) would not owe their salvation to Paul's faithful witness for Christ. Yet if we were to speak to Paul today, he would not boast about that. He would be the first to tell us that there is no way to explain his life, his apostolic ministry, and the impact he had for Christ, by looking at his own abilities. Christ had transformed his life, and whenever he was weak - least likely to trust in his own abilities - God breathed power through his ministry. The application for us is clear. If we desire an experience like Paul's, we must learn his lesson, and share his outlook. If we want the power of Christ to revolutionize our own lives - and extend itself to others - then we too must be weak to be strong. We must allow our weaknesses to lead us to rely solely on God's strength — not on our own abilities. The more we learn to release our limitations to God in recognition of our weakness, the more Christ's power will make its home in our lives. When our human frailties and limitations become most evident to ourselves, we will find the truest experience of God's strength at work in our hearts. Our handicaps will then become Christ's opportunities to show Himself strong on our behalf. *The secret of spiritual strength is learning to delight in our weaknesses; to genuinely choose to embrace them. We must continually nourish and foster the awareness that it is through those weaknesses, that the power of Christ is most effective in our lives.*

The Apostle Paul, and Nick Vujicic - have something in common. Despite their limitations, they knew that God loved them and had a purpose for their lives. This fact allowed them to seize their opportunities. It's the same for you and me. When our problems are at their worst - when it hurts the most and our own strength is all but gone - the grace of God will prove itself sufficient. God has a purpose for each of our lives. There is work for us to do. Remember, we are saved by grace; yet the Lord has planned something for each of us:

"For we are God's masterpiece. He has created us anew in Christ Jesus, so we can do the good things he planned for us long ago." Ephesians 2:10 NLT

God's love for us in Christ - is beyond all attempts to describe it. We are each fearfully and wonderfully made (Psalm 139:14). We must not allow our limitations to keep us from believing that God will use us in ways we cannot yet imagine — if we will only dare to trust Him.

Perhaps like Paul, others have considered you a "nobody" or a "nothing", at some point in your life (see 12:11). None of God's children are "nobodies". Many great pastors, evangelists, missionaries, and those of great spiritual influence in all walks of life, entered their work feeling ill-equipped for what God called them to do. However, the very limitations that made them seem to be "nothing" in the world's eyes - were what God used to bring them to their place of power. Their secret was 'to yield themselves and their weaknesses - completely to God'.

"My grace is sufficient for you, for my power is made perfect in weakness."

"For when I am weak, then I am strong."

If we allow these words to take hold of our hearts, then *the same power that raised Jesus from the dead* will produce a deeper walk with God than we would otherwise ever know. Here then, are five key principles for allowing the power of Christ to rest upon our lives:

• *A true experience of spiritual strength and power comes only by giving all glory to God.*

• *When faced with a serious weakness or limitation — the first thing to do is bring our problem straight to God.*

• *Our experience of spiritual power deepens as we learn to trust God's "No's".*

• *Our spiritual life grows as we learn the total sufficiency of God's grace.*

• *The secret of spiritual strength is learning to delight in our weaknesses; to choose to embrace them. We must continually nourish and foster the awareness that it is through those weaknesses, that the power of Christ is most effective and evident in our lives.*

The Bible gives us many wonderful examples of these principles at work in the lives of God's servants. People who saw themselves as nobodies; yet were called by God to obedient faith. Even though conscious of their weakness - and knowing full-well that their calling was beyond all their abilities - they dared to believe God. What they discovered was that by God's grace — nothing was impossible. God's power was made perfect through their weakness, and God's mighty acts became evident for all the world to see. These folks were not "super saints". Like Elijah, their human nature was just like ours (cp. James 5:17). They came to their 'place of power' only by yielding themselves and all their weaknesses in total surrender to God. In Hebrews 11 (the great hall of faith), we find many individuals who saw the impossible happen - by taking God at His word. They were commended for their faith, but do we suppose this was due to their own great abilities? No. Their faith points us to Jesus; the one 'who began their faith and made it perfect' by completing in their lives the promises God made to them (Hebrews 12:2). With many of these saints, it's not difficult for us to find evidence that God's power was conspicuously at work through their weakness. We read of those like Noah; who built a 450 foot long ark that could carry 20,000 tons of cargo, and did not complete it until he was 600 years old (give that some thought!). There was Abraham and Sarah, who conceived a child promised by God, even though he was 100 years old, and Sarah was 90. Some time later, this same Abraham was about to sacrifice his son Isaac, the one through whom God had said his descendants would be counted. While it is true that he reasoned God could raise the dead — imagine the grace he would need - to be able to take a knife to his own son - a child he had waited 25 years for. This entire scene of Abraham's obedient faith was truly a demonstration of God's power made perfect through man's weakness. Later in Hebrews 11, there is a reference to several other individuals and their exploits of faith:

"32 And what more shall I say? I do not have time to tell about Gideon, Barak, Samson and Jephthah, about David and Samuel and the prophets, 33 who through faith conquered kingdoms, administered justice, and gained what was promised; who shut the mouths of lions, 34 quenched the fury of the flames, and escaped the edge of the sword; whose weakness was turned to strength; and who became powerful in battle and routed foreign armies." Hebrews 11:32-34 NIV

We immediately note some of those mentioned as 'those blessed with a spiritual faith' — but who the Bible declares had lowly thoughts of themselves (as did Gideon, Barak, and David). These men recognized their weaknesses, and God worked powerfully on their behalf. Then there is one like Samson - in whose life the grace of God is expressly displayed to us in his weakness - despite the fact that it took the loss of both of his eyes to humble him. There, in his greatest humiliation and sorrow, we see the power of God most prominently on display, as he destroys more of God's enemies in his 'death' than he had in his 'life' (see Judges 16:23-30). We realize from this and many other Biblical examples, a remarkable feature of scripture that distinguishes the 'exploits of these men of faith' from the 'attainments and triumphs of the people of the world'. Namely that the Bible never glosses over the infirmities of these individuals through whom faith so often worked — and the weakness that preceded their victories. They, like us, were often afraid and remonstrated with God over His calling on their lives - due to a honest assessment of their own limitations. There are many other examples in the Bible which we could cite as an illustration of how God shows Himself strong through human weakness. People like Joshua, Job, Daniel, the three Hebrew children (Shadrach, Meshach, and Abednego), and Peter, along with many others. To exemplify these principles, let us focus next on three such notable individuals (Joseph, Moses, and Hezekiah) "whose weakness was turned to strength" (Hebrews 11:34). By looking at relevant episodes in their lives, we will be better able to understand why 'delighting in our weaknesses' provides us with the most unobstructed vision of God's power at work in us.

Joseph

More than once, the Bible shares with us the wonderful story of an individual who rose from obscurity to become among the most powerful men in the world. Joseph is one such person. His life pictures for us in dramatic ways - the power of God working out His intended goals through human weakness. The story of Joseph was referenced earlier as a notable example of how God's plan for someone 'encompassed their suffering and overrode the intentions of evil'. The significant events in his life are found in Genesis 37:2 - 45:28; with additional mention until Genesis ends in 50:26.

When we meet Joseph at age 17, he is being sent on a mission by his father (Jacob) to check on the welfare of his brothers - who were out pasturing their sheep. He is wearing the beautiful robe (traditionally referred to as "a coat of many colors") which was given to him by his father. This robe was a token of the favoritism shown to him, and it represented his father's intention to grant him the largest portion of the inheritance. Joseph's older brothers hated him because he was his father's favorite son — and even more so because of the dreams God gave him; dreams that portrayed Joseph as the future family leader, and who would be elevated to a position of authority over the whole clan of Israel. We are told that Joseph's brothers resented him for this, and typically would not even speak a kind word to him. As the story continues, Joseph catches up to his brothers who were caring for their sheep at Dothan. Despite being alienated from his brothers, we find Joseph to be a young man of good character. He is faithfully checking on their welfare - in obedience to his father's wishes - despite the way they treated him. Most of us are familiar with what happens next. The cruel brothers throw the helpless Joseph into a cistern, and ultimately sell him into slavery to a group of passing Midianite traders on their way to Egypt. To make matters worse, they dip his beautiful robe in goat's blood, and deceive their father into believing he had been killed by a wild animal. Young Joseph arrives in Egypt with the slave traders, and is sold to an Egyptian officer named Potiphar - the captain of Pharaoh's palace guard. Despite this injustice, we are told repeatedly that *"the Lord was with Joseph"*. As a result, Joseph was soon put in charge of Potiphar's entire household and property, and became his personal steward. Consequently, the Lord blessed Potiphar's household for Joseph's sake. Some time later, Potiphar's wife tries to seduce Joseph - who had grown into a very handsome man. After failing in her efforts to do so, she falsely accuses him of attempted rape. Joseph possessed a godly wisdom that enabled him to resist the temptation of immorality with this ungodly woman. Nevertheless, he becomes the victim of her cruelty and thus her husband's outrage. Potiphar then has him thrown into prison in disgrace. There, unjustly imprisoned, we find the Lord once again showing His faithful love to Joseph. Joseph soon became a favorite of the prison warden — who placed him in charge of everything that happened in the prison.

After an undisclosed amount of time, we find Joseph correctly interpreting the dreams of Pharaoh's chief cup bearer and chief baker. These officials had offended Pharaoh, who angrily put them into the same prison where Joseph was. (It is worthy of note — that Joseph was careful to give all glory to God. He said to these men, *"God is the only One who can explain the meaning of dreams. Tell me your dreams."* Genesis 40:8 NCV) Joseph's faith in God never wavered. He knew he had been kidnapped and unjustly imprisoned. So according to the interpretation of the dreams, he asked the chief cup bearer to *"remember him before Pharaoh"* when he was restored to his former position some three days hence. The cup bearer forgot all about Joseph however, and didn't give him another thought. Joseph remained in prison for another two years. At that time, Pharaoh had two dreams - which none of his magicians or wise men could interpret. Finally, Pharaoh's chief cup bearer remembered Joseph and spoke up. He testified to Pharaoh that Joseph could interpret dreams, and that the interpretations came true. Pharaoh then summoned Joseph to interpret his dreams. In the amazing scene that follows, we have an Israelite slave confounding the wisdom of the world. Joseph is now 30 years old; having been enslaved and imprisoned for some 13 years. Here he stands (as a convicted felon of sorts), before the most powerful ruler on earth. In Genesis 41:15-16 NLT, Pharaoh asks Joseph to interpret his dreams. *"It is beyond my power to do this."*, Joseph replied. *"But God can tell you what it means and set you at ease."* The result? Joseph became the second most powerful man in Egypt, and was put in charge over all the land. The nation is saved from the coming famine, and people from everywhere around the world come to Egypt to buy grain from Joseph. Most importantly — God's people are blessed and preserved.

Observe here God's Arithmetic at work. At every opportunity, Joseph gave all glory to God. When faced with his own limitations, he brings the matter first to God, and then applies God's wisdom to every situation. Whenever he faced an unfair setback or injustice in his life, he trusted God's "no's" without complaint or bitterness (toward God). God did not save Joseph from the cistern or from the cruelty of his brothers — although he was innocent of any wrongdoing. He was not spared the ignominy of slavery, the false accusation of rape, or the long years spent in prison — despite being a man of integrity and faith. In each unpleasant circumstance, he was compelled to learn the total sufficiency of God's grace. Finally, as one of the most powerful men in the world, he grew in the consciousness that God was the one at work in his weakness - to show the limitless scope of His power. He obtained this understanding despite the odds against it; that his dreams would be fulfilled, and that he would be ruler over all of Egypt. Listen to the words he spoke to his newly reconciled brothers:

"7 *But God sent me ahead of you* to preserve for you a remnant on earth and to save your lives by a great deliverance."

8 "So then, *it was not you who sent me here, but God.* He made me father to Pharaoh, lord of his entire household and ruler of all Egypt." Genesis 45:7-8 NIV (italics mine)

Then, again, we find his final words of forgiveness to these same brothers who feared his reprisal:

19 But Joseph said to them, "Don't be afraid. Am I in the place of God? 20 You planned evil against me; God planned it for good to bring about the present result — the survival of many people." Genesis 50:19-20 HCSB

Joseph's life and experience with God remain an inspiration for us. Among the many great lessons of his life, are the same words Jesus spoke to Paul: "My grace is sufficient for you, for my power is made perfect in weakness." Whenever I entertain thoughts that my life has little value – a 'nobody' far too weak for God to ever use for His glory - I remember Joseph. His story reminds me that I serve the God of the impossible; a Sovereign whose power has no limits. I face no adversity that cannot be turned to His glory, if only I will submit to His plan and delight in my weaknesses — so that the power of Christ may rest upon me.

Moses

As we move forward in holy history, our *second* notable individual is the one man above all others — in whom we observe the power of God made perfect in weakness. This is a man so great, that until the coming of Jesus, there was no prophet like him (see Deuteronomy 18:15; Acts 3:18-26). That man is Moses. God said of Moses that he was a very humble man; more humble than anyone else on the face of the earth (Numbers 12:3). *'That there was no one else like him'* - can also be seen from this same passage - when Moses' brother Aaron and his sister Miriam were criticizing him behind his back. God then called them all together and said this:

"Listen to my words:
When there is a prophet among you,
I, the LORD, reveal myself to them in visions,
I speak to them in dreams.
But this is not true of my servant Moses;

he is faithful in all my house.
With him I speak face to face,
clearly and not in riddles;
he sees the form of the LORD.
Why then were you not afraid
to speak against my servant Moses?" Numbers 12:6-8 NIV

We might suppose that a man like this, with whom God spoke *"face to face"*, would be a proud man. Like Paul, Moses had received *"surpassingly great revelations"*. Yet we do not read that he was boastful or arrogant, but rather that he was humble beyond all others. I believe he is shown to be so humble because he had learned from life's experiences how weak he was in himself. In addition, anyone who is granted that kind of familiar intimacy with the 'presence and power of God', would also be made profoundly aware of their personal weaknesses, limitations, and frailties.

As we read the story of Moses, there are many occasions in his life that we can identify where his human frailties are most evident. For example, we could survey his experience before Pharaoh, where the obstacles to God's promises were so extraordinary that we see him crying out to God in his helplessness (see Exodus 5:22; 6:12,30). There are also those times during Israel's wilderness wanderings, when the people's rebellion left Moses overwhelmed (see Exodus 17:4; Numbers 11:10-15, 21-22). Many times, both Moses and Aaron were compelled by the fear of God to prostrate themselves on the ground; to plead with God on behalf of His errant people (Numbers 14:5,10; 16:4,19,22; 20:6). Then there was Moses' failure at Meribah, where in frustration he struck the rock in defiance of God's command (thus failing to demonstrate God's holiness), and was forbidden to enter the promised land (Numbers 20:1-13). While all these incidents are evidence of Moses frailties, there is one occasion in his life where we find the most distinct contrast between

God's power and Moses' sensibility of his own weakness. That occasion, is Moses' call from God to deliver Israel from slavery in Egypt (Exodus 3:1-4:17). In order for us to understand Moses' reaction to God's call, we must bear in mind the events that led up to that time in his life.

Moses was born in Egypt under the most perilous circumstances. Hidden from danger at birth by a God-fearing mother, he was found by Pharaoh's daughter - floating in a reed basket in the Nile River. She took him to Pharaoh's palace as her own child, where he was taught all the wisdom of the Egyptians, and was powerful in his speech and actions (Acts 7:22). When Moses was about 40 years old, he killed an Egyptian to rescue a Hebrew slave. His action discovered; he fled from Pharaoh and lived as a foreigner in the land of Midian. There he married, raised a family, and lived the next 40 years of his life as a lonely desert shepherd (Acts 7:30, and cp. Exodus 7:7).

These events from Moses' life, paint the picture of the man we find at Mount Sinai in Exodus chapter 3; tending the flock of his father-in-law Jethro. By this time, Moses is eighty years old. Any expectation he once had of being Israel's deliverer (Acts 7:25) was now all but gone. The hardships of life in the harsh desert wasteland had no doubt taken their toll. We find then, an elderly man, who for forty years had endured all the discomforts the desert could dish out. Much of this time he was alone; for shepherding is a solitary work, with little opportunity to depend on the help of others. All the accolades from his life as an Egyptian prince, were now a distant memory. Instead of the fame and treasures of Egypt, all he knew was the obscurity of nomadic life in the desert. All these elements of Moses' life, were used by God to prepare him for the task that lay ahead. When it came time for God to reveal to the world His mighty power, Moses was ready to understand (as Paul later would) that: *"When I am weak, then I am strong"*.

We come now to that special day in his eightieth year, when Moses was tending his flock at Mount Sinai. There, God called to him from the midst of a burning bush:

"Moses! Moses!"
And Moses said, "Here I am."

5 "Do not come any closer," God said. "Take off your sandals, for the place where you are standing is holy ground."
6 Then he said, "I am the God of your father, the God of Abraham, the God of Isaac and the God of Jacob." At this, Moses hid his face, because he was afraid to look at God.

7 The LORD said, "I have indeed seen the misery of my people in Egypt. I have heard them crying out because of their slave drivers, and I am concerned about their suffering. 8 So I have come down to rescue them from the hand of the Egyptians and to bring them up out of that land into a good and spacious land, a land flowing with milk and honey — the home of the Canaanites, Hittites, Amorites, Perizzites, Hivites and Jebusites. 9 And now the cry of the Israelites has reached me, and I have seen the way the Egyptians are oppressing them. 10 So now, go. I am sending you to Pharaoh to bring my people the Israelites out of Egypt." Exodus 3:4-10 NIV

God said to Moses that He had heard the cries of His people and had come down to rescue them. To do this, "I am sending you", God told him (v.10). Moses now responds to the Lord with a series of excuses, trying to convince Him that He had the wrong man. By this time in his life, at age 80, Moses was well aware of his personal weaknesses, lack of ability, and past failure. Had God allowed it, he would have missed the opportunity of a lifetime; an opportunity to experience the almost unimaginable deeds God would accomplish through his life as Israel's deliverer and lawgiver. We must listen carefully now to all of Moses excuses. Each of them reflects a personal limitation that Moses believed would hinder God from doing what He declared He would do.

Moses' first excuse is found in v.11 NIV:

But Moses said to God, "Who am I that I should go to Pharaoh and bring the Israelites out of Egypt?"

God, you need a great man for such a task, not an old man like me. Not only am I an unworthy nobody, but how in the world do you expect someone like me to accomplish this?

God replies:

"I will be with you. And this will be the sign to you that it is I who have sent you: When you have brought the people out of Egypt, you will worship God on this mountain." (v.12)

Don't worry Moses, the issue isn't who you are, it's who I am. Your influence doesn't matter. *I will be with you.* When you all get back and worship me at this mountain, you'll really understand what I mean.

Moses' second excuse (v.13):

Moses said to God, "Suppose I go to the Israelites and say to them, 'The God of your fathers has sent me to you,' and they ask me, 'What is his name?' Then what shall I tell them?"

While this excuse is a bit difficult to understand, a couple of ideas may help us. Moses may have felt that he didn't have all of the answers, and he needed more information (much of which God will provide in verses 16-22). Or, when he says that the people may ask "What is his name?", what they would actually be asking was a question about God's nature and character. In other words, did God genuinely care? Could He really help? Would He keep His promises? Can we truly depend on Him?

God said to Moses, "I AM WHO I AM. This is what you are to say to the Israelites: 'I AM has sent me to you.'"

God also said to Moses, "Say to the Israelites, 'The LORD, the God of your fathers — the God of Abraham, the God of Isaac and the God of Jacob — has sent me to you.' "

"This is my name forever,
the name you shall call me
from generation to generation." (vv.14-15)

The Lord's reply, sharing the divine name, is His assurance to His people that He is *the Living God*. He is the God who is beyond all human history and can enter and direct it. He is the God who alone holds the future. He is the eternal God, with no beginning and no end, and He remains unchanging. He is the self-existent God, who has no limits, and who is always personally present with His people. There is no other God like Him, and none who can challenge Him. All of this is meant as God speaks, "I AM WHO I AM". He does care about His people. He is faithful to His promises. He is able to do anything He says. Nothing is impossible for Him.

Moses' third excuse (4:1):

"What if they do not believe me or listen to me and say, 'The LORD did not appear to you'?"

Moses' resistance to God almost seems to be an argument here, since God had just said to him that they *would* listen to him (3:18). Perhaps Moses' mind flashed to that time long ago when they wouldn't listen to him - although he was a prince (Exodus 2:13-14). It's more likely that by this time, Moses was so aware of his own unimportance, insignificance, and personal inadequacy, that he was sure that no one would believe him. He was still focusing on self doubt, instead of on what God had told him. Their discussion continues..

2 Then the LORD said to him, "What is that in your hand?"

"A staff," he replied.
3 The LORD said, "Throw it on the ground."

Moses threw it on the ground and it became a snake, and he ran from it. 4 Then the LORD said to him, "Reach out your hand and take it by the tail." So Moses reached out and took hold of the snake and it turned back into a staff in his hand. 5 "This," said the LORD, "is so that they may believe that the LORD, the God of their fathers — the God of Abraham, the God of Isaac and the God of Jacob — has appeared to you."

6 Then the LORD said, "Put your hand inside your cloak." So Moses put his hand into his cloak, and when he took it out, the skin was leprous — it had become as white as7 "Now put it back into your cloak," he said. So Moses put his hand back into his cloak, and when he took it out, it was restored, like the rest of his flesh.

8 Then the LORD said, "If they do not believe you or pay attention to the first sign, they may believe the second. 9 But if they do not believe these two signs or listen to you, take some water from the Nile and pour it on the dry ground. The water you take from the river will become blood on the ground." Exodus 4:2-9 NIV

While God was not about to change His mind with respect to His choice of Moses - and not withstanding Moses' doubts - God did recognize that Moses would need assurance of His presence and power. The Israelites would also need proof that God had authenticated Moses as His messenger. So God provides him with these three miraculous signs; to give him all the credibility he would need. But Moses wasn't finished.. Moses' fourth excuse (4:10):

Moses said to the LORD, "Pardon your servant, Lord. I have never been eloquent, neither in the past nor since you have spoken to your servant. I am slow of speech and tongue."

Lord, I'm just not a good speaker. I've never been good with words, and even now since you've been speaking with me, I still have this problem. I speak too slowly, and I just won't be able to respond as I should. I get all tongue tied, and I won't have the right words. Lord, I'm pleading with you here. I just can't do this. My words will be tripping all over themselves while I'm struggling to find the right thing to say. But God wasn't finished either..

11 The LORD said to him, "Who gave human beings their mouths? Who makes them deaf or mute? Who gives them sight or makes them blind? Is it not I, the LORD? 12 Now go; I will help you speak and will teach you what to say." Exodus 4:11-12 NIV

God's words here may sound strange on the surface, but I believe Moses understood exactly what God was telling him. My personal paraphrase of this would be, "Look Moses, I'm well aware of how you speak and of what your mouth can and cannot do. I made everyone's mouths, ears, and eyes. I know when someone cannot speak, hear, or see. Just go, and *I* will help you speak, and *I* will teach you what to say."

We see God here saying to Moses (as He did to Paul), that it isn't about your weakness. Your limitations are not a hindrance to my power. In fact, they will only make it more evident that it is I who am at work - not you. But Moses has one more card to play (v.13). . .

But Moses said, "Pardon your servant, Lord. Please send someone else."

Lord please, anyone but me! Now Moses is desperate. He really doesn't want to go. Yet I don't believe it was as much rebellion on his part, as it was 'an inability to see past his own inadequacies and imperfections'. But God now tells him that enough is enough:

14 Then the LORD's anger burned against Moses and he said, "What about your brother, Aaron the Levite? I know he can speak well. He is already on his way to meet you, and he will be glad to see you. 15 You shall speak to him and put words in his mouth; I will help both of you speak and will teach you what to do. 16 He will speak to the people for you, and it will be as if he were your mouth and as if you were God to him. 17 But take this staff in your hand so you can perform the signs with it." Exodus 4:14-17 NIV

We are told here that God got angry with Moses. Not because of Moses shortcomings — but because of his attempt to circumvent God's clear call on his life. He is trying to escape the call of *I AM*, to be His chosen instrument. But there were to be no more excuses. So God essentially says to him: "All right, you're worried about your speaking ability. I'm going to help you get started on this. What about your brother Aaron? I know he speaks well. In fact, I've already sent him to meet up with you. Not only will he be glad to see you, but he will be happy to help you, and I will be with you both. Now take your staff and get going."

As we review this encounter that Moses had with God, and we consider it along with the other events in his life, there are two themes that are most significant. One, is Moses' keen awareness of his weakness. The other, is how God chose to allow His great power to rest upon him. Both of these motifs run throughout Moses' life. It can be clearly seen from them that God's strength was made perfect in his weakness — the very weakness that Moses imagined was a direct hindrance to God's plan for him. Was Moses mistaken about his limitations? Was he just fooling himself when he thought he was inadequate to heed God's call? No, he wasn't. He was quite correct. Not about his complaint that God had chosen the wrong man, or about what he supposed God could or could not do through him. But regarding his assessment of his own abilities, he was right on target. Here he was, an eighty year old man, with no personal power, facility, or prestige to commend him. He had no experience as a prophet, and no superior knowledge to suit him for the task. He had no sense of adequacy in himself, especially when it came to his speaking ability. Although Moses thought he had nothing to offer God — (quite unknown to him at the time) God had actually been building into his life 'the kind of experience he would soon need' to lead such a great people. His 'years as a shepherd in the wilderness of Sinai' were invaluable as preparation for leading God's flock during their forty years of wilderness wandering. Additionally, God would use Moses' 'earlier life experience in Egypt' to provide a deeper understanding of his people's culture and needs; not to mention his familiarity with Egypt's royal protocols. Still, none of that was what qualified Moses for such a high position of leadership. God uniquely prepares us for His call on our lives — but it is not the preparation itself which allows us any prior claim on what He must do. It is by *God's own sovereign choice* that He calls us to a task. It is His own providence to build into our lives the kind of experiences that He chooses to use in the display of His power. God had prepared Moses for eighty years for the mission to which He would call him. Those long difficult years were certainly not wasted. Yet it was not Moses' own preparation — but *God's all sufficient grace* which would make Moses adequate for the responsibilities that lay ahead.

So it was in this lowly state that Moses appeared before Israel (and later before Pharaoh) with only a staff in his hand. If we could have seen Moses then, we would not have been very impressed. Yet it was through this humble man that God began to reveal Himself to the world through His mighty acts of power. It's evident from the scripture that neither God's people, nor Pharaoh, glorified Moses as he stood before them. In fact, the recurring rebellion of Israel, and the constant criticism Moses faced, demonstrate to us that in his own person - he was never perceived as someone special. The incident in Numbers 12, where Moses' siblings Aaron and Miriam "suppose themselves to be at least his equal" - make this point to us as well. Even they (who knew God had specially chosen Moses) were not impressed with his person, nor afraid to speak against him. In contrast, whenever Moses spoke for God, everyone could see that it was **I AM** who was doing the work. Despite Moses' outward appearance, the Lord always showed Himself strong on his behalf. The contest between Moses and Pharaoh (who thought himself a god), was really between the gods of Egypt and Moses' God. The ten plagues upon Egypt were not a display of Moses' might and power - but of the omnipotent acts of I AM. It was not to 'make Moses' name great' that God performed such miracles - but to make His own name known. Witness God's declaration to Pharaoh:

*Then the LORD said to Moses, "Get up early in the morning, confront Pharaoh and say to him, 'This is what the LORD, the God of the Hebrews, says: Let my people go, so that they may worship me, or this time I will send the full force of my plagues against you and against your officials and your people, so you may know that there is no one like me in all the earth. For by now I could have stretched out my hand and struck you and your people with a plague that would have wiped you off the earth.' **But I have raised you up for this very purpose, that I might show you my power and that my name might be proclaimed in all the earth."***
Exodus 9:13-16 NIV (bold print mine)

So we see then that God's power was made perfect through the weakness of his chosen spokesman. For while Moses was weak in himself — God showed Himself strong so that all the earth would know His name.

Here is a fitting time to mention that even the Lord Jesus himself, in his humanity, went through an experience like Moses. Isaiah said of Jesus:

"There was nothing beautiful or majestic about his appearance,
nothing to attract us to him.
He was despised and rejected —
a man of sorrows, acquainted with deepest grief.
We turned our backs on him and looked the other way.
He was despised, and we did not care." Isaiah 53:2b-3 NLT

As with Moses, there was nothing in Jesus' appearance that impressed his opponents. And like Moses, Jesus appealed to His works to authenticate Himself as God's Son, who had been sent into the world:

"Don't believe me unless I carry out my Father's work. But if I do his work, believe in the evidence of the miraculous works I have done, even if you don't believe me. Then you will know and understand that the Father is in me, and I am in the Father." John 10:37-38 NLT

Moreover, on the cross, the Father showed Himself strong through the apparent weakness of His crucified Son, so that the whole world might know His salvation. We can barely imagine such a divine marvel; looking up to a Messiah on a cross - and finding God's power there. Yet John said:

"Just as Moses lifted up the snake in the wilderness, so the Son of Man must be lifted up, that everyone who believes may have eternal life in him." John 3:14-15 NIV

And Paul declared:

"For the message of the cross is foolishness to those who are perishing, but to us who are being saved it is the power of God." 1 Corinthians 1:18 NIV

Undeniably, *the cross of Jesus Christ is the power of God made perfect in weakness.* For when he speaks of the crucified Christ, Paul says:

"But to those whom God has called, both Jews and Greeks, Christ the power of God and the wisdom of God. For the foolishness of God is wiser than human wisdom, and the weakness of God is stronger than human strength." 1 Corinthians 1:24-25 NIV

As we return to view Moses' life as a whole, we see at work here all the principles that lead us to spiritual power.

First (the rare exception of his failure at Meribah notwithstanding) – Moses, more than any other person, *gave all glory to God.* In order to experience the blessings of the covenant, Israel had to learn God's holiness. When they reverenced His holiness, and gave Him the glory He deserved, they would inevitably experience His power. Moses stands out as the model of a man who pointed others to God's holiness - without the slightest hint of self promotion. *Second* — we see that anytime Moses was faced with his own weaknesses and limitations (as well as the failings of others), *he immediately and without hesitation - brought the matter to God.* In the company of Jesus and Paul, we would be hard pressed to find in scripture another intercessor like Moses; who understood the weaknesses of humanity, and the faithful love and mercy of God. Over and over, when Israel's sin aroused the Lord's anger, Moses entreated Him on their behalf. In doing so, he always appealed to God's faithfulness and the honor of His own great name, rather than to any sense of worthiness on the part of His people. *Third* — like us, *Moses had to learn to trust God's "No's".* When Moses tried to escape his calling, God said no. While judging the people of Israel, he had to trust God's decisions implicitly. Whether moral law or ceremonial law, when God said no - it was absolute. His directions are always in the best interests of His people. Every "no" was meant for their highest good, even as it is for ours. As the 'pillar of cloud by day' and the 'pillar of fire by night' moved, it taught His people that God's "yes" and "no" must be obeyed. The entire generation that died in the wilderness - was for us, an object lesson - that God's commands and prohibitions must be trusted (cp. 1 Corinthians 10:1-11). When we ignore God's "no", there is always a cost, and we do so at our own peril. Throughout Moses' lifetime, he discovered that when God said no, there was always the blessing of His power behind it. *Fourth* — *Moses learned in every situation - to trust the total sufficiency of God's grace.* Over and over again, God provided for his needs. When he required credentials for ministry, God gave them. When he needed help getting started, God sent his brother who could speak well. When he was afraid, God calmed his fears. When he lacked wisdom, it was ready for him (cp. Exodus 18:13-26). For forty years in the wilderness, two million people needed health, protection, animals for sacrifice, and the daily provisions of food and water. God gave them manna, water from the rock, comfort in every sorrow, the blessing of good health, and a faithful new generation of children. Moses watched as God miraculously provided for all the various needs of the vast hosts of Israel. Even unto the one hundred twentieth year of his long life, Moses lacked for nothing in every need, every danger, and every situation he faced. Such was the abundance of God's grace, that even at the time of his death - his eyesight was clear, and he was as strong as ever (Deuteronomy 34:7). ***Finally***, Moses remains the portrait of a man *who maintained the steadfast awareness that his weaknesses were always God's opportunities to show Himself most effectively strong - as He worked to accomplish His purposes throughout Moses' life.* Whether he was standing boldly before Pharaoh, the nation of Israel, or the very presence of the Almighty God Himself — Moses remained the most humble man on earth. His genuine spiritual power grew, as face to face with God he learned his own weakness, and saw how despite his personal inadequacies - *no man could stand before him all the days of his life* (see Deuteronomy 31:6-8; Joshua 1:5).

Hezekiah

We come now to the *third* notable individual through whom God manifests His awesome power - despite their conspicuous and public weakness. We move forward several hundred years after the time of Moses, to a tumultuous time in Israel's history. The year is 716 B.C.; a little over 200 years since Israel's prosperous days under King Solomon. During this period, God's judgment over the nation's apostasy had grown progressively worse. The northern kingdom of Israel (with its capital in Samaria) had been overrun by the Assyrians in 722 B.C.. Her citizens had been deported, and many foreigners had come to take up residence in the land. In the southern kingdom of Judah, the situation was hardly any better. Wicked King Ahaz had neglected and closed down the great Temple of God. Ahaz himself worshiped foreign gods, and was spreading false worship throughout the land. In the midst of this spiritual darkness, God raised up a new king — Ahaz's son Hezekiah.

Hezekiah was the sole ruler in Judah from 715-686 B.C.. He was 25 years old when he began to reign, and his reign lasted 29 years (2 Chronicles 29:1; Isaiah 36:1; 2 Kings 18:13). Hezekiah was one of Judah's best kings. The scriptures say of him that:

"Hezekiah trusted in the LORD, the God of Israel. There was no one like him among all the kings of Judah, either before him or after him. He held fast to the LORD and did not stop following him; he kept the commands the LORD had given Moses. And the LORD was with him; he was successful in whatever he undertook. He rebelled against the king of Assyria and did not serve him. From watchtower to fortified city, he defeated the Philistines, as far as Gaza and its territory." 2 Kings 18:5-8 NIV

At every opportunity, we find Hezekiah seeking the Lord. His reign begins by immediately repairing and reopening the temple. Levites and priests sanctify themselves, and their service is restored. Sacrifices to God begin again, and all the proper religious ceremonies are reinstated. Once again the Lord is praised with music and the singing of Psalms.

Then, in an unprecedented attempt to restore the nation's unity, Hezekiah invites people throughout the entire nation to celebrate Passover in Jerusalem. Shortly thereafter, pagan shrines throughout the entire land are destroyed, and things seem to finally be looking up. Unfortunately, Hezekiah faced two big problems. Each of them will expose a weakness — and allow us a glimpse into how *God's all-sufficient grace* led to a demonstration of His power through Hezekiah's life.

It was sometime just before 701 B.C. (at 39 years of age) that Hezekiah became deathly ill. The story of his illness is found in 2 Kings 20:1-11, 2 Chronicles 32:24, and Isaiah 38:1-8, 21-22. Isaiah the prophet, who was ministering during this time (740-685 B.C.), was well acquainted with Hezekiah, and came to visit him. We pick up the narrative in 2 Kings 20:1b:

He gave the king this message: "This is what the LORD says: Set your affairs in order, for you are going to die. You will not recover from this illness."

2 When Hezekiah heard this, he turned his face to the wall and prayed to the LORD, 3 "Remember, O LORD, how I have always been faithful to you and have served you single-mindedly, always doing what pleases you." Then he broke down and wept bitterly.

4 But before Isaiah had left the middle courtyard, this message came to him from the LORD: 5 "Go back to Hezekiah, the leader of my people. Tell him, 'This is what the LORD, the God of your ancestor David, says: I have heard your prayer and seen your tears. I will heal you, and three days from now you will get out of bed and go to the Temple of the LORD. 6 I will add fifteen years to your life, and I will rescue you and this city from the king of Assyria. I will defend this city for my own honor and for the sake of my servant David.'"

7 Then Isaiah said, "Make an ointment from figs." So Hezekiah's servants spread the ointment over the boil, and Hezekiah recovered! 2 Kings 20:1b-7 NLT

Here we find Hezekiah a relatively young man in the prime of his life. He has faithfully followed the Lord, and he had been influential in helping to bring spiritual renewal in the land. Also, the time was almost upon him when the nation would need his spiritual leadership as it faced an imminent threat from the Assyrians. At just such a time, Hezekiah became terminally ill. God's own great prophet has come to bring him the sad news that he would soon die. To make matters worse, Hezekiah had no son. There was no one to succeed him; no one to carry on the Davidic line of kings. So here he is, sick, helpless, and sorrowful. The city is in danger, and Hezekiah is disconsolate without an heir. What can he possibly do? He does what Paul did, what Joseph did, and what Moses did. He does the same thing that Job, Daniel, Abraham, Jacob, David, Jeremiah, Nehemiah, Ezra, and countless others did. He does what our Lord Jesus did while on earth, when faced with a desperate situation (Hebrews 5:7). He does what we must do when all seems hopeless, and all our strength is gone. *He seeks the face of God.* In utter weakness and humility, he prays to the Lord; reminding Him of the single-minded devotion he has shown Him. Now we must not suppose here that Hezekiah is simply boasting about his faithfulness - as if he were trying to place God in his debt, or trying to make God think that He owed him something. Hezekiah was calling to mind a promise of God; asking Him to remember that promise, and to exalt His own great faithfulness. God had made King David a promise (see 1 Kings 2:4) that if his descendants would follow Him faithfully with all their heart and soul, and live as they should, then one of them would always sit upon the throne of Israel. Hezekiah was crying to God - that he had done his best to fulfill this condition. He besought the Lord to remember His promise, and not let him die without a son to continue David's line. And sure enough, God heard him; as He always will - when we dare to stand on His faithful covenant promises. In Christ, all the promises of God are "Yes" in Him (2 Corinthians 1:20). We are never on more solid ground in prayer, than when we can take a promise of God - and plead it in sincerity before His throne. For no matter what the situation, or how impossible the circumstances, God will honor His word - whether it is through our life or through our death. The subsequent events in Hezekiah's life, will soon bear testimony to this. So God remembered His promise, and now he makes Hezekiah a promise. He tells him that not only will He add fifteen years to his life, but He will save the city from the king of Assyria. He will do so to honor the promises He made to David, and for the honor of His own great name. Herein is a great lesson for us. God will always honor His word, for His integrity can never be impeached. In Christ, we need never despair. For no matter how desperate our need - despite our own limitations - everything we face has been foreknown — and abundant grace has been provided for us in Jesus. Out of his weakness, Hezekiah was made strong; and three days hence, he would be back worshiping God at his beloved Temple. It's interesting to note that God's promise so overwhelmed Hezekiah, that he actually asks God (through Isaiah) for a sign that these things would happen. Here is God's answer from 2 Kings 20:

9 Isaiah answered, "This is the LORD's sign to you that the LORD will do what he has promised: Shall the shadow go forward ten steps, or shall it go back ten steps?"

10 "It is a simple matter for the shadow to go forward ten steps," said Hezekiah. "Rather, have it go back ten steps."

11 Then the prophet Isaiah called on the LORD, and the LORD made the shadow go back the ten steps it had gone down on the stairway of Ahaz.

The stairway of Ahaz was a set of steps used as a sundial. People could tell by the position of the shadow on the steps what time of day it was. Hezekiah reasons that the shadow normally goes forward anyway, but it would really assure him of the Lord's power if it went backwards. Interesting thinking on his part, since it would be just as difficult to advance the earth's motion as to reverse it; but it was all the same to God. So the Lord makes the shadow go back the ten steps it had gone down on the stairway. I'm not even going to try to explain such a miracle; except to say that we serve an awesome and compassionate God. God was not only tender with Hezekiah's weakness - but by doing this, He gives us another lesson that His word will always come to pass; and that nothing is too hard for the Lord (Genesis 18:14; Jeremiah 32:27). Also from this demonstration, we see once again how God's power is perfected in weakness. The contrast could not be clearer between the helplessness of Hezekiah, and the all-sufficient grace and power of the Lord.

We might suppose that Hezekiah and his people would be greatly humbled at this point. Hezekiah even composed a beautiful psalm of praise to God, to celebrate his recovery (see Isaiah 38:9-20). Surprisingly, this was not the case. We have now this interesting interlude between Hezekiah's recovery from his illness, and the Assyrian invasion of Jerusalem which took place shortly thereafter. It seems that the king of Babylon had sent envoys to Hezekiah, along with a get-well letter and a gift, because he heard that Hezekiah had been sick. The truth of the matter was that the Babylonian king was an enemy of Assyria, and he was seeking allies in his rebellion against them. Here is what happened. . .

13 Hezekiah received the envoys and showed them all that was in his storehouses — the silver, the gold, the spices and the fine olive oil — his armory and everything found among his treasures. There was nothing in his palace or in all his kingdom that Hezekiah did not show them.

14 Then Isaiah the prophet went to King Hezekiah and asked, "What did those men say, and where did they come from?"

"From a distant land," Hezekiah replied. "They came from Babylon."

15 The prophet asked, "What did they see in your palace?"

"They saw everything in my palace," Hezekiah said. "There is nothing among my treasures that I did not show them."

16 Then Isaiah said to Hezekiah, "Hear the word of the LORD: 17 The time will surely come when everything in your palace, and all that your predecessors have stored up until this day, will be carried off to Babylon. Nothing will be left, says the LORD. 18 And some of your descendants, your own flesh and blood who will be born to you, will be taken away, and they will become eunuchs in the palace of the king of Babylon."

19 "The word of the LORD you have spoken is good," Hezekiah replied. For he thought, "Will there not be peace and security in my lifetime?" 2 Kings 20:13-19 NIV

The Bible's own commentary on this is found in 2 Chronicles 32:25-26, 30-31 NIV:

"But Hezekiah's heart was proud and he did not respond to the kindness shown him; therefore the LORD's wrath was

on him and on Judah and Jerusalem. *26 Then Hezekiah repented of the pride of his heart, as did the people of Jerusalem; therefore the LORD's wrath did not come on them during the days of Hezekiah."*

"30 It was Hezekiah who blocked the upper outlet of the Gihon spring and channeled the water down to the west side of the City of David. He succeeded in everything he undertook. 31 But when envoys were sent by the rulers of Babylon to ask him about the miraculous sign that had occurred in the land, God left him to test him and to know everything that was in his heart."

Hezekiah had pridefully shown the Babylonians all the Temple treasuries as well as his armory. It appears that by doing so, he was seeking their support against the Assyrians rather than trusting the Lord. He had become proud of his wealth and his military power. God knew all too well that the nation's repentance was incomplete, and that Hezekiah himself still had a long way to go in his walk with God. So the Lord allowed this as a test, one that revealed the weakness that was still there, but needed to be brought to light. To their credit, Hezekiah and his people repented of their pride, but God knew that the people had not truly changed. Through Isaiah, God had already declared the exile of the nation (cp. Isaiah 10:3-4; 22:1-14); but he would spare this generation due to Hezekiah's prayers (as we are about to see). It's somewhat unusual that this entire episode with the Babylonian envoys was recorded in holy writ — but God gave it to us for a reason. We discover here *two concepts* relevant to our discussion. *First*, it emphasizes again that along with Hezekiah and the citizens of Judah - we may become proud of our spiritual blessings. And *Second*, we are reminded that when God allows personal weakness and external trial to seem to be at work against us - it's only to prepare us for a further demonstration of His grace, a larger opportunity for faith, and the unfolding in our lives of His power — power made most unmistakable in our weakness.

If Hezekiah has any pride remaining - it's about to be shattered. We come now to the most prominent incident of his life. A scene so astounding — that it will speak to all future generations. It reminds us of the weakness of man, and of the mighty power of God on behalf of all who will dare to trust Him - when all hope seems lost. Let's set the stage. . .

It was not long after Hezekiah began to be a co-regent with his father - that the Assyrians under Shalmaneser V and his successor Sargon II - defeated the northern kingdom of Israel in 722 B.C.. We noted earlier that many citizens of the north had been deported, and that foreign residents had been brought in to inhabit the land. Move forward several years - to the time of Sargon's death in 705 B.C. When his son Sennacherib came to power, it fomented widespread rebellion among Assyria's subject nations. Hezekiah, seizing the opportunity he believed to exist during this change of government, refused to continue to pay the tribute to Assyria, that his father Ahaz had begun (see 2 Kings 16:7-9). Sennacherib responded to this insurgence by invading Judah, and conquering its fortified towns. Hezekiah knew he had made a mistake, and was now in big trouble. He sent word to Sennacherib, and tried to appease him by sending a large tribute. Sennacherib demanded and received 11 tons of silver and a ton of gold. In his desperation, Hezekiah even had to strip the gold from the doors of the temple to come up with this payment (2 Kings 18:14-16). Despite this last-ditch attempt by Hezekiah to avert disaster, Sennacherib decided he had enough. Hezekiah recognized that Sennacherib was about to wage war against Jerusalem. After consulting with his officials and military advisers, he set about to prepare the city for the siege (2 Chronicles 32:3-8). What happens next is so significant that it takes two full chapters in the Bible to recount it — and both chapters are repeated twice for our instruction (Isaiah 36-37; 2 Kings 18-19). There are even additional insights provided in 2 Chronicles 32. The story of Sennacherib's invasion of Jerusalem cannot be condensed here without losing the sense of atmosphere, mood, and effect of what really took place. Therefore, to gain a thorough appreciation of the feeling of terror and apprehension in the hearts of Hezekiah and his people, I encourage you to pause briefly and read the story in its entirety from Isaiah 36-37.

It's not within our scope here to provide a detailed analysis of these events. What I hope to do — is set forth those particulars that capture the principles we have looked at so far in this chapter. In the search for spiritual power in our lives; what does Hezekiah have to show us? God has been at work in Hezekiah's life to bring him and his people into a growing relationship of trust in Him. He wanted to emphasize to the nation that His covenant blessings could still be experienced if only they would keep looking to Him in faith. With this in mind, we make the following observations:

First, Hezekiah was finally coming to realize that bringing his problems to God in prayer *had to become a top priority.* We are told here that on at least two occasions, Hezekiah sought the Lord's help in this crisis. Isaiah 37:1 states that he tore his clothes and put on sackcloth (as a sign of mourning and prayer), and went to seek the Lord in His temple. In verses 14-15 of this same chapter, we find Hezekiah once again going to the temple. This time, he takes Sennacherib's threatening letter with him — and in a striking picture of the intimacy of prayer, he spreads the letter out before the Lord, and asks Him to look at it!

"Hezekiah received the letter from the messengers and read it. Then he went up to the temple of the LORD and spread it out before the LORD. And Hezekiah prayed to the LORD:" Isaiah 37:14-15 NIV

I have always loved this scene. It is so human; so very easy for us to identify with. When we face a crisis or a threat in our lives, there may be some form of written communication or other tangible item that represents to us the distress we are experiencing. That Hezekiah spread his letter out before the Lord - is very instructive for us. It's not that Hezekiah wasn't aware that God already knew the content of Sennacherib's letter. In the same way; it's not that we don't know that God is already aware of all the details of our problems and circumstances. What's taking place here is that Hezekiah wanted and needed a personal interaction with God; one where he could ask God to see the letter for Himself (as it were), and then enter into a conversation with Him about the matter. This is the nature of prayer. We serve a *living God,* and we want to have a very personal and private discussion with Him about whatever is troubling us. Bringing along tangible proof of our problem, such as the letter Hezekiah brought, has a way of arousing our emotions, focusing our attention, and reinforcing the reality of our relationship with our heavenly Father. God seems to us (if it were possible) even more real; and the object we brought has the effect of engaging our spirit in a deeper face to face encounter with the one who always provides us mercy and grace to help us in our time of need (Hebrews 4:16).

There is yet another mention of prayer during this time, in 2 Chronicles 32:20 NIV. We are told that, *"King Hezekiah and the prophet Isaiah son of Amoz cried out in prayer to heaven about this."* I have always thought that due to the accounts in Isaiah and 2 Kings - this is simply a reference to their individual prayers to God. In fact, this is the only place we learn that *Isaiah* prayed about the situation as well. But what if this isn't a reference to their individual prayers? What if Isaiah joined Hezekiah — and they prayed together about Sennacherib? If so, it is another beautiful picture for us of how important and helpful it can be to seek out a prayer partner in our time of need. When godly people are in distress, it can be a powerful encouragement to seek out a supportive brother or sister in Christ - and pray through a matter *together*. It will not only strengthen their mutual faith, but it will allow the Holy Spirit to keep them both keenly attuned to what He may be trying to tell them. They will be better enabled to understand the will of God through their accord in the Spirit; and Jesus will be in their midst to provide such grace as they may need (cp. Matthew 18:19-20).

The *second* thing we see in Hezekiah's experience, is that he learned the importance of *giving all glory to God.* The prayer that Hezekiah offered in the temple — is one of the most profound intercessory prayers in all of scripture. We could spend a great deal of time learning how to pray successfully from his example. Look at Isaiah 37:16:

"LORD Almighty, the God of Israel, enthroned between the cherubim, you alone are God over all the kingdoms of the earth. You have made heaven and earth."

In these two short sentences, Hezekiah is acknowledging several characteristics of God. He is the Lord Almighty (or the Lord of Hosts), sovereign over all nations, and sufficient in power for any situation. He is the God of Israel, enthroned between the cherubim; a reminder that He is the God of the covenant that was made with the nation. Thus, He is just in all His ways, and ever faithful to His promises. He alone is God over all the kingdoms of the earth; the only true God, and the one who controls the destiny of all mankind. He is

God the creator; the one who made heaven and earth. Then in v.17, Hezekiah goes on to say that the Lord is the *living God*. He has eyes and ears to see and hear the distress of His people; unlike idols made of wood and stone who cannot even help themselves (vv.18-19). He is the living God who is able to respond to the prayers of His people.

As we have noted many times, any sense of spiritual power must begin with a confession of our own weakness, and an acknowledgment that it is the Lord alone who is worthy of all praise and glory. So as his prayer begins, Hezekiah appeals first to God on that basis — that He is God Almighty, the Creator, the faithful covenant keeping God, sovereign over all men and nations, and filled with compassion toward all who call upon His name. If we would hope to have any power in prayer - we must learn to pray as Hezekiah did - giving all glory to God. Don't miss v.20 as well. Hezekiah does indeed ask for deliverance, but notice his appeal:

"Now, LORD our God, deliver us from his hand, *so that all the kingdoms of the earth may know that you, LORD, are the only God.*" *(italics mine)*

As he prays here to be rescued, it is with an eye toward the glory of God. If we would see God's power at work for us, we must imitate Hezekiah's example. When we listen to him pray, it is not unlike the model prayer the Lord Jesus gave us in Matthew 6:9-13. Both prayers begin and end with God's glory. To experience that glory for ourselves, we must go and do likewise.

The *third* lesson we are reminded of from Hezekiah, is that it's best to *trust God's ways, and to obey His prohibitions.* When God says "no", it's always for a reason. Hezekiah didn't start out understanding this — but he did come to learn it. His father, King Ahaz, was tested by God in a similar situation, but failed the test. Ahaz never learned to trust in the Lord. His story is found in 2 Kings 16 and Isaiah 7. When Ahaz learned that Syria and Israel were allied against him, he was afraid. The Lord through Isaiah encouraged him to be a man of faith; because without faith, he would not know God's protection (Isaiah 7:9). God told him that he must not trust in man, but in Him. Ahaz, however, refused to trust the Lord. Instead, he turned to the Assyrians for help. As a result, the Lord became a snare for Him - as with all Israel and Judah - rather than a source of help and safety. Thus Isaiah declared:

"The LORD Almighty is the one you are to regard as holy,
he is the one you are to fear,
he is the one you are to dread.
He will be a holy place;
for both Israel and Judah he will be
a stone that causes people to stumble
and a rock that makes them fall.
And for the people of Jerusalem he will be
a trap and a snare.
Many of them will stumble;
they will fall and be broken,
they will be snared and captured." Isaiah 8:13-15 NIV

We must pause here for a moment to take note of how wonderfully the Lord weaves and incorporates all of scripture together. For even as Ahaz and Israel refused to trust the Lord - and thus were caused to "stumble" and "fall" - so all who fail to trust in Christ will never know God's provision for their sins. Jesus is the "stone" that God has designated as the foundation of our faith. All who reject the "stone"will find to their everlasting shame that *He* is the one whom God has made the cornerstone of salvation.

"See, I lay a stone in Zion,
a chosen and precious cornerstone,
and the one who trusts in him
will never be put to shame."
Now to you who believe, this stone is precious. But to those
who do not believe,
"The stone the builders rejected
has become the cornerstone,"
and,
"A stone that causes people to stumble
and a rock that makes them fall."
They stumble because they disobey the message — which is
also what they were destined for.
1 Peter 2:6-8 NIV (cp. also Isaiah 28:16; Psalm 118:22-23;
Luke 2:34; Romans 9:32-33; Matthew 21:42)

As we return to Hezekiah, we see that unlike his father Ahaz, Hezekiah had learned to regard God as holy, and to fear only Him. He did falter briefly with the Babylonian envoys, but ultimately he gave God alone *first place in his life*. Instead of placing his trust in an arm of flesh or in any other god, Hezekiah determined that the Lord alone was God (Isaiah 37:20). He understood that when God said, "Yes, you may" or "No you may not" — His wisdom could be trusted. For as Paul told the Corinthians:

"This foolish plan of God is wiser than the wisest of human plans, and God's weakness is stronger than the greatest of human strength." 1 Corinthians 1:25 NLT

Hezekiah discovered that through the "weakness" of trusting in the Lord, the greatest of human strength (Sennacherib) would be confounded. [So also in the weakness of the cross of Jesus Christ — all other paths to salvation are shown to be nothing but foolishness.] When we learn to take

God at His word, and to accept His prohibitions, we too will find at the end of the day that His ways are always best for us. We can never prosper when we go against God's "No's" (see also Numbers 14:39-45 for another example of this).

The *fourth* observation we make from this crisis, is that Hezekiah found God's grace was all he needed, and that *God's power was perfected in his weakness.* The faith that Hezekiah placed in the Lord was vindicated. Though totally helpless against the terrifying might of Assyria, God sustained him and provided everything he needed. At the outset, Hezekiah tried to make his own preparations for the coming siege. His efforts are described in 2 Chronicles 32:1-8 NLT. The first thing he did was to ensure that Sennacherib's army would not have access to the city's water supply. To accomplish this, Hezekiah organized the building of an underground aqueduct. This tunnel connected the fresh waters of the Gihon spring outside the city, to the pool of Siloam located inside the city. The tunnel itself is almost a third of a mile long and six feet high. It is one of the most famous engineering feats of ancient times. In addition to this, we read in v.5: *"Then Hezekiah worked hard at repairing all the broken sections of the wall, erecting towers, and constructing a second wall outside the first. He also reinforced the supporting terraces in the City of David, and manufactured large numbers of weapons and shields."* Finally, he placed military commanders over all the people, and gathered them together in the public square, in front of the city gate. There he encouraged his people by saying (v.7-8):

"Be strong and courageous. Do not be afraid or discouraged because of the king of Assyria and the vast army with him, for there is a greater power with us than with him. 8 With him is only the arm of flesh, but with us is the LORD our God

to help us and to fight our battles." And the people gained confidence from what Hezekiah the king of Judah said.

Although these provisions for the upcoming siege were eminently practical and strategic — it turns out that God had His own ideas. To his credit, Hezekiah had the courage to speak those words that greatly encouraged his people. Even in this, we see the grace of God at work; providing the inner strength they would all need, to face their fearful situation. Then after all these preparations, we read that Hezekiah took Sennacherib's letter to the temple and prayed. It was shortly thereafter that God gave him a promise of deliverance through Isaiah:

"But I know where you are
and when you come and go
and how you rage against me.
Because you rage against me
and because your insolence has reached my ears,
I will put my hook in your nose
and my bit in your mouth,
and I will make you return
by the way you came."
"Therefore this is what the LORD *says concerning the king of Assyria:*
"He will not enter this city
or shoot an arrow here.
He will not come before it with shield
or build a siege ramp against it.
By the way that he came he will return;
he will not enter this city,"
declares the LORD.
"I will defend this city and save it,
for my sake and for the sake of David my servant!"" (Isaiah 37:28-29, 33-35 NIV)

Hezekiah had prepared for an actual battle; but he was about to learn that the battle belongs to the Lord. To demonstrate His all-sufficient grace - and to show that victory rests on His own arm alone - God did not use Hezekiah's military weapons, strategies, or the city's bulwarks. Instead, we read (v.36-37):

"Then the angel of the LORD went out and put to death a hundred and eighty-five thousand in the Assyrian camp. When the people got up the next morning — there were all the dead bodies! So Sennacherib king of Assyria broke camp and withdrew. He returned to Nineveh and stayed there."

God could have employed human means (as He often does) to accomplish His plans and purposes. Here however, the Assyrians are slaughtered, and Hezekiah doesn't have to lift a finger. For the same purpose as when Moses stood before Pharaoh - so that the world might know His name - God triumphs all on His own. No one could mistake any strength on Hezekiah's part with the power of God — power now made perfect in weakness. All who heard of this would know that the God of Israel fought for His people. For us, as with Hezekiah; no matter how grave the situation — the power of God in Jesus Christ is more than enough for anything we may need: "My grace is sufficient for you".

Finally, we see from the outcome of these events, that Hezekiah arrived at a settled place of humility. He had learned to *delight in his weakness - and to give all glory to God.* As a result, the blessing of God rested upon the remainder of his life:

"So the LORD saved Hezekiah and the people of Jerusalem from the hand of Sennacherib king of Assyria and from the hand of all others. He took care of them on every side. Many

brought offerings to Jerusalem for the LORD and valuable gifts for Hezekiah king of Judah. From then on he was highly regarded by all the nations." 2 Chronicles 32:22-23 NIV

See now the faithfulness of God that corresponded to the attitude of Hezekiah. God continued to take care of His people, and protect them from all who would threaten them. They had peace and rest on every side. People from everywhere came streaming to Jerusalem bringing gifts to the Lord; for His fame had once again become known to the nations. For Hezekiah, because he had given all the glory to God - God honored Hezekiah. Not only were gifts given to the Lord, but many *valuable* gifts were given to Hezekiah! To crown his faith and humility, God made it so that Hezekiah himself was highly respected among all the surrounding nations. Herein we see the principle that God will always honor those *whose service honors Him* (cp. John 12:26).

God's Arithmetic - while well within reach of the humble - is always beyond the grasp of the proud. They cannot fathom such knowledge; it is too high for them. We who belong to Jesus Christ - have the path to spiritual power set before us. It belongs not to the great or the strong, but to those who acknowledge their own weakness, and rely wholly on Christ's strength. It is not the mighty who will inherit the earth, but the meek (Matthew 5:5). It is not by our own resources that we learn to find contentment in all our limitations and circumstances — but through the all sufficient grace of Jesus:

"Not that I was ever in need, for I have learned how to be content with whatever I have. I know how to live on almost nothing or with everything. I have learned the secret of living in every situation, whether it is with a full stomach or empty, with plenty or little. For I can do everything through Christ, who gives me strength." Philippians 4:11-13 NLT

It is not those who place their confidence in wealth, fame, or talent, who drink from the rivers of living water; but those who trust in the Lord - that will soar on eagle's wings:

"He gives power to the weak
and strength to the powerless.
Even youths will become weak and tired,
and young men will fall in exhaustion.
But those who trust in the LORD will find new strength.
They will soar high on wings like eagles.
They will run and not grow weary.
They will walk and not faint." Isaiah 40:29-31 NLT

Where are you today in your spiritual life? Do you hunger and thirst for a deeper experience of the resurrection power of Christ? Are you discouraged by all you lack; your failures, shortcomings, inadequacies, and weaknesses? Do you feel your life was meant for more than the disappointment of lost opportunities? Are you pleading with God to remove the obstacles in your life that seem to be preventing fruitful service to Him? Have you decided that life just doesn't add up? Listen once again to Paul. Ask God to give you that same outlook as he had. Pray now that He will show you that your weakness is no hindrance to His power. Seek the eyes to see, the ears to hear, and the heart to understand - that the power of Christ is made perfect in that very weakness which is so distressing to you. When grace helps you choose to *"delight in weaknesses, in insults, in hardships, in persecutions, in difficulties"* — you will discover a spiritual strength that you never thought possible. Along with all the great saints of the Bible, you will find that: ***"When I am weak, then I am strong"***.

Hi-Def Pictures
Of God's Children

ஒ௫௸ஒ

*W*e live in a world where technology is the order of the day. If a significant event occurs halfway around the world, we know about it in a matter of minutes. All of our various media devices strive to be the first ones to bring the events into our living room; it could just be our TVs, but more often lately it's a computer or other Internet-connected gadget (like a smartphone or tablet). It isn't enough that news outlets simply bring us this information. They all compete to deliver it to us in a format that will communicate the information in the clearest possible way. The sounds and images they present, are all designed to impact us in a precise manner; one which we will best understand or appreciate. With that goal in mind, news networks utilize the latest in video technology to bring us the clearest and sharpest possible images. But even the highest-quality recorded images cannot be delivered to us without a device that allows us to view them with that same high-quality. Visiting a store that sells these devices, presents us with a wide array of choices. Let's take television for example. You almost can't even buy one anymore that is not "HD" (high-definition). Your first choice is if you want a TV that presents its images by means of a Plasma, LCD, or LED screen (did someone say 3D?). Then there are other factors to consider and select from, such as; refresh rates, contrast ratios, availability of connection ports, screen size, brand name, price, and a host of other technical features. Perhaps the most vital consideration when making your TV decision - is known as Vertical Resolution. Vertical Resolution refers to the total number of visible lines as counted from the top of the TV screen to the bottom. These lines are made up of small dots called pixels. Individual pixels are too small for us to notice, but as vast numbers of these pixels work together rapidly changing color and brightness, a picture is created. The best Vertical Resolution quality for TVs available today, consist of 1,080 horizontal lines of pixels (with progressive scan). This is commonly written as 1080p. Everyone wants a 1080p image on their device or appliance, because it's the nearest thing to actually being there. The images are sharp and crystal clear. The point of having such high-definition images, is to make what we see *as real to us as possible*. By viewing them, our minds are better able to grasp the most complete meaning of what they represent. In other words, the reality of an event is presented to us in such a way that there is no confusion or mistake about what we are seeing. Our view is not obscured, and we experience the next best thing to being there ourselves. This idea of creating the best high-definition images — can be translated into the realm of Christian character. Let's first discuss why such images are vitally important for the world to see.

In the world of Marketing, the 'pinnacle of success' is when a person or organization achieves the status of a "brand." The brand represents not only the person or organization itself, but also a highly publicized and marketed "image" of what the brand-sponsor wants you to think of whenever the brand name is mentioned. Examples of some well known brands are: "Coke", "Armani", "Apple", "Starbucks", "Ferrari", and "NASA", just to name a few. Once achieved, the status and popularity of a brand may last a long time. Alternately, a brand can quickly lose its status if the brand name is tarnished. This can occur for a *personal brand name* if that person acts in a way that is contrary to the brand, or brings disgrace to it in a way that has a negative impact on the public. This can also occur for a corporate brand, if a product fails to live up to the high standards of quality or efficiency that the brand has set. For instance, if a car manufacturer has a large-scale recall due to the production of a defective vehicle or component — the brand name can be adversely affected. To bring this into the spiritual realm, let's suppose for a moment that God also has His own brand. It's not a brand that He wants to market for profit to stockholders; nor is it a brand designed to mask the true nature of what it represents. It is a brand that He wants known - so that the entire world might know His truth, and experience His love. God's brand is Jesus Christ. Jesus is the Son of God; of whom we are told, "The Son is the radiance of God's glory and the exact representation of His being" (Hebrews 1:3 NIV). In a magnificent hymn to the Son, the Apostle Paul presents amazing truths about Him in Colossians 1:15-20 NLT:

Christ is the visible image of the invisible God.
He existed before anything was created and is supreme over all creation,
for through him God created everything
in the heavenly realms and on earth.
He made the things we can see
and the things we can't see —
such as thrones, kingdoms, rulers, and authorities in the unseen world.
Everything was created through him and for him.
He existed before anything else,
and he holds all creation together.

Christ is also the head of the church,
which is his body.
He is the beginning,
supreme over all who rise from the dead.
So he is first in everything.
For God in all his fullness
was pleased to live in Christ,
and through him God reconciled
everything to himself.
He made peace with everything in heaven and on earth
by means of Christ's blood on the cross.

We see from this passage that Jesus Christ is the *Creator and Sustainer* of the Universe. He is supreme over everything that exists - and *all the very fullness of God* can be seen in Him. To see Jesus - is to see God. To know Jesus - is to know God. Since God has determined that an accurate representation of His brand is so important in sharing the message of His love with everyone, He has chosen a way to ensure that it is well represented everywhere in the world. For this reason, God has commissioned a people - otherwise known as His Church - to represent His brand the world over. Jesus is the head of the Church - which is His body. The true Church of God has many names. Some call us "believers." Some prefer "followers of Christ" or "disciples." Most publicly however, we are known as "Christians." In order to accurately represent God's brand in the way He desires, a Christian must demonstrate in their life *the character of God*. This means that a Christian's behavior should look exactly like Jesus' behavior. Christian character should look exactly like Jesus' character. For many people in our society, the word "Christian" conjures up a mental image of a certain kind of individual. This image is often very stereotyped or generic. It's also often not a very favorable one. Perhaps it's more accurate to say that the image is a "fuzzy" one.

Lamentably, we (who make up the church) often present an image of God's brand to the world which is not only fuzzy, but distorted as well. Our character often lacks the clarity, focus, and distinctiveness, which should mark us as true follows of Jesus Christ. Because of this, many people label us as "hypocrites." We are viewed as professing to be true followers of Jesus Christ — but our lack of behaving with a Christ-like character belies that profession. I've already noted the importance of having "high-definition images" to demonstrate to people in a clear and unmistakable way, what they are viewing. Throughout all of the snapshots of character which constitute vital Christian living, there are unique qualities (that God has made plain) which will effectively identify us with His brand. When the world sees these qualities evidenced in a Christian's life, they will be seen as a *high-definition picture* of what a child of God looks like. Anyone who observes such qualities on display, will recognize with maximum clarity, that what they are seeing is an individual who is acting just like Jesus would act – thereby showing themselves to be one of His true disciples.

There are many aspects of character which would improve our image as followers of Christ. Almost everyone recognizes that some of these qualities have a universal appeal. For instance, 'a person of integrity' is highly respected in all decent societies. So also are those who have high moral standards, strong family values, or who show love to all the people in their lives. Among the pantheon of qualities of holy character, there are *three* in particular that are unrivaled. In my view, the Bible presents these three as most distinctively telling the world that a person is a genuine follower of Jesus Christ. They are what I call **"Hi-Def Pictures of God's Children"**; for they portray the uniqueness of Jesus' life and character in the most recognizable ways. In God's Arithmetic, a person who exercises these qualities of character *will best reflect His brand.* The actions of this individual allow those who are watching to spiritually "add two and two together"; to realize they are seeing a Hi-Def Picture of a true child of God.

Love for enemies

The *first* of these distinct qualities of character — is "love for enemies." Here are some of the more salient passages of scripture that emphasize this:

If your enemy is hungry, give him food to eat;
if he is thirsty, give him water to drink.
In doing this, you will heap burning coals on his head,
and the LORD will reward you.
Proverbs 25:21-22 NIV

On the contrary:

"If your enemy is hungry, feed him;
if he is thirsty, give him something to drink.
In doing this, you will heap burning coals on his head."
Do not be overcome by evil, but overcome evil with good.
Romans 12:20-21 NIV

You have heard the law that says the punishment must match the injury: 'An eye for an eye, and a tooth for a tooth.' But I say, do not resist an evil person! If someone slaps you on the right cheek, offer the other cheek also. If you are sued in court and your shirt is taken from you, give your coat, too. If a soldier demands that you carry his gear for a mile, carry it two miles. Give to those who ask, and don't turn away from those who want to borrow.

You have heard the law that says, 'Love your neighbor' and hate your enemy. But I say, love your enemies! Pray for those who persecute you! In that way, you will be acting as true children of your Father in heaven. For he gives his sunlight to both the evil and the good, and he sends rain on the just and the unjust alike. If you love only those who love you, what reward is there for that? Even corrupt tax collectors do that much. If you are kind only to your friends, how are you different from anyone else? Even pagans do that. Matthew 5:38-47 NLT

*To you who are ready for the truth, I say this: **Love your enemies**. Let them bring out the best in you, not the worst. When someone gives you a hard time, respond with the energies of prayer for that person. If someone slaps you in the face, stand there and take it. If someone grabs your shirt, giftwrap your best coat and make a present of it. If someone takes unfair advantage of you, use the occasion to practice the servant life. No more tit-for-tat stuff. Live generously. Luke 6:27-30 MSG*

*I tell you, **love your enemies**. Help and give without expecting a return. You'll never — I promise — regret it. Live out this God-created identity the way our Father lives toward us, generously and graciously, even when we're at our worst. Our Father is kind; you be kind. Luke 6:35-36 MSG*

Throughout the years I attended college and seminary, I had the opportunity to hear a great many renowned Christian speakers. On one such occasion while in seminary, I became aware that Richard Wurmbrand would be speaking at a church not far away. Here is a brief biography of Rev. Wurmbrand's life[7]:

"Pastor Richard Wurmbrand was an evangelical minister who spent fourteen years in Communist imprisonment and torture in his homeland of Romania. He was one of Roma-

nia's most widely known Jewish Believer leaders, authors, and educators. In 1945, when the Communists seized Romania and attempted to control the churches for their purposes, Richard Wurmbrand immediately began an effective "underground" ministry to his enslaved people and the invading Russian soldiers. He was eventually arrested in 1948. Richard spent three years in solitary confinement, seeing no one but his Communist torturers.

His wife, Sabina, also Jewish, was a slave laborer for three years. Due to Pastor Richard Wurmbrand's international stature as a Messianic Jewish leader, diplomats of foreign embassies asked the Communist government about his safety. They were told he had fled Romania. Secret police, posing as released fellow prisoners, told his wife of attending his burial in the prison cemetery. Pastor Wurmbrand was released in a general amnesty in 1964. Realizing the great danger of a third imprisonment, Christians in Norway negotiated with the Communist authorities for his release from Romania. The "going price" for a prisoner was $1,900. Their price for Wurmbrand was $10,000. In May 1966, Pastor Richard Wurmbrand testified in Washington before the Senate's Internal Security Subcommittee and stripped to the waist and showed 18 deep torture wounds covering his body. His story was carried across the world newspapers in the U.S., Europe, and Asia. Read a portion of this report. <u>*Communist Exploitation of Religion Pastor Richard's Testimony from 1966.*</u>

Pastor Wurmbrand has been called "the Voice of the Underground Church." His books are best sellers in over fifty languages."

By this time (around 1980), I had become aware of Pastor Wurmbrand's ministry: "The Voice of the Martyrs." I had also read his best selling book: "Tortured For Christ." His physical appearance was frail and elderly, and he was not necessarily a great preacher in any traditional sense. So why did people pack churches and listen with rapt attention when he spoke? In my case, I went to hear him because of what I had heard regarding his reputation as a believer. It was said that "to listen to him — would be the closest you would ever get to hearing an Apostle speak." What then was it about Richard Wurmbrand that marked him as being like an Apostle of Jesus Christ? I believe that beyond his absolute dedication to the cause of Christ; the distinguishing characteristic that made him apostle-like, was *the love he showed toward his enemies*. To endure the suffering of solitary confinement and savage beatings for 3 years for the sake of Christ - is surely a remarkable display of courage and faith. Even more conspicuous and singular, is to show the love of Christ toward those who would treat you so cruelly. As Pastor Wurmbrand looked into the faces of his captors, he saw the potential for an Apostle Paul or the Philippian jailor. When I listened to him speak, I did so not only because he bore in his body the *marks* of the Lord Jesus, but also because he bore in his heart the *love* of the Lord Jesus - toward those who had so brutally abused and persecuted him. To hear this man, and to learn his story, was to truly see a Hi-Def picture of the life and Spirit of Jesus.

Followers of Jesus who read these scripture passages and desire to obey God, must be very puzzled by them. On the surface, it doesn't make a lot of sense to love our enemies. They certainly don't 'deserve' to be loved. In fact, our sense of justice tells us that they may indeed deserve much worse! I'm sure there are *some* situations where we perceive someone as our enemy, because we suppose that they are mistreating us — but actually, it is only we who are covering up our own sinful behavior, while blaming others who oppose us. Here in these scriptures however, God is not saying to "love your enemies" because *you* may really be the one who is in the wrong. There is more meaning in "demonstrating love for our enemies" than God simply advising us that we're not qualified to determine a person's actions as unjust. All of us at some point have been mistreated by an individual or a group in a manner that was objectively unjust, unfair, unmerited, or just plain wrong. In fact, when we follow Jesus faithfully, it may indeed result in just that kind of mistreatment or persecution. Therefore, when Jesus exhorts us to "love our enemies", it is not some kind of religious 'fiction' that allows for the fact that we may be the ones who are in the wrong. Rather, it is because "human nature apart from God" carries an inevitable tendency toward sin, that we will all be mistreated by others at some point, as we strive to live godly lives in Christ (2 Timothy 3:12).

Furthermore, here's some news that may come as a shock to you: Not everybody likes you. There will always be those who want to hurt you, simply because they don't like you — whether you did anything to cause them to feel that way or not. So why does the Lord Jesus exhort us to love our enemies? Does God have any reason for it? Is there a point to it? Wouldn't "loving our enemies" allow those who do wrong to "get away with it" - and suffer no consequences for their actions? Not at all! A review of these passages of scripture, provides us with **several reasons why it is important to love our enemies.**

First, when we retaliate in kind, it only perpetuates hatred and ill-will. The way to overcome evil - is not with more evil. Evil is overcome by good (Romans 12:21). This is God's Arithmetic. It is the way He triumphs over sin and evil. The cross of Christ is the best example of this. In the greatest single act of love, goodness, submission, and self sacrifice the world has ever seen, God has totally defeated death, the Devil, and sin. Jesus sheds His blood - and evil is destroyed forever. He did this, not for His friends, but for His enemies (see Romans 5:8-10)! It may not make sense to the carnal eye, but it is blessedly true. When the Church does good to those who wrong us, we are living under the power and banner of God's true victory. His triumph will be our triumph. Christ's reward will be our reward. We will live and reign together with Him! In Romans 12:20 where Paul speaks of acts of kindness to an enemy that "will heap burning coals on his head", the Message reads: "your generosity will surprise him with goodness." When we return good for evil, it may be the first thing God uses to help a person see themselves as He sees them. The unkind actions of our enemies toward us - may become evident to them as sin; and our acts of kindness - may be the starting point that leads them to repentance and faith.

The second reason it is important to love our enemies, is that it assists the progress of our transformation into the likeness of God and Christ. Matthew 5:45 NIV:

"In that way, you will be acting as true children of your Father in heaven. For he gives His sunlight to both the evil and the good, and He sends rain on the just and the unjust alike."

Luke 6:35-36 MSG states in part:

"Live out this God-created identity the way our Father lives toward us, generously and graciously, even when we're at our worst. Our Father is kind; you be kind."

The Spirit of God enables us to act toward the undeserving just as He does. As we obey Him, we become more like Him. Something of the beauty and permanence of what we will become in Christ - is infused into our character now.

The fragrance of such love for our enemies - will make it obvious to all - that we are indeed a Hi-Def picture of what a child of God should be. Matthew 5:46-47 (NLT) adds still another reason to love our enemies:

"46 If you love only those who love you, what reward is there for that? Even corrupt tax collectors do that much. 47 If you are kind only to your friends, how are you different from anyone else? Even pagans do that."

Jesus' words make it plain here — that as we show God's love to people who do not love or care for us - we are distinguishing ourselves from the rest of the world as His disciples. Everyone loves those who love them in return. But *we who love those who do not love us in return* are making it evident that we are followers of Jesus.

The command of God to "love our enemies" also embodies further blessing for our spiritual life. We are also told to pray for them:

"Pray for those who persecute you!" Matthew 5:43 NLT

"When someone gives you a hard time, respond with the energies of prayer for that person." Luke 6:28 MSG

When we entreat the Lord for those who mistreat us, several things ensue: That person receives God's help and mercy. Our feelings of hatred and resentment begin to be transformed toward healing. Our minds and thinking patterns are renewed toward conformity with the mind of Christ. Through such prayer, we begin to learn the spiritual habit of "thinking" love toward everyone. Therefore, praying for enemies is really teaching us *how* to pray. If we form the habit of asking God for His mercy toward our enemies, we will also be growing in our understanding of how to pray for our friends and loved ones as well. All of our prayers will start to flow under the umbrella of grace. Not only will we discern right from wrong, but all our intercession for others will be colored with the proper proportions of justice, mercy, patience, strength, and gentleness. We will better learn *how* to ask, *what* to ask, and *when* to ask for it. Our inner life will grow in grace. In conjunction with this, most translations of Luke 6:28 state, *"bless those who curse you."* This brings love for enemies into the realm of our speech as well. Just as with prayer, when we begin to actually speak aloud a blessing on those who spitefully use and persecute us, it affects all our speech as well. We become more conscious that all of our words need to be gracious; seasoned with salt. We also become more aware of the real power of the spoken word. The ancient Hebrews were aware of this. Words spoken have substantive power. They have power to bring about an actual blessing or a curse. We know that the words God speaks have power, for he declares:

"The same thing is true of the words I speak. They will not return to me empty.
They make the things happen that I want to happen,
and they succeed in doing what I send them to do." Isaiah 55:11 NCV

Therefore as we learn to speak godly words of blessing to our enemies, we make a very real difference that will impact them. As we learn to speak godly words to everyone, we discover that our speech makes a powerful difference in the environment we create around us. Thus, to bless even our enemies, is to assimilate the development of speech in our daily lives which has the power to heal, as well as to encourage and draw people to the Savior whom we represent.

<u>Yet another reason we love our enemies, is that we develop an attitude of service to others, along with a spirit of generosity.</u> The examples Jesus uses in Matthew 5:40-42 and Luke 6:29-30, put into practice the power of overcoming evil with good. As we give to an enemy (and submit to them in this manner by going the extra mile, and by not retaliating in kind) we are really submitting to God. This is nothing other than the very life of Christ imparting His own love through us. We are learning to depend completely on the Spirit of our Savior who declared, *"Even the Son of Man did not come to be served, but to serve, and to give His life as a ransom for many."* (Mark 10:45 NIV). To treat an enemy with an open hand of generosity, is to exhibit divine love in its purest form. The same principle applies here as with prayer and speech. If we can respond to the demands of an *enemy* by "going the extra mile" with a heart of love, service, and generosity — then how much more will we be able to love *everyone* God places in the daily orbit of our lives?

Indirectly, as we love our enemies, we are reminded pointedly of how much God has done for us. Luke 6:35-36 NCV states:

"But love your enemies, do good to them, and lend to them without hoping to get anything back. Then you will have a great reward, and you will be children of the Most High God, because He is kind even to people who are ungrateful and full of sin. Show mercy, just as your Father shows mercy."

Before we came to know Christ, that is exactly who we were - *those who are ungrateful and full of sin!* Our Father has shown mercy on *us*. The Apostle John reminds us of this, by telling us how to respond to God for sending His Son to be the sacrifice for our sins:

"Dear friends, since God loved us that much, we surely ought to love each other. No one has ever seen God. But if we love each other, God lives in us, and His love is brought to full expression in us." 1 John 4:11-12 NLT

To love our enemies - is to be reminded of how we were formerly enemies of God. It is to realize that absolutely no one is beyond redemption. No one is beyond His grace. No one is beyond the power of God to save, to forgive, to reconcile, and to restore a sinner into fellowship with Himself. The grace of God in Christ is limitless. There are no boundaries to it. Therefore, to love our enemies - is to be the truest kind of ambassador for Jesus; showing to them the highest resolution Hi-Def picture of the all encompassing love of God.

Earlier in our discussion, I suggested that to "love our enemies" may not always make sense to us as Christians. We might feel that those who do us wrong are "getting away with it"; that they are suffering no consequences for their actions. One final thing that loving our enemies teaches us - is that this is not the case. When we act in love toward those who mistreat us, we are learning to put ourselves and our entire circumstance into the hands of God. To those who are suffering for the sake of Christ, the Apostle Peter offers these words of encouragement:

"So if you are suffering in a manner that pleases God, keep on doing what is right, and trust your lives to the God who created you, for He will never fail you." 1 Peter 4:19 NLT

The admonition in Romans 12:21 to "overcome evil with good" (as quoted above) is preceded by the following:

"Don't hit back; discover beauty in everyone. If you've got it in you, get along with everybody. Don't insist on getting

even; that's not for you to do. "I'll do the judging", says God. "I'll take care of it."" Romans 12:17-19 MSG

God will take care of it. Such simple words, yet so very difficult to live by. How often when we are wronged, is our first reaction to get back at someone! The first thing to come to mind is usually not: "How can I discover the beauty in this person?" However, when we truly come to terms with this truth, it will transform the pain in our relationships. God says "He will do the judging"; we are set free. Judgment is not our burden. Our burden is to allow the love of Christ to flow through us. It is God's burden to determine how to take care of the person who has wronged us. We must come to trust this as a fact with all our heart. When we learn to make a practice out of committing our cause to God, just as it is, in all its entirety — when we learn that we do not have to retaliate because God has promised to handle the matter on our behalf — then and only then will we find peace when we are treated unfairly - and have the freedom to truly love those who have wronged us. As it is with many of the deep teachings of the Spirit - this is a matter of faith. It's a decision on our part to trust God when we are hurting and don't understand what is happening to us. It's a confidence that God, the Righteous Judge, will do right by us, and for everyone concerned. It's a sure hope that all will turn out well for us. This hope is not based on unsubstantiated wishful thinking. It is based on God's infallible promises, undergirded by His love for us - which declare that He will only and certainly do us good.

"Can anything ever separate us from Christ's love? Does it mean He no longer loves us if we have trouble or calamity, or are persecuted, or hungry, or destitute, or in danger, or threatened with death? (As the Scriptures say, "For your

sake we are killed every day; we are being slaughtered like sheep.")

No, despite all these things, overwhelming victory is ours through Christ, who loved us.

And I am convinced that nothing can ever separate us from God's love. Neither death nor life, neither angels nor demons, neither our fears for today nor our worries about tomorrow — not even the powers of hell can separate us from God's love. No power in the sky above or in the earth below — indeed, nothing in all creation will ever be able to separate us from the love of God that is revealed in Christ Jesus our Lord." Romans 8:35-39 NLT

Forgiveness

The *second* quality of character that constitutes this set of Hi-Def Pictures of God's Children — is forgiveness. It can be readily seen that a willingness to forgive the wrongs done to us - is inseparable from love toward enemies. They are both flawless facets of the same divine jewel. To love one's enemies, pray for them, bless them, and do good toward them - is not possible without the same spirit of love and mercy involved in forgiveness. To illustrate the importance of forgiveness, let's take a brief look at a conversation between Jesus and the Apostle Peter. This conversation takes place in the context of one of Jesus' long discourses in the book of Matthew. In this instance, Jesus had been discussing various aspects of the standards in personal relationships that need to exist among the community of God's people. (Matthew chapter 18 includes instruction on humility, sensitivity, compassion, and discipline.) As Peter listened to Jesus discuss the proper way to confront a situation when another believer sins against us, it got him thinking. This led to the following conversation between them in vv.21-35. Here, in this dialogue, Jesus concludes His teaching with a lesson about forgiveness:

"21 Then Peter came to him and asked, "Lord, how often should I forgive someone who sins against me? Seven times?"

22 "No, not seven times," Jesus replied, "but seventy times seven!"

23 "Therefore, the Kingdom of Heaven can be compared to a king who decided to bring his accounts up to date with servants who had borrowed money from him. 24 In the process, one of his debtors was brought in who owed him millions of dollars. 25 He couldn't pay, so his master ordered that he be sold — along with his wife, his children, and everything he owned — to pay the debt."

26 "But the man fell down before his master and begged him, 'Please, be patient with me, and I will pay it all.' 27 Then his master was filled with pity for him, and he released him and forgave his debt."

28 "But when the man left the king, he went to a fellow servant who owed him a few thousand dollars. He grabbed him by the throat and demanded instant payment."

29 "His fellow servant fell down before him and begged for a little more time. 'Be patient with me, and I will pay it,' he pleaded. 30 But his creditor wouldn't wait. He had the man arrested and put in prison until the debt could be paid in full."

31 "When some of the other servants saw this, they were very upset. They went to the king and told him everything that had happened. 32 Then the king called in the man he had forgiven and said, 'You evil servant! I forgave you that tremendous debt because you pleaded with me. 33 Shouldn't you have mercy on your fellow servant, just as I had mercy on you?' 34 Then the angry king sent the man to prison to be tortured until he had paid his entire debt."

35 "That's what my heavenly Father will do to you if you refuse to forgive your brothers and sisters from your heart." Matthew 18:21-35 NLT

The story Jesus tells, is quite arresting. It grabs your attention from the beginning, and does not let go - even after the stunning climax. Such a story is meant to cause us to think soberly about what is taking place, and how we are to apply it in our relationships with others. I do not believe we are supposed to listen to this story with the ears of a scholar. I think we are meant to hear it with the ears of a person like Peter; someone who may be struggling with just how much mistreatment, harm, or fault we have to put up with from someone. I love Peter. He always seems to be saying the things everyone else wanted to, but were too afraid to ask. Here in verse 21, it sounds a little like he is not only making a serious inquiry to Jesus, but at the same time trying to impress Him a bit as well. Popular in that society, was the idea that a good man would be willing to forgive someone three times. So Peter goes beyond that when he asks Jesus if he should forgive someone seven times. We see then in Peter, a little of what seems to be the best in ourselves. . . A Christian may say to God:

"Look Lord, I know as a believer I ought to forgive others their sins against me. I know that most people think we shouldn't have to do this, but at least everyone recognizes that forgiveness is a noble thing. So Lord, I think I'm big enough to overlook a few offenses. I'm going to take the high road. I will keep on forgiving this really annoying person - but only up to a point. I'm no pushover Lord. I have my limits. But to honor you, I'll go beyond what most people would do. After all, what more could you want of me? It's only fair." . . . With that, we pat ourselves on the back, cast a glance over at Jesus, and say to ourselves, "What a good person am I!"

As our story begins, Peter looks at Jesus for a response. While a part of him might have been seeking approbation, another part of him was really seeking answers. How many times should I really forgive someone? When is enough, enough? What does God really want of us when people do us harm? Even God didn't always forgive His people, right? Where are the boundaries? What are the limits? Just how much should we forgive? Jesus first replies to Peter with a brief answer, and then explains it further by sharing this penetrating parable. Jesus' parables are not intended to confuse us. They are meant to deepen our understanding in matters pertaining to the Kingdom of God. As this parable moves toward its climax, we are gently yet progressively compelled toward a deeper understanding in this matter of forgiveness. Jesus would have us clear on at least these key precepts:

• *There is no limit to forgiveness.* This is the meaning of Jesus' initial response to Peter where he says:

"No, not seven times — but seventy times seven!" In God's Arithmetic, seventy times seven is not pure multiplication. It is, as we noted earlier, God's way of looking at this matter. It is not about the numbers per se, but about the weight God places on the higher virtues of love, character, and mercy. We are to learn the deeper meaning of what it is to live together in the Kingdom of God. What Jesus brings

to light here is not new. It is in essence the true meaning of what God had always been speaking to His people. For as the prophet said:

"No, O people, the Lord has told you what is good,
and this is what He requires of you:
to do what is right, to love mercy,
and to walk humbly with your God." Micah 6:8 NLT

At the core of forgiveness is the love of mercy. This is what Jesus will make plain in the parable that He shares.

• *God, our great King, values each of us so much, that forgiveness cost the death of His Son.* Jesus' story begins with the Kingdom of Heaven being compared to a great King who decided to bring his accounts up to date. One great day, the Bible tells us, the great King of the Universe will indeed bring all accounts up to date.

"And I saw a great white throne and the one sitting on it. The earth and sky fled from His presence, but they found no place to hide. I saw the dead, both great and small, standing before God's throne. And the books were opened, including the Book of Life. And the dead were judged according to what they had done, as recorded in the books." Revelation 20:11-12 NLT

Those of us who read Matthew's gospel, do so from this side of the cross and resurrection. We know that God gave His only Son, to die in our stead (John 3:16). Jesus paid the debt for our sins that we could never pay ourselves. The extent of this mercy, and the measure of what our God and Savior has sacrificed for us, can never be fully understood. The Bible's message that God loves each of us with an infinite and self-sacrificial love - cannot be debated or denied.

To understand the importance of forgiveness in our relationships, we must begin by holding in our mind's eye a vision of the Son of God dying on the cross for our sins. We must see the love of the Father in sending the Son to be the Savior of the world (1 John 4:13-15). Only then will the full meaning of Jesus' parable become clear to our seeking hearts.

• *There is no comparison between the debt that we owe to God and the debt that someone owes to us.* The contrast in the story between the two debtors - is key to the meaning of Jesus' parable. He paints in the most vivid terms of His day, the relative inequality between the debt the first servant owed the king, and the debt his fellow servant owed to him. Literally, the first servant's debt to the king was "10,000 talents." The talent was the highest unit of currency in use at that time. The translation above lists the modern equivalent as millions of dollars. The real point however is not in the amount itself - but that the debt was completely impossible to pay. The amount exceeded the total tax revenue of all the province of Galilee! An insurmountable debt was forgiven this servant by his merciful king. In contrast, his fellow servant owed him 100 denarii. The actual relative value of this amount to the "10,000 talents" is not simple math. Various Bible translations and commentaries have tried to express the relative difference in modern terms. The underlying point, and the thing that would have been instantly clear to Peter and the disciples, is that this smaller amount of debt was **insignificant** by comparison with the amount of debt the king forgave the first servant. This is God's Arithmetic — and the meaning intended by Jesus that must not be missed. The key to understanding why we must forgive others from the heart - lies in just this. Look above at verses 32-34. Don't miss this! We are the servants who have been forgiven such tremendous debt. It is therefore evil to not forgive our fellow servant who has a debt to us. The great King will not tolerate such a lack of mercy.

• Jesus concludes His parable with sober words that are both *a warning and an encouragement.*

33 "Shouldn't you have mercy on your fellow servant, just as I had mercy on you?' 34 Then the angry king sent the man to prison to be tortured until he had paid his entire debt."

35 "That's what my heavenly Father will do to you if you refuse to forgive your brothers and sisters from your heart."

This is a warning that if we are not willing to foster within ourselves a spirit of forgiveness, then we should not expect the forgiveness of God.

"Blessed are the merciful,
for they will be shown mercy." Matthew 5:7 NIV

"There will be no mercy for those who have not shown mercy to others. But if you have been merciful, God will be merciful when he judges you." James 2:13 (NLT)

"If you forgive those who sin against you, your heavenly Father will forgive you. But if you refuse to forgive others, your Father will not forgive your sins." Matthew 6:14-15 NLT

If you have not yet experienced the full pardon for your sins that Jesus Christ is offering to you, then you may come and freely receive His forgiveness for all your sins. You must realize however - the inestimable sin-debt you owe to God. You must also realize that it will no longer be possible for you to withhold that same love to others which God has shown to you. A person who absolutely refuses to forgive others their sins - demonstrates that they have never experienced God's forgiveness. Jesus' somber words are: *"Then the angry king sent the man to prison to be tortured until he had paid his entire debt. That's what my heavenly Father will do to you if you refuse to forgive your brothers and sisters from your heart."* The debt of our sins to God - must be paid. If you will not accept that Jesus paid this debt for you, then you will have to pay it forever yourself:

"Whoever believes in Him is not condemned, but whoever does not believe stands condemned already because they have not believed in the name of God's one and only Son." John 3:18 NIV

There is a warning here also for us as believers. *We cannot expect to live in daily fellowship with our Heavenly Father, and experience His blessing in our lives, if we refuse to forgive others.* The unwillingness to forgive someone - is like a slow-working poison. It gradually affects our outlook towards life. It puts a dark color on all of our relationships. We are left angry and bitter. We begin to feel that life is unfair, and that God does not care about us. It prevents the possibility of reconciliation with the one who has wronged us. It can cause us to speak ill of our brothers and sisters. God's cause is damaged as we nurse our grudge. Others see us living with spite and hatred - instead of with the love of our God. We may overreact to even innocent actions of others toward us, allowing our bitter spirit to cloud our judgment of their motives. We cannot move forward in our lives or in our spiritual growth, because the channel between God and us is clogged with emotional debris. To progress and keep this matter in balance, it is critical to know with certainty that *God recognizes that there are some very terrible things that people do to each other.* He is not ignorant or uninformed about the pain in our lives; caused by those who have wronged us. In fact, the Bible tells us in no uncertain terms that Jesus walks with us in our times of pain and weakness. He empathizes with us, and He is always there for us and able to help. One of my favorite promises from God which addresses this, is found in Hebrews 4:15-16 NLT:

"This High Priest of ours understands our weaknesses, for he faced all of the same testings we do, yet he did not sin. So let us come boldly to the throne of our gracious God. There we will receive his mercy, and we will find grace to help us when we need it most."

God is also well-aware that there are times when extending forgiveness to others will be a process we walk through. Some hurts are so painful - that only time and the thoughtful prayer and support of others - will allow us to overcome our pain, and to forgive the one who has harmed us. God will work in us and along side us, to help overcome the ugly scars that the sins of others have caused. There are occasions when it is mentally and emotionally healthy and needful to take the time necessary to heal and forgive. Forgiveness cannot be forced, coerced, or induced by guilt into existence. Sometimes, forgiveness must be a process — a work in-progress. As a believer in Jesus, you must however be *willing* to forgive; no matter how long it takes. Bring your pain to God. Ask Him to help you. As you do, you will find His grace sufficient to redeem your suffering. He will take His own triumphant love, and gradually infuse it into your heart. Through the power of His Spirit within you, you will find victory over your suffering. You will discover that God is able to take even your heartache - and make it a blessing both to yourself and others. The Apostle Paul reminds us of this in 2 Corinthians 1:3-5 MSG:

"All praise to the God and Father of our Master, Jesus the Messiah! Father of all mercy! God of all healing counsel! He comes alongside us when we go through hard times, and before you know it, He brings us alongside someone else who is going through hard times so that we can be there for that person just as God was there for us. We have plenty of hard times that come from following the Messiah, but no more so than the good times of His healing comfort — we get a full measure of that, too."

I noted above that Jesus' parable was also an encouragement for us. I think you will see that this has been evident throughout our whole discussion. *In teaching us about forgiving others, Jesus has also been teaching us about the boundless love of God. Anyone may come to Jesus, our great King, and find a full and complete pardon for all of their sins.* What's more, as God's children, we may come to Him daily, and find forgiveness, healing, and fellowship with Him. In Jesus' model prayer, He reminds us to entreat our Father: *"And forgive us our debts, as we also have forgiven our debtors." Matthew 6:12 NIV.* By learning to pray this way, we are reminded daily of the need to forgive others, and of the power of God living in us which makes it possible to do so.

All of this brings us full circle. Why is forgiveness such a clear Hi-Def picture of God's Children? It's because as we demonstrate forgiveness in our relationships, it prominently characterizes what the gospel states is *God's greatest offer to every person — the forgiveness of sins.* When we are seen freely forgiving others (and also not keeping a record of their wrongs), those who observe us will pause to think. They will ask themselves how we could possibly forgive a person who has committed such a wrong against us. To all appearances, our act of forgiveness will look very different from what their sense of justice might demand, or from any behavior

423

they are used to seeing. Yet by God's grace, we may have opportunity to share with them why we are able to forgive. We can let them know that we are acting like Jesus - and that we are His followers. We can tell everyone that we are forgiving the sins of others, because Jesus has so wonderfully forgiven ours. We can share the good news that Jesus is alive — and that no matter what a person has ever done wrong, Jesus offers the forgiveness of their sins, and a relationship with God that leads to everlasting life. Thus as we forgive the sins of others, we create a Hi-Def picture of the extravagant offer made by divine love to those who don't deserve it.

In July of 2012, a terrible tragedy took place in Aurora, Colorado. A crazed gunman marched into a movie theater and brutally attacked the patrons. Twelve people were killed, and another 58 people were wounded during the incident. Among the wounded is a man named Pierce O'Farrill. A recent news blog shared the following story about Mr. O'Farrill, who is believer in Jesus Christ:

It would be understandable for the victims of the Colorado theater shooting and their families to want retribution.

But Pierce O'Farrill, a 28-year-old who was shot three times in the Aurora massacre, says he has forgiven the suspected shooter in last week's Aurora, Colo., massacre.

"Of course, I forgive him with all my heart," O'Farrill told reporters shortly before his release from the Univ. of Colorado Hospital on Wednesday. "When I saw him in his hearing, I felt nothing but sorrow for him — he's just a lost soul right now."

O'Farrill — a staffer at the Denver Rescue Mission, a Christian charity organization that helps "people at their physical and spiritual points of need, with the goal of returning them to society as productive, self-sufficient citizens" — told the Denver Post he would eventually like to meet the shooter.

"I want to see him sometime," O'Farrill, one of 58 people wounded in the shooting, said. "The first thing I want to say to him is 'I forgive you,' and the next is, 'Can I pray for you?'" [8]

Mr. O'Farrill's forgiveness stands in stark contrast to the feelings of the brother of one of the other shooting victims; a man who could not even bring himself to attend the hearing of the gunman, for fear that he might try to "get his hands on him" in order to avenge his sister's death. Many comments were made by readers of this news blog. Some readers, like this woman's brother, felt that the gunman was not fit to live. Others could not understand how Mr. O'Farrill could forgive him, because they supposed that by doing so, O'Farrill was expressing a desire that the gunman be released (and not be held accountable to the law for his crimes). But Pierce O'Farrill was not seeking the gunman's release, or an escape for him from the consequences of his actions. What Mr. O'Farrill did was a reflection of his relationship with Jesus. What he was seeking for this gunman is an experience of God's love. As hard as it is for us to understand, God loves this gunman. Not because he deserves it - his actions were cruel and inexcusable - but it is even for one such as he, that Jesus died on the cross. Mr. O'Farrill recognized that behind this terrible crime, was a lost soul for whom Jesus died. By forgiving the sins committed against him, this courageous follower of Christ presents a Hi-Def picture to the world, of the extravagant offer of divine love to those who don't deserve it. Yet despite any misunderstanding, most of those who commented on this incident admired the genuineness of Mr. O'Farrill's faith and compassion - and recognized in him the love of Jesus Christ.

Love one another

"Let me give you a new command: Love one another. In the same way I loved you, you love one another. This is how everyone will recognize that you are my disciples — when they see the love you have for each other." John 13:34-35 MSG

It was during the time of the "Jesus Movement" that I came to place my faith in Jesus Christ. I was a young man; not yet out of my teens. Had you met me during this time of my life, one thing you would have noticed unmistakably, was that I was a very excited new believer. Everywhere I went, I told people that I was a follower of Jesus. I also searched eagerly for others who were also His followers. As I was somewhat naive in my new faith, I supposed that everyone who had the name "Christian", believed as I did. Anytime I saw a Christian bumper-sticker on a car driving by, I proudly held up my index finger to let that person know that I too was a Christian. (For those of you who were not necessarily around for this — this gesture to someone during the time of the Jesus Movement, identified you as a fellow believer.) These days, I'm somewhat more careful in how I gesture to people. (Unless you have a secret code book that explains all the various gestures people use nowadays, you might want to be careful how one is interpreted!) In any case, one thing I had come to learn, was that not everyone who I supposed was a true Christian, really was. This was quite shocking for me as a young believer. It seemed almost instinctual to me that all Christian people would want to identify themselves to each other. That way, we could enter into an immediate bond of love and fellowship which I thought should characterize all true believers in Christ. As I grew in my new faith and knowledge of God's Word, I learned that essentially yes, I was correct. True disciples of Christ should indeed want to acknowledge and love each other. Correspondingly, I came to learn that not everyone that called themselves "Christian" would demonstrate God's love toward those who also called themselves "Christian." This lack of love on the part of so-called Christians toward their fellow believers, has always saddened me. I later learned from various teachings of Jesus, that God would one day ultimately separate the true believers from the false. Even so, I marveled at how some seemingly 'religious' people could attend church, and yet have no genuine concern for those who joined them in worshiping Jesus. As a new believer, I did not understand these so called 'religious' people. Why would anyone who did not truly know and love Jesus personally, attend church anyway? What did they hope to gain? (Of course now I understand the reasons for this quite well — but that's another conversation.) The issue here is the truth that *a credible disciple of Jesus will in fact acknowledge other disciples - and demonstrate love for them.* Only as they do, will they exhibit themselves as a Hi-Def picture of a child of God.

It may seem strange to take the idea of Christian love for one another, and make it the choice as the *third* Hi-Def picture of a child of God. So before we go any farther into that, there is something important to consider first. . . Anytime we begin to discuss Jesus' command to love one another, a question will inevitably spring to mind: Aren't we supposed to love *everyone* - and not just our fellow disciples? This is a valid question to address before getting back to 'Jesus' emphasis on love for one another'. There is a connection between the love we are to show toward all people, and the love we are to show toward fellow disciples of Jesus. The two are not dissimilar; they are in fact quite interconnected. Jesus could never have meant that we should love one another, and yet not love the rest of the people in the world. Biblical exhortations to love our fellow man are plentiful. A useful example of this, is found in Luke 10:25-37. This is the well known story Jesus told of the "Good Samaritan." When a religious scholar was discussing with Jesus *"the way to obtain eternal life"*, Jesus asked the man his opinion on the matter. The scholar answered, *"Love the Lord your God with all your heart and with all your soul and with all your strength and with all your mind; and Love your neighbor as yourself."* Jesus replied that he was indeed correct. The man then asked Jesus, *"and who is my neighbor?"* He did not ask this question merely to obtain information. He was in fact seeking to justify his lack of love for others, and to find a loophole for himself. In response, Jesus told the story of the Good Samaritan. The story ends with Jesus making it clear to the religious scholar - *that our neighbor is anyone who is in need of our help and mercy.* It is evident then; that our Lord desires His followers to love all people. It is also plain that we must love Jesus' followers as well. We can hardly love people in general - and not love Christ's followers in particular! That would be foolish on the face of it. It would be like showing love toward everyone we meet - except for those in our own immediate family. In loving everyone, we love Jesus' disciples also. It's safe to say that showing God's love to others - is a vital quality in successful Christian living. The well known "Love Chapter" by the Apostle Paul in 1 Corinthians 13 (NLT) is a further example of this.

If I could speak all the languages of earth and of angels, but didn't love others, I would only be a noisy gong or a clanging cymbal. If I had the gift of prophecy, and if I understood all of God's secret plans and possessed all knowledge, and if I had such faith that I could move mountains, but didn't love others, I would be nothing. If I gave everything I have to the poor and even sacrificed my body, I could boast about it; but if I didn't love others, I would have gained nothing.

Love is patient and kind. Love is not jealous or boastful or proud or rude. It does not demand its own way. It is not irritable, and it keeps no record of being wronged. It does not rejoice about injustice but rejoices whenever the truth wins out. Love never gives up, never loses faith, is always hopeful, and endures through every circumstanProphecy and speaking in unknown languages and special knowledge will become useless. But love will last forever! Now our knowledge is partial and incomplete, and even the gift of prophecy reveals only part of the whole picture! But when full understanding comes, these partial things will become useless.

When I was a child, I spoke and thought and reasoned as a child. But when I grew up, I put away childish things. Now we see things imperfectly as in a cloudy mirror, but then we will see everything with perfect clarity. All that I know now is partial and incomplete, but then I will know everything completely, just as God now knows me completely.

Three things will last forever — faith, hope, and love — and the greatest of these is love.

Paul also prefaced those timeless words by saying: *"So you should earnestly desire the most helpful gifts. But now let me show you a way of life that is best of all." 1 Cor.12:31 NLT*

It is without question then - that *love for others is indispensable to living as a true follower of Jesus.* Having established this, we must now address the question of why Jesus' new commandment in John 13:34-35, focuses so distinctly on love for fellow believers - rather than love for all mankind. We must also discover why obedience to this commandment qualifies as such a Hi-Def picture of a child of God.

As we read these verses again, Jesus makes a very clear statement. He says, *"This is how everyone will recognize that you are my disciples — when they see the love you have for each other."* There is something about the special love we exhibit toward our brothers and sisters in Christ, which grabs the attention of outsiders. Something that witnesses to them that we are true disciples of Jesus. When an unbeliever steps into a church gathering, they immediately start to form impressions of the disciples who are present. This is the case whether the number of disciples is large or small. Those impressions will mostly be based on the way they are treated - and the way those present treat each other. There is no fooling ourselves about this. Unbelievers attending our gatherings are quite perceptive in this regard. They are watching and observing us - and the way we worship God. Are they made to feel welcome? Does anyone personally greet them? Do those in attendance seem kindly-disposed toward each other? Does anyone care about what's going on? Is everyone interacting in an orderly and unified way? The truth is, when we gather as believers, we are creating a certain type of social-spiritual atmosphere. This ambiance consists of body language, speech, and the display of personal relationships (such as handshakes and hugs). It also consists of the way we converse together, and of the general esteem with which we regard each other (shown through our interactions). There is a sort of "Christian society" that we demonstrate - no matter what the purpose of our gathering is. It may be for worship, teaching, acts of charity, fellowship, holidays, or any social occasion. In other words, those who do not believe in Jesus, will take immediate note of what we as "Christians" are like. When we make the general impression that declares we genuinely love God and one another — the visitor is compelled to realize that we are true disciples of Jesus. This is of course not to downplay the role of the Holy Spirit. The Spirit's expression is in fact *highlighted* through our interactions. Only through His ministry - will the presence and power of God be seen and felt at our gatherings.

In a discussion regarding prayer, Jesus declared that: "For where two or three gather together as my followers, I am there among them." (Matthew 18:20 NLT). It is in fact the Holy Spirit who makes Jesus known (John 15:26). Assuredly then as we love one another — Jesus is being made known. Not just in a general way that a person might observe as we act in love toward everyone — but in a specific way; the context of Jesus' disciples relating and acting toward one another with acts of love. It is there among Christians, that an outsider sees first and foremost - our proclamation of the life of Jesus on display. As we love one another in this way — we are keeping Jesus' commandments. The Father is glorified, and we bear much fruit proving ourselves to be His disciples (See John 15:4-17).

So why then does obedience to *Jesus' command to love one another*, qualify as a Hi-Def picture of a child of God? The Apostle John (who wrote the words we have been examining) had a great many years to reflect upon their full meaning. The letter of 1 John provides us with a more detailed understanding of the importance of this command. There are four distinct passages in the letter which highlight John's perceptiveness in a powerful way. In all of them, John declares unequivocally that failure to keep this command of Jesus - shows that we do not love God at all, nor do we truly belong to Him. These passages are; 1 John 2:7-11, 3:11-18, 4:7-24, and 5:1-5. A concise review of some of these key verses will make John's meaning plain:

2:9-11 NLT If anyone claims, "I am living in the light," but hates a Christian brother or sister, that person is still living in darkness. Anyone who loves another brother or sister is living in the light and does not cause others to stumble. But anyone who hates another brother or sister is still living and walking in darkness. Such a person does not know the way to go, having been blinded by the darkness.

3:14-18 NLT If we love our Christian brothers and sisters, it proves that we have passed from death to life. But a person who has no love is still dead. Anyone who hates another brother or sister is really a murderer at heart. And you know that murderers don't have eternal life within them.

We know what real love is because Jesus gave up His life for us. So we also ought to give up our lives for our brothers and sisters. If someone has enough money to live well and sees a brother or sister in need but shows no compassion — how can God's love be in that person?

Dear children, let's not merely say that we love each other; let us show the truth by our actions.

4:7-8 NLT Dear friends, let us continue to love one another, for love comes from God. Anyone who loves is a child of God and knows God. But anyone who does not love does not know God, for God is love.

4:20-21 NLT If someone says, "I love God," but hates a Christian brother or sister, that person is a liar; for if we don't love people we can see, how can we love God, whom we cannot see? And he has given us this command: Those who love God must also love their Christian brothers and sisters.

Even a casual reading of these verses makes their meaning unmistakable. To claim to be a child of God, and yet not demonstrate a practical love for our brothers and sisters, means that:

- We are blind and still living in spiritual darkness.

- We are still spiritually dead and do not have eternal life within us.

- We are really murderers at heart.

- We do not know what real love is - since Jesus' sacrifice for us has not translated into sacrificial love practiced in our lives.

- Our refusal to show compassion for a brother or sister in need - proves that God's love is not in us.

- When we claim to be God's child — the truth of the claim can be only be shown by our actions.

- Love comes from God - and is His very nature. Refusing to love one another shows that we do not love God at all.

- To say, "I love God", is totally incompatible with a lack of compassionate love for His children.

- Our failure to love our brothers and sisters makes our claim to love God - an outright lie.

The Bible's meaning is unmistakable; that the truth of our claim to be a disciple of Jesus - will be revealed by evident practical expressions of love toward our Christian brothers and sisters. It is for this reason that *love for one another* is the final of our Hi-Def pictures of a child of God. Such love marks us distinctively as Jesus' disciples, and it affirms His statement that: *"This is how everyone will recognize that you are my disciples — when they see the love you have for each other."*

One last point to consider here. I noted earlier how Jesus' statement connecting our discipleship and our love for one another, is very important. There is another statement He made in John 13:34 MSG which could be easily overlooked, but is just as remarkable:

"Let me give you a new command: Love one another. *In the same way I loved you*, you love one another." (Italics mine)

Jesus' directive for His disciples to love — "*In the same way that I loved you*" — must not be overlooked. It is here that He tells us the *manner* in which we are to love one another. So what does it mean 'to love each other in the same way that Jesus has loved us?' Think of how the disciples who were sitting with Jesus during the Last Supper might have understood this. To make it personal, imagine how John (who wrote this gospel) may have thought back on how Jesus had loved him. He would have remembered how just a few short years earlier, Jesus had called him from his life as a fisherman, to follow after him and be His disciple. He would think with gratitude about how Jesus had taught him what it means to know God, and to enter His Kingdom. He would think about how Jesus had given his life meaning and purpose; far greater than he had ever known or thought possible. All of the life lessons he had heard Jesus speak of, and all of the things he had seen Him do, would have come readily to mind. There were lessons about how to relate to others from all walks of life; about how to spend time wisely and live responsibly; about how to pray to God; and about how to trust God to meet all his needs without needless anxiety. In short, John would have thought about the caring and compassionate way that Jesus treated him, and how He had met all the deepest needs of his life. He would call to mind the difference that the love of Jesus made in his soul — a difference which led him to realize that God had put him in this world for a reason, and that he in-turn could make a real difference in the lives of others. Does this sound familiar? It should, because John's story is our story as well. This is the way Jesus has loved each of us. He gave His life with no thought of Himself; so that we can become all that God means for us to be. For the first disciples, as well as for us

— loving one another as Jesus has loved us - means to live a life motivated by service to others; a life that makes every person we meet feel valued. A life lived *proclaiming God's love for us* as central in everything we do.

Consider what took place just prior to Jesus' issuance of this new command 'to love one another as He had loved them' (this manner of love which invests primarily in others). The story is found in John 13:1-17. Here we find Jesus getting up from the supper table, setting aside His outer robe, and wrapping a towel around His waist. He poured water into a basin, and began to wash the feet of His disciples. Then He dried their feet with the towel that was wrapped around Him. When He had finished, He put His outer robe back on again, and returned to His place at the table. We learn from Luke's gospel (22:24) that this entire scene was preceded by an argument among the disciples about which of them would be considered the greatest. It's most likely that it was right after this dispute that Jesus washed the feet of His disciples. John tells us in his gospel account, that after Jesus returned to the table, He declared to them all:

"Do you understand what I was doing? You call me 'Teacher' and 'Lord,' and you are right, because that's what I am. And since I, your Lord and Teacher, have washed your feet, you ought to wash each other's feet. I have given you an example to follow. Do as I have done to you. I tell you the truth, slaves are not greater than their master. Nor is the messenger more important than the one who sends the message. Now that you know these things, God will bless you for doing them." John 13:12-17 NLT

The main idea universally recognized from these words, is that *an attitude of humble genuine service* should characterize those who follow Jesus. Since the Son of God gave up so much to live among us as a servant — we who follow

Him, and bear His message to others, must pattern our lives after His example. This essential truth is an echo of another saying of Jesus' in Matthew 20:28 NLT: *"For even the Son of Man came not to be served; but to serve others, and to give His life as a ransom for many."* It was following this foot-washing that Jesus gave the new command to His disciples *to love one another as He had loved them.* This compelling object lesson by their Lord and Master (which intervened during their dispute) would have been fresh on their minds as they heard this new command. When Jesus spoke to them of 'loving one another as He had loved them', it would have been clear from His actions that this kind of love involved a willingness to do humble service on behalf of others. There was no longer any room for pride among them. Consider also Jesus' further words to them (as recorded by Luke) during the course of these events. Here, His words focus not only on the importance of humble service, but on the connection between servant leadership, and true greatness:

Then they began to argue among themselves about who would be the greatest among them. Jesus told them, "In this world the kings and great men lord it over their people, yet they are called 'friends of the people.' But among you it will be different. Those who are the greatest among you should take the lowest rank, and the leader should be like a servant. Who is more important, the one who sits at the table or the one who serves? The one who sits at the table, of course. But not here! For I am among you as one who serves." Luke 22:24-27 NLT

Shortly after this model of humble service, John records one of Jesus' prayers. In this prayer, Jesus asks the Father that the disciples be made one in heart and mind - as He and the Father were one - so that the world would know that God had sent Him. As Jesus lived in the hearts of His disciples, their unity would also attest to the rest of the world that God loved the disciples in the same way as He loved Jesus (John 17:21-23). After they listened to Jesus pray those words, the disciples would soon understand what we must also understand — that only by loving each other as Jesus loved them - in the manner of a selfless servant - would the world acknowledge them as authentic followers of their Lord. When the world recognizes by this essential love for one another that Christ lives in us, it gives credibility to our witness that the Father sent the Son to be the Savior of the world.

Finally, as we tie all these threads together, we see *in the cross* the ultimate expression of the way Jesus loves us. The sacrifice Jesus made on the cross for the sins of the world, defines for us what divine love really looks like:

"God showed how much He loved us by sending His one and only Son into the world so that we might have eternal life through Him. This is real love — not that we loved God, but that He loved us and sent His Son as a sacrifice to take away our sins. Dear friends, since God loved us that much, we surely ought to love each other. No one has ever seen God. But if we love each other, God lives in us, and His love is brought to full expression in us.

And God has given us His Spirit as proof that we live in Him and He in us." 1 John 4:9-13 NLT

It's only when we survey the cross, and experience a new life from God (a life bestowed through His Spirit), that we learn the extent of God's love for us and how we are to love each other. When we love each other as our Lord has loved us, we show to everyone that He lives in us. Then, His love can mature into the full expression of what He intended when He saved us. This in turn gives us the confidence to know that we truly belong to God.

It is only because God first loved us — that we are able to love one another (1 John 4:19). **This is God's Arithmetic.** God loves you freely. You embrace His love. Then, that same love from Jesus living in you - is extended through you to others. His love flows and multiplies to the world though all His children. **It all adds up — and the sum is eternal life in Christ:**

"And we know that the Son of God has come, and He has given us understanding so that we can know the true God. And now we live in fellowship with the true God because we live in fellowship with His Son, Jesus Christ. He is the only true God, and He is eternal life." 1 John 5:20 NLT

When Gain Is Loss

For much of my life, I have been an aficionado of science fiction. I especially enjoy the movies, television series, and novels, which are imaginative and creative. You know, the ones that portray the future in exciting or thought-provoking ways. One of my favorite science fiction movies is "The Matrix". (Warning: If you haven't seen this movie — mild Spoilers ahead!) The movie asks the question: "What if virtual reality wasn't for fun, but was being used to imprison you?" The central character and hero of the movie, is a man named Thomas Anderson. Mr. Anderson works for a software company by day, and is a computer hacker by night, under the alias 'Neo'. When Neo finally meets a mysterious man named Morpheus, he learns some shocking news — Nothing of what is going on around him is real. Morpheus offers Neo a choice. He can continue with the fiction of his daily life, or he can learn the truth about what he believes is reality. Neo chooses to learn the truth, and awakens to find himself in the 'real' world. It turns out that Neo, like most of the human race, is a victim of The Matrix (a massive system of machines which have taken control of our minds, and created the illusion of a real world). So in the world of this science fiction adventure, people go through their entire lives living in a virtual dream-world. They never realize that their whole reality is a false one, and that they are prisoners of their own minds; blinded from the truth of their existence.

I have no intention here to try to interpret the specific symbolism in this movie which its writers may have intended. But I do want to use its plot to make a unique comparison to a truth put forth in the Bible; one which always comes to mind as I watch this movie. Please bear in mind that this is not an exact comparison, but only a pronounced one. We will use it to lead us into our larger discussion of *the truth and reality of the salvation that God has provided for us in Jesus Christ*. It has been said that "truth is often stranger than fiction". Most people would be surprised to learn that (like those in The Matrix) we are also living in a world where our reality is neither what we believe it is, nor what it appears to be. Furthermore, we are also prisoners and slaves — not of machines, but of what the Bible calls "sin"; and we are oppressed and blinded by an unseen power of evil.

The Bible teaches that God is Spirit (John 4:24). He is the King eternal, immortal, invisible, the only God (1 Timothy 1:17). He lives in unapproachable light, and no one has seen Him or can see Him (1 Timothy 6:16). These basic truths about *the reality of God,* are held by several of the world's great religions (Judaism, Christianity, Islam). Each of these acknowledges that there is a realm which exists around us - a reality beyond our own - that is the dwelling place of God and other great hosts of spiritual beings. The Bible teaches the reality of this invisible realm, and its effect on the world in which we live. Spiritual reality is not provable by the scientific method; yet we can see its effects by the good and evil so evident in our vast societies of people. Just like those in The Matrix (who never realized that there is more to reality than the world around them), our world needs to awaken to the truth of its spiritual condition. It was our Lord Jesus

Christ who spoke of this need *for all people to experience a spiritual rebirth*:

"Very truly I tell you, no one can see the kingdom of God unless they are born again." John 3:3 NIV

He went on to say that although this new spiritual birth was very real, it does not occur by natural means. Like the wind which is invisible, but can be seen by its effects; so the work of the Spirit of God can be seen in people's lives, but not explained:

"Humans can reproduce only human life, but the Holy Spirit gives birth to spiritual life. So don't be surprised when I say, 'You must be born again.' The wind blows wherever it wants. Just as you can hear the wind but can't tell where it comes from or where it is going, so you can't explain how people are born of the Spirit." John 3:6-8 NLT

Jesus is the only one who can enlighten people as to their spiritual need, and open their eyes to the truth:

"I am the light of the world. Whoever follows me will never walk in darkness, but will have the light of life." John 8:12 NIV

At the time Jesus spoke those words, He was teaching at the Temple in Jerusalem. The teachers of religious law, and the religious experts known as the Pharisees, had just brought to Jesus a woman caught in the act of adultery. These men were not so much concerned for the woman, as they were in trying to trap Jesus into saying something that they could use against Him (John 8:6). In a wonderful display of God's wisdom, Jesus refutes their hypocrisy by saying, *"Let any one of you who is without sin be the first to throw a stone at her." (John 8:7)*. Upon hearing these words, the woman's accusers all left, leaving Jesus alone with her. Jesus promptly forgave her sins, and started her on the path to a brand new life, despite the mistakes of her past. It was not long after this (when Jesus had resumed teaching in the Temple) that He was once again confronted by the Pharisees. It was immediately after He claimed to be the light of the world, that the Pharisees (who were still stung by Jesus' recent rebuke of their deceitfulness) entered into a fierce dispute with Him regarding the claims He was making about Himself. During this dispute, Jesus made clear His unique authority as the Son of God — and in the process, He also makes known the absolute reality of the spiritual world or "Kingdom of Heaven":

"Once more Jesus said to them, "I am going away, and you will look for me, and you will die in your sin. Where I go, you cannot come."

This made the Jews ask, "Will he kill himself? Is that why He says, 'Where I go, you cannot come'?"

But He continued, "You are from below; I am from above. You are of this world; I am not of this world. I told you that you would die in your sins; if you do not believe that I am He, you will indeed die in your sins."

Who are you?" they asked.

"Just what I have been telling you from the beginning," Jesus replied. "I have much to say in judgment of you. But He who sent me is trustworthy, and what I have heard from Him I tell the world."

They did not understand that He was telling them about His Father. So Jesus said, "When you have lifted up the Son of Man, then you will know that I am He and that I do nothing on my own but speak just what the Father has taught me. The one who sent me is with me; He has not left me alone, for I always do what pleases Him." Even as He spoke, many believed in Him." John 8:21-30 NIV

Among the notable ideas in this passage, is that Jesus is not from this world. He was sent by the Father (God) from the unseen world (above), and was soon to return to that realm (cp. Acts 1:9-11; Luke 24:51). This truth, that there is an invisible reality beyond our own, is also evident later in John's gospel, as Jesus responds to the Roman governor Pontius Pilate:

Jesus said, "My kingdom is not of this world. If it were, my servants would fight to prevent my arrest by the Jewish leaders. But now my kingdom is from another place."

"You are a king, then!" said Pilate.

Jesus answered, "You say that I am a king. In fact, the reason I was born and came into the world is to testify to the truth. Everyone on the side of truth listens to me." John 18:36-37 NIV

Another prominent idea from Jesus' dispute in John 8, is that if the self-assured religious experts refused to believe that He was the Messiah - uniquely divine and speaking as only God can - then they *would die in their sins (vv.21,24).* As if this were not shocking enough, Jesus goes on to tell them (those Jews at the Temple who believed what He said):

"If you hold to my teaching, you are really my disciples. Then you will know the truth, and the truth will set you free." (vv.31-32)

To this, the Jews responded:

"We are Abraham's descendants and have never been slaves of anyone. How can you say that we shall be set free?" (v.33)

This honest response on the part of these Jews as they sought the truth about God - is exactly what so many people from all the world's religions would say today. "How can you say to us that we will be set free — just to who or what do you think we are enslaved?" The sad fact is that (like those who were trapped in The Matrix) all humanity is - in reality - also imprisoned. We see this in Jesus' response:

Jesus replied, "Very truly I tell you, everyone who sins is a slave to sin. Now a slave has no permanent place in the family, but a son belongs to it forever. So if the Son sets you free, you will be free indeed."
(vv.34-36)

Every human being is a slave to sin. This includes all of us; *"for all have sinned and fall short of the glory of God" (Romans 3:23)*. Thus, like those in The Matrix, all individuals apart from Christ - even the most religious people - are blind to this slavery and to the truth *that there is only one way to freedom* – faith in God's Son Jesus Christ.

Finally, after Jesus tells His inquisitors that their hearts were closed to the truth - and that only He could set them free — He reveals to them that they are blinded and encumbered by a terrible power of evil:

"Why is my language not clear to you? Because you are unable to hear what I say. You belong to your father, the devil, and you want to carry out your father's desires. He was a murderer from the beginning, not holding to the truth, for there is no truth in him. When he lies, he speaks his native language, for he is a liar and the father of lies. Yet because I tell the truth, you do not believe me! Can any of you prove me guilty of sin? If I am telling the truth, why don't you believe me? Whoever belongs to God hears what God says. The reason you do not hear is that you do not belong to God." John 8:43-47 NIV

Consider also 2 Corinthians 4:4 NCV:

"The devil who rules this world has blinded the minds of those who do not believe. They cannot see the light of the Good News — the Good News about the glory of Christ, who is exactly like God."

Forget the Matrix! This is the harsh reality under which all humanity actually lives. The truth is out there - in the Word of God. The truth that our spiritual condition has placed us all in great peril. Unless God had intervened, we were all destined to die in our sins. Only Jesus Christ can open our eyes, turn us from the power of Satan unto God, forgive our sins, and give us a place among God's people; who are set apart through faith in Him (Acts 26:18). Jesus is unlike all others. There is no prophet, priest, or religious leader of any kind, who claims to be the Lord Himself (John 8:58) and has declared:

"Very truly I tell you, whoever obeys my word will never see death." John 8:51 NIV

God's Arithmetic <u>is all about how we are to view our
lives. It is learning the basics about what is true and real; as
God has revealed it to us; and then ordering our lives in a
way that honors Him.</u> It is beginning to see the world as God
sees it, to measure our existence as He does, and to allow
His Word to shape our reality — instead of trying to shape
our own. Throughout the course of writing this book, I have
experienced a persistent gentle urging to cover a specific passage of scripture in our discussion of God's Arithmetic. Since
I have been unable to find another suitable place to include
it, I determined to dedicate this last chapter to focus on that
passage. Although God's Arithmetic was written primarily
for those who have already made a commitment to follow
Jesus — there may be some who are reading this, that have
not yet made such a commitment. Therefore, I conclude our
journey together with *two* goals in mind. *First*, is that those
who love our Lord Jesus Christ may gain a new appreciation
- that to know Him better and better - is the highest goal we
may attain to. *Second*, is that those who have never trusted in
Jesus for their salvation - may come to realize that nothing in
all the world compares with the surpassing value of having a
personal relationship with Him.

The passage of scripture I referred to in the previous
paragraph, is found in the third chapter of Paul's letter to the
Philippians, with an emphasis on verses 7-11. To begin our
discussion on what it means to know Jesus Christ, we need
to look at two of His parables. These concise parables are
closely related to each other, and they set the stage for our
look at the radical transformation that took place in Paul's
life. The first one is found in Matthew 13:44 NIV:

*"The kingdom of heaven is like treasure hidden in a field.
When a man found it, he hid it again, and then in his joy went
and sold all he had and bought that field."*

What we have in this parable, is a man who has spent his life accumulating wealth and material possessions. He happens upon a hidden treasure in a field that is so invaluable - that he gladly sells everything he owns to obtain that *true* treasure. He is willing to give up all that he has, in order to possess something far more precious and valuable.

The next two verses in Matthew 13 (45-46), give us the second parable which carries the same idea as the first:

"Again, the kingdom of heaven is like a merchant looking for fine pearls. When he found one of great value, he went away and sold everything he had and bought it."

Here is a merchant who goes around seeking pearls. One day, he chances upon a special pearl - one of great value. Like the man who sold his possessions to buy the field, this man sold everything he owned, in order to obtain a treasure he considered far more valuable.

It's always amazing to me the things that our culture places value on. We become so absorbed in our accumulation of "stuff", that we forget:

". . . we brought nothing with us when we came into the world, and we can't take anything with us when we leave it."
1 Timothy 6:7 NLT

So in these parables, Jesus is not telling us to go treasure hunting for material wealth. The treasure in the field, and the pearl of great value, are Jesus Himself. There is so much in this world that we assume has value; and sure, in the everyday business of life, it does. But in God's Arithmetic, there is something of such surpassing value, that if we could only see the truth — we would gladly give up everything and anything to possess it.

Before the Apostle Paul came to know Christ, he was a man who had almost all of the advantages this world could offer. He was an eminently religious man, who lived among God's chosen people. He had obtained an established position in life, earned the respect of others, and was convinced that he was entitled to the favor and blessing of God. One day, his world was shattered when he met Jesus Christ on the road to Damascus. As we look at Paul's experience in discovering the truth about Christ, we too may find that everything in this world we thought was gain to us (by comparison) — is actually nothing but loss.

Our reading begins in chapter three of Philippians, where Paul speaks to the church about his personal salvation experience. Here in this chapter, he talks with us about his background in Judaism, and how it contrasts with the life he found in Christ. Prior to his conversion (recorded in Acts 9), Paul was a prominent person in the Jewish faith, and he enjoyed all the benefits that were his due in that regard. Yet after his decision to follow Christ, there was no comparison between his appraisal of his former life as a Pharisee, and what he had now gained through his personal knowledge of Christ. Paul describes Christian living as *a constant striving toward the goal of maturity in Christ*. He exhorts the Philippian church (as well as us) to join him in the quest for spiritual maturity.

The first six verses of this chapter, are a warning against false teachers who were pridefully asserting how their own efforts and worthiness had achieved (for themselves) a right relationship with God. These false teachers were Jewish legalists (commonly referred to as Judaizers) who insisted that Christians obey the law of Moses, along with their faith in Christ, as a requirement for salvation. Their particular emphasis was on the 'rite of male circumcision' as a necessity for obtaining right standing before God. Paul actually begins this chapter with a reminder for the believers to always rejoice in the Lord (v.1). Such a reminder may seem out of place as he writes to us about false teachers, but it really is a good place to start. Why is that so? Think of it like this: As we center our lives in Christ, and remember that *He alone* is sufficient for our salvation, we have a continual source of joy. This joy reminds us that Jesus has set us free from sin - through His cross and resurrection - *apart from any works of our own.* The better we understand this, the greater our joy will be. For as we reflect on our salvation and the finished work of Christ, it becomes easier to distinguish the true gospel from the false. In other words, our new freedom in Christ brings joy, while the false teaching of legalism robs us of it. So Paul begins with a reminder for the Philippians to rejoice in the Lord, because their joy stands in direct contrast to the trouble caused by the false teachers. Their joy would serve as a reminder of the truths Paul had taught them, and as a safeguard against those who would steal it away.

Paul had warned the church about these false teachers before, as well as the dissension they cause; but it never hurts to share those things again (v.1). Many Christians today are always seeking the latest and greatest in unfamiliar, trendy, and so called 'ground breaking' teachings about the scriptures. In my personal study of the Bible, I have always found the Apostles placing an emphasis on reminding us *of the truths we have already been taught.* For those of us who have been Christians for any length of time, it isn't so much "what we *don't* know", but "putting into practice what we *do* know" — which is most needful for our spiritual growth. That's not to discourage us from studying the Word of God to gain new insights into its teachings; but it is the tried and true teachings of the faith - not the offbeat and the unfamiliar - which keep us safe and progressing toward the goal of spiritual maturity. Remember the warning of Jeremiah 6:16 NLT:

This is what the LORD says:
"Stop at the crossroads and look around.
Ask for the old, godly way, and walk in it.
Travel its path, and you will find rest for your souls.
But you reply, 'No, that's not the road we want!' "

Here, to the Philippians, Paul reminds us of the safest path of all. It is the path of salvation in Christ alone - marked out by faith - that will keep us from the high sounding and empty philosophies of false teachers. To that end, Paul begins with a warning:

"2 Watch out for those dogs, those people who do evil, those mutilators who say you must be circumcised to be saved. 3 For we who worship by the Spirit of God are the ones who are truly circumcised. We rely on what Christ Jesus has done for us. We put no confidence in human effort, 4 though I could have confidence in my own effort if anyone could." (Philippians 3:2-4a NLT)

Paul calls these false teachers 'dogs' — and he doesn't mean they are like cute puppies. This is a derogatory term that suggests that these people were acting like scavenger dogs; stalking members of the church in order to convert them into their own disciples, and mislead them to their way of thinking. These teachers were evil workers — not because they sought to keep the Mosaic law, but because their 'gospel of salvation through the law' was directly opposed to *the true gospel of salvation by grace alone*, through faith in Christ. They insisted on mutilating the flesh. (i.e. They required that males be circumcised according to the law of Moses, before their faith in Jesus would be sufficient to obtain a right standing before God.) Paul describes them as mutilators, not because he was opposing the law or the rite of circumcision per se, but because of the importance of making clear that circumcision has no relationship to salvation. No one has to be circumcised in order to be in right standing with God. He drives this point home in verse 3, by declaring that the true people of God are not those who are trying to earn salvation by circumcision or any human effort. The true people of God are those who have trusted in Christ alone, and who follow and serve Him by God's Spirit. They put no confidence in human effort for their salvation, but instead rely completely on God's grace, and only on what Christ has done for them. The truly 'circumcised' are those who God leads by His Spirit, and who trust in Christ alone for their right standing with God. This is exactly the same idea that Paul put forth in Romans 2:28-29 NLT:

For you are not a true Jew just because you were born of Jewish parents or because you have gone through the ceremony of circumcision. No, a true Jew is one whose heart is right with God. And true circumcision is not merely obeying the letter of the law; rather, it is a change of heart produced by God's Spirit. And a person with a changed heart seeks praise from God, not from people.

As Paul continues to highlight the error of those who believe that any human effort whatsoever can make them right with God, he shares his own experience of salvation. He begins in vv.4-6, by laying out the grounds for the confidence he placed in his own efforts to obtain a right relationship with God, before he knew Christ. Paul believed that if anyone had good reason to be confident in their own efforts to get right with God, it was him! In fact, if others thought they had good reason to trust in their own achievements to obtain right standing with God, Paul thought he had even more:

"Indeed, if others have reason for confidence in their own efforts, I have even more! 5 I was circumcised when I was eight days old. I am a pure-blooded citizen of Israel and a member of the tribe of Benjamin — a real Hebrew if there ever was one! I was a member of the Pharisees, who demand the strictest obedience to the Jewish law. 6 I was so zealous that I harshly persecuted the church. And as for righteousness, I obeyed the law without fault." (Philippians 3:4b-6 NLT)

Let's see if we can understand the reasons Paul gives for his pre-Christian confidence in believing he had obtained God's favor. As we examine his self-reliance, we can also observe the same means that so many people today trust in for their salvation — and why they mistakenly believe that God is pleased with their own efforts to be made right with Him.

<u>First, he was circumcised when he was eight days old</u>. Circumcision 'on the eighth day' was the command that God had given Abraham and to Moses (Genesis 17:12; Leviticus 12:3). It was a sign that identified a person as a part of the covenant community, and a reminder to remain faithful to that covenant. So Paul is stressing the fact that he had been born into the Jewish faith, and had observed its ceremonies since his birth. From the beginning of his life, he had observed the rites that his family believed were essential to salvation. Almost every religion in the world has these types of rites and rituals; which are believed to help them get their lives right with whatever god they worship. These rituals take many forms, and go by many names. There are ceremonies, symbolic acts of worship, sacraments, masses, routines, washings, baptisms, disciplines, self-denials, liturgies, customs, observances, styles of dress, and any number of other behavioral conventions. Yet as Paul will make plain,

there is not a single rite or ritual of any kind that has any value whatsoever - in terms of making a person right with God.

Next, Paul was a pure-blooded citizen of Israel. Racially, he was a true Israelite, who could trace his descent through Jacob and all the people of promise. He is saying that by birth, he is one of God's chosen people; a claim that is not uncommon today, and seemingly not without merit. In Romans 9:3-5, Paul recounts the blessings of being an Israelite. To them, belong the adoption as sons, the glory, the covenants, the giving of the law, the temple services, and the promises. Theirs are the forefathers, and from them by physical descent, came the Messiah. God had in fact given the Israelites all of those privileges. So Paul says, "I am one of those that God had specially chosen; those He intended to save, redeem, and bring to eternal glory. If a person's race could save them, mine certainly would." Tragically, this is all too commonplace today. Many people assume that if their parents are Christians, then so are they. "I was born into a Christian family, so I too am a Christian." Some even try to affirm this identity by baptizing their children as infants; so as to assure their place in the covenant community. But the truth is that "no family status in the world" can grant you right standing with God. This is so — no matter what religion your family belongs to. Being part of a Christian family — or any other religious family — is no guarantee of any standing with God. Also, what is true for a family - is true for a nation. Being born into a Christian nation (or any other nation) is no assurance that God accepts you. As Paul will make clear — a right relationship with God *is personal and individual*, and has nothing to do with race or any virtue gained by birth.

<u>Along with being an Israelite, Paul belonged to the tribe of Benjamin</u>. The tribe of Benjamin was one of the very elite tribes in Israel. You may recall that Benjamin was the youngest child of Jacob, and the brother of Joseph. His mother Rachel died during his birth, and he was the only one of the twelve patriarchs to be born in the promised land (Genesis 35:17-18). It was from the tribe of Benjamin that the first king of Israel had come; and it may well be that Paul (whose Hebrew name was Saul) was named after him. Benjamin, along with Judah, were the only tribes to stay faithful to the house of David, after the kingdom divided under Rehoboam. Centuries later, when the exiles returned from Babylon, it was again Benjamin along with Judah, which made up most of the community that would rebuild the temple in Jerusalem under the leadership of Zerubbabel (Ezra 1:5; 4:1). Not long after that, it was Mordecai (a Jew from the tribe of Benjamin) that was responsible for the deliverance of the Jews; as told in the book of Esther. Every Jew would know the names of Mordecai and Esther, since the annual feast of Purim was initiated to commemorate that very deliverance. So when Paul says that he is from the tribe of Benjamin — he is stating that not only is he an Israelite, but that he belongs among the most noble and elite citizens of Israel. Thus, by his birth heritage and tribal position, he was looked upon as one of the ranking members of the aristocracy of Israel. In today's world, every nation has its privileged classes. Some people, by wealth or position, are part of the social elite. Others, based on religious leaders in their family or on their own clerical titles, are part of a 'spiritual elite'. None of these things impress God; who is no respecter of persons. No position or rank of any kind, secular or religious, entitles a person to the forgiveness of their sins and acceptance before God. No rank of any kind has anything to do with salvation. Paul will make it unmistakably clear to the Judaizers and everyone else, that no one, privileged

Jew or otherwise, has any implicit merit or status in the sight of God. There is absolutely no such thing as an inherited standing before God.

At this point, Paul moves from what he has inherited, to what he has personally achieved. To the false teachers who believed it was necessary to keep the law of Moses in order to be right with God, <u>Paul now lists his credentials</u> as a person who could do so — if such a thing were even possible. He begins by stating that <u>he is a real Hebrew</u>, if there ever was one — a Hebrew of Hebrews. At the time Paul lived, there were large numbers of Jews living in every city and country all over the world. Despite the strong influence of greco-roman culture, these Jews faithfully maintained their own religion, customs, and laws. But quite often, they forgot their own language. This was because they lived in a Greek-speaking environment, and it was necessary to speak Greek in the course of daily life. There are many parallels to this today; people who choose to maintain their ancestral religious or cultural distinction - while having to learn and practice the language of the country they have chosen to live in. A "Hebrew" was a Jew who had deliberately (and often with great effort) retained the Hebrew language. These people could speak Greek, but they also spoke Hebrew, which was their traditional and historical language. Paul, although born in the Gentile city of Tarsus, was brought up and educated in Jerusalem, at the feet of a prominent rabbi (Acts 22:3). He was able to speak Hebrew when it was necessary for him to do so (e.g. Acts 21:40). He had maintained the language, traditions, and customs of his people; never deviating from them. According to his testimony in Acts 26:4-5, all the Jews knew about his way of life, and would acknowledge that he had strictly and resolutely lived that way. Paul was well-known in the Jewish community as a young man, and he was recognized for his gifts. Even the Jewish high priest and the whole council of elders, knew of his devotion to Hebrew tradition (Acts 22:5). Paul was like many of us who start out in life with a religious tradition handed down to us from our parents and ancestors. We grow up and maintain loyalty to those traditions, in order to fit in comfortably with our society - and because that's the way our family has always been. We've all met people who have told us that they adhere to their religious traditions because it's part of their family heritage. The Bible teaches that no one's loyalty to tradition has any value as a means of salvation. Salvation is provided to us on God's terms alone, and those terms are that we must *personally* receive Jesus Christ as our Lord and Savior. While our traditions may help us to seek and find the Lord, or establish a stable life in our society, they are worthless on their own in terms of obtaining the forgiveness of sins - and entering the Kingdom of God. This is true even for Christians. Growing up in a traditional Christian family certainly has its advantages; just as growing up in a Jewish family had advantages for Paul. By growing up in a godly household among Christian believers and influences, a child can be given a Biblical framework of understanding, as well as a wide variety of opportunities to learn the truth about Jesus Christ. But ultimately, those traditional influences only have value when that child or young person comes to their own decision about who Jesus is — and then receives a personal intimate knowledge of Him for themselves. No one is exempt from making their own personal decision for Christ. No one can be "grandfathered" into the faith through family or religious tradition - exempting them from trusting in Christ entirely on their own accord. When Jesus said, *"I am the way and the truth and the life. No one comes to the Father except through me.";* He was not only declaring that He is the only way to know God and experience salvation, but also that each of us must *personally* come to God through Him — no one can do it for us. There is no tradition that can add to who Jesus is, what He done for us, or to our need to come to God through Him alone.

The next of Paul's personal achievements - is that <u>he was a member of the Pharisees</u>; who demanded the strictest obedience to the Jewish law. The Pharisees were a sect of Judaism who never numbered more than six thousand. Their name means '*The Separated Ones*'. These individuals had chosen to separate themselves from the common tasks of everyday life, in order to make their sole aim 'to keep even the smallest detail of the Mosaic law'. By stating that he was a Pharisee, Paul claimed that as a Jew, he was among the most religious of his people. There was no demand of his religion that he had not gone to great lengths to observe. Originally, the Pharisees were a very noble group of men. They came into being at a time between the Old and New Testament; when many Jews were questioning the authority of Scripture, and compromising the godly values that were set forth in God's Word. Today, we might compare them with those religious fundamentalists whose zeal to protect the interpretation of whatever scripture they hold as sacred, causes them to take a narrow-minded legalistic view of God's truth. The really sad thing was that by the time of Jesus — their zeal had taken them to a place where they came to believe that their 'strict adherence to the law' is what saved them. That was their proverbial 'fatal flaw'. Additionally, they tended to severely criticize those who did not apply the law as they did. This often resulted in a distorted understanding of the law's intent for people, and it brought them into severe conflict with Jesus on many occasions. That isn't to say that all of them were the kind of religious hypocrites that Jesus rebuked. Many of them were very devoted serious-minded Jews, who were trying their very best to achieve right standing with God through their religion. In fact, as it turned out there were many thousands of Jews in Jerusalem who would later come to believe in Jesus - and remain zealous for the law (see Acts

21:20). So Paul tells us that before he knew Christ, he was part of a group of elite religious Jews who were zealous for God's law as the means of salvation. It is also very possible based on what Paul told us about his heritage, that his parents were Pharisees, or that he came from a line or tradition of Pharisees. In any case, it's clear that Paul took his religion to the very highest possible level. He knew the law, he interpreted the law, he guarded the law, and he lived by the law. He was a very very religious man.

As we consider the modern world, we see that it's filled with all manner of religious devotion. In almost every nation, there are the trappings of religion. We find people who worship in churches, mosques, synagogues, and temples of every kind. We see all manner of religious activity, along with its accompanying clothing and fashion. All over the world, there are religious adherents making great personal sacrifices and undertaking terrible burdens to show themselves pleasing to God, or otherwise marking their progress toward whatever salvation they believe in. There are Pastors, Elders, Bishops, Overseers, Imams, Rabbis, Gurus, Swamis, Priests, and countless other religious leaders, all trying to assist their followers in achieving a life that is pleasing to God. Millions upon millions of people are devoted to Christianity, Islam, Hinduism, Buddhism, Judaism, and a variety of other traditional religions. Even among the non-religious, there is a kind of almost 'religious' devotion to a particular belief or philosophy. What does God make of all this? Which form of religion is most pleasing to Him? What kind of religious devotee impresses Him? Which religious sacrifices merit His favor and approval? The answer is *none of them*. According to the Bible, salvation comes not through any 'form' of religion, but from the arrival of a <u>person</u>:

"For God so loved the world that He gave His one and only Son, that whoever believes in Him shall not perish but have eternal life." John 3:16 NIV

"Salvation is found in no one else, for there is no other name under heaven given to mankind by which we must be saved." Acts 4:12 NIV

It is Jesus Christ alone who can save sinners. Everything that is necessary for a person to be made right with God - was accomplished when Jesus died on the cross, and rose from the dead. It is as we come to Him, trusting in what He has done for us, and putting our lives completely in His hands, that we find a living Savior; one who takes us into a personal relationship with Himself, and becomes our sole assurance of eternal life.

There are many people in the world today who say it doesn't matter what you believe, as long as you are sincere. If anyone was ever sincere in their religion, it was Paul. Paul was so sincere in his Judaism and zeal for God, that he went so far as to kill others to protect his religion. (How's that for sincerity?) He said, *"I was so zealous that I harshly persecuted the church." (Philippians 3:6).* Paul was so sincere, so zealous in his love for God's law and the Jewish people, so identified with what he believed was God's will — that he *hated* anything he thought offended God, or blasphemed His name. As he learned of the burgeoning Christian church in Jerusalem and elsewhere, it ignited his zeal. This zeal for the law and honor of God - was inflamed even more when Stephen, the first Christian martyr, was brought before the Jewish Sanhedrin; and was stoned to death for his testimony about Jesus. Acts 7:58 (NLT) tells us that Paul was there as a witness when Stephen was being stoned, and that he played a role in the event. As Stephen was about to die:

"His accusers took off their coats and laid them at the feet of a young man named Saul."

Then, as Stephen died, we're told in Acts 8:1 (NLT) that:

"Saul was one of the witnesses, and he agreed completely with the killing of Stephen."

On the very day that Stephen was killed, a severe persecution broke out against the church in Jerusalem, and Saul (Paul) was one of their ringleaders:

"But Saul was going everywhere to destroy the church. He went from house to house, dragging out both men and women to throw them into prison." Acts 8:3 NLT

This zeal Paul had to protect Judaism from what he thought was a threat from the Christian community, grew even more — right up until the time that Jesus Himself called a stop to it by appearing to him on the road to Damascus:

"Meanwhile, Saul was uttering threats with every breath and was eager to kill the Lord's followers. So he went to the high priest. He requested letters addressed to the synagogues in Damascus, asking for their cooperation in the arrest of any followers of the Way he found there. He wanted to bring them — both men and women — back to Jerusalem in chains." Acts 9:1-2 NLT

Paul's reputation for violence against the church was so great, that even Ananias - the man whom God sent to heal Paul's blindness after Jesus had appeared to him - had this to say about him:

"But Lord," exclaimed Ananias, "I've heard many people talk about the terrible things this man has done to the believers in Jerusalem! And he is authorized by the leading priests to arrest everyone who calls upon your name." Acts 9:13-14 NLT

Paul would have wiped out the Church, killing every Christian had he thought it necessary - all because of his sincere zeal for his religion. Even the Judaizers (whom Paul is speaking *against* in our passage from Philippians) would never have done anything like that! So if anyone was ever sincere in their religion, it was Paul. But ultimately, despite his great sincerity, Paul the persecutor would come to see the truth about Christ.

Many times in my life, I've heard people say that it doesn't matter what religion you are, as long as you're sincere. They will say that there are many roads to heaven, and as long as a person is sincere in their beliefs, God will accept them. Unfortunately, according to the Bible, this is not true. It is no more true to say that all sincere religious beliefs make a person right with God — than to say that if a person sincerely believes they can fly, then it is safe to jump off of a tall building. There are a great many sincere religious people in the world today. People who make every effort, often at costly sacrifice to themselves, to live in a way that they believe will merit God's favor and acceptance of them. They earnestly pray, perform good deeds, go to church, live by the golden rule, and live as respectable members of their community. But the Bible teaches that no amount of religious works can ever possibly be enough to earn the forgiveness of sin and right standing before God. It is *faith in Jesus Christ alone* which brings us salvation. The real underlying problem, is that many people refuse to accept the existence of *absolute truth*. Paul was sincere, as were the Jews of his day, but their zeal was not according to knowledge. Paul makes this clear in Romans 10:2 (NIV) where he says:

"For I can testify about them (the Jewish people) that they are zealous for God, but their zeal is not based on knowledge."

Religion can be very sincere, yet also very different from the truth. Only God Himself has the right to determine the conditions that will allow a person to be made right in His sight — and only the Bible reveals the truth regarding those terms of acceptance. I have been asked on many occasions by those with whom I have shared the gospel, 'what makes me think that Jesus Christ is the only truth about salvation?' What makes the Bible the *only* true and reliable guide for obtaining a right relationship with God? There are several ways to answer this question, depending upon how genuine a person's desire is to know the truth.

In some instances, I will speak of Israel's history; beginning with how God chose one man (Abraham).

Then, through that one man's descendants born of God's promise, He created for Himself a nation as His own special possession. It was through this nation (Israel), that God revealed Himself to the world through His mighty acts - from a people chosen to show forth His holiness and praise to all the earth.

Sometimes I speak of the Bible as a work of literature; noting its unparalleled beauty and complexity, and the unmatched genius of the words and stories in its pages. At other times, I have spoken of the Bible's spiritual unity; and how despite the variety of authors from across more than a millennia, every one of its 66 books fits together perfectly — as it portrays the nature of God, and the salvation offered to mankind through Jesus Christ. There is also the Bible's prophetic unity; seen in the way that the words of the prophets never fail to come true, and the incredible number of prophecies from across the centuries that were fulfilled in Christ. As if this weren't enough, there are also the claims that the Bible makes about itself - to be the only divinely inspired Word of God.

"All Scripture is God-breathed and is useful for teaching, rebuking, correcting and training in righteousness, so that the servant of God may be thoroughly equipped for every good work." 2 Timothy 3:16-17 NIV

This claim (cp. Heb.4:12-13; 2 Peter 1:20-21), along with the detailed history of the formation of the Biblical canon - is enough to guarantee the truth of the Bible's message. We could also speak at length on the discoveries of archeology; how again and again they show the Bible to be trustworthy and historically reliable. Yet for those who remain unconvinced that the Bible alone is true, there remain the greatest proofs of all. There are two evidences that provide for the honest-thinking individual, the most compelling confirmation of the truth found in the Bible. First, the great centerpiece and foundation of the proof of our salvation — is the resurrection of Jesus Christ. No one else has ever been raised from the dead by God's Spirit, and declared to be the powerful Son of God (Romans 1:4). No one in human history has claimed the authority to lay down their life of their own freewill, and then take it up again — and then actually done it!

"The reason my Father loves me is that I lay down my life — only to take it up again. No one takes it from me, but I lay it down of my own accord. I have authority to lay it down and authority to take it up again. This command I received from my Father." John 10:17-18 NIV

Anyone who has ever honestly examined the evidence for the resurrection of Jesus Christ — has had their lives changed forever. There is no shortage of books and testimonies available from those who have done this; even from those who initially set out to disprove it! If Jesus is indeed alive, and is a living presence to all who will seek Him, then it leads naturally to the second compelling evidence for the truth of the Bible: The radically changed lives of those who have personally met Jesus Christ, and trusted Him. There are simply no words to explain away the countless lives that have been transformed by the gospel of Jesus Christ. These are the lives of Apostles, martyrs, and untold millions of people since the first outpouring at Pentecost, up to the present day. For nearly 2,000 years, Jesus Christ has been powerfully changing lives. He provides forgiveness, and continues to set people free from sin, sorrow, addictions, distress, guilt, hopelessness, fear, and despair. How do we explain this? Hallucinations? Positive thinking? Clever rhetoric? Self-help? Go to any genuinely Christian church in all the earth, and ask people to tell you what Jesus Christ has done for them — and the whole world couldn't contain all the books that would be written with the stories of their lives. *"Jesus Christ is the same yesterday and today and forever." (Hebrews 13:8 NIV).* Thus, the truth of the Bible is written on the heart of every person who follows Him; and it is plain for anyone to see. Jesus is alive now and forever:

"Therefore He is able to save completely those who come to God through Him, because He always lives to intercede for them." Hebrews 7:25 NIV

The last personal achievement Paul lists for himself (before he trusted in Christ), is that 'regarding the righteousness that the law could produce' - he was blameless. What does that mean? It means that no one observing his life could find fault with the way he was keeping the law of Moses. All the demands that the law required - he appeared to fulfill. Paul was not claiming that he never struggled with sin, or that he was a perfect human being (cp. Romans 7). But as far as a person was able to; he lived up to the outward standards set forth in God's law, and was a model Jew. Anyone in the Jewish community who looked at his track record, would find that he had not omitted anything he was supposed to do, as far as they understood the law of God. So Paul rounds out his list of personal achievements by declaring that he thought himself righteous enough to stand before God, since he had blamelessly fulfilled the external requirements of the law to the best of his ability.

We started this study with Paul warning the Philippians against the false teachers known as Judaizers. The Judaizers were claiming that in addition to faith in what Jesus has done, it is necessary to be circumcised, and to keep the law of Moses, in order to be in right standing with God. Paul began with the premise (v.3) that those who are the true people of God - are not those who are who trying to earn salvation by adding circumcision or any other human effort to what Christ has done on the cross. The true people of God are those who have trusted in Christ alone, and follow and serve Him by God's Spirit. They put no confidence in human effort for their salvation; but instead rely completely on God's grace, and solely on what Christ has done for them. The truly 'circumcised' are those who God leads by His Spirit, and who trust in Christ alone for right standing with God. Then, to confirm his warning about the falsehood these teachers were spreading, Paul said, "Look, if anyone had good reason to be confident that their own efforts could bring them salvation, it was me." So he laid out his credentials in vv.4-6 to show those false teachers, and everyone else, that he had as much right to speak as they did. By doing so, he prepares us for the contrast he makes in vv.7-11. A contrast between his own righteousness, and the righteousness that comes from knowing Christ; a righteousness granted by God alone - and based on faith. So now as Paul shares what he discovered for himself when he trusted Christ — he not only establishes the meaning of salvation for the Philippians, but he rebukes the Judaizers and anyone else who has confidence that their own efforts can put them right with God:

"7 But whatever were gains to me I now consider loss for the sake of Christ. 8 What is more, I consider everything a loss because of the surpassing worth of knowing Christ Jesus my Lord, for whose sake I have lost all things. I consider them garbage, that I may gain Christ 9 and be found in Him, not having a righteousness of my own that comes from the law, but that which is through faith in Christ — the righteousness that comes from God on the basis of faith. 10 I want to know Christ — yes, to know the power of His resurrection and participation in His sufferings, becoming like Him in His death, 11 and so, somehow, attaining to the resurrection from the dead." Philippians 3:7-11 NIV

What happened to 'Paul the Pharisee' after living the life he described in vv.5-6 that changed him into the person who could make these statements here in vv.7-10? You may be familiar with the story of Paul's conversion in Acts chapter 9:

"Meanwhile, Saul was still breathing out murderous threats against the Lord's disciples. He went to the high priest and asked him for letters to the synagogues in Damascus, so that if he found any there who belonged to the Way, whether men or women, he might take them as prisoners to Jerusalem. As he neared Damascus on his journey, suddenly a light from heaven flashed around him. He fell to the ground and heard a voice say to him, "Saul, Saul, why do you persecute me?"

"Who are you, Lord?" Saul asked.

"I am Jesus, whom you are persecuting," He replied. "Now get up and go into the city, and you will be told what you must do."

The men traveling with Saul stood there speechless; they heard the sound but did not see anyone. Saul got up from the ground, but when he opened his eyes he could see nothing. So they led him by the hand into Damascus. For three days he was blind, and did not eat or drink anything." Acts 9:1-9 NIV

It's easy to suppose that this appearance of Jesus to Paul in a blinding flash of heavenly light overrode his will, and compelled him toward a radical change in the course of his life. However, that is not the case. In our choice to trust in Christ, God never circumvents human volition, nor rides roughshod over it. Paul's encounter with Christ was not the first time he had ever heard of Him. Paul was present for Stephen's sermon, and he knew full-well what the Christians were claiming about Jesus. It was those very claims that led to Stephen's death. Jesus claimed to be the Son of God, and the Messiah. His followers were proclaiming a gospel of grace, and declaring that *faith in Jesus* for salvation was more important than the law of Moses and their temple. They were saying that Jesus the Messiah died on the cross as a sacrifice for sin, and that He had risen from the dead. As we noted earlier, all of this infuriated Paul, and ignited his zeal; because he thought this was all heresy - and a threat to the Jewish faith. When Jesus then appeared and confronted Paul on the road to Damascus, the Holy Spirit began to enlighten his hard heart, and caused him to consider the truth about Jesus for the first time. I imagine this would be a serious wake up call for Paul, because someone he had believed to be dead, he now knew (in no uncertain terms) was alive! Later, as Paul stood before King Agrippa, he would recount this event, and tell us that Jesus said to him, *"It is hard for you to kick against the goads?"* (Acts 26:14). In other words, "Saul, why are you persecuting me? You are only hurting yourself by fighting me." At that point, Saul was compelled by his vision of Jesus - to do some serious evaluation of both himself and his understanding of the scriptures. Paul was well acquainted with the scriptures, and it was not many days later that he was preaching in the Damascus synagogues, and proclaiming that Jesus was indeed the Messiah. In fact, we're told in Acts 9:22 that Saul (Paul) grew more and more powerful, and baffled the Jews living in Damascus by proving (from the scriptures) that Jesus is the Messiah. For someone like Paul (who had only recently been breathing our murderous threats against the Christians) to move so quickly to being able to *prove* from the scriptures that Jesus is the Messiah — means that God must have opened his eyes to see Jesus for the first time - within those scriptures with which he was so familiar. After Jesus confronted him, the Holy Spirit illuminated Paul's understanding, and helped him to see the truth already present in the Word of God. With all of this in mind, we return to Philippians 3:7-11; to discover the meaning of what Paul understood when Jesus cast aside his self-righteousness — and became to him the one true "pearl of great value" which mattered more than all else.

Now that Paul had encountered the living Christ, and learned the truth about Him from the scriptures, he came to a new understanding about the reality of his relationship with God.

"But whatever were gains to me, I now consider loss for the sake of Christ." (v.7)

Everything Paul possessed by inheritance and achievement: ritual, ceremony, race, religious heritage and privilege, tradition, devotion, sincerity, zeal, and the outward keeping of Mosaic law; all he had counted on to put him into favor with God - he now realized could not do so at all. To express this contrast clearly, Paul borrows words from the business world of accounting. The word *gains* was used to describe a profit, and the word *loss* signified a financial loss. *Loss* also carried the idea of damage or disadvantage. The significance in these words - is that Paul is taking an accounting of his relationship with God. As if visualizing his life on a spiritual ledger, he weighs all that he previously believed was to his advantage in earning God's favor. All of that which was on the "plus" side of the ledger, he moves to the "minus" side. In other words, Paul is telling us that when he learned the truth about Jesus, he realized that all of his *own* efforts to get right with God - really just left him spiritually bankrupt. All of his attempts to earn God's favor apart from Christ, were actually a hindrance or disadvantage when it came to entering into a *right relationship with God*. For the first time in his life, Paul saw clearly that having a right relationship with God - was not a matter of his own effort or works - but came only through faith in Christ. He now knew that most everything he previously thought was true in his relationship with God, was actually false.

Accepting the truth about our lives is a difficult proposition, even in our everyday affairs; much less in our relationship to God. I was watching a popular television show about a famous successful Chef, who goes about trying to help struggling restaurants avoid a total failure of their business. In one episode, as the Chef was pointing out various truths regarding the quality of the food, the incompetence of the wait staff, the lack of kitchen cleanliness, and the poor performance of management — the restaurant owner was in complete denial. It was obvious to the viewing audience, as well as to the owner's wife, that changes had to be made, and hard choices were needed — if the business was to avoid bankruptcy. But sadly, the owner's ego was getting in the way, and he refused to humble himself to acknowledge the truth about the conditions in his establishment. It was only after he ran away and reflected soberly on what he had been told (and on what the consequences of his failure to listen to the truth would be), that he was able to acknowledge that he might be wrong. When he returned a day or so later to see the changes that his wife and the Chef had initiated, he finally decided to accept the truth about the condition of his business, and determined to give it another go. Like this restaurant owner, none of us enjoys hearing the truth about our failures and shortcomings. Yet it's only *a willingness to be honest with ourselves* about the true condition of our lives, which allows us to change and grow. This is supremely so when it comes to our relationship with God. The world is filled with people who are trapped by their ego, their religion, and the beliefs they have been taught. They are blind to the truth of what the Bible teaches about Jesus Christ and the salvation He brings. Unwilling to even acknowledge that what they believe about God may not conform with the truth of His Word — they are destined to face the consequences of their failure to accept the truth: The wages of sin is death (Romans 6:23); and we must all stand before the judgment seat of God (Romans 14:10-12; 2 Corinthians 5:10; Hebrews 9:27).

Jesus Christ is the truth about God. He alone reveals to us our true spiritual condition. It is only through a personal relationship with Jesus that we can know God - and experience the forgiveness of our sins, and the gift of eternal life. His death on the cross to pay the penalty for our sins - is a reality that many cannot accept. Our human nature is so corrupt; that we refuse to believe *that there is nothing we can do for ourselves* - to get into a right relationship with God. We compare ourselves with others, and we think - "we are not as bad as that". The fact is there are billions of people in the condition Paul was in, before he met Christ; everything they would like to believe is true about their relationship with God - is actually false. But the good news is that even though Paul was blind to the truth, and was a terrible sinner, God opened Paul's eyes. From his example we can understand that there is no one beyond the grace of God; no one so hard of heart or sinful that God cannot reach them. We may not all be privileged to a vision of Jesus (as Paul was), but the very same Holy Spirit that opened Paul's eyes to God's Word - will open our eyes to the truth - if we are willing to humble ourselves, and come to God with an honest open heart.

Paul has told us that everything he previously thought was an advantage to him in obtaining a right relationship with God, he now considered a loss. His own works and self-righteousness were actually a hindrance which prevented him from seeing the truth about what Christ had done for him. So he placed all those things on the negative side of his spiritual ledger, and placed Christ alone on the positive side. But even more than that, he weighed everything and all things that he might ever suppose would bring him God's favor through his own strength — and placed them *all* on the negative side of the ledger:

What is more, I consider everything a loss because of the surpassing worth of knowing Christ Jesus my Lord, for whose sake I have lost all things. I consider them garbage, that I may gain Christ and be found in him.. (v.8)

Anything that might possibly stand between Paul and his personal relationship to Christ, he disregarded as a total loss. Why? The infinitely surpassing worth or value of *knowing Christ* cannot be compared with any attempt to *earn* merit before God. Since it's clear that for Paul, the very heart of salvation is *knowing Christ*, we must be clear on what he means by this. To know Jesus Christ is very different from knowing *about* Him. Just knowing the facts about Jesus (where he lived, when he died, what he taught, etc.) is very different from actually knowing *Him*. Take celebrities for example. We can read all about celebrities; their lifestyle, their families, their clothes, their likes and dislikes, and any other number of facts about their lives. Yet that doesn't mean we *know* them; it only means that we know a lot of facts about them. We do not know them personally or by experience. Many modern countries participate in representative or presidential elections. If I agree with what a candidate believes, and I actively go campaign or raise funds for them, I may stand for that person — but I do not actually *know* them. When we study the actual Greek and Hebrew words that mean "to know", we gain a rich understanding of what the Bible means by *knowing* Christ. Knowing Christ begins, as we acknowledge that when He died on the cross and rose from the dead, He did so for us. Yet it is far more than simple mental assent to what He did. To know Christ - is to enter into an actual relationship with Him; a relationship where we *trust Him* to personally forgive our sins, and restore our broken relationship with God. It is a deep intimate spiritual communion of love with Him that surpasses any natural human apprehension. We become so acquainted with Him in this bond of holy love, so closely united together, that we no longer even see our own existence apart from our identity in union with Him. Deep within ourselves, in a way that cannot always be put into words, we experience Christ, and we recognize His personal living presence.

Knowing Christ is not a one time experience (like a handshake with a person we may never see again). It affects our lives forever, with a consciousness that He is deeply familiar with all our ways, and knows everything about us. We grow in an awareness that Christ knows us better than we even know ourselves. To know Jesus is to *experience life with Him each day*, in all its up's and down's; in our joys and in our sorrows. It is to receive from Him the inner strength and comfort that only His grace can provide, as we face hardship and suffering. Along with this, to know Christ is to receive the gift of His Holy Spirit; to be always aware of His presence within us; and to understand that He loves us personally - with a bond that can never be broken or denied.

In the popular movie Avatar, there are scenes between the hero Jake, and his wife Neytiri, that capture for me the essence of what it means to know someone in this way. When the two greet each other after having been apart, they gesture affectionately and say, "I see you". By this, they do not mean merely that they are looking upon each other with their eyes alone, but that they see beyond their outward appearance, and into each others hearts. They perceive the love and affection for each other which is always present in their lives - now fully awakened by their personal reunion. It is a very special bond of love and intimacy that knows what the other person is thinking and feeling; a bond that can only be known by the two of them, and no other. Such is the way we know Jesus. He "sees" us, and we "see" Him. Our life and our thoughts are so bound together with His — that He shares His mind and heart with us, and we join with Him in His ministry of love to others; working together for the salvation of all mankind. This is what Jesus means in Matthew 7:23 NIV, when He tells those who merely claim to stand for Him:

"Then I will tell them plainly, 'I never <u>knew</u> you. Away from me, you evildoers!' "

And, it is what He means in John 10:14 (NIV) when He says:

"I am the good shepherd; I <u>know</u> my sheep and my sheep <u>know</u> me. . ."

So when Paul says that he would disregard everything as a total loss for the surpassing value of knowing Christ — that is the kind of knowledge that he is speaking of. Then to add an even more personal touch to it, he calls Christ Jesus *"my Lord"*. Not only is Christ Lord over all, but He is <u>*my*</u> *Lord.* I have an interest in Him, a bond with Him, an intimacy with Him for which I count everything else as loss. What's more, as if Paul hadn't said this strongly enough, he says, *"for whose sake I have lost all things. I consider them garbage, that I may gain Christ.."* Now this word *garbage* is a slang term used only here in the New Testament. The word was used to describe the leftovers that remained at the end of a meal or banquet. Thus it came to be used for the scraps that were thrown to the dogs. Later it was used of human and animal waste. The idea is that every effort that Paul had previously made to get into a right relationship with God by his own striving - was a total waste. He considered those efforts as filth, garbage, refuse, dung, rubbish, worthless trash, completely without value; all a waste. All the things he had formerly valued so highly; his social status, possessions, the respect of others, career, lifestyle, heritage, accomplishments, and position in the world — all of it was nothing but rubbish when compared with gaining Christ as His Lord, and being found in a life-giving relationship with Him. Now, to round out the long thought he began in v.7, Paul tells us what it means to know Christ and be found in Him - as far as God's law is concerned. More than anyone else, Paul realized that he could never be good enough to earn God's favor now, or when he faced the final judgment. So he expresses his longing to be united with Christ this way:

"..not having a righteousness of my own that comes from the law, but that which is through faith in Christ — the righteousness that comes from God on the basis of faith". (v.9)

For us to know Christ in the way Paul has just described — is also to *receive the righteousness that comes from God.* To properly understand this, we must see that Paul is teaching us that <u>there are only two approaches to being right before God</u>: 1) We can try to become right before God *from the law,* or 2) we can seek this standing *based on faith*. These two approaches are said to be different here (v.9) in three ways. They are different in *where they originate* (either from man, or from God). They are different in *their ground or basis* (resting on either the law, or on Christ). (And) They are different in *the way by which they are received* (either through works of the law, or by faith in Christ). Righteousness is a legal term. It is used here by Paul to indicate right standing with God based on one's relation to His law. If a person is found to fall short of the perfection in God's law in any way - whether in action or intent - they can never be declared righteous (or "justified") in His sight (Rom.3:20,23; Gal.2:16, 3:10-14). As a Pharisee, Paul believed that only by keeping God's law - could a person have any hope of being declared righteous before God. But when God saw fit to reveal His Son to Paul, he understood that God's law is so holy, and man is in such a sorry state, that no person can ever hope to keep the law to earn God's favor. Paul realized, that even the law itself - though inherently holy, just, and good - is powerless to enable a person to overcome the sin in their life. In addition, the law cannot create in someone either the desire to keep it, or the perfection required to be declared right in God's sight (cp. Rom.7). As Paul came to this understanding, he realized that prior to knowing Christ, he had been living in a false reality. His approach to becoming right with God *based on the law* was in error. Such an approach could not help him now, nor had it ever been able to help anyone. The only hope any human being has of being declared righteous before God - is based on faith (Rom.3-4; Gal.3). What Paul discovered, is that God sent His Son into the world to do for us what we could not do for ourselves. Our sins had to be atoned for. A righteousness had to be established which would serve as a basis for our acceptance before God. A way had to be found to enable those who God accepted - to live rightly before Him; both now and forever. None of these things could be accomplished by the law, but God did all of this on our behalf through Jesus Christ. *Solely by His grace*, He took the initiative to save us — when we were all totally helpless to do any of those things for ourselves (Rom.5:6-8). By the blood of Jesus Christ, our sins are put away (Rom.3:25; Heb.9:11-14, 24-26; 1 John 1:7, 2:2, 3:10). By the perfect life of Jesus Christ, there is a righteousness that is imputed to us that is so pure, that even the holy law of God will find no fault in us (Rom.4:24, 10:9-10). Through the resurrection of Jesus Christ, our lives are transformed, and sin will be done away (Rom.7:24-8:30; 1 Corinthians 15:51-57). All that is required on our part is *faith*. Jesus took our place; paying the penalty that the just law required. He lived so that we could have His righteousness. He died on the cross so that our sins could be forgiven. He rose from the grave so that in relationship with Him, we could have a brand new life. To put this another way, God has declared that He will count us as righteous if we will trust the righteousness *He has provided* — instead of trusting in a righteousness we try to earn on our own. He alone has provided the means by which anyone may be made right with Him, now and forever. God reaches out to each of us; calling us to trust Him by placing our faith in Jesus Christ. Jesus is alive;

a living presence who offers us a choice. If we will take Him as our personal Lord and Savior — if we will trust Him, and believe that He has done for us what we cannot do for ourselves — He will save us. We will have *"peace with God through our Lord Jesus Christ"* (Rom.5:1). We will *know* the good shepherd, and He will *know* us.

Now that Paul has declared the surpassing value of knowing Christ, and receiving His righteousness by faith, he states his desire to press on to maturity. He sets his heart on experiencing Christ in the most meaningful possible ways:

"I want to know Christ — yes, to know the power of His resurrection and participation in His sufferings, becoming like Him in His death.." (v.10)

As Paul moved forward toward the goal of experiencing all that God intended for him in this new life with Christ, it became clear in his mind what he needed in order to grow in the grace and knowledge of Jesus (cp. 2 Peter 3:18). Central to this growth are the three phrases in v.10 that are intimately connected together.

First, Paul wants to experience more and more the power of Christ's resurrection. This "power" refers to the dynamic spiritual energy that raised Christ from the dead, and is now at work in the lives of believers. It is the very power that Paul prays God will use to strengthen our inner spirit from His glorious unlimited riches in Christ (Ephesians 3:14-21). It is this power that roots us in God's love, and enables Him to do infinitely more in our lives than we can ask or imagine. It is Christ's resurrection power that gives us spiritual life, transforms us into His image, equips us to minister in His name, and will one day give us a resurrection body. It is the power to overcome trials, and to make us strong when we are weak; and it is the power we need to be bold as we witness to the truth. It is this same power that helps us in our daily struggle against sin, keeps us from falling away, and allows us to feed continually on the living presence of our Savior.

Second, as we live in this power in the here and now, we can participate in Christ's sufferings. Paul did not mean by this that we suffer on the same level as Christ, or that our sufferings have the same meaning as His. What he meant is that his own sufferings *as a Christian* brought him into even closer communion with Christ. Jesus lives within us. As we partner with Him in Christian service and conformity to the will of God, we share in the same kind of suffering in this world as He experienced while submitting His life to the will of His Father. As Jesus suffered in this world, so will we. As our great High Priest, He identifies tenderly with the sufferings of His people (Heb.4:15-16). Our suffering may or may not come from beatings or imprisonment, but it might come from the hardship and loneliness that is our lot; as we devote ourselves to the will of God. In the times when we may feel most forsaken, the Spirit of God will in due course make Himself known to us for our comfort and joy. He will also use our helplessness to deepen our dependence on Him; and so we will truly know Him more and more as He draws near to us in our time of need. This is what Paul had in mind. As he walked in Jesus' footsteps, and suffered for His sake, he would come to know Him as an intimate spiritual comforter that can always be relied upon. By sharing together in the same kind of suffering that Jesus endured as He walked in this world, Paul would experience an ever deepening sense of intimacy with Him - as he was being conformed more and more into His likeness.

Third, as he lived in that kind of daily fellowship with Jesus, the Spirit would conform him to Christ's death; i.e., to the same attitude Jesus had as He surrendered Himself in obedience to God, and to the self sacrifice that led to His cross (see Philippians 2:5-8). Paul desired to walk in the newness of life; the life that was imparted to him when he came to trust in Christ, and was united with Him in His death and resurrection (Rom.6:1-11). This life involves being led by the Spirit, and experiencing His power in our lives. It is to die to ourselves, take up our cross, and follow after Jesus. It is a life of fellowship in the will and service of God; sharing with Jesus in whatever suffering that may entail. It is to know that as He was in this world - so are we; but we are not alone. He lives within us, and as we share in His life, we know Him personally more and more; experiencing the comfort of His presence, and the limitless resources of His grace.

The last phrase in this passage (from verse 11) is a bit challenging — as it seems to imply that Paul had doubts about experiencing the resurrection from among the dead. Certainly that was not the case, as there are many places where he expresses his confidence in the certainty of the resurrection, and in the promises of God (e.g., 1 Corinthians 15; 2 Corinthians 5:1-8; Romans 8:38-39; Philippians 3:20-21). So what does he mean when he says:

"... and so, somehow, attaining to the resurrection from the dead." (v.11). . .?

Some Bible students see this simply as an expression of Paul's humility, or the uncertainty regarding the outcome of his trial in Rome. The grammatical sense of his words is that in whatever way things happened, no matter what the outcome of his circumstances might be, sooner or later he would experience the resurrection to eternal life. He says, "Whatever my case might be, I will continue to know Christ, and so one way or another, I will experience the resurrection from the dead." My own paraphrase of this would be:

"And so by whatever means God sees necessary to bring me through, I will finally attain to the resurrection He has planned for me."

As we have listened to Paul in these verses from Philippians 3, we have seen a life characterized by faithful service to Christ. If we want to grow in grace - and in this same knowledge of Jesus as Paul described - it will mean that we must learn to look at life as he did and learn a new value system. For Paul, there was nothing compared to the surpassing value of knowing Christ more and more. This was the highest value and his highest goal — and he was willing to sacrifice his own ambitions and desires when Christ's call compelled him to do so. No cost was too great, and nothing in this life was worth more than to become what God wanted him to be. So we too must ask ourselves whether there are any practices in our lives that are displeasing to the Lord — if we desire to move forward in spiritual maturity. Paul goes on to express his passion this way (vv.12-15 NLT):

"I don't mean to say that I have already achieved these things or that I have already reached perfection. But I press on to possess that perfection for which Christ Jesus first possessed me. No, dear brothers and sisters, I have not achieved it, but I focus on this one thing: Forgetting the past and looking forward to what lies ahead, I press on to reach the end of the race and receive the heavenly prize for which God, through Christ Jesus, is calling us.

Let all who are spiritually mature agree on these things. If you disagree on some point, I believe God will make it plain to you. But we must hold on to the progress we have already made."

In our progress as disciples, what actions and attitudes have become more Christ-like because of God's power at work in us? What areas of our lives still need improvement so that we can give priority to faithfully serving Christ? Do we agree with Paul in this pursuit of maturity — or are we content with the status quo? Is there a hunger in our hearts for a closer walk with the Lord, and a deeper experience of His love and power? Will we learn from the past, yet press on from where we are — to take hold of all that God has for us in our relationship to Christ? The image Paul leaves with us, is that life is like a race. We must always be straining toward the finish line, and making progress toward the goal. Then if our attitude is something less on these points than what it should be — God will make that clear to us (v.15).

This chapter was written from the burden on my heart that anyone who might be reading this but has not yet trusted in Christ for salvation - would do so. For as we discussed earlier:

"What good is it for someone to gain the whole world, and yet lose or forfeit their very self?" Luke 9:25 NIV

Perhaps like Paul, you thought you had it all worked out. But now you realize that everything you were taught was true when it comes to knowing God — is not what you believed it to be. Getting right with God is simultaneously the easiest thing in the world to do, and also the most difficult. It is the most difficult because we must let go of everything we believe is on the "plus side of the ledger" (all our own efforts to make ourselves right with God). We must admit that they are all of no value, and can never merit His favor. But the good news is that once we have reached that place - and acknowledged our helplessness before God - we will see in the cross of Christ that everything necessary for our salvation has been fully provided for - once and forever. All that remains is for us to personally receive Jesus as our Lord and Savior by inviting Him into our hearts through a simple act of faith. God's salvation is not complicated. It is not something far away or hard for us to reach. It is very near to us; close at hand. It is as close as our mouth and our heart. It is the message of faith that we proclaim:

If you declare with your mouth, "Jesus is Lord," and believe in your heart that God raised Him from the dead, you will be saved. For it is with your heart that you believe and are justified, and it is with your mouth that you profess your faith and are saved. As Scripture says, "Anyone who believes in Him will never be put to shame." For there is no difference between Jew and Gentile — the same Lord is Lord of all and richly blesses all who call on Him, for, "Everyone who calls on the name of the Lord will be saved." Romans 10:9-13 NIV

I join my heart with the Spirit of God and the Apostle Paul, urging you to trust in Jesus Christ. His offer to everyone is a new life, and a new beginning:

Therefore, if anyone is in Christ, the new creation has come: The old has gone, the new is here! All this is from God, who reconciled us to Himself through Christ and gave us the ministry of reconciliation: that God was reconciling the world to Himself in Christ, not counting people's sins against them. And He has committed to us the message of reconciliation. We are therefore Christ's ambassadors, as though God were making His appeal through us. We implore you on Christ's behalf: Be reconciled to God. God made Him who had no sin to be sin for us, so that in Him we might become the righteousness of God. (2 Corinthians 5:17-21 NIV)

In God's Arithmetic, there is nothing of higher importance or value than entering into a personal relationship with Him. He wants you to be reconciled to Him and to "become the righteousness of God". I hope what I have written adds up for you, and that you have come to a deeper understanding and appreciation of God's amazing arithmetic! Also, if this book has helped you to come to faith in Christ, or if it has helped to deepen your walk with Christ, I would like to hear from you. Please feel free to contact me through my website at www.godsarithmetic.com.

Endnotes

1. http://www.hoopsofhope.org/, and http://www.austingut-wein.com/
2. David Platt, Radical (Colorado Springs: Multnomah Books eBooks, 2010) Chapter 8
3. ibid. Chapter 1
4. Have You Heard of the Four Spiritual Laws? © 1965-2012 Written by Bill Bright. Copyright Bright Media Foundation®. All rights reserved. Used by Permission. No part of this booklet may be changed in any way or reproduced in any form without written permission from Bright Media Foundation.
5. Streams in the Desert, p.155. Compiled by Mrs. Charles E. Cowman. Zondervan Publishing House, Copyright 1965 Cowman Publications Inc.
6. http://www.attitudeisaltitude.com/
7. http://members.cox.net/wurmbrand/wurmbrandbio.html
8. "Colorado shooting victim on James Holmes: I forgive him with all my heart" blog, By Dylan Stableford, Yahoo! News, The Lookout - Thursday, July 26. 2012 - http://news.yahoo.com/